COMPETITION AS A DYNAMIC PROCESS

COMPETITION AS
A DYNAMIC PROCESS

By

JOHN MAURICE CLARK

GREENWOOD PRESS, PUBLISHERS
WESTPORT, CONNECTICUT

Library of Congress Cataloging in Publication Data

Clark, John Maurice, 1884-
  Competition as a dynamic process.

  Reprint of the 1961 ed. published by Brookings
Institution, Washington.
  Includes index.
  1. Competition. I. Title.
[HB238.C5 1980]   338.6'048   79-26651
ISBN 0-313-22300-9

Reprinted with the permission of The Brookings Institution

Reprinted in 1980 by Greenwood Press,
a division of Congressional Information Service, Inc.
51 Riverside Avenue, Westport, Connecticut 06880

Printed in the United States of America

10 9 8 7 6 5 4 3 2 1

THE BROOKINGS INSTITUTION is an independent organization devoted to nonpartisan research, education, and publication in economics, government, foreign policy, and the social sciences generally. Its principal purposes are to aid in the development of sound public policies and to promote public understanding of issues of national importance.

The Institution was founded December 8, 1927, to merge the activities of the Institute for Government Research, founded in 1916, the Institute of Economics, founded in 1922, and the Robert Brookings Graduate School of Economics and Government, founded in 1924.

The general administration of the Institution is the responsibility of a self-perpetuating Board of Trustees. In addition to this general responsibility the By-Laws provide that, "It is the function of the Trustees to make possible the conduct of scientific research and publication, under the most favorable conditions, and to safeguard the independence of the research staff in the pursuit of their studies and in the publication of the results of such studies. It is not a part of their function to determine, control, or influence the conduct of particular investigations or the conclusions reached." The immediate direction of the policies, program, and staff of the Institution is vested in the President, who is assisted by an advisory council, chosen from the professional staff of the Institution.

In publishing a study, the Institution presents it as a competent treatment of a subject worthy of public consideration. The interpretations and conclusions in such publications are those of the author or authors and do not necessarily reflect the views of other members of the Brookings staff or of the administrative officers of the Institution.

Foreword

This volume by a distinguished economist critically examines the dynamic character of modern competition, appraises the inadequacies of equilibrium theory, and suggests a new approach to the study and interpretation of competitive activities in the economy.

Empirical studies of competition have been an interest of Brookings for many years. *Big Enterprise in a Competitive System*, by A. D. H. Kaplan in 1954, *Pricing in Big Business: A Case Approach*, by A. D. H. Kaplan, Joel B. Dirlam, and Robert F. Lanzillotti in 1958, *The Price Discrimination Law: A Review of Experience*, by Corwin D. Edwards in 1959, are recent studies in the series.

A new attempt to explain competition in all its diversity and to judge its effectiveness as a regulative force in the economy has long been overdue. As modern industry and trade have shown their dynamic character in innovation, product differentiation, competitive rivalry, and organizational change, the inadequacies of theory have become more and more glaring both for purposes of explanation and for normative judgments regarding the adequacy of competition.

The problem needed an author who could appraise both theory and practice and who could develop more fruitful approaches to an understanding of the competitive process. In John Maurice Clark these qualifications are ideally combined, and Brookings was delighted when he agreed to undertake the study.

The present volume does not offer a unified theory; instead it offers a conceptual approach to the study of competition as a dynamic process. It is a pioneering contribution that is rich in insights and suggested lines of investigation.

The study was a project of the Economic Studies Division, directed by Ralph J. Watkins. An advisory committee consisting of Corwin D. Edwards, Richard B. Heflebower, A. D. H. Kaplan, and Mark S. Massel made helpful comments on the manuscript. To them and to others who reviewed the manuscript and made suggestions, the author and the Institution are especially grateful.

The study was financed mainly with funds from the Ford Foundation.

The views expressed in the study are those of the author and do not necessarily reflect the views of the Ford Foundation, those serving on the advisory committee, or on the staff of the Brookings Institution.

Robert D. Calkins
President

September 1961

Author's Preface

The present volume is an elaboration of a line of inquiry dating from the author's article entitled "Toward a Concept of Workable Competition," in the June 1940 number of the *American Economic Review*. This article was an attempt to find an escape from the negative conclusions stemming from the Chamberlin-Robinson group of theories, in which it appeared that all feasible forms of competition in industry and trade are defective in the same direction in which monopoly is defective, from the standpoint of the services competition is supposed to render. In the present study, I am shifting the emphasis from "workable" to "effective competition"—a term I think I borrowed from Blackwell Smith—because "workable" stresses mere feasibility and is consistent with the verdict that feasible forms of competition, while tolerable, are still inferior substitutes for that "pure and perfect" competition which has been so widely accepted as a normative ideal. And I have become increasingly impressed that the kind of competition we have, with all its defects—and these are serious—is better than the "pure and perfect" norm, because it makes for progress. Some departures from "pure and perfect" competition are not only inseparable from progress, but necessary to it. The theory of effective competition is dynamic theory.

Thus the inquiry goes back to my father's basic conception that the analysis of static equilibrium, for which he is chiefly known, is properly not an end, but an introduction to the study of dynamics, in which it should find its fulfilment. In the pursuit of this endlessly receding goal, I reached the conclusion that it requires something more than offsets from static models in the light of inductive evidence, important as these are. It requires a fresh equipment of dynamic tools of analysis, which will introduce into such basic concepts as demand functions and cost behavior the element of time, change over time, and especially the processes involved in the initiation of changes and adjustment to them, including anticipations and uncertainties. This brings in the time sequence of moves and responses in competition as an active process and the corresponding interplay between aggressive and defensive forms of competition, which are complementary to one another and both necessary, but which have different requirements as to structure of industry and motivational perspective of firms. Of the essence of the picture are innovations and their diffusion, and competition in products and sales promotion, as well as in prices.

If the present study could promote an understanding acceptance of such dynamic tools of analysis as are suggested above, and a readiness to make real use of them, this might be its greatest service, making some contribution to the means whereby the multitudes of factual cases, instead of being mere specific exceptions to the existing array of equilibrium models, may be subject to more systematic interpretation in terms of appropriate dynamic categories. If this objective is to be effectually promoted, the writer must test the import of his tools of analysis by making his own attempts to apply them. At this point the threat of failure looms large, in that readers whose conception of theory is identified with models of determinate equilibrium are likely to decide that no theory has been produced.

Actually, dynamic theory cannot be confined to models of determinate equilibrium—as should be self-evident. Different combinations of size of firm, character of product and of customers, motivational perspective, and other factors can bring about diverse results, and this must be recognized in any account that is faithful to the facts. What may be hoped is that the cases may fall into significant categories, and that the indicated tools of dynamic analysis may point to the rationale by which the results arise from the determining conditions even if no unique result can be deductively predicted. This is the attempt I have made, whether destined to succeed or fail.

Some critics may object to what may appear a disproportionate amount of space devoted to the problems of competition over distance. Aside from the fact that the writer has had more contacts with these problems than with some others, he has long felt that this was the largest and most conspicuous neglected area of problems in the theory of competition. It has been so ever since Cournot set the precedent of bypassing it.

Acknowledgements should begin with the works of Professor Chamberlin and Mrs. Robinson, which furnished the point of departure of the present study, and in some sense the orthodoxy from which it diverges. Next come the many able students of concrete conditions, among whose works the writer has found examples, or germs, of those dynamic tools of analysis which appear to deserve wider use. More particular thanks are due to the members of the editorial advisory committee who have contributed their reactions on the entire manuscript, and whose suggestions have been valued, even where the revisions made in response may not appear adequate. The Brookings staff have been endlessly helpful. And especial gratitude is due to President Calkins for the generous patience with which he has followed the slow progress of this work. The writer would be happy to think that the work might turn out to merit the support he has given it.

John M. Clark

Westport, Connecticut
September 1961

Contents

CHAPTER 1

Preliminary Survey

1. Forecast of the Argument

This volume is an experimental attempt at a fresh approach to the study of competition as it exists in a modern industrial economy, with primary reference to the United States. This statement presupposes two things: that competition still exists as a dynamic force to an extent that makes it worth thinking about, and that our thinking about it is in a state that leaves room for a fresh approach. As to the first, the continued existence of effective competitive forces is not to be too easily taken for granted. One cannot ignore the question whether such forces have ceased to have a role of any importance under the conditions modern industrialism imposes. The views of outstanding economists range from those who think competition has ceased to be effective, to those who think it is more effective than ever before.[1] Certainly competition cannot be thought of, as our predecessors used to think of it, as a simple and self-acting regulator, maintaining itself as a part of the "obvious and simple system of natural liberty." If it remains effective, it does so in altered ways, different from those reflected in textbook theories. Furthermore, we have deliberately repudiated the full action of this regulator with respect to farm prices and production, labor bargaining, and a growing list of other sectors of the economy.

---

[1] The first view might be represented by Joan Robinson, "The Impossibility of Competition," in *Monopoly and Competition and Their Regulation*, E. H. Chamberlin, Ed. (1954), pp. 245-54; also by J. K. Galbraith, *American Capitalism: The Concept of Countervailing Power* (1952). The second view might be represented by S. H. Slichter, "How Stable is the American Economy?" *Yale Review* (June 1950), p. 582; also by David Lilienthal, *Big Business: A New Era* (1953), especially p. 387.

Having given it such divided support, can we reasonably expect it to remain effective in the sectors where it is still wanted, chiefly in the realm of industry and trade? Such questions demand serious consideration.

It is the author's belief that, while competition as it used to be conceived has changed its character and has been dislodged from full control in important spheres, *competitive forces* persist, more pervasively and effectively than existing theories typically give them credit for. The operation of these forces is loaded with imperfections and faces serious threats, and these should not be minimized. One may remark in passing that these imperfections include some that are (imperfectly) reflected in the theorems of formal economic theory, plus some others. Yet if the constructive features of competitive forces can be preserved, they offer us something better than the models labeled "pure competition" by E. H. Chamberlin and "perfect competition" by Joan Robinson—better because they have somehow managed to combine competitive incentives with the mass production and applied science that are nowadays essential to dynamic progress. And for appraising dynamic progress, "perfection" is an irrelevant criterion.

As to the opportunity for a fresh approach, our thinking about competition appears to be in an unsettled state that is presumably transitional. Our mental pictures have been responding to the enormous changes that have been taking place in the economy itself, and this response has not reached final conclusions—as presumably it never will. In the field of theory, the most challenging opening seems to be for an approach that would shift the emphasis from competition as a mechanism of equilibrium to competition as a dynamic process. This shift has far-reaching implications, which this volume will explore. The task needs to begin at the bottom, with the basic concepts; and the material does not lend itself to the kind of precisely determinate conclusions that equilibrium theories are accustomed to producing. Hence the results may be disappointing to many theorists, who may reject them on the ground that they do not constitute a formulated theory. But it would be premature to conclude that the attempt is not worth making. Many things have combined to persuade the author that the time is ripe for such an experiment, and that the materials lie ready at hand.

Changing economic conditions have been reflected in the two major divisions of economic study: industry-by-industry study of facts and conditions, and theoretical interpretations; also in the character of the liaison between the two types of study. The author, being a theorist, has a special concern with the theoretical interpretations, always from the primary standpoint of the service they can render as aids to understanding the facts and dealing with them. From this standpoint he has felt an uneasiness about the state into which the subject has fallen, and especially about the representativeness of the picture which the textbook type of theory gives. In later chapters we shall examine the antecedents of this type of theory and the main stages by which it reached its present development, and then examine it critically, as a basis for suggesting a modified treatment.

For the present it may suffice to identify this type of theory by its central concepts and conclusions, as exhibited in the works of Chamberlin and Robinson.[2] In place of concentrating on the contrasting cases of "free competition" and monopoly, their analysis focused on the intermediate area. Incidentally to delimiting this intermediate area, added attention was paid to defining the limiting cases of "pure" or "perfect" competition. The analysis is characteristically epitomized in diagrammatic models leading to equilibrium results in terms of price, cost, and output. For these models, the crucial distinction hinges on the character of the demand schedule for the product of a single seller. In the case of consolidated monopoly, this individual-demand schedule is identical with the demand schedule for the product of the entire industry, with whatever elasticity it may have. In the competitive limiting case (pure or perfect) the individual-demand curve is horizontal, the market affording a price at which the seller can dispose of his entire output, while at any higher price he can sell nothing.

The conditions necessary to this horizontal schedule include: (1) large numbers, so that the impact of one seller's supply on the market is negligible; (2) a homogeneous product—so conceived in the minds of the purchasers—so that they have no preferences among suppliers that the smallest price-differential will not overcome; (3) for this purpose there must be the kind of market in which buyers are aware of the offerings and have unobstructed access to them.[3] "Perfect competi-

[2] See E. H. Chamberlin, *The Theory of Monopolistic Competition* (1933) and subsequent editions; and Joan Robinson, *Economics of Imperfect Competition* (1932).

[3] Joan Robinson apparently derives an equivalent result by defining the perfect market as one in which the buyers are all alike in their preferences. *Economics of Imperfect Competition*, pp. 18, 89.

tion" as Chamberlin conceives it calls for perfection in various further characteristics, in the theorist's discretion, but notably including perfect knowledge and mobility of the factors.[4] Perfect mobility, if attainable, might make "pure competition" more endurable than it frequently is in practice, when factors are committed to a situation from which they cannot escape without loss. Mrs. Robinson's analysis is explicitly conceived in a static setting.[5] And equilibrium models in general afford no positive interpretation of the forces of progress. What "perfect knowledge" might mean in a dynamic economy baffles the present writer's imagination: he can claim no perfect knowledge of what forms of economic action might result, and he tends to regard it as an unprofitable speculation. Pure competition can be approximated chiefly in agriculture; but "perfect competition" in any full sense seems imperfectly defined, though clearly unattainable.

The intermediate cases include, in Chamberlin's system, competition among differentiated products (monopolistic competition) and small numbers (oligopoly). The first leads to a sloping individual-demand curve; the second may do so, or may present other peculiarities. Joan Robinson presents her entire analysis in terms of horizontal versus sloping individual-demand curves. Especially where numbers are small, the individual-demand curve is affected by the seller's expectations about the responses his rivals may make to his actions. As we shall see, widely different results may be deduced according as he is conceived as expecting their outputs to remain unchanged, their prices to remain unchanged, or either to change responsively. In the most extreme case, he may expect his price moves to be duplicated promptly enough to neutralize their competitive effect.

Pure competition, with unhandicapped freedom of entry, is pictured as equating price to cost at the optimum scale of production. In contrast, competition with sloping individual-demand curves (and free entry) is presented as equating price with cost at a scale of production smaller than the optimum, and therefore at a level of cost and price

[4] *The Theory of Monopolistic Competition*, p. 6.
[5] See *Economics of Imperfect Competition*, p. 16. It should go without saying that the use of equilibrium models as tools of analysis or as normative criteria implies no belief that these models are precisely fulfilled in the *actual world*. Any sensible theorist who uses such models will, if he is at all careful, disclaim any implications as to their literal fulfilment, as Chamberlin does, and as my father did in his *Distribution of Wealth*, which is universally accepted as a static theoretical model.

higher than the optimum. This appears as an inferior result in terms of a statically desirable cost-price-output adjustment. "Inferior to what?" We shall not fail to ask this question, and the result is a warning against implicitly accepting any sweeping unfavorable judgment applying to all cases involving sloping individual-demand curves. Chamberlin has stated that pure competition is not the ideal. Since people want differentiated products to choose between, the ideal involves "monopolistic competition, and hence implies some kind of selling effort, as well as price, as determinants of demand."[6] It also includes qualitative as well as quantitative criteria.

Meanwhile, the Chamberlin-Robinson types of analysis, with their common features and differences, have had a formative effect on the thinking of a generation of economists. Even those who dissented at points, could not ignore this pioneering, systematized interpretation of certain outstanding features of modern industry and trade, which previous simpler competitive theories had not reduced to system. The resulting picture is selective, on a principle that appears to contain a built-in bias, inherent in the method used, toward an unfavorable judgment. It depicts, or lends itself to the depiction of, defects like those of monopoly as built into the inherent structure of modern business rivalry. Such defects do exist, undeniably, and we do well to give serious attention to them, and to search earnestly for remedies. But are they as widespread, as serious, and as inevitable as the theories represent them? The author believes that a closer examination will show that they are not, and are outweighed by the capacity for growth and improvement.

Judged by performance, this defective system has somehow achieved an advancing productiveness that has placed it in the forefront of the world's economies, and has diffused the benefits of increasing real income among the population to an extent undreamed of, even as recently as the beginning of the present century. In J. K. Galbraith's view, according to theory we should be suffering all the ills associated with monopoly. Why aren't we? When the facts fail to verify a prediction derived from a scientific hypothesis, the natural conclusion is that the situation contains elements of which the hypothesis has not taken sufficient account. Galbraith's suggestion is that, while competition has lapsed into passive ineffectiveness, a rough substitute that can

---

[6] See "Product Heterogeneity and Public Policy," *American Economic Review* Supplement (May 1950), pp. 86, 92.

do much to deprive monopoly of its arbitrary power is found in the organization of "countervailing power" by those who encounter the power of monopoly. Others conclude that competition is more widespread and effective than it is sometimes given credit for. These include theorists who do not follow monopolistic-competition theory to its most disturbing conclusions, and also observers of practices. Among the latter are some foreign observers—notably the late Professor William Rappard and Mr. Graham Hutton—seeking an explanation of American productiveness, and finding it in part in a greater competitiveness of the American economy as compared to the European. This finding does not imply "perfect" cost-price relationships. Much imperfection in this respect appears clearly compatible with strong competitive incentives to efficient production and innovation.

If one is searching for elements insufficiently accounted for in existing theories, factual studies are an obvious place in which to look. Such studies have found current theories, of the period since 1933, "a fruitful source of new hypotheses for empirical study."[7] But they have also turned up many types of behavior and elements of motivation departing from those for which formal theories have found room. Wherever these findings are essentially and directly concerned with dynamic process and with change over time, they are bound to depart from theories that are focused on tendencies to equilibrium.

It is a commonplace that the facts depart from any feasible theoretical formulations, and the latter are supposed to serve, not as letter-perfect descriptions of the facts, but as points of departure for understanding them. But investigators show a real desire to extend understanding to the dynamics of the facts; and for this purpose an essentially static theory leaves a formidable gap to be bridged. Is not this gap too wide for the best service which a theoretical point of departure might render to the student of facts? Viewing the liaison from the other end, how are students who are not themselves engaged in these particular types of empirical studies to assimilate the results for their own use and benefits? They do not get much help from a mere injunction that each case needs to be considered on its individual merits.

[7] Joe S. Bain, "Price and Production Policies," in A Survey of Contemporary Economics, Vol. 1, Howard S. Ellis, Ed. (1948), p. 153. Cited by Chamberlin, "Full Cost and Monopolistic Competition," The Economic Journal (June 1952), p. 323. Bain also says this use of theoretical price analysis "can be a curse if the investigator becomes preoccupied with an unduly narrow range of questions, as propounded by a simplified theory."

Those who attempt to apply general theories have long been accustomed to being told that their conclusions are true in theory but not in fact. Investigators of departures from general theories are likely to be baffled by an opposite reaction, finding that departures which they cite are freely accepted as true in fact, but not in theory, and therefore of no significance for a theorist. Thus they become mere facts, divorced from (or contributing nothing to) any generalized interpretation of the economy. If this merely refers to existing forms of theory, it leaves open the question whether forms of theory can be developed in which these facts, or some of them, would fit significantly. Judgment that this is impossible would be premature, tending to sterilize inquiry. All this constitutes a challenge to identify significant categories of facts not yet assimilated theoretically, to define their significance, and thus to rescue them from the status of "mere" facts. No doubt each case will always include some unique factors; but the challenge is to widen the scope of analysis.

It is natural to hope that from inductive, case-by-case studies, fresh and fruitful generalizations may ultimately emerge. So far, the results have not been woven into a unified general theory, with good reason—they point in too many different directions. The utmost that could be hoped for consists of generalizations, each representing an important type of case. But even in this limited sense, is the hope of fresh generalizations wishful thinking and doomed to disappointment in a field in which every instance seems to differ from every other, in ways that appear important when viewed at close range?[8] Perhaps this is the case. Perhaps such fresh generalizations, in the sense of conclusions, are the wrong thing to look for—at least in the present stage of exploration. Perhaps, before fresh general conclusions can be expected to emerge, or instead of fresh general conclusions, what one should look for consists of an equipment of raw materials and tools of analysis. This material is so varied as to be baffling to one who tries to interpret it. Such an equipment might be used to improve the liaison in both directions.

As already noted, it would not yield precisely determinate models, such as theorists have a habit of demanding. In this field such models are bound to be far from the facts. But the limitations of existing theo-

[8] Economists working for the OPA and the NRA had the common experience of finding that each was dealing with an exceptional industry—none appeared "normal."

retical models go deeper than the models themselves, down to the tools of analysis with which the models are built—for example, timeless (static) demand curves and cost curves. To change these into concepts of movement over time can have a profoundly transforming effect on the character of the picture that emerges. Such movements over time may be self-reversing, self-limiting, or indefinitely progressive, and their effects differ accordingly. Leads and lags become important, also differences between anticipations and realized results. The attempt of the present volume will be to work toward assembling and identifying an equipment of dynamic tools of analysis (most of which can be found scattered in writings outside the integrated structure of formal theory), to apply them in some leading types of cases, and to indicate what kind of difference they make.

These differences affect many things. Dynamic standards of appraisal are different from static; so also are dynamic cost-price relations. The relation of competition and monopoly to the conditions of innovation and product differentiation invite more analysis than they have yet received. Some things rated as "imperfections" turn out to have positive uses under favorable conditions, while some characteristics of "perfect competition" become suspect when found under the actual conditions of modern industry and trade.[9]

The results resist expression in a neat series of diagrams. This is especially true as trade practices evolve with time. In the light of this evolution, there can be no guarantee that competition will persist indefinitely. It is not likely to endure much longer than our own vigilance against tendencies toward monopolistic restraints. And such vigilance is seldom literally "eternal." Nevertheless, competitive forces appear more durable than particular historical forms of competition in which they have been embodied.

In following out this line of investigation, we shall trace, in broad outlines, changes in the character of the economy that have affected the character of competition since our early and primitive ideas about it were formulated in a period of small units, relatively simple techniques, and little fixed capital. Paralleling this, we shall trace the corresponding changes in our ways of thinking about competition, helping to explain the stages by which our thinking arrived at its present

[9] An outstanding example is the proposition that there can be only one price for a given product in a perfectly competitive market. In contrast antitrust authorities find "identical prices" evidence of collusion.

state. Then this present state of thinking will be critically examined, with primary attention to its basic tools of analysis (which are static). Substitute tools of a dynamic character will be suggested, and these will then be applied to certain characteristic propositions of current theory. Some particular situations and practices will be examined. Finally, some attempt will be made to present and appraise the over-all picture of the economy, in the light of the differences between different sectors of it, in terms of the forms competitive forces take and their relative strength and effectiveness.

2. What is Competition?

Competition is an indispensable mainstay of a system in which the character of products and their development, the amount and evolving efficiency of production, and the prices and profit margins charged are left to the operation of private enterprise.[10] In our conception of a tenable system of private enterprise, it is a crucial feature that the customer should be in a position (as Adam Smith put it) to exert effective discipline over the producer in these respects. Otherwise, government would feel constrained to undertake discipline over these matters —as it does in the field of public-service industries. It is competition that puts the customer in this strategic position, hence its crucial character. It is the form of discipline that business units exercise over one another, under pressure of the discipline customers can exercise over the business units by virtue of their power of choosing between the offerings of rival suppliers. Competition presupposes that businesses pursue their own self-interest, and it harnesses this force by their need of securing the customer's favor. By reason of this discipline, business, which is profit minded, has to become production minded as a means of earning profits dependably.[11]

[10] The reader need hardly be reminded that this system includes many public controls to protect such values as safety, health, conservation, and truth in advertising.

[11] The phrase "profit minded" is used deliberately, to avoid the implication that business is solely and uniquely governed by an unrealistically precise "maximization" of profits. Cf. below, Chaps. 5-7.

This has its seamy side, as when the pressures of competition toward reducing money costs of production lead to substandard wages and working conditions, which increase the human costs of industry or lead to deterioration of the quality of products. These defects arise from a variety of causes: handicapped or relatively inefficient employers may be forced to make up for their disadvantages by lower money wages and may be able to do so because the competition they face as hirers of labor is less compelling than their competition as sellers of products; or customers may be poor judges of products, or certain qualities of products may be inscrutable. These are defects of a serviceable institution. In an impossibly perfect, omnipresent, and equal competition, they would presumably not arise; but that is an unattainable ideal. In the actual market place they have to be dealt with, and mitigated, by a variety of public and private measures adapted to the causes at work, including the "countervailing power" of organized labor, which uses anticompetitive pressures and has its own seamy side. Many of the remedies are themselves subject to abuse.

These defects are responsible for the view held in some quarters that it is the inherent tendency of competition to sacrifice serviceability to "vendibility" and to debase or impair the human values it touches. These things can happen; but if they were the whole story, the system of private business would not exhibit the strength it does today. Remedies that sustain the "level" of competition are in the interest of the business community, as well as the broader community of citizens. This is a more generally applicable course of action than the one envisioned a half-century ago by Gerald Stanley Lee, in a small volume entitled *Inspired Millionaires,* based on the idea that there existed men of wealth whose dominant motive was to use it to benefit humanity. To such a person, his first prescription was: "get a monopoly." Free yourself from the competitive compulsions that force you to squeeze down costs and prevent you from putting human values first.

The attraction of this procedure might have been somewhat dimmed by a hard-headed contemplation of the methods by which monopolies are established and defended. The element of truth in the prescription might better have been expressed in terms of organizing one's processes of production efficiently enough to give a margin of superiority affording leeway for experiments in promoting human values, not all of which need justify themselves by increasing profits. This, being consistent with competitive checks, would have been more clearly defensible.

A secure monopoly—if such a thing exists or can exist in industry or trade—might be able to save some of the wastes of competitive marketing. After spending part of the savings on public-relations advertising, it might choose to give the public some share of the resulting net economy. Indeed, there are quite cogent reasons why it might do this, or at least might refrain from exploiting to the utmost its immediate power over profits. Nevertheless, we would oppose such a monopoly, regardless of its good performance, because this performance would rest on its arbitrary choice. It would have power, if it chose, to make larger profits by giving the customer less for his money rather than more. The choice to give him more would depend too much on its enlightenment and good will.

While the good performance of our economy is more dependent on such qualities than many of us realize, our resources in this direction are limited. They are already heavily taxed or overtaxed by the requirements of good faith and responsibility in many relationships essential to the economic process and concerned with maintaining the level of competition. They would surely be overtaxed by laying upon them the whole burden of making economically correct decisions in the central matter of amounts produced and prices charged. In such decisions the opposition between private and community interest, is direct and powerful. Hence we do well to seek to keep these decisions subject to forces that are visibly and tangibly cogent, after the fashion of impersonal and competitive "economic law." So we are unwilling to leave in uncontrolled private hands the kind of power that goes with monopoly.

The patent system, with its grant of temporary legal monopoly, is less of an exception than might seem on the surface, as will appear later when we discuss innovation. Innovations are first selected and their value tested by their success in competition with existing practice. If innovation is to be stimulated by public policy, it is hard to devise a totally different system that would not depend more on arbitrary or bureaucratic judgment. Imperfections in the operation of the system present difficult problems, as we shall see, but do not destroy this general principle.

When an industry is recognized as a "natural monopoly," controls of the public utility kind are resorted to, imposing an enforceable obligation to render adequate service at reasonable charges. But we would quite rightly shrink from extending this system to the whole of industry and trade. And where effective competition exists, the customer does not need this sort of protection. Given a chance to choose between the offers of rival producers, his protection rests with his own ability to make an intelligent choice, plus his willingness to take the trouble involved. As to his ability, when he is faced with the inscrutable qualities of many products of modern applied science, there are difficulties, as we shall see, and there are various things that can be done about them, starting with various ways of giving the customer the most appropriate kinds of information. Minimum standards of quality may be set, publicly or privately, and some harmful products may be prohibited. But public control of output and price is not called for to meet this kind of need.

The customer can put pressure on the producer to create a supply corresponding to demand, produced at economical cost and sold at a price reasonably related to cost. "Consumer sovereignty" may be effective in this primarily quantitative sense; but it should be noted with some emphasis that this is not all there is to serviceability. Serviceability depends on how well the customer's patronage reflects those needs and interests that are properly identified with his welfare—using the term in its generally accepted meaning. This is more than an economic problem—a fact which is often used as a pretext for ignoring its economic aspects. The forces shaping our wants include the arts of salesmanship, at a time when our increased consuming power makes it disturbingly easy to become so preoccupied with the *mélange* of trifles or worse that salesmanship offers that we lose something really indispensable—a sense of worthwhile purpose in life.[12] At the utilitarian level, we shall accept consumer sovereignty as an agency that is demonstrably limited and fallible, in need of practical aids to getting what is wanted—aids that can be furnished. Yet with all its defects this

[12] Cf. Barbara Ward, *New York Times Magazine,* May 8, 1960. She said that in the frivolous and ridiculous choices we make, "the modern moralists see . . . more than the virtuosity of the ad man . . . a society corrupted . . . by a scale of choice that . . . finally extinguishes all sense of the proper ends of man." Here the economic goal of affluence is indicated, jointly with the failure of individuals to meet the moral challenge that arises as material necessities are conquered and marginal striving moves on to things of less and less human importance.

agency is indispensable in a society in which the task of shaping worthwhile lives is basically voluntary, rather than dictated by central authority.[18]

So far we have been speaking of the effect of competition, from the standpoint of the alternative choices it offers to the customer, but without trying to define competition as an activity of the producers. For the present purpose, the most useful kind of definition is one that is full enough to suggest some of the important differences in degree and kind of situation, objective, and activity that the realistic student should be prepared to encounter. This kind of definition might also help to explain why competition is so many things to so many different people. They may take hold of it at different points and encounter different aspects, like the blind men and the elephant. Our elephant should have legs, tail, trunk, tusks, and ears. The following definition is framed with this in mind.

Competition between business units in the production and sale of goods is the effort of such units, acting independently of one another (without concerted action), each trying to make a profitable volume of sales in the face of the offers of other sellers of identical or closely similar products. The pursuit of profits includes attempting to minimize losses if that is the best the situation permits. The process normally involves rivalry, though this may or may not be direct and conscious. In perhaps the chief example, the case of staple farm products sold on organized exchanges, the rivalry of the growers is indirect and for the most part unconscious. In contrast, business units consciously attempt to get customers away from their rivals by the relative attractiveness of their offers. To the extent that the customer does his choosing effectively, the way to secure his business is to offer him good value for his money, backed by dependable information about the product. To the extent that he is incompetent or otherwise unable to choose effectively, specious selling appeals and scamped products have their opportunity. Business firms as buyers are better equipped and more competent than most consumers, and the methods of selling to them reflect this. But even with business buyers, the

[18] Cf. the symposium on our national purpose, Life, *The National Purpose* (1960). Here, because our society is of the sort indicated above, the problem of individual purpose is largely bypassed, and with it the problem of national purpose relative to the individual citizen. As J. K. Galbraith has indicated, the affluent society presents its own special problems and is not an unambiguous gain.

seller must bring his product to their attention. There may be rivalry between products not closely similar—this is ordinarily called "substitution" rather than "competition." We shall later examine the problem of defining the distinction between them.

Rivalry may be active or latent. In the latter case it has its most visible effect when it becomes active; but if this possibility influences the conduct of active competitors without waiting for the latent rivalry to become active, then latent competition as such has some effectiveness. It may come from the potential entry of new firms, but it is nowadays often a matter of an existing producer branching out into a new type of product or a new market. Much of the most formidable competition takes this form.

Where profits are attainable, competitors may aim at the largest feasible short-run profit, or at a profit thought of as reasonable and probably the best attainable in the long run. The point in either case is that the feasible profit and the methods of pursuing it are limited by the return for which other competitors are willing and able to produce goods and offer them to buyers. The aim may be to excel the attractiveness of their offerings, or to equal it, or to come as near equaling it as possible, in cases in which the rival has something that is, at least for the time being, inescapably superior as a sales appeal. In the latter case, the first firm is under pressure to find ways of improving the appeal of its offerings. Or the aim may be merely to secure enough business to survive.

The attempt to excel may be called aggressive competition, in effect if not in intent; it may or may not be aimed at a particular rival's business. The attempt to equal a competitor's offer or minimize a rival's advantage is clearly defensive. Under competition the one implies the other, and it takes both kinds to make an effectively competitive situation—certainly in industry and trade and probably in agriculture. A proper understanding of the processes of competition in industry and trade requires a recognition of the different and complementary roles of aggressive and defensive actions. This distinction has been recognized, but its basic importance does not appear to have been developed.

Overlapping this, but not coextensive with it, is the distinction between moves of an initiatory character, including moves responding merely to the general situation in which a competitor finds himself, and responses precipitated by specific moves of a rival or rivals—

responses of the nature of parries or ripostes. They may imitate the rivals' moves, or may be countermoves of a different sort. Initiatory moves may be aggressive, as defined above; or they may be made by a competitor who is in a defensive situation, in an attempt to improve his position by trying something fresh. This distinction between initiation and response has been more fully recognized than the distinction between aggression and defense. In fact, it is the basis of that theory which claims that effective competition occurs only when firms making initiatory moves disregard the responses their rivals will make. Where competitors are few and a competitive action by one has a substantial impact on his rivals, they are virtually certain to make some kind of response. If the initiator of the move does not have foresight enough to anticipate this, experience will soon drive it home to him. To assume that he ignores it requires him to be far more stupid than businessmen are. If competition really depends on this kind of stupidity on the part of businessmen, its prospects are not good.

Fortunately, this pessimistic view contains only part of the truth, and a part that is seldom fully controlling. Businessmen are not only able to anticipate that rivals will respond, but to devise moves of sorts that cannot be easily and quickly neutralized by rivals' responses. And it is not necessary that all should initiate such moves; if some do, resulting competitive pressures will spread, not instantly or in precisely predictable forms, but, in general, effectively. For this purpose, it is important that firms differ in situations and perspectives. Fewness does not eliminate the incentive to improve productive efficiency or to increase the attractiveness of the product; and the resulting differences tend to spill over into price competition, often of irregular sorts. Anticipation that rivals will respond does not carry certainty as to how prompt or effective the responses will be. This uncertainty allows some firms to hope that, as the outcome of initiating a competitive move, they may end with an improved relative market position, which will mean increased profits for them, after profits in the industry as a whole have reached a normal competitive state. There are a variety of conditions that may lead some firms to this kind of an expectation, including the hope of avoiding a worsening of the firm's market position if it fails to make competitive moves when other firms are doing so. At the best, gains may be progressive over time. This, in nonmathematical language, is a rudimentary explanation of the paradox of competition, whereby single firms see an advantage in actions that tend to eventuate in reduced profits for the entire industry. This explanation supplies some essential elements that are left out of the simplified theoretical model that runs in terms of an "individual demand function" substantially more elastic than the industry function.

The forms which this condition may take hinge on the different means competitors may use in making their offerings attractive to customers. These include the selection and design of a product, selling effort to bring it to the favorable notice of potential customers, and price. The appeal of a seller's offer is a joint resultant of all three. Nevertheless, it has meaning to distinguish "competition in price" from competition in selling effort or product design. Any one of the three may change while the others do not. Indeed, estimates of the probable effects of such single variations are implied in the attempt to devise the most effective joint combination. But all three are tied together by the fact that they all need to be appropriate to one another and to the type and level of market demand the seller is aiming to reach.

The attempt to attract the customer's trade, in this three-sided appeal, costs money, whether it takes the shape of a high-quality product, an expensive selling campaign, or a low price. To make a profit on this money outlay or sacrifice, efficient and economical production is needed; and the more economical the production, the more effective the selling inducements can be made, consistently with profits. Therefore, though low-cost production is not a direct act of rivalry (a producer *may* reduce his costs and pass none of the benefit on to his customers), it is an essential enabling factor and as such is part of the whole process. A struggling competitor may have to reduce his costs if he is to stay in business at all. So it may be added as a fourth means of competitive appeal.

Most of these responses take time and involve uncertainty, starting with the responses of the customers that determine how effective the initial move is, after which rivals' responses take further time. The outstanding exception is an openly quoted reduction in the price of a standardized product. Here response can be prompt and precise; and the expectation of such responses can interfere with the competitive incentive to reduce prices and tends to shift price action to the more irregular forms, which create problems of their own, or to increase competitive emphasis on moves in the field of product and selling effort, which present a different array of problems as to the conditions of effective and serviceable competition. Competition over distance also presents its special problems in identifying serviceable forms of competitive price behavior. All in all, the conditions of serviceable competitive behavior in price, product, or selling effort leave much to be defined.

For example, does competition improve or deteriorate quality? Actually, it can do either or both. How can we judge the conditions determining whether the range of quality offered corresponds to the range desired or misrepresents it? By what criteria can we appraise the productiveness or wastefulness of the indispensable function of advertising or balance its informative and perverting effects on the guidance of demand? Would genuine competition drive prices down to marginal cost? Whose marginal cost, and short-run or long-run? The simplified formulas of abstract theory have too-often bypassed such questions. Or would genuine competition cause prices to fluctuate continually with every change in the relation of "demand and supply" (or rather, of demand and productive capacity)? If a given price remains unchanged for weeks or months, is price competition nonexistent during those intervals?

To answer the last question first, the decisive fact seems to be that the purpose of a firm in setting a price on its goods is to sell the goods at the price that has been set. If a price is set competitively, it would be absurd to claim that the price competition ended with the setting of the price and before any goods had been sold. The selling of the goods is part of the price competition. What remains is an arguable question how often prices should change, and such questions do not belong in a definition. The same applies to the other controversial questions about how competitive prices should behave. A definition should facilitate the study of such questions, not foreclose it by purporting to give a final answer.

Perhaps some of the difficulties can be reduced by accepting the consequences of the proposition that effective competition requires both aggressive and defensive actions. A second saving consideration is that price competition must, in reason, include some way in which prices can rise, on occasion, without concerted action. Some conceptions appear to leave room only for price reductions except when demand exceeds capacity. As to specific behavior, it is clear that price competition is something different for a wheat grower, a cement manu-facturer, an automobile producer, or Macy's department store.

For the competition to be effective, the crucial thing seems to be that prices be independently made under conditions that give some competitors an incentive to aggressive action that others will have to meet, whenever prices are materially above the minimum necessary supply prices at which the industry would supply the amounts de-manded of the various grades and types of products it produces. What profit or loss a given competitor will individually make will depend on whether he is a high-cost or a low-cost producer, and on whether the industry is shrinking or expanding.

It may be worth while calling attention to certain things that this definition does *not* set up as essential characteristics of competition. It does not limit it to cases in which the seller merely accepts a going price, which he has no power to influence. It does not define compe-tition as a struggle to excel, after the simile of a race, in which there can be only one winner. It does not incorporate the effort to maximize profits—still less their actual maximization—as part of the definition of competition. The definition needs to leave room for competing firms that may conceive their aims in ways not necessarily inconsistent with the attempt to maximize profits, but including elements that are formulated in different terms. Perhaps the chief trouble with the conception of maximization is its implication of a precision which is unattainable and can be misleading. Secondarily, the meaning of profit maximization is ambiguous unless the time perspective that controls the firm's policy is carefully specified. Incidentally, and para-doxically, the producer who is likely to be trying hardest to maximize his profits is the one who is not making any—he is struggling for survival.

Finally, the definition does not require that each form of competi-tion should be active at every moment, in the sense of new technical methods, new products, new selling tactics, or changed prices. All these may remain unchanged between active moves and may still em-body the resultant of active and effective competitive forces. If so, this implies that preparedness is under way for further moves as occasion may present the need or the opportunity. Of course, this preparedness may lapse into ineffectiveness; but the producer who allows this to happen in his own establishment is likely to find himself fatally out-classed. And if preparedness is active, it is likely to eventuate in action.

3. Noncompetitive Elements—Matters of Degree

The character of a definition is commonly shaped not only by the thing one wants to define, but in hardly less degree by the things one wants to distinguish it from. In the case of competition, the obvious antithesis is "monopoly"; and this is still a useful concept, though in the field of industry and trade it is seldom or never encountered full strength, either as to the scope of its coverage or the completeness and security of its control within this scope. It is like competition in this respect. The situations one has to deal with are intermediate between the two theoretical extremes. By way of a starting point, the distinguishing feature of monopoly is unified control over what can usefully be thought of as "one product" (including some degrees of differentiation) extending over the scope of what can usefully be thought of as "one market."

It includes control of production and sale already existing within the field, plus control of entry from outside, or obstacles to entry that have equivalent effect. It is limited by the rivalry, not of variants of the "same" product, but of different and "substitute" products. This distinction is often clear enough for all practical purposes, though it is commonly impossible to draw a sharp and precise boundary. Unified control may cover any or all of the four means of competitive rivalry already discussed: methods of production, selection and design of product variants within the scope of the "product" covered, selling effort, and price. To start with control of price, as is commonly done, it includes control of the price differentials between the variants of the "line" produced. And it needs to be backed by control of output.

Methods of control start with complete consolidation, but do not end there. Consolidation of less than the whole field may be sufficient for control if the remaining rivalry is too weak to be effective. The other method of unified control is concerted action, and this exhibits numerous gradations. There are implemented and enforceable agreements, including "cartels," unenforceable agreements, and informal understandings; and they may set prices directly or may involve trade practices having a bearing on prices. The hazy boundary line is reached when antitrust authorities attempt to infer agreement or understanding from "conscious parallelism" of behavior. If this were accepted as a universal principle, it would prove too much; any orderly market behavior would be evidence of collusion. Or if one seller reduced his price, a rival who met the reduction would be acting collusively. In that case, normal defensive competition would be tainted. Here the conditions of the particular case need to be studied to decide whether an inference of understanding of a noncompetitive sort is warranted, or whether the parallelism is such as might result from independent action. In either case, the further question remains whether the *results* of such parallelism are such as to impair or preclude effective competitive rivalry.

The scope of unified control exhibits fully as wide gradations as the method, ranging from the control of one producer's product variant, which is in active competition with others, to control of all possible substitutes, which gives the fullest degree of monopolistic power. This, and "perfect competition," constitute the two extremes of an array and will be regarded in the light of limiting cases for the purposes of this study. One may grant that the producer of a product that is differentiated from others' products has something unique, but mere uniqueness is not identical with monopoly. If it exists only because others, being free and able to imitate it as closely as they choose, have chosen to allow the difference to persist, the writer would contend that, far from having a significant monopoly character, such imitable uniqueness is of the essence of competition in quality, which explores customers' preferences and adapts its offerings to them.

Cases in which imitation or nonimitation is fully optional shade off into cases in which, while there are no legal or technical obstacles to imitating the product, there may be practical difficulties about equaling the sales appeal of an established and successful brand, the difficulties lying in the realm of sales promotion. These difficulties are largely a matter of consumer ignorance and inertia—though it is invidious to give such disparaging names to such a useful trait as habit or to anything as inevitable as the inability to be a connoisseur of every product. The problem divides itself into the question whether such differentiated products are exposed to competitive forces that limit their profits to something like a competitively "normal" level and the extent to which this competition centers on giving the purchaser more serviceable value for his money. As to the last, conditions range from supplies sold to an industrial firm with an efficient purchasing department, to the often-mentioned case of pharmaceuticals and toilet articles, in which the customer pays for branded products many times the price at which he could freely purchase their chemical constituents. Here is waste, mostly in small driblets; and to remove it via consumer education may be an over-laborious and costly remedy.

Competition via low prices with low-cost selling, against high prices with high-cost and high-powered selling, faces difficulties in a country as rich as ours, but has, in various forms, made some headway and may have unexploited possibilities. These would appear to depend more on a type of dealer known to be specializing in this kind of appeal than on the inclusion of this sort of product among the offerings of dealers who also offer the highly advertised brands, and who may not help the consumer to find the cheaper items. In extreme and important cases, where the evil is judged serious enough, public "yardstick" competition is available as a logical remedy, but beset with too many pitfalls to be undertaken lightly.

It is sometimes considered that any product differentiation always affords some shelter from competition, in the form symbolized by a "sloping individual demand curve." This may be taken to mean that if my price rises relative to my rivals', by an increase in mine or a decrease in theirs, I will not at once lose all my business. However, the amount I do stand to lose may be quite a sufficient competitive incentive, especially as it may turn into a continuing shrinkage unless I do something to mend or stabilize the situation.[14] In that case, my sheltered position merely gives me time to appraise a competitive threat and meet it, rather than affording me a monopolistic position. We shall see later that a "sloping individual demand curve" affords no assurance of a price that would yield profits above total economic cost. In fact, even possession of a monopoly is not by itself a guarantee of being able to make any profit.

This brings us to the class of products that are different and that cannot be freely imitated; either because the product is patented or because of physical differences, as between aluminum and plastics. This is the area of substitutes. Here substantial shelters from competition may exist, though applied science is busy breaking them down

---

[14] This involves the writer's contention, which will be discussed later, that competition may be effective without driving a seller's price down to his own short-run marginal cost.

and may often do so about as fast as they are created. The product may be an effective substitute for a number of others for different uses and at different points in its demand structure. It may be encroaching or encroached upon, superior or inferior for a given purpose at a given price relationship. And it would seem that it is only the product that, under given conditions, is superior, which gets any shelter from competition out of the fact that the other product cannot, by imitation, wipe out the difference between them. The inferiority of inferior products gives them no monopolistic advantage! Except for patented products, rivalry between substitutes is commonly superimposed on competition among the producers of each. But where it is dynamically active, it may be the more formidable kind of rivalry—it can threaten the existence of an entire industry, as competition within the industry cannot. Defense against such a threat might call for research into new uses, coupled with adaptation of the product.

Unified control of a superior substitute has limited monopoly power, within the limits of its superiority. Unified control of an inferior substitute might assist it to strengthen its defense against its superior rival —provided it used its power in this way. This would mean combined financing of research and adaptation, plus a possible drastic rationalization, to make it a more athletic contender. But if it merely held prices high enough to enable all members of the threatened industry to stay in business in the face of declining volume, it would make its position worse. The temptation to do this would be great, since declining sales for the industry would have caused competition within its ranks to become painfully severe.[15]

It is obvious that the more substitutes are brought under unified control, the greater is the degree of monopolistic power. But these higher degrees of supermonopoly power are so clearly contrary to public policy that we need waste no time in analyzing them, in a study concerned with monopoly only secondarily and only as it sets boundaries on the area of effective and desirable competition.[16]

[15] These remarks find reflection in the conditions pictured in the report of the Canadian Restrictive Trade Practices Commission on the retail coal trade of Winnipeg (Ottawa, 1956). Its volume of sales had been shrinking for five years, due to the increasing use of oil as a substitute fuel. Its remedy was an agreement sustaining prices.

[16] This condemnation would not automatically apply to a competitive firm that hedges its risk of being displaced by a substitute product by branching out, competitively, into the production of the threatening substitute.

In the next chapter we shall trace some of the outstanding stages in the evolution of our thinking about competition, correlating them with developments in the economic conditions and practices this thinking undertook to interpret. We shall see that the thinking evolved, partly by its own internal processes of increasingly precise formulation and partly by way of response to changing economic conditions and practices. Regarding the latter, we shall limit our attention to major changes that have had an important effect on the conditions of competition and that are, in one way or another, reflected in our present thinking about it.

CHAPTER 2

How Our Thinking About Competition Took Shape

1. Adam Smith: Conditions and Theories Interact

The theme of this chapter is the relation between the evolution of competitive conditions and practices, and the evolution of our thinking about them. It rests on the idea that we can better judge our current thinking about competition if we understand something of the processes by which it reached its present shape. These processes include contrary tendencies. Theorizing has, quite naturally, lagged behind changes in the conditions and practices it is trying to interpret. It appears that one contributory reason for this lag has been that theory brought preconceptions to the task. It was preoccupied with formalizing, by its own deductive methods, selected seminal ideas of a long-dead philosopher whose writing, in his time, had the touch of prophecy and whose prescient insights had enduring relevance. To a limited extent these ideas have influenced business practice. The philosopher in question was, of course, Adam Smith, who generalized about competition in the infancy of the industrial revolution, and naturally could not foresee all the later changes. He stressed the services competition rendered in a way that placed it in the center of the system of free exchange, which was destined to become dominant during the following century.

As a prophet of competition, one of the notable things about him was that he said unfinished things about it; things that had implications that he did not spell out and some of which were not fully compatible with one another or with the automatic continuance of effective competition. Perhaps his most seminal statement in this connection was: "The price of monopoly is upon every occasion the highest which can be got. The natural price, or the price of free competition, on the contrary, is . . . the lowest which the sellers can commonly afford to take, and at the same time continue their business." He had already defined natural price as covering the natural or prevailing rates of wages, profit, and rent, supporting the inclusion of profits by a theory of opportunity cost.[1] Later he noted that inequalities in the force of competition, due to obstructions to free mobility of factors, sustain unnatural inequalities in wages and profits, implying that competition, if made more equal by free mobility, would reduce these inequalities in the "component parts of price."[2]

This key statement by Smith does two things: it treats the problem in terms of two "pure" conditions, full and free competition and complete monopoly, and it lends itself to the definition of these conditions in terms of their contrasting results, both loosely defined. Thus it left it to later students to make the statements of results more precise, and to analyze the conditions that were necessary to bring about these more precisely defined results. This subsequent process produced the theory of "pure and perfect competition," which came to command interest largely as a way of explaining why actual competition did not produce the precise results theorists had come to expect or to demand of it. The theories that were offered as alternatives will be critically examined in the chapter that follows.

Smith did not demand or expect perfection; he accepted without apparent undue concern the idea that prices might stay for considerable periods above their "natural level"—largely due to trade secrecy—while they could not stay equally long below it.[3] He noted one instance of competition said to have been ruinously severe—this was "competition of the few"—when, between 1698 and 1701, the old and new East India Companies and several independent traders were competing. But Smith was unimpressed when the company later used this episode as an argument for its monopolistic privileges.[4] He said that "good management . . . can never be universally established but in consequence of that free and universal competition which forces

---

[1] *Wealth of Nations*, Book 1, Chap. 7, pp. 60-62, especially p. 61. All page references are to the Modern Library Edition of 1937.

[2] *Ibid.*, Chap. 10, pp. 118, 129.

[3] *Ibid.*, pp. 60, 62.

[4] *Ibid.*, Book 5, Chap. 1, p. 706.

everybody to have recourse to it for the sake of self-defence."[5] This defensive aspect will be stressed in the present study, and its application extended.

Smith saw the tendency of town traders to combine, making one of his most famous pronouncements in this connection.[6] His remedy was to do nothing to facilitate their meeting and communicating. In an age of telephones and trade associations, this negative policy appears insufficient. But Smith's real reliance was on the belief that voluntary agreements require unanimity. In other words, he trusted the power of a single competitively minded maverick to render impotent a purely voluntary agreement of a noncompetitive sort. It remains for us, in the light of subsequent experience, to judge whether he was unduly optimistic about the power of the lone dissenter. Effective competition is still dependent on the power of the most competitively minded minority to set a competitive pace that the others are constrained to follow.

Possibly more pregnant, though well-nigh neglected, are the implications for competition of Smith's famous proposition that "the division of labour is limited by the extent of the market." It is quite possible to read into this the implication that the economies of scale are such that a single firm, serving the entire market, is necessarily more efficient than any larger number. This is the conventional definition of a "natural monopoly." Smith obviously did not draw this inference with regard to the sizable markets of large towns, or the larger markets brought within reach by economical methods of transportation. But his picture of the rural craftsman, who might be twenty miles distant from his nearest competitor, is not a fully competitive picture, nor is the small-town mercantile enterprise whose unit cost is high because its necessary profit must be earned from a small turnover.[7] Here was a set of problems: Competition and the economies of size, the balancing of these against costs of transport in reaching out for a larger market, and the problem of competition between spatially separated producers. Smith left them at loose ends, and others were strangely slow in recognizing that this is an integrated structure of problems, essential to an understanding of competition as it operates.

[5] *Ibid.*, Book 1, Chap. 11, p. 147.
[6] *Ibid.*, Chap. 10, pp. 126-29. The famous passage referred to is the one, p. 128, beginning: "People of the same trade seldom meet. . . ."
[7] *Ibid.*, Chap. 3, p. 171; cf. Chap. 10, pp. 112-13.

Perhaps one important reason for neglect of the obvious case of the local near monopoly is that where demand is too sparse to support more than one merchant or artisan of a given sort in a considerable area, it is also too sparse to make him rich. He is also a member of the local community; and if he constitutes a problem, it is a personal one, not a general one inviting wide attention, as does the incursion of outside financial interests. This matter of attitudes tends to escape economic theorizing. For the larger-scale problem, Alfred Marshall's distinction between internal and external economies of size and concentration stands out as one major contribution, but it came over a century after the *Wealth of Nations*. In the meantime, emphasis among theorists had shifted from Smith's nonprecise realism in the direction of precisionist deductive analysis.

2. *The Deductive Trend*

The pioneer of this trend was, of course, Ricardo; but it has sometimes been neglected that the problems that preoccupied him and determined his most controversial formulations were those of the violent changes in values resulting from the Napoleonic wars. John Stuart Mill paid his respects to the importance of deductive models when he said that "Only through the principle of competition has political economy any pretension to the character of a science"; but in the same breath he warned against the assumption that the demonstrable tendencies of competition are fully carried out in actuality, noting that they are commonly displaced, or at least modified, by customary practices.[8]

The writer whose work concerns us more was Augustin Cournot, whose *Researches into the Mathematical Principles of the Theory of Wealth* appeared in 1838, and was translated into English in 1897, interest in his work having revived after long neglect.[9] Cournot defined "unlimited competition" in terms of what we should now call an infinitely elastic individual-demand curve for each producer in the market in question, requiring infinite numbers. He also dealt with costs

[8] *Principles of Political Economy* (1848), Book II, Chap. 4.
[9] For our purposes, the key chapters are 6, 7, 8, and 10.

of transportation between markets, but only on the assumption of "unlimited competition" in each market, the reason being that the introduction of local "monopolies" (in trading contact with one another's market areas) would create "a complicated problem . . . of very little interest for economic theory."[10] An inquiry might be pertinent: If a problem is important in practice, what more is needed to make it of interest to economic theory? This problem of spatial competition became too important to be longer ignored, in the United States if not in Europe, as it became the type of competition in large-scale industry. But the treatment employed by Cournot became standard, bypassing the problem of competition between spatially separated single producers or small localized groups. Worse, it has at times been misapplied to this problem by economists who took it for granted without recognizing that for that problem fresh analysis was necessary.[11]

To represent the small-group case, Cournot constructed his well-known model of duopoly, producing a determinate result intermediate between monopoly and "unlimited competition." This precipitated critical discussion in which various alternative solutions were proposed by J. Bertrand, Alfred Marshall, F. Y. Edgeworth, and Irving Fisher.[12] Cournot's solution assumed that A varies his output on the assumption that B's output will be unchanged. Bertrand assumed that A varies his price on the assumption that B's price will be unchanged, resulting in what we should call "cutthroat competition." Edgeworth modified this with an oscillatory solution that was ingenious, not fully convincing as it stood, but suggestive of neglected possibilities. Fisher found it more rational to assume that A expected B to make some response to A's actions; and this became the basis of the theory of the oligopoly stalemate. Marshall's treatment was more comprehensive and realistic. With this exception the outcome came to have the appearance of an intellectual exercise, capable of yielding well-nigh any result, according to the different assumptions that might be fed into the hopper of the deductive machine.

[10] *Researches into the Mathematical Principles of the Theory of Wealth*, Chap. 10, p. 118.

[11] Examples of misapplication include F. A. Fetter's theoretical treatment of delivered prices and freight absorption, and Harold Hotelling's exploratory article: "Stability in Competition," *Economic Journal* (March 1929), pp. 41-57. This will be discussed below, Chap. 11, Sec. 6, and delivered prices in Chaps. 14 and 15.

[12] This discussion is traced by E. H. Chamberlin, *The Theory of Monopolistic Competition* (1933), Chap. 3.

Each of these precisionist models produced results that bore an intriguing resemblance to some actual condition; but the assumptions that produced these results in the models were often different from the conditions that brought about the observed results, or omitted decisive elements. And important classes of cases were omitted, particularly those in which fewness is combined with competition at a distance.

As to the powerful marginal method of analysis, it is interesting and perhaps significant that its application to industrial price-making was a late development. It was led up to by the recognition of complications and imperfections due to constant and variable costs, as well as by the economies of large-scale production. Only considerably later were these problems analyzed in fully marginal terms, with variations depicted as continuous, making the infinitesimal calculus applicable and yielding models of precise equilibrium, in which imperfect or monopolistic competition was interpreted in terms of the intersection of curves of marginal revenue and marginal cost. Meanwhile marginal-cost pricing was urged by some as a normative criterion. Problems persist, especially in regard to coordinating the treatment of variations of output within the capacity of existing equipment and changes in the scale of the equipment, together with the differing time perspectives involved. There are also problems of discontinuous changes, unsuited to treatment by the infinitesimal calculus. We shall be examining these problems in later chapters.

3. Conditions Change in the Nineteenth Century

In tracing the course of conditions and practices, along the way to the emergence of the characteristic problems of today, it is time to shift the center of attention to the United States, having taken note of certain key points of European origin in the theoretical equipment with which we faced our emerging problems. Crucial transforming factors, forming an interwoven whole, included internal transportation, soon dominated by the railroad; industry with mass production for ever-growing markets; the corporation, including later the holding company; an improved banking system; and an agricultural revolution—mechanical, chemical, and biological—which made agriculture an expanding industry in terms of output and use of capital, increasingly a cash-crop operation, and a shrinking industry in terms of personnel. We may start with the agricultural revolution.

The cotton gin, introduced at the end of the eighteenth century, was followed by an endless series of more general mechanical devices, beginning with improvements in primitive plows and going on to cultivating and harvesting machinery. These made agriculture more capital-using and increased its dependence on a cash crop, marketed under conditions of pure competition. Scientific fertilizers and selection of strains of animals and crops added enormously to productivity, while processing operations largely left the farm, and many of them, like flour-milling, meat-packing, and cotton textiles, became mass-production operations. So also did the production of farm equipment.

The total group of operations that go into the end products, chiefly food and textile products, and including the production of capital equipment and the distribution of the products, is still a large group. The farm is still an important factor as a source of materials for processing, and the internal combustion engine has enormously increased the role of the farm as a customer for mechanical equipment, including trucks, tractors, and passenger cars.[13] This makes it a major customer of the oil industry. It is the operations taking place on the farm itself that have been spectacularly shrinking in their economic dimensions; and it is these operations to which the standard theory of pure competition fully applies. Thus it remains true that the sector of our economy most fully exemplifying "pure competition" shrank to a small minority sector, even before price supports took large sectors of staple-crop farming out of the fully competitive area.

When agricultural productivity was lower, farming occupied a large majority of the gainfully employed population and was correspondingly more self-sufficing. Except for exportable staples—chiefly cotton, tobacco, and wheat—the cash crop was naturally a minority element in the aggregate. In 1959, with less than 10 per cent of the gainfully employed population engaged in agriculture and producing more than enough for the rest, the cash crop had necessarily become the major dependence, except for handicapped fringes, which remain largely

[13] It is estimated that the average farm has an investment in machinery of $20,000 per worker, substantially more than the average industrial plant. *New York Times*, March 27, 1960, Business Section, pp. 1, 5.

self-sufficing. This made staple agriculture competitive in a way in which self-sufficing farming was not. The latter had contended with the soil and the elements, but not with the market prices resulting from other farmers' activities. Now it became committed to that form of competition to which the theoretical model of "pure competition" applies most unqualifiedly, including a price literally governed by "supply and demand"—a nontypical phenomenon in the modern economy—and with seasonal difficulties in adjusting supply to demand, compounding the secular difficulties of adjusting increasing productivity to a relatively inelastic demand for raw farm products. With this went greatly increased capital investment and monetary costs plus added hazards due to the contingencies of specialized crops, making competition more severe than the prevailing theory contemplated. All this led to the policies of price supports with which we are still wrestling. It appears that the imperfections of competition can include undue severity as well as undue leniency. This suggests the possible usefulness of revisions of competitive theory, both as a reflection of reality and as a standard of what is desirable.

In rural areas, in early and mid-nineteenth century, this country had the small local store or workshop, while the itinerant peddler, tinker, cobbler, or bricklayer played an important part. They were largely local monopolies, as already noted, but not the kind that generate antimonopoly movements. Later, the mail-order house became an effective competitor, though offering a service substantially different from that of regular retailers and requiring a price differential to enable it to compete. Later still, the automobile widened the rural buyer's shopping area. There is little or no evidence that earlier and more primitive conditions were closer to "perfect competition" than conditions of today. Chiefly, both the producer and his market were on a smaller scale and perhaps marked in some respects by more mobility. It is, of course, true that competition is not what it used to be—it never was, because it was always evolving. But that is not saying that it ever had the neat and determinate quality our theories tempt us to imagine that it used to have. We need to be on our guard against this form of homesickness for an historical past that is mythical.

Turning to the mechanical revolution, Eli Whitney's achievement of interchangeable parts, in his epoch-making musket contract at the turn of the century, laid the basis for the economies of mass production when and if a sufficient market appeared. Later, it was carried to a higher power by the technique of the assembly line. During the first decade of the century Eli Terry achieved cheap clocks by mass production methods, at first with wooden works, and used the itinerant peddler to reach the necessary market. The technique was continued by Seth Thomas. At the same time the New England textile industry was being founded on the basis of the mechanical knowledge which Samuel Slater had brought from England, stored in his memory. The railroad, by making larger markets accessible, made progressively larger-scale units feasible. The great development of agricultural machinery came after 1830, and what one might call its heroic period was contemporary with the first three decades of the railroad. It was from 1835 to 1846 that Lucy Larcom worked in the Lowell textile mills, beginning at the age of eleven and emerging to become a teacher and writer and a symbol of a bygone time when native daughters accepted spartan conditions, and published a textile mill literary journal. Westfield, Massachusetts, attained pre-eminence in the making of buggy-whips, and at one time had more than forty firms producing them. This was a case in which the dominant competition was between firms in the same location, thus fitting the standard theory. It must have been a case in which Marshallian external economies were more important than the internal economies of scale, favoring local concentration without bringing about monopolistic consolidation. It was also a vanishing type, coexisting with contrasting types that were becoming more prevalent.

4. Fixed Capital and Subcost Competition

The Civil War gave a great impulse to manufacturing. It was followed by a period of vigorous expansion, interrupted by the major economic crises in 1873 and 1893. The wartime inflation was followed by a period of declining prices, lasting until 1897. It is perhaps not necessary to determine how much, if anything, this general downward trend of prices had to do with the emergence into prominence of conditions of "cutthroat competition" and theories about it. The theories attributed it to heavy fixed investment and costs, a considerable part of which were constant, independent of output within wide limits, so that, in present-day terminology, marginal cost was less than average cost, and active competition tended to drive prices down toward marginal cost as a limit. This was combined with differential pricing, adjusting price concessions to competitive necessity, which was not uniform over the extensive markets that such firms reached.

This condition became painfully evident in the case of railroads, built ahead of traffic and having a heavy minimum investment. The condition was at first identified as something special, to which the accepted standard laws of normal competitive price did not apply. As one observer put it: "We have learned that a railroad is not like a soap factory," implying that a soap factory does not face the condition in which marginal cost is less than average cost and the resulting problems of pricing. Later, it was discovered that in this respect a soap factory is like a railroad.

This principle was not thought of as extending to agriculture, presumably because agriculture was not thought of at the time as marked by large fixed capital, and more especially because it was thought of as operating under "diminishing returns," from which it was concluded that its marginal costs exceeded average costs. This involves a confusion of principles, inherited from classical economics and continued by Marshall, at least terminologically. The present writer has analyzed this confusion elsewhere.[14] Briefly, in a farm as a going organization, problems of constant and variable costs appear, and, given its capital commitments and the inelasticities of the basic working force of the family farm, its marginal cost is frequently below its average cost in a way that makes competition more severe than the theoretical "normal."

In retrospect, it appears that the tendency to "cutthroat competition" in mass-production industry was most marked in the early stages of this form of competition, and when new competitive contacts were being encountered as the railroads broadened the boundaries of market areas. It also appears that this extra-severe competition took place largely via "discriminatory" pricing; and that this was a many-sided problem with which standard theories were unprepared to deal adequately. It had been ruled out of standard treatments of competition, following Cournot's assumption of "unlimited competition" at every point of production: an assumption that should have been seen to be

[14] See *The Economics of Overhead Costs* (1923), pp. 71-72, 79, 87-90, 343-47, 447.

irrelevant to the competition between spatially separated large producers. It has been designated as something only a monopoly could practice, classifying its customers according to how much their trade would bear, on profit-maximizing principles for each class. In its new embodiment it appears in a variety of roles: as a practice tending to make competition unduly severe, as sheer favoritism, or as a predatory weapon for extinguishing small competitors and building a monopoly.

5. Competition and Discrimination

The problem of discrimination was argued first with reference to railroads, which competed directly only at junctions of competing roads. These points were granted lower rates than intermediate points, where competition was of the indirect sort concerned with enabling local shippers to compete with their rivals on other rail lines. Or a road might give a promising shipper a special rate, hoping to profit by the business he got away from his competitors. If the shipper was already strong, he might take the initiative and exact especially favorable treatment. This sort of abuse figured in the early history of Standard Oil. Regulation under the Interstate Commerce Act of 1887 and subsequent amendments attacked such personal discrimination and set limits on local discrimination, starting with the long- and short-haul clause and going on to rate formulas based on mileage.

As to discrimination between commodities, the structure of class rates was worked out by joint action, hence noncompetitively, and competition centered in commodity rates, applicable to large-volume and low-grade traffic. Higher rates applied to more valuable freight, which could bear the higher charges without drying up the traffic in the absence of a competitive alternative. This theory became obsolete when railroads became subject to competition of trucks and air transport, which bid formidably for the traffic that had been charged the highest rates. This competition tended to have a subcost character and has been restrained by the Interstate Commerce Commission, thus interfering with the process by which competition, where it works, assigns business of different sorts to the agency that can handle it most efficiently. Here is a form of competition which is not left free and which, as a practical matter, can hardly be expected to be made equal. It may be an example of the kind of problem that lies outside the scope regularly adopted by general economic theorizing, being technically involved and relegated to an administrative agency, before which specialists will debate it.

6. Moves to Soften Competition

Attempts to escape the rigors of competition in the late nineteenth century produced agreements and pooling arrangements, as well as attempts to build consolidated monopolies. After 1890, the antitrust law stood in the way of outright agreements, and later, predatory and unfair competition came within its purview. In the steel industry a movement of vertical integration involved the building of considerable excess capacity, leaving the industry vulnerable in the face of Andrew Carnegie's competitive tactics of shading prices where and as it might be necessary to get orders that would keep his plant capacity busy. This was felt as a formidable threat; and the urge to escape from it led to the formation of the U. S. Steel Corporation, to the Gary dinners, and to the Pittsburgh plus pricing structure. This last presented discrimination in a new guise, raising problems with which standard theory was not equipped to deal. These will be taken up later.

As time went on, large-scale industry appeared to have learned how to get on with the tendencies to destructively severe competition, and to keep them in bounds most of the time, while agriculture was manifestly distressed. These facts were revealed by inductive studies before they were analyzed theoretically. World War I yielded studies of costs and prices, made with a view to price controls, which exhibited the facts of differences in costs between different producers in the form of "bulk-line" charts. In these, price typically covered more than the average operating expenses of producers accounting for the bulk of the industry's output, leaving the high-cost tail, typically in the neighborhood of 12 per cent of industry output, for which operating expenses

exceeded price. While the data lacked standardized accounting precision, the general character of the results may be accepted as significant.

In 1920 Eliot Jones published a revealing study under the title "Is
Competition in Industry Ruinous?"[15] The title indicates that the theory
of ruinously severe competition was prevalent. The theory was used,
among other things, as a rationalization for the formation of "trusts."
Jones's findings indicated that the competition of modern large business enterprises, with large fixed capitals, did not as an observed fact
force prices below a normal return. As other studies have showed, it
has been the trades largely composed of small enterprises, easy to
enter with inadequate capital and managerial know-how, where average incomes have been "abnormally" low. Meanwhile surveys of farm
incomes supported the view, long accepted as common knowledge,
that these incomes were too low for economic health.[16]

The depression of the thirties brought such a collapse that in the
worst year, the net earnings of industry as a whole were a minus
quantity. Under this pressure, the NRA was established as an experimental laboratory in mitigating ruinous competition by various
methods installed in supervised codes formulated by industries under
exemption from the antitrust laws for this purpose, though "monopoly"
was still, somewhat ambiguously, forbidden. The plan included an
attempt to revive purchasing power through wage increases. For mitigating competition, one frequent device was open-price reporting.
Provisions against cutting prices below cost were attempted, but ran
into unexpected complications due to differences in costs between
competitors. The industry-average cost as a minimum encountered objections as too high for the purpose of a bottom limit on competition,
while firms had to be allowed to meet the prices of rivals, whose costs
might be lower than their own. Thus the provisions in their final shape
tended to afford less protection than their advocates had expected.
After the demise of NRA, resale price control was frequently employed: a method by which competing producers of branded goods
can, in effect, specify the dealers' margins instead of leaving them

[15] *Quarterly Journal of Economics* (May 1920), pp. 473-519.
[16] One debatable feature of these surveys resulted from charging, as a deduction
from the return on farming, 5 per cent interest on the market value of the land,
which was high because voluntary buyers paid prices that capitalized its rental
return at rates in the neighborhood of 3 per cent.

to be set by the competition of the dealers. This leaves the final resale price subject to the competition of rival branded products. This competition involves a balance between the competitive need for a moderate final price and a margin for the dealer that gives him an incentive to push the brand in question.

With all this factual background, the stage was set for a favorable reception to a fresh theoretical analysis of varieties and degrees of competition and mixed conditions. The character and direction of this analysis was further influenced by another transformation which may prove even more pregnant. The industrial applications of science had multiplied to the proportions of a new phase of the industrial revolution. One major effect was to increase the economies of large-scale conduct of industrial research, with side effects facilitating diversification of huge firms. Fully as spectacular was the proliferation of novel products, with its inevitable accompaniment of producers' creation of demand on a mass scale. This may fairly be called the product revolution.

7. Applied Science and the Product Revolution

The nineteenth century phase of the industrial revolution was, like the eighteenth century phase, mainly concerned with increasingly efficient and massive production of end products of generally familiar sorts, with which consumers were at least acquainted. The new products which multiplied were mainly means of production: a major exception being the telephone. Corresponding to this, competitive theory had concentrated on output and price as the crucial competitive variables. A new era came into being with the addition of a chemical revolution to the mechanical and electrical revolutions and the internal-combustion engine, pouring out for the consumer— I had almost said "pouring out upon him"—an endlessly increasing flow of new end products, many of them made of synthetic materials unknown a few years before, or employing chemical additives or preservatives, with the properties of which government agencies could not keep up, while the consumer's unaided judgment was obviously inadequate.

It is clear that this proliferation of products brings indispensable benefits, along with much that is inane or frivolous or worse. It is inseparably bound up with the utilization of increased power of production and with putting an increased per capita income in forms in which it will be wanted. And new and synthetic materials relieve the pressure on some important scarce materials furnished by nature. There is no possibility of turning back; and only a very few extreme nonconformists have chosen to do so, by seceding from modern economic civilization. The process is one of exploration, and exploration involves risks and wastes. New products cost many lives, but they save many more. There is a price to be paid, much of which can be paid in the form of protections to the consumer and aids to his task of selecting goods.

Automatically, the differentiated product has become an economic variable at least as important as price, along with the methods of selling effort and demand creation that necessarily go with product differentiation. These changes have revolutionized the status of consumer sovereignty and the conditions of its exercise. They have added the requirements of honest and informative labeling to the more primitive requirements of business honesty and fulfillment of contracts, which have always been basic to a serviceable business system. For economic theory, the implications were profoundly disturbing. The relation of consumer and producer is no longer a one-way street, but a mutual, two-way interchange. Demand determines what producers will create, while producers influence and stimulate demand. This two-way relationship is an undeniable economic fact. The response of economic theory to this fact has been of two sorts: to adapt its analysis to the fact, or to exclude the fact in the interest of preserving customary theoretical analysis.

Thus one branch of pure theory applied the name "welfare economics" to a structure of deductive analysis based on an emphatic and rigorous insistence on accepting the consumer's choice between rival offerings as the ultimate criterion, for purposes of economic science, of the relative contributions of these offerings to the consumer's welfare. This attitude precluded any inquiry into the conditions making for effective or ineffective exercise of consumer sovereignty, or any concern with the problems that underlie the Pure Food and Drug Act or the Federal Trade Commission's requirements of informative labeling. The reader will not need to be told that the present study will not accept this kind of inhibition on inquiry in the name of science.[17]

The minimal effect of the product revolution on economic theory has been to render inadequate the comfortable two-dimensional scheme of variables—output and price—and to add product and selling effort as variables, making a four-dimensional scheme and turning the relation between producer and demand into a two-way street. While the man in the street has a fair working conception of how these added variables operate, it is no easy task to combine them into a manageable model, assuming that business decisions are guided by the kind of understanding that is generally available for the purpose and requiring for its interpretation and application only such understanding as is available for guiding public policy in a self-governing society.

This is perhaps the culminating challenge which this latest industrial revolution has presented to economic theory, to bring itself into closer touch with economic processes and problems in ways that involve enlarging its scheme of variables. It is this challenge that Chamberlin undertook to meet in his study of the theory of monopolistic competition, as did also Joan Robinson, in a somewhat different but complementary way. These two works ushered in the period of thinking about competition that the present study takes as its point of departure.

8. The Growth of Inductive Evidence

In the meantime, inductive knowledge has been expanding enormously. Cases under the antitrust laws have turned the legal searchlight on practices suspected of monopolistic character or tendencies, while industry studies have multiplied. This increasing flow of inductive material would presumably have been welcome to Adam Smith or Marshall, though even they might have found the flow somewhat overwhelming in its volume. Cournot, on the other hand, might have felt that the new materials presented complicated problems, of very little interest for economic theory. However, the increasingly evident

[17] This particular inhibition appears to have been relaxed, leaving this branch of inquiry in a state the present writer will not attempt to appraise.

importance of some of these complicated problems might have impelled even Cournot to enlarge the assumptions with which his models undertook to deal. Be that as it may, the product revolution and the flow of inductive material are main factors in bringing about the present state of thinking about competition, which will be commented on in the chapter that follows.

CHAPTER 3

Current State of Thinking
About Competition

1. Introduction

In the preceding chapters we have traced some of the main things that have happened to change the character of economic conditions and practices during more than a century and three quarters since our basic conceptions of a freely competitive economy were first comprehensively formulated. We have concentrated on features that affect the character of competition in substantial ways that call for recognition in our thinking on the subject. Paralleling this, we have traced some of the phases through which our thinking has gone, with special attention to the ways in which it has reflected these changes in conditions without fully describing them, and has also reflected our growing factual knowledge about them. Not less important have been the devices of abstract analysis employed by theorists. These may be variously described as severe simplifications of reality or as hypothetical models, some elements of which are creations of the scientific imagination. In either case, the models aim to isolate certain elements, in order to study their tendencies as they would operate in a situation simple enough to free them from the disturbances and complications that always modify their action in practice.

This brief and selective survey has been made in the belief that we can understand better the state our economy is now in by being reminded of how it arrived at that state; and that we can better understand the present state of our thinking by being reminded of "how we got that way." Such a perspective should serve as a warning against any tendency to assume that either conditions or our thinking about them have reached a final terminus. The current state of thinking is directly an outgrowth of the last preceding stage of thinking in its relation to conditions; and tends to focus on some unfinished business which that last preceding stage presented. In the process, it is likely to forget some things that were remembered in earlier stages and that may still deserve attention. Thus it may in turn leave some unfinished business.

In the present chapter, we shall try to appraise the state which thinking on competition has now reached—or perhaps one would better say, to diagnose it. The purpose is certainly not to praise those who have made notable contributions to this development—their accomplishments speak for themselves. Neither is the purpose to blame them for not achieving the impossible and producing a simple and unified theory that explains all the baffling complex facts. It is rather to understand the strong points and the limitations of our present equipment and the inherent difficulties that account for the limitations; all being intended to serve as a rationale for an experimental approach to a modified attack on these difficulties. This starts with an equipment of a different sort, as suggested in the opening chapter. The difficulties it faces, and its limitations, will at least be different from those faced by approaches of the prevalent types.

2. Empirical Types of Study

We saw in the opening chapter that inductive studies proceed on a case-by-case basis, indicating that they do not find the existing equipment of general principles sufficient to explain all or most of the highly diverse behavior they encounter. As to standards by which the serviceability of existing practices may be appraised, much the same is true. The student trying to pass judgment on specific cases must weigh opposing considerations that differ not only quantitatively but qualitatively. For example, in the promotion of consumer demand, elements of indispensable information and interested manipulation are so thoroughly intermingled that any attempt to unscramble them involves subjective judgment at some point, not to mention the part advertising plays in supporting newspapers and magazines and making them available to the purchaser at prices that cover only a fraction of their total cost of production.

It is also true that with the partial exception of "full-cost pricing," empirical studies have not yielded fresh generalizations of a comprehensive sort. They do not appear likely to furnish a structure comparable in scope with that of analytical theory, in spite of the fact that the makers of such studies include persons eminently competent for theoretical thinking. The reason appears to lie partly in the baffling diversity of the material and partly in the indeterminate character of the behavior it reveals. "Indeterminateness" in this case means that the results are not precisely determined by the limited number of variables that are manageable for purposes of theoretical analysis. For example, an elaborate study of automobile demand, made in 1938, revealed an unwieldy number of determinants, among which price appeared secondary to income and a number of other factors, price elasticity appeared indeterminate within wide limits, with the most probable value insufficient to enable any feasible change of prices to overcome other more potent factors.[1]

As this example makes clear, the "case by case" type of study does not mean that the concepts of general theory play no part. They are used and useful. But it does mean that no one or two such concepts can be counted on to dominate a particular situation; and that the facts of the case must be appealed to in trying to decide how important any one factor is. Also it means that the effect of single factors cannot be counted on to follow any determinate quantitative formula. To put it briefly, the concepts of theory suggest some of the things a student should look for; but he also needs to be looking for other things and to be prepared for the unexpected. And these concepts cannot tell the student in advance what he will find. Their predictive value is extremely limited and can lay no claims to accuracy.

Most important of all, perhaps, when the student of cases comes in contact with the forces dealt with by general theory, he encounters them in a different form. The theoretical models are uniformly presented as operating toward an equilibrium, the nature of which is determined by the conditions that are given at the start. And the nature of this equilibrium is the main thing studied, typically with only in-

[1] See *The Dynamics of Automobile Demand* (1939), especially "Factors Governing Changes in Domestic Automobile Demand," by C. R. Roos and Victor von Szeliski, pp. 21-95.

cidental attention to the processes by which this equilibrium is supposed to be reached; generally conceiving them in hypothetical terms, rather than in terms of the actual time patterns and rates of movement involved. But the student of cases finds his material in motion, never reaching equilibrium, reacting to disturbances from outside and to its own self-generating changes, in a pattern in which leads, lags, and rates of movement are of the essence of the problem. The tools with which equilibrium models are built do not take one far in analyzing such material; but if the student describes it as he finds it, he may be describing something that has general application and that could be generalized into a tool of dynamic analysis, usable by other students dealing with other materials. If this were done, it might be a large step toward achieving such generalizations as inductive study is capable of yielding, in view of the diverse nature of the material.

This diversity is a tremendous obstacle, but it should not be regarded as hopeless. As to that, the state of modern medical therapy may be suggestive. The whole subject of allergies, of course, is one in which the differences between individuals are the essence of the matter. But in other fields—tuberculosis has recently been mentioned in the news—the need of adapting treatment to the individual's pattern of reactions is playing an increasing part.[2] One wonders whether these adjustments may be handled by finding constants for gauging each individual's dosage or other treatment, or whether these constants may turn out to be variable over time or under different conditions. However that may be, the difficulties of inductive economics do have counterparts in other fields.

3. Concepts Developed Under Antitrust Laws

The case-by-case method presents special features where the cases arise under the antitrust laws. This is only in part because of the obvious fact that the arguments are developed ex parte by counsel for opposing sides. Equally important is the fact that the standards of

[2] *New York Times,* Dec. 31, 1956, letter to the Editor by Philip Houtz, Executive Director, National Jewish Hospital, Denver.

judgment that can be applied to the facts are circumscribed by the law. Where the private investigator may be concerned with the conditions he finds existing, whatever they may be, and with judging whether they are satisfactory by competitive criteria, the law is directed at things people have done to affect these conditions. The existence of a monopoly, or of inadequately competitive conditions, may not be, in and of itself, a violation of antitrust law, but acts of monopolization are violations. This distinction makes a real difference which can be important, but its exact importance is not easy to appraise.

There remains the question whether a condition of monopoly has actually been created by the acts in question, or is likely to result from them, or whether trade of a competitive character has been restrained. Section 7 of the Clayton Act forbids mergers the probable effect of which is substantially to lessen competition. The statute is silent on any possibility that competition might previously have been too severe, so that a lessening might be in the public interest, but the statute opposes lessening by action of the interested competitors. It is in this light that one should construe the possible implication that in the eye of antitrust law competition can never be too severe. In application, the provisions against mergers are unlikely to be interpreted in ways that would result in the enforced perpetuation of unduly severe competition. Mergers of weaker firms reducing inequality of competition at the expense of reducing numbers, present a difficult problem.

The Robinson-Patman amendment forbids discrimination in price that is of a character likely to injure competition either among the customers who pay the discriminatory prices, or among the sellers who practice the discriminations. It is of interest that "injury" is a qualitative concept, while "lessening" is, at least on its face, purely quantitative. The provision against unfair competition introduces a further qualitative concept of an elastic sort. All in all, things seem to be moving closer to a status in which legality hinges on the boundary between practices judged desirable and those judged harmful from a competitive standpoint. The latter are attacked primarily by the negative method of identifying prohibited practices, but orders issued after a finding of illegality sometimes have a positive character; at times an order to "cease and desist" may in effect define what must be done.

However, this border line is bound to lack precision. This leaves business men and their legal advisers with a difficult choice between such caution as may fail to explore the legality of all borderline practices and the risks of legal action if they do explore them. They are under pressure to follow policies adapted to promoting their economic interests as shaped by the necessities and expediencies of the situations in which they find themselves, hoping to keep on the legal side but unable to be sure of doing so until their practices have survived a legal test.[3] It seems that some of them do not or cannot avoid taking chances, and the legal concept of competition evolves with the growing mass of cases decided, though not all possibilities may be adjudicated.

The picture of competition that emerges from this process, indefinite as its outlines are, differs appreciably from the models of theory. It pays little attention to the requirements of pure or perfect competition. Though attackers and defenders of certain practices have at times attempted to score argumentative points by claiming that these practices conform to, or depart from, certain supposed features of pure or perfect competition, it would be less easy to find such reasoning accepted in the governing judicial decisions or made the basis of remedies applied. However, inferences may still be drawn, rightly or wrongly, going beyond the letter of decisions or orders or the facts of cases decided. The basing-point question, which will be examined later, exhibits these somewhat baffling legal-economic crosscurrents.

Antitrust authorities appear in general to acquiesce in unused capacity, such as does not result from restrictive practices of a monopolistic character. This is in contrast to perfect competition theory, under which unused capacity *must* result from monopolistic restrictions. Corwin Edwards may impliedly go further, where he defines as a limit on size consistent with competition, that a firm's rivals should have enough capacity to take a substantial proportion of the firm's business.[4] This could have a long-run or a short-run application, and in the latter case would seem to imply unused capacity. Antitrust authorities appear also in general to accept product differentiation as

[3] Such tests can absorb much time, money, and executive attention. If a complaint is issued, the cheapest way out for both sides may be the acceptance of a consent decree, leaving the legal-economic issue unsettled. If a borderline practice does not bring a complaint, this does not prove legality; it may merely mean that the enforcement agencies have not gotten around to acting on this issue.

[4] See *Maintaining Competition* (1949), pp. 9-10.

enriching the range of alternatives the buyer is given to choose from, and as a competitive rather than a monopolistic feature, so long as the freedom of competitors in this respect is not interfered with.[5] This involves, of course, acceptance of trade-marks and competitive advertising, always in a context of restraints on false or misleading statements. As to patents, the antitrust viewpoint is concerned to prevent the extension of a patent monopoly beyond the scope of the invention for which it was granted. This viewpoint shows concern when techniques are kept out of use.

In short, the concept of competition that has grown out of the antitrust laws is not confined to price competition, but accords a place to competition as affecting productive techniques and quality and design of products. As to productive techniques, it is especially concerned that access of producers to good and efficient techniques should be as wide as is consistent with the essential purpose of the patent system. This system is built around the principle of stimulating innovation in products and technical methods by offering inventors a temporary monopoly in the particular inventions each has made, on condition that their specifications are publicly disclosed. Antitrust policy has combated extensions of this into a basis for industry-wide monopoly, or the perversion of it into a means of obstructing the use of techniques. There is a tendency to regard it as qualified by a public interest that it be not used to hold techniques out of use. Problems arise where the massing of patents appears to have outgrown the original view of their function, or where the technical facts disclosed may appear insufficient to convey knowledge of the kind intended. In some antitrust cases where compulsory licensing has been prescribed as a remedy, a requirement has been added that additional "know-how" be made available. For our present purpose, however, it is sufficient to note that this is a balanced conception of competition—one in which the aspects of productive techniques, improved and differentiated products, and price all play a part.

[5] Corwin Edwards has recently named, among three main characteristics of competition, the availability of "a considerable number of alternatives. . . . The larger the number of alternatives available at a given point, and the greater the variety that is to be found in these alternatives, the more fully the situation may be described as competitive." *Big Business and the Policy of Competition* (1956), p. 2. Cf. pp. 86-87, where quality competition is recognized, but with stress on its defects.

4. Other Governmental Attitudes

Antitrust action, being directed against restraints of competition, may tend to develop an unspoken presumption that competition can be defective only in the direction of being too weak, never too severe.[6] Whether or not this is the case, attitudes expressed in other areas of governmental policy have in various ways sanctioned restraints on competition, on the assumption that it can be unduly severe, from the standpoint of the public interest. The most obvious and important examples are the exemption of labor unions from the antitrust laws and price supports for agriculture. But hardships in bituminous coal mining led to an elaborate though transient experiment in minimum price-fixing for this highly competitive industry, threatened by rising costs and by competition from substitute fuels.

As the preceding chapter indicated, price-cutting in the depth of the depression of the thirties was officially regarded as a ruinous excess of competition, and led to the short-lived NRA, under which industries adopted codes that combined maintenance of wages with restrictions on competitive price-cutting. After this was invalidated in the Schechter case, elements of it persisted under the Wagner Act and the acts supporting resale price maintenance. Finally, competition in rates between railroads and trucks has been restricted by the Interstate Commerce Commission, on the ground that it could go to cutthroat lengths without materially benefiting the transportation service as a whole. Here the crucial fact appears to be a difference in the character of the service rendered by the two agencies, about which no consensus has been reached whether it does or does not call for a price differential to equalize the competitive appeal of the two services to the customer. This appears to define a type of case in which destructively severe competition is peculiarly likely to arise, because

[6] Nominal exceptions that sustain the rule include predatory competition, the ultimate aim of which is to lessen competition by eliminating competitors; also discriminations of similar effect, under the Robinson-Patman Act. The "rule of reason" is not necessarily an exception, so long as it relates to the degree of restraint of competitive action, and does not hinge on the reasonableness of resulting prices.

one rival insists on a differential the other is unwilling to concede. One cuts rates in the attempt to establish a differential the other insists on canceling by an equal reduction in its own rates.

5. *Summary of Empirical Studies*

In concluding this characterization of inductive studies, we may ask what is meant by their having a "case-by-case" character. This obviously applies to their individual departures from available theories, such theories being still used as points of departure. The student of conditions may feel that he "understands" such departures, but not sufficiently to feel safe in extrapolated prediction; hence he may properly be cautious in attempting fresh generalizations. But this gives little help to the many who necessarily lack the inductive student's wide background of factual knowledge. For them, tentative generalizations, so far as they are feasible, would be important aids toward understanding.

As things stand, such inductively derived generalizations are few, and largely take the shape of cautions against drawing too confident conclusions, either from theoretical models or from such devices as concentration ratios, which are employed to simplify and quantify the structural features of modern industries and trades. The empirical student naturally tends to try to pick out well-marked structural types and identify them with types of competitive behavior, and with degrees of effectiveness or ineffectiveness of competitive pressures. But the structural types so far identified and employed in this way do not seem sufficient to determine all the important variants of behavior or all the factors responsible for effective or ineffective competition.

Perhaps the nearest thing to a widespread observed behavior pattern consists of "full-cost pricing," with the variations and deviations that go with it. Here there are both questions for descriptive study, as to the prevalence of the pattern and the deviations from it, and questions of the rationale underlying both the pattern and the deviations. So far, it appears about equally possible to construe it as a manifestation of far-sighted monopoly, limited by potential competition, oligopoly of a similarly farsighted sort, workable competition or, finally, a "minimax" policy in accord with the "theory of games." But in either case, it differs from the patterns which most people, rightly or wrongly, associate with the prevalent kind of theoretical models.[7] It is closer to the older Marshallian idea of a "normal competitive price," before that general idea was displaced by the present growing assortment of special cases. The chief difference is that it is conceived as being deliberately adopted as a matter of policy, anticipating the result which economic forces would bring about, rather than waiting to be brought to this result as the outcome of a process of trial and error.

6. Theoretical Thinking

Theoretical thinking about competition is in a paradoxical state. The author assumes that there is something that deserves to be called a prevalent form of theoretical thinking; but if so, it appears to be prevalently used as a point of departure in an extremely literal sense—something from which nearly everyone departs. This prevalent point of departure consists mainly of various forms of the model-building approach that took fresh shape in the 1930's and is still proliferating. It is compounded of two tendencies, one making for greater realism, the other working in the opposite direction. It undertakes to interpret some of the types of modern departure from earlier simple concepts of competition, stressing especially the effects of large size and small numbers and differentiated products. This looks toward greater realism. But it does this via a revival of the type of analysis initiated by Cournot, consisting of models, generally in graphic form, the aim and end of which is the mathematically precise definition of a state of

---

[7] It is interesting that E. H. Chamberlin, in discussing the case of small numbers and differentiated product, mentioned something like full-cost pricing as one of the possibilities. (*The Theory of Monopolistic Competition*, 1933, p. 105.) This appeared five years before the pioneering empirical study of Hall and Hitch. But Chamberlin can hardly be said to have incorporated full-cost pricing into his structure of theory, since he does not account for it or attempt to resolve its apparent incompatibility with the pursuit of maximum profit, as conceived in terms of the perspectives governing the form which the pursuit of profits takes in his other cases.

stable equilibrium toward which the model demonstrably tends. This static character, plus the requirements of mathematical precision, lead away from realism in some ways that appear rather important. They impose limitations on the extent to which these models can reflect the behavior of actual, dynamic economic situations and the forces that operate on them.

7. Judgments Fostered by Prevalent Theories

On the normative side, the prevalent type—or types—of theorizing have one outstanding common characteristic, which they share in varying ways and in different degrees. They tend to a finding that every feasible form of competition in industry and trade is defective in the same direction in which monopoly is defective, and to an extent that may be equivalent to the defects of monopoly, or less, or in some cases even more. One should hasten to add that this is less true of the formulators of theories, than of others who interpret the theories and apply them. The formulator may state a key idea of his theory in overly simple, precise, or positive terms; but he then typically proceeds to qualify it. But the overly positive statement tends to have more impact on the reader, and is likely to be the thing that stays with him, and determines the version of the theory that gets disseminated, especially in text books, where anything that can be presented in a two-dimensional diagram has a virtually invincible advantage in exposition.

This is true of the theories that have been dominant during the past quarter century, especially those of E. H. Chamberlin. In relation to his theories, the present study could be regarded as an attempt to build a positive treatment on assumptions, many or most of which Chamberlin admits or leaves room for as exceptions or departures, but the significance of which he does not develop. When so developed, the results turn out to be contradictory to some of the diagrammatic theorems with which Chamberlin's exposition starts, and from which it diverges.

For a theory to find business conditions and practices defective is not *per se* a fault in the theory. These conditions and practices have many and serious defects; and a vital service the theorist should render consists in the kind of methodical criticism made possible by a professionally detached point of view, which adopts criteria and compares with them not only actual performance but the inherent tendencies of various prevailing conditions. I shall attempt to follow this method, but with dynamic rather than static criteria and estimates of tendencies. I am persuaded that the precisionist model-building type of theory finds business monopolistically defective for what are in part the wrong reasons. At important points it disagrees with the kinds of judgments already mentioned as growing out of contact with antitrust and other problems. One such disagreement is the finding of an "element of monopoly" inherent in all differentiation of products; another point calling for heavy qualification is the imputing of a monopolistic result to all situations where fewness leads to an expectation that one's rivals will respond to one's actions.

With regard to the latter, the author has already contended that expectation of some kind of response need not mean expecting that one's competitive moves will be neutralized, though it may affect the nature of the moves in ways that raise problems for critical analysis. The model of fewness is an oversimplification of the kinds of situations typically found, in which firms are of different sizes, and there may be a few big concerns and a larger number of various smaller sizes; or there may be a situation of "chain oligopoly," in which a single firm is in active competitive contact with a limited number of others, but these are in contact with still others, in a ramifying series. This presents the problem of the response of a firm whose competitors in one direction have reduced their prices, while those in other directions have not. Something similar may occur in terms of quality gradations.

Such situations may or may not lead to monopoloidal results, depending on accompanying conditions, which remain to be more fully analyzed. But prevailing theories tend to stress the simplified model of "interdependence," and the conclusion that this situation leads of inherent necessity to a monopolistic result (in the sense of price and output policies aimed at maximum profit for the industry as a whole) or a result differing from this only in minor degree.[8]

Similarly, product differentiation carries with it many defects, in-

---

[8] Chamberlin's formal theorem on this point presents a rigorously monopolistic result (*The Theory of Monopolistic Competition*, p. 49) while in later comments he qualifies this.

cluding abuses of skimped or deteriorated quality, waste and perversion of selling effort, and the need for better-organized guidance for consumers. These are combined, as we have seen, with positive services that are not only important but essential. Instead of stressing these problems, prevailing theory stresses the uniqueness of each differentiated product as an element of monopoly or a shelter from competition—Joan Robinson has even spoken of it as something business men think of as competition, which destroys competition as an economist views it.[9] A monopolistic character is ascribed to the mere existence of the kind of demand described in theory as a "sloping individual-demand curve."[10]

As against this, it seems clear that differentiation brings in an added dimension of competition; and I shall argue that on balance and in the light of available remedies for accompanying defects, this outweighs any contrary effects it may have, especially in the light of progressive effects over time. In that light it appears that the kind of demand that goes with differentiation is favorable rather than unfavorable to a healthy kind and degree of competition, unless the slope of the demand function is unduly steep, representing the existence of stubbornly strong customers' preferences or other resistances to the transfer of customers from one supplier to another; or unless it brings advantages of size that unduly reduce numbers and restrict free entry. In these cases, product differentiation would afford a substantial shelter from competitive pressure. But in more usual kinds of cases, it is quite consistent with competition vigorous enough to result in prices no higher than a normal competitive level for the industry, while for a particular producer they might be no more than enough to

[9] See "The Impossibility of Competition," in *Monopoly and Competition and Their Regulation*, E. H. Chamberlin, Ed. (1954), pp. 245-54, especially p. 246. It may not be intended to imply that destruction is complete; but Mrs. Robinson had defined "competition" in terms of "very high" cross-elasticities of demand between producers of the same commodity.

[10] This defines a condition in which the amount a single producer can sell varies inversely with the price he charges in a more or less continuous relation; in contrast to a condition in which he can sell his whole output at the going price, and nothing at any higher price, or to a condition in which the smallest possible reduction of price, if not met by competitors, would enable a producer to take away from his rivals all the business he could handle. This last is the nearest approximation to a literal "horizontal individual-demand curve" that is feasible in most cases in industry and trade, where goods are generally sold at quoted prices rather than on organized exchanges.

cover cost in the economic sense, and might be lower than that. Where they are higher, this may or may not be a worthwhile payment for a service of product innovation. This, of course, leaves plenty of problems. The matter will be gone into more fully later, after examining the relationships between short-run pressures and long-run norms of cost-price relationships.

8. Influence of Methods of Analysis

If this critical judgment on the conclusions drawn from current theories is warranted, the cause presumably does not lie in any anti-business bias on the part of the originating theorists themselves, though the wide adoption of insufficiently qualified versions of these theories undoubtedly reflects an unfavorable view of the behavior of prices, especially their resistance to the reductions that old-fashioned competition would have been expected to bring about in response to either declining demand or reduced costs. This behavior of prices is a fact calling for critical examination; but the same critical examination needs also to be applied to the standards by which these modern forms of price behavior are judged. In that matter, it appears to be a case in which the conclusions derived from current theories are influenced by the techniques employed. As to conclusions drawn from the precisionist models, the theorists may be said to be the prisoners of their own techniques and tools of analysis. The remainder of this volume may be regarded as an attempt to develop the meaning of this proposition and to show how much difference it makes.

One incidental and unnecessary limitation of this sort results from assuming that all competitors can be represented as having identical cost curves and demand curves. This obviously simplifies exposition. As a result, however, it less obviously imposes impossible requirements on the substance of the theory, requiring that each producer shall encounter competitive forces that drive his price down to *his own* marginal cost. This calls for a horizontal individual demand curve. The troublesome difference between short-run and long-run marginal cost is disposed of by the expositional device of the "envelope curve," the substantive implications of which will be critically analyzed later.[11] Alfred Marshall was more realistic on both counts, at a deliberate sacrifice of precision.

A more substantial limitation of these model techniques arises from their static character, as models of equilibrium. This leads to the introduction of elements that have no purpose except to enable the model to yield an impossibly precise result. Such elements are unnecessary, once the goal of static precision is abandoned. Equilibrium means, for this purpose, an adjustment which the self-interested actions of independent economic units tend to bring about or to restore if disturbed. It is a condition that no one has an interest in doing anything to alter, though all are free to do so. The theories being discussed have added a new type of equilibrium to the older competitive type: namely, the oligopoly type, in which there is an adjustment, at prices higher than competitive prices would be, an adjustment that may not be thoroughly satisfactory to any one of the oligopolists, but which each is willing to leave undisturbed, because if he disturbed it, he would be worse off.

A static model does not have to deny or ignore all change or movement.[12] The regular method of deriving such a model is to start with a random adjustment and show in what direction it must change and at what point the change will stop. If any departure from this stopping-point, in either direction, will start a movement back toward it, that identifies it as a level of stable equilibrium. For our purpose we may define statics as a selective attitude of the investigator toward his subject matter, in which movement is regarded as tending to an ultimate equilibrium, and this equilibrium is the primary object of interest. The movement may involve dynamic elements—the order of events in time and the speeds of different adjustments. If these dynamic elements are allowed to take charge, the final equilibrium may vanish, and the treatment become fully dynamic. Examples would include W. C. Mitchell's theory of business cycles, the corn-hog cycle and J. A. Schumpeter's theory of innovation and imitation. As to the theory of competition, the writer is persuaded that fuller recognition of these dynamic elements is capable of generating a picture of an

[11] See below, Sec. 10.

[12] More precisely, a "static" adjustment in the present connection means action that repeats itself in a uniform pattern or cycle of production and sale.

institution far more serviceable than the impression ascribed, rightly or wrongly, to prevalent types of theory. Of the defects which theory finds, some remain, others vanish or become unimportant, and still others call for fuller recognition.

The most characteristic and effective criterion by which competition is appraised, in the prevalent type of theory, is a static criterion. It may be defined as a price equal to cost at the scale of production at which cost is least (and therefore where marginal cost equals average unit cost); character of products and demand for them, and technical efficiency of production, being given (that is, treated as constants). When one reflects on the full implications of this criterion, it appears that it eliminates progress by assumption and the conclusion is inescapable: this allegedly desirable condition is something nobody really wants, including the theorists whose models impliedly set it up as a desideratum. They do not want techniques to be static, or diversity of products to be wiped out, and complete homogeneity of products would threaten competition worse than differentiation does. This cost-price criterion is only one of a number, but it happens to be the one that can be presented—in exaggerated form—in the diagrams theory knows how to use, and which text-book writers favor for their kind of exposition. This gives it an impact out of proportion to its importance.

9. Conceptions of "Demand Curves"

Equilibrium is treated as determined by curves of demand as a function of price, and of cost as a function of output. The requirement of a horizontal individual demand curve has already been mentioned. In industry and trade this means a market in which the smallest feasible price differential will cause all the customers to shift to the lower-priced sellers, up to the limit of the latter's capacity. (This limit may be important.) Within it, any seller can, by a negligible reduction in his profit-margin per unit, sell a substantially increased number of units and thus increase his total profit—or vice versa if the price differential is against him instead of in his favor. This last is important because the threat of losing business is a more compelling incentive than the prospect of an increase; and this compulsion may be imposed on a producer by competitors whose costs are different from his own. Some of them may make profits at prices that do not cover his costs. Differences between short-run and long-run marginal cost, as will appear presently, afford a further reason for holding that the "horizontal individual demand curve" is neither necessary, nor even favorable, to competition of full effectiveness, in modern industry and trade.

The usual conception of a demand curve needs to be elaborated in several ways, to bring out its full competitive import. First, a two-dimensional curve is necessarily timeless and therefore misses the most important feature of elasticity of demand, namely, its capacity to bring about expansion or shrinkage that is progressive over time, if the necessary conditions can be maintained. ("Necessary conditions," we may remember, include more than price.) An opposite problem occurs when present sales are made wholly or partly at the expense of future sales. What determines the outcome and how should such cases be handled by business men or theorists? The time-dimensions of demand are sometimes allowed for by saying that long-term demand curves are more elastic than short-term.[13] But it is doubtful that this device does full justice to the importance of progressive response over time, while with longer time perspectives a simple change in price becomes increasingly inadequate to represent the active variables at work.

Second, we are dealing with "cross-elasticities" of demand; and one of the most important things about them, from the standpoint of their competitive effect, is the fact that if, for example, one firm gets $10,000 in sales away from a rival or rivals, this may represent a 10 per cent gain to the successful competitor and a 1 per cent loss to the loser or losers or vice versa, according to the relative sizes of their sales of this product and the number of firms among which the impact is distributed. Thus the relevant elasticities are different, in what we have called the aggressive and defensive directions, or for larger and smaller competitors; and these differences are essential for an understanding of the strength of competitive forces.

These distinctions are inconvenient for theory, in its legitimate striving for simplification; but they cannot be safely ignored, if competitive

[13] The writer has used this device; see "Toward a Concept of Workable Competition," *American Economic Review* (June 1940), pp. 241, 246. His present comments on the limitations of the device apply to his own use of it.

forces are to be adequately depicted. One of the widest divergencies of view in this field is between those who think small competitors are helpless in an industry "dominated" by a few big concerns, and those who think a few concerns that are relatively small but vigorous can introduce effective competitive pressure into an industry in which otherwise what might be called the "truce of giants" might prevail.[14] This leaves us with the question: assuming that both conditions are possible, what determines which will prevail in any given case? As to that, there would seem to be room for hypotheses which inductive study might test.

10. Variation of Cost: Long-Run vs. Short-Run

In the treatment of cost, theory encounters difficulty in the simultaneous operation of two kinds of variation of cost with output: varied utilization of a given productive equipment—which we may for convenience call "short-run" variation—and variation involving long-term change—typically expansion—in the capacity of the productive equipment, spoken of as an increase in the "scale" of production.[15] These two kinds of cost curve are typically combined for theoretical purposes by imagining a numerous series of plants of different sizes, each with its "short-run" curve of unit cost which descends with increased output until optimum capacity is reached and then ascends in the familiar U-shaped fashion. The long-run curve of unit costs with increased "scale" is depicted as an envelope enclosing the short-run curves and tangent to each of them. This long-run curve is necessarily much flatter than the single short-run curves. It represents the firm as avoiding the high unit cost of working at a small fraction of capacity

[14] For an example of the first view, see Corwin D. Edwards, *Big Business and the Policy of Competition* (1956), pp. 44-45, 76-77. For a recent example of the second view, see Willard Arant, "Competition of the Few Among the Many," *Quarterly Journal of Economics* (August 1956), pp. 327-45. Arant cites (p. 337) W. A. Paton, *Shirtsleeve Economics* (1952), p. 193, and Dexter M. Keezer, *Making Capitalism Work* (1950), p. 228.

[15] P. J. D. Wiles, *Price, Cost and Output* (1956), proposes the terms "partial adaptation" and "total adaptation" of the plant and its operation to differences of output. This adds something to the concepts at issue; but for present purposes the more familiar terms appear serviceable, if understood. Wiles' objections to them will be discussed below, in Chap. 6, Sec. 7.

by building a smaller plant; or avoiding the prohibitive cost of trying to work beyond optimum capacity by building a larger plant. This reflects the kind of adjustment that businesses actually make—so far as they can.

The trouble is that, as is the way of mathematical constructions, it ascribes to this adjustment an impossible precision, inconsistent with the facts of normal fluctuations and the inevitability of piecemeal growth. By making the envelope curve tangent to the short-run curves, it gets rid—on paper—of the awkward discrepancy between short-run and long-run marginal costs, since the two are identical at the point of tangency. By doing this, it makes—perhaps quite unconsciously—one of the most violently unrealistic of static assumptions. It assumes that, for any given output, a plant can be built precisely adapted to that output and can then be operated indefinitely at precisely the output for which it is adapted. That is, output remains constant. Or alternatively, it assumes that the plant can be rebuilt as fast as output changes with no added cost resulting from this continual rebuilding.

This may be a mere feat of abstraction; but it has what looks like a significant relation to the attitude that interprets excess capacity as a wasteful abnormality and an evidence of monopoly or "elements of monopoly." Of course, it can be that; but some amount of it is a natural adaptation to growth, fluctuation, and provision for peaks, and uncoordinated construction by competing firms. A firm that hopes by vigorous competition to enlarge its share of a business will not succeed unless it has capacity to handle the hoped-for increase in sales volume. If there are several such firms, this holds for each of them. A firm whose orders have shrunk, leaving it with some margin of unused capacity, may feel that it now faces competition, as it did not when its order books were full. Such considerations appear to outweigh a purely formal deduction from a geometrical model.

The upshot is that most concerns cannot be expected, most of the time, to be operating at their optimum capacity. Their short-run marginal cost will be sometimes below total cost per unit and sometimes above; but most of the time below. Under a rigorous application of the theory of marginal-cost pricing, prices would fluctuate drastically, and profits would be made only at times when concerns were operating beyond their optimum capacity; that is, unless demand were stabilized at a full-capacity level *in each industry and trade,* and this seems too much to ask of any stabilization policy. And most economists would probably hold that this kind of extreme price flexibility should not be expected to bear the burden of maintaining stable levels of industrial production. As a corollary, it appears that if product differentiation moderates cross-elasticities of demand enough to enable producers to get some margin above short-run marginal cost, this mitigates pressures toward ruinously severe competition. And if rivalry between differentiated products is vigorous, the industry as a whole is not likely to make monopoly profits.[16]

The shape of the long-run cost curve, as presented in theory, becomes an issue because certain theories hinge on the use of a U-shaped curve with a definite optimum scale of production, and a curvature such that departures from this optimum in either direction entail materially increased costs. This is contrary to the limited available evidence, which seems typically to indicate no clearly marked and precise optimum scale of production. There is a minimum scale necessary to approximate standard economy; but beyond this, the curve seems typically to flatten out over most of its length; and most of the productive capacity seems to be spread over a range in which, while costs vary for numerous reasons, trends traceable to scale of production are too small to be of controlling effect. So far as this evidence goes, these firms do not seem to be behaving in accord with the theories that depict them as taking advantage of a sloping individual-demand curve in ways that limit their scale to less than the optimum; or pricing for a profit, which then attracts new entries, which split up the business until costs are raised by reducing sales volume per firm, and firms are left making zero profits on a smaller and less economical volume than they might have had if they had been less grasping in the first place.[17] These theories represent something that can happen,

---

[16] Joan Robinson sees this problem in a darker light, as a well-nigh insoluble dilemma. On one side is what might be called a theory of natural oligopoly successful firms tending to grow until oligopoly results. On the other side, where competition persists, it tends on balance of good and bad times to a subnormal average return, driving firms to seek shelters through collusion or product differentiation, which, as we have seen, Mrs. Robinson regards as anticompetitive from an economist's standpoint. Between these forces, little room is left for competition. See Robinson, *op. cit.*, pp. 245-54.

[17] The outstanding theory here referred to is Chamberlin's well-known "tangency theorem": see *The Theory of Monopolistic Competition*, pp. 81-93, especially pp. 84, 88, 90, and 92. The substantial character of the excess cost envisioned is entirely due to the exaggerated curvature of the cost curve employed. If product differentiation increases costs, as it may, it is mainly in other ways and for other reasons. One notes that this model excludes advertising (cf. p. 102).

but is not typical. Firms expand well beyond the point indicated by these theories. If their policies have harmful effects, they would appear mainly to take different forms. Without attempting at this point to resolve all the questions involved, it appears that there is reason for reconsidering these theories, and we shall do so later.

This leads to the question of time perspectives and degrees of foresight prevalent in modern business. The three main grades of foresight contemplated by prevalent theories are: (1) the competitor who ignores his rivals' probable responses and therefore acts competitively; (2) the firm that anticipates rivals' responses and therefore prices monopolistically, without anticipating the new entries this policy will attract. This represents an intermediate degree of short-sightedness. (3) The firm that has enough foresight to be governed by potential competition, which means that it avoids the kind of profits that would attract an exaggerated flow of entries and thus defeat itself. ("Full-cost pricing" might be an example of this.) In addition, there is: (4) the kind of foresight that takes the shape of devising forms of competitive moves that will not be promptly neutralized by rivals' responses. This may be reinforced by: (5) the expectation that others will devise such hard-to-neutralize moves, and that the original firm may be better off if it moves early rather than belatedly, or if it at least undertakes defensive preparedness. It seems that prevailing theories stress types (1) and (2), to the relative neglect of types (3), (4), and (5); and that more realistic study might lead to a more just emphasis.

11. Summary

To sum up this attempt at an appraisal of prevailing types of theory, we have seen how they have reacted to two dominant features of modern industry: large size with limited numbers, and product differentiation. These two features carry with them serious defects and dangers. From among these, theory selects for main emphasis certain ones which its analytical tools can handle, thus introducing a selective bias into its standards of judgment. It focuses on problems that can be solved in terms of output and price as determined by demand curves and cost curves. From the simplified (and static) models thus constructed, and by the criteria to which they lend themselves, certain unfavorable conclusions are reached. (1) When producers get few enough to realize that their rivals will respond to their competitive moves, they tend to price monopolistically instead of engaging in competitive contests to gain business at one another's expense. (2) Product differentiation and a "sloping individual-demand curve" are monopolistic features, necessarily and inherently involving some of the defects of monopoly.

These criticisms are a formidable challenge, but are not the final word. Monopoloidal results of the sorts suggested *may* happen, but they are not inevitable. A re-examination of the whole case would—the writer is persuaded—lead to a more balanced judgment. This means re-examining the basic concepts, starting with the standards of judgment and the aims of business policy and going on to the complex patterns of behavior of which demand curves and cost curves afford simplified pictures. One is reluctant to introduce added complexities, but it seems that this cannot be avoided without excluding some of the important competitive forces at work. And the effects may not be all in the direction of increased complexity. When a firm recognizes its own uncertainty, its reactions may be simpler than those of the hypothetical firm of theory, with its impossibly precise knowledge of marginal revenue and marginal cost and of the point at which the two curves intersect.

CHAPTER 4

What Do We Want Competition To Do For Us?

1. Connection Between Gain and Serviceability

The preceding chapter criticized normative criteria derived from models of precise static equilibrium, but defended the theoretical method of adopting criteria and comparing them with competitive performance and the inherent tendencies of actual competitive conditions. The logical alternative would seem to start by asking ourselves directly what we want of competition, without reference to equilibrium models, and what the necessary conditions and consequences are. Since what we want includes dynamic progress, this dictates the conditions we should be prepared to accept. We want competition to help us secure a large and growing real productive power per capita, actively used, well directed toward desired results (including voluntary leisure), and distributed in ways we can approve. This statement bristles with questions it does not answer, some of which can be sources of conflict.

For example, there is the choice, which we settle in one way and the Soviets in another, between present consumption and investment for future increase in power to produce and consume. There is no way of proving that the market yardstick by which we settle this choice of values is correct, with or without effective competition. But we do divide our annual increase in resources between these two uses, and our system requires that we so divide them. If, thirty years ago, some authority had decided that all resources going into increased investment, including research and development, should be diverted into

63

increased consumption, today consumers would have less as a result. But also, under our system, unless consumption increases vigorously, investment will lag, and production with it. It is a commonplace that our system gives more weight to consumption than the Soviets do.

Another question is at least equally fundamental. We want gratifications from goods and services, public and private and including the gratification that goes with progress; and these are produced by an organization shaped primarily by the pursuit of monetary gain. It follows that before we can accept the system as serviceable, it must satisfy two prerequisites. First, it must operate in a setting and by methods such that dollar gain shall represent social serviceability to an extent that we can accept as a tolerable, though necessarily imperfect, approximation. "Vendibility," while it cannot be made completely identical with serviceability, must be adequately related to it; and monetary expenses must be similarly related to the social sacrifices of production, including those representing opportunities foregone.

Secondly, monetary gains must be self-limiting in some acceptable fashion. This is the modern substitute for the medieval idea of a "just price" yielding an income suitable to one's station in life. Having abandoned the ideas of customary status embodied in this standard, we accept as a substitute a system of freedom to acquire as much income as one can by business methods. This has been spoken of as a system of unlimited acquisition; and it is true that no quantitative ceiling has been set on the size of incomes, though an income tax that is highly progressive in the upper brackets is an effective expression of public policy unfavorable to extreme and excessively concentrated acquisition. A prior limitation operates through the "rules of the game" of business acquisition: rules intended to make income depend on serviceability so far as general rules can bring this about, and recognizing the inevitability of many loopholes.

The most pervasive agency operating in this direction is competition, which tends ideally to limit business incomes to the minimum necessary supply prices of the factors of production, including the services of enterprise. In this general fashion we depend on business competition to give us an economy in which it is safe—well, reasonably safe—to allow people to *pursue* unlimited income, because what they can get is, by competition, both limited and conditioned on serviceability, and what they can keep is limited by a progressive income tax.

Needless to say, this leaves much unfinished business for the rule makers, as conditions and practices evolve.

Under unrestrained competition a firm may profit by tactics that are predatory or fraudulent, by debasing the product, endangering the safety or health of consumers or workers or innocent third parties or impairing labor conditions in other ways, by wasting irreplaceable natural resources or deteriorating a community by neglect of the impact a productive establishment can have on surrounding values. It may promote or obstruct the requirements of national defense. And if one firm can gain a competitive advantage by such disserviceable methods, its rivals may feel that competitive pressure is forcing them in the same direction, and the constructive force of competition can be perverted.

To make it work for serviceability rather than the opposite in all these respects and others calls for a multitude of conditioning factors, starting with the basic law of personal and property rights and contract, implemented by dependable guidance, and going on to an array of more specific controls and general standards of responsible conduct. This whole body of standards, formal and informal, constitutes what has been spoken of above as the "rules of the game" of competitive business.[1] Insofar as these rules work in the direction of the public interest, they are sometimes spoken of as maintaining or raising the "level of competition." They need to be supplemented by an understanding acceptance of the tests of serviceability by enough competitors to influence the tone of the whole. Standards reluctantly accepted under social pressure may come to command the interest of management in their own right. In psychological terms, they may become "internalized." Progress of this sort may be spearheaded by firms strong enough to have an option of policy.

It is never safe to assume that the relation between profitability and serviceability is automatic, and our best efforts cannot hope to make it perfect. But it can turn the forces of competition largely in constructive directions, resulting in a combination of adequate discipline and flexible responsiveness to the wishes of those most directly concerned, which is preferable to the defects and abuses of direct authoritative control of production, price, and all that goes with them.

[1] These matters are discussed in the author's *Social Control of Business*, 2d ed. (1939).

2. Survival of Competition

Obviously, if we are to secure certain benefits that we desire from competition, the first requisite is that competition should survive. Only slightly less obvious is the corollary, that it should have the characteristics necessary to survival—and should operate in an environment that will permit it to possess these characteristics. And when it comes to defining the necessary characteristics, these are determined by the dangers that threaten it and which it must be able to avoid or resist. As to the environment, assuming that it includes a public opinion that wants competition to survive, it does not necessarily follow that this public opinion will realize, and tolerate, the characteristics competition needs for survival. The requirements it sets may be too lax, permitting rivalry to extinguish itself; or may be too meticulous, wiping out the necessary zone of individual discretionary choice, by trying to eliminate every objectionable feature. Both defects may occur at once, in different areas of action. Possibly the danger of laxness is the greater in the realms of policy; but it would be a bold man who would claim to know where the line should be drawn.

First and most obvious among the threats is the fact that a firm or an industry can make more profit if it does not compete, so that a desire to end competition is quite natural and may be hard to circumvent by public policy. Economists of the competitive school who viewed competition as a simple corollary of freedom were forced to recognize that this included freedom to agree not to compete. Thinking in terms of an economy of numerous small enterprises, they trusted in the instability of such agreements (if not formalized in cartels) and the tempting opportunities they afford to members of the trade who hold out from the agreement, and especially to outsiders who would enter.

Modern conditions of size and concentration create more of a problem. Free entry on the necessary scale is not so easy (though the diversification movement adds a fresh source of well-heeled new entries from other industries, in the shape of new departments of existing strong firms). Where there are a few firms of dominant size and strength, they may reach a *modus vivendi*, without clear violation of the antitrust laws, and may be able to exert enough disciplinary pressure over the irregularities of smaller concerns to keep them within limits which the leaders are prepared to tolerate. What are the means of countering the danger that competition might become ineffective by this kind of route? In this country, they start with a competitive tradition and acceptance of antitrust policy, at least "in principle," by business. They go on with alert interpretation and enforcement of this policy, in which perhaps the most difficult and delicate task is to distinguish between the kind of understandings and disciplinary measures that prevent competition from rendering its essential services and practices that merely maintain market conditions in which orderly but effective rivalry can proceed. The condition described, too simply, by the expression "You can't make people compete if they don't want to" needs to be transformed into a condition in which those who want to compete will be able to exert controlling pressure on those who do not, rather than the dominant control being the other way around. Success is not guaranteed, but neither is failure certain.

Another familiar statement is that competition is self-extinguishing because the strong eliminate or absorb the weak. If competitive strength were measured solely by productive efficiency, this would mean that the industry in question is the kind that economists class as a "natural monopoly," in which economies of large-scale production continue up to the point at which one unit absorbs substantially the whole market. In a market of the size of the American, this condition may be discounted as not existing in serious degree, so far as physical production goes, with qualifications as to firms with multiple plants, diversified regionally or productwise.[2] Sources of larger optimum size might be found in the economies of massive research or massive advertising, and especially in some cases in advantages of distribution by a network of exclusive agencies. This last raises perplexing problems extending beyond manufacturing productivity and illustrated in the automobile industry, or on a smaller scale in hearing aids.

[2] It is significant that it was only in his early work, "Some Aspects of Competition, 1890," in *Memorials of Alfred Marshall,* A. C. Pigou, Ed. (1925), pp. 256-91, that Marshall rated the ingenuity and enterprise of many small firms ahead of the advantages of fewer and larger firms in promoting technical progress. In *Industry and Trade* (1919), p. 249, this motif is reduced to the more modest statement that it is well if the economies of size stop somewhere.

A further problem has its roots in the contention that the modern large corporation has something close to perpetual life, exempting it from the sequence of youth, maturity, and declining vigor and enterprise, which Alfred Marshall stressed.[3] As a result, there is a greater chance for competitive superiority by whatever means attained, to work cumulatively over time, rather than being limited by the fluctuating fortunes of a kind of competition in which all are exposed to major shifts of relative power and position.[4] This may lead to natural oligopoly, rather than natural monopoly, or may fortify single-firm leadership. This tendency may be accentuated by factors in which competitive strength depends on other things than productive efficiency. Against using these kinds of competitive strength to establish a clearly monopolistic degree of unified control, the antitrust laws afford a fairly effective deterrent. As against the growth of a dominant few, the case is less clear. There are indications that leading firms voluntarily tend to avoid acquiring more than a minority of the market for an entire industry—perhaps a minority of 30 per cent to 33 per cent. The same rule may tend to hold for fairly distinct segments of the national market, such as the Pacific coast. For less distinct market segments, distinguished either in terms of areas or of particular products, a leading concern might permit itself larger percentages of control: for example, U. S. Steel's percentage of heavy plates and shapes in the midwestern market.[5]

Preservation of competition against self-extinction may require safeguards against abusive use or undue extension of the legal monopoly granted by the patent system. This privilege is intended as an incentive to innovation, limited in time and to the particular innovations covered, which should soon pass into the public domain, to benefit

[3] Cf. *Principles of Economics*, 5th ed. (1907), Book IV, Chap. 11, Sec. 6, and Chap. 13, Sec. 1.

[4] Relative positions fluctuate. (See A. D. H. Kaplan, *Big Enterprise in a Competitive System*, 1954, especially Chap. 7.) The remaining question is one of degree. The automobile industry is a disquieting instance in which firms of secondary size have shown resilience in meeting threats, while lesser firms have either gone under or merged in the attempt to gain viable secondary status.

[5] The writer has been told that this amounted to 90 per cent or more, as of 1956. The chief argument for the disallowed Bethlehem-Youngstown merger was that it would introduce strong competition into this market, more economically than either company could do this by itself. This would, of course, still be an extreme example of competition of the few, substantially a case of duopoly.

the economy in general. But it may be extended, both in time and in coverage, or abusively used for monopolizing purposes, outside its original purpose. These problems will be taken up in Chapter 8.

Among general structural conditions favorable to the persistence of competition, the efficiency necessary to survival should not require such large size as to permit only a few firms, and differences of efficiency should be moderate enough to make wars of extermination uncertain and costly. Short of such wars, most of the less-advantaged producers should be able to survive by accepting lower returns than the stronger firms, meanwhile working to improve their relative status. This condition is helped if no one firm is best in all parts of its operations—and it generally is not.

A third threat to the persistence of competition consists of a tendency of rivalry to go to lengths at which even efficient firms lose money and are impelled to resort to some kind of curbs, if the entire industry is to avoid real disaster. As we have seen, this problem was prominent during the late nineteenth century, when massive fixed investment was having its early impact. Under excess capacity, unrestricted competition tended to drive prices toward short-run marginal cost as a limit, this being less than average operating expenses. Resulting losses did not eliminate excess capacity with any readiness. Expanding industry was not exempt, and it was even suggested that a similar squeeze might result from bidding up the prices of the factors of production. The problem was naturally accentuated when substantial shrinkages of demand occurred, either for particular products or in general—notably in the depression of the thirties.

One way of stating the requirement involved is that the impact of short-run pressures on cost-price relations should not be so much more severe than the long-run standard of minimum necessary supply price as to prevent industry from being able to adapt competitively to fluctuations and vicissitudes. From this standpoint the most favorable condition appears to be one of growth, with innovations calling for frequent readjustments, but without massive recessions.[6] The threat of ruinous competition does not appear acute in this country at present. Is this because vicissitudes have been mild or because competition is ineffective? As late as 1951, Joan Robinson argued for the "impossi-

---

[6] Cf. Dexter M. Keezer, *Making Capitalism Work* (1950), p. 227.

bility of competition" on the basis of its tendency, unless restricted, to drive prices too close to short-run marginal cost.[7]

Destructive competition is the reverse of the conception that competition automatically becomes ineffective through the effects of fewness and product differentiation. The two may be tied together by the proposition that if the dilution of competition does not occur naturally, it will have to be brought about deliberately. This pair of questions will occupy much of this volume. For the present we may merely note that it defines, as a condition for the survival of competition, that it should be strong enough to be effective without being so strong as to be intolerable. The model of "perfect competition" combines these two qualities, though in a form both unattainable and undesirable. The remaining problem is whether a tolerable approximation can be attained under the conditions of modern and progressive industry. It will, of course, lack the precision of the "perfect" model of theory.

3. Allocation as a Dynamic Process

Assuming that we want a dynamically progressive system, it appears self-evident that we do not want a system that will actually reach a state of complete "static equilibrium." It may even be misleading to speak of the economy, or the various parts of it, as tending *toward* an equilibrium, since that may be taken to imply that such an equilibrium exists as a desirable goal, and that the economy could approach it as a limit, until it differed by less than any assigned quantity.[8] This is an abstraction; but it is the static version of something we do very much want in the actual, dynamic world, but which, for such a world, needs to be restated. We want resources allocated between different uses by

[7] See "The Impossibility of Competition," in *Monopoly and Competition and Their Regulation*, E. H. Chamberlin, Ed. (1954), pp. 145-54.

[8] In my father's statics, this requires the imaginary stoppage of growth and progress, a price we should be unwilling to pay. In a stagnant economy, the processes of adjustment would stagnate also; hence he held that in a dynamic economy the ever-changing static goals are approached more closely than they would be in a stationary state. Cf. John B. Clark, *The Distribution of Wealth* (1899), p. 404; and especially *Essentials of Economic Theory* (1907), pp. 195-96.

the actions of persons, no one of whom needs to be aiming at, or even conceiving, the whole economy-wide resultant. The resulting allocation does not have to be the one best possible. The only persons likely to worry about that are theoretical economists, overly impressed with the burden of hypothetical omniscience which they bear. Even theoretical "welfare economics" seems nowadays to be foregoing the concept of a definable single best allocation, largely as a result of its view that the utilities of different individuals are incommensurable.[9] On the other hand, an idea of rough commensurability, in terms of some kind of "social minimum," seems to underlie social policy.

In this same key, what we want may be defined as a system in which the persons who control economic resources are free to change their uses, and do change them, when they think they see a chance of making some of the resources more productive than they are, by enough to outweigh the costs and uncertainties of the change and to overcome any sheer inertia that may be involved. In the case of uncommitted resources, the costs of movement are minimal, but the uncertainties remain. Generally, these resources have some sort of market value, against which any particular use has to bid in order to secure them. To be profitable such a use needs to offer a prospect of greater productivity than that reflected in the general market value of the factors called for. Business firms, in grasping such opportunities, reduce the particular differentials in potential productivity from which the opportunities arise, while others are continually being created.

The process is beset with errors, uncertainties, time-lags, and tendencies to undercorrection or overcorrection—witness the corn-hog cycle already mentioned—and fresh changes create fresh differentials without waiting to see if existing ones will ever be completely ironed out. The point is not that differentials disappear in a perfect equilibrium, but that they perform a service—to stimulate useful movements—and in performing it they become self-limiting, not capricious but kept within bounds that, however elastic, spell organization rather than chaos. The important thing is that the remaining differentials should be due to the natural factors just discussed, rather than to

[9] Cf. Melvin W. Reder, *Studies in the Theory of Welfare Economics* (1947), pp. 14-15, 38. The same is true of Kenneth Arrow's more recent contributions, which include recognition of people's desires for collective adjustments, and the imperfections of voting as a method of composing their differences.

monopolistic obstacles to movement. This is what the author understands by the proposition that the static forces are acting in a dynamic economy.

4. Productive Efficiency

One of the most essential services of competition is to act as a spur to efficient production. By this is meant, of course, efficiency in real terms. From this standpoint one of the first services of competition is to establish the kind of market for the factors of production already spoken of, reducing mere exploitation of bargaining advantages to a minimum. In the case of the market for organized labor, of course, the most obviously active forces making for an approximate going rate are not competitive, and whatever competitive forces are at work operate as conditioning factors and mostly well below the surface.

Areas of cheap labor still exist, and it is not clear that these differentials are dwindling. Locations differ in the combined economy of transportation of materials inward to the establishment and of products outward to the market area or areas. We may assume that production is located in the light of these advantages—possibly with the aid of "linear programing"—and that conspicuous openings for economies of this sort are taken advantage of. Not all such differentials will be eliminated. In any case, from the standpoint of economy-wide efficiency, we are primarily interested in the kind of dollar economy that is to be had by more efficient location and use of the factors of production and not by buying them below the market rate. Later we shall encounter the problem whether or how far it is desirable that workers in technically advancing industries should for that reason receive higher wages than other workers.[10]

We may distinguish in a general way what may be called routine efficiency of management from acts of distinctive innovation, since they raise somewhat different problems. Routine efficiency may be roughly defined so as to leave room for improvement or deterioration in the effectiveness with which essentially similar methods are applied. Here the bearing of competition is comparatively simple. Com-

[10] See especially Chap. 18, below.

petitors try to reduce costs, under the conditions already indicated, and if one succeeds, relative to the level of costs that determines his selling conditions, he gets the full benefit as long as his relative gain holds. This is reversed if he falls behind; and in this sense he has a maximum incentive to economy and efficiency. But if his output is very small, he may lack some of the enabling conditions, including the ability to afford to devote good and adequate managerial talent to improvement. From this standpoint, it pays to spend a more expensive grade of management to save a dollar apiece on a million units of output per year than on ten thousand. Small firms that cannot offset this handicap may drop out.

The normal competitive assumption is that a more successful firm will want to use at least part of its advantage in ways that will increase its share of the business. If it succeeds, its original source of superiority is likely to persist up to the point at which the firm outgrows its original type of organization. Some firms refrain from trying to grow beyond this point, whether owing to limited capital, desire to retain personal control or preference for the simpler type of management operation. By natural selection, the largest and strongest firms in an industry or trade are those which have grown beyond this point, and have successfully met the accompanying challenge of administrative reorganization.

This process means a stiffening of the competitive pace. However, so long as it is confined to what has been called routine efficiency, it is likely to be gradual and limited. More rapid and far-reaching advances spring from innovation; and these involve temporary innovational monopolies and partial monopolies, reactions of competitors, and the delays and obstacles they face. We want innovation; but we also want its necessary conditions reconciled with those of an economy that retains its generally competitive character. These problems will be taken up in Chapter 8 below.

By contrast to competitive conditions, a secure monopoly—if such a thing exists—can be efficient and has the entire output of the industry on which to realize the benefits of its improvements in efficiency. This condition of incentive it possesses in maximum degree. But its incentive lacks one dimension: no increase or decrease in its proportionate share of the business is at stake; its survival does not depend on meeting the standards set by the rest of the industry. Its ability to earn continued profits above the competitive minimum does not depend on

keeping ahead of rivals who are doing their best to catch up or to surpass it. It is not forced to wage a determined struggle against the
forces of bureaucratic decay that naturally attack big organizations.
Actually, it is impossible to imagine a monopoly as absolute as this in
any substantial branch of industry or trade. Any close approach to
bureaucratic decay will invite rivals to come into being.

So much for a summary of the part we want competition to play
in the advance of productive efficiency. It is inevitably imperfect, if
only because the processes involved all take time—innovation, expansion of sales, imitation, obsolescence. But even competition which,
pricewise, is decidedly imperfect, can exert strong pressure, both on
productive techniques and toward diffusion of resulting gains.

5. Product Differentiation

American consumers want an adequate variety of goods to choose
from, including the development of new products. This is an inevitable
accompaniment of the expanding standard of living that results from
increasing the efficiency of productive processes. We could not use
our increasing consuming power unless we bought new products, and
new grades of old ones. As we take part of our gains in shorter working
hours, industries arise to cater to our increasing leisure. As the general
rise in incomes spreads over forms of production in which the gains of
mass production and applied science do not accrue, these things become more expensive, and substitutes are sought—notably household
appliances and prepared foods to replace old-fashioned domestic service. We, as consumers, could not invent all the things we would choose
to use if offered; we leave that to the producers, who produce what
they think we can be induced to buy. The consumer, insofar as he
can be said to be sovereign, has the last word, not the first. And that
is enough, if he can exercise it effectively.

But can he? It is around this question that the drawbacks of modern
product differentiation center. In accepting product differentiation, we
accept the multitude of problems of customer choice and guidance
that go with it. Synthetic substitutes, food additives, new mechanical
devices, multiply the problems of judging products beyond the ca-

pacity of the ordinary consumer, though industrial purchasers are in a different class in their ability to test the materials and subassemblies they buy. Competition impels numerous large producers to protect their own reputation and that of their products by testing the products, often quite rigorously, for the features of performance on which customer satisfaction or dissatisfaction will depend. But this does not guarantee that all "bugs" are eliminated. There are many dangers to health and safety against which public safeguards are needed, and many products that might contain dangers about which the necessary knowledge does not exist. "Adulterants" may be harmful, may merely reduce the positive serviceability of the product, or may be useful economizing of scarce materials without reduction of serviceability. Food additives multiply faster than the Food and Drug Administration is currently able to investigate their effects on health.[11] Improvements that increase the durability of products may in some circumstances reduce total demand and therefore raise special problems of incentive, which will be discussed later (Chap. 10, Sec. 3).

What is needed starts with knowledge that would cover the most serious dangers. On the basis of such knowledge, compulsory safety standards might be improved. As a result there might be less excuse for excluding new products—for example, new construction materials —merely on the ground that they have not been proved safe and thus converting the safety regulations into barriers to protect existing producers against legitimate competition of new and improved methods and materials. Within the range of permitted products, we may assume that producers will promote their own, and the constructive character of their competition for the customer's favor hinges on his having as much dependable information as he can and will use, to enable him to appraise their conflicting claims and sift out the objective information they contain. The system includes general prohibitions against false or misleading statements, some specific requirements of information on ingredients, also testing by both public and private agencies. So far as consumers are concerned, a crucial limiting factor is the unwillingness or inability of the majority to spend the time and effort required to take full advantage of the testing services that are available.

Another point is that, in this matter of consumer choice and its guidance as the key to effective competition in quality, such competi-

[11] Anthony Netboy, "Cancer Fighters Turn to Food Additives," in the *New Leader*, Feb. 18, 1957, pp. 20, 21.

tion gains nothing from the very large number of sellers that is represented, in what has here been called "accepted theory," as necessary for effective competition in price. The typical single buyer can make successful comparisons between only a limited number of makes of differentiated products; a large number forced on his attention would confuse choice rather than promote it. If a large number is available, the result may be a market in which each buyer is actively comparing only a few, but different buyers' lists overlap, so that a chain of selective comparisons covers the market. This may be more marked if stores in a particular town or small area carry goods chosen from a limited number of brands, the sales of which are pushed in this particular area.

The upshot is that, while one brand might have superior appeal, no one could quickly scoop the market, because there is no one that enters into every buyer's active focus of comparison. This is reinforced by differences of taste, so that some consumers would prefer brand A and others brand B, even if all of them made careful comparisons of these two brands. This minimizes the likelihood, discussed above, that competition will automatically lead to monopoly. It would naturally lead to some instability in the shares of business done by different producers and would eliminate some of the least successful. But if brands are changing actively, there is no great likelihood of one maintaining superiority long enough to drive out all the others.

Within the latitude offered by imperfect consumer knowledge, there is room for opposite kinds of misleading tactics, roughly classifiable as artificial differentiation of products essentially alike and superficial likeness of products that differ in the less observable features of serviceability. Improvement in consumer knowledge would reduce the scope for both, but there is no prospect of eliminating them under free private enterprise.

To sum up a subject on which volumes could be written without exhausting it, three types of problems may be distinguished in general terms: the qualitative question of adequacy of consumer choice and two quantitative questions, that of wasteful multiplication of selling effort and that of the sensitiveness with which demand may shift, momentarily or progressively, between the brands of different sellers in response to sales appeals in quality, selling effort, and price. The qualitative and quantitative questions are related. On the qualitative side, much imperfection is unavoidable, for reasons already briefly suggested. They concern the relation between sales appeal, momentary or sustained, and consumer satisfaction, and between both and ultimate serviceability, in matters in which the consumer may benefit or suffer without ever tracing the result to its cause and therefore without interpreting it in terms of satisfaction or dissatisfaction with the particular product that may be responsible.

As to the quantitative question of cross sensitiveness of demand, it bears on whether competition between differentiated products leads to monopoloidal profits or destructive rivalry and losses, and whether it is consistent with an efficient scale of operation. There is presumably some optimum range of cross-sensitivity of demand (momentary or progressive) well short of the immediate and infinite elasticity of theoretical "perfect competition," though it would be hopeless to attempt to measure it. Criteria would include: (1) that short-run competitive pressures arising from unused capacity should not depart too drastically from a long-run normal; and (2) that new products and product variants should be developed and find market acceptance fast enough to cause total demand to keep pace with increasing productive power, but not faster than producers of displaced products can make a healthy adjustment. There can be no guarantee that the forces at work will lead to such an optimum. Nevertheless, there is reason to judge that if definable abuses are restrained, the result may give us progress at a cost we should be willing to pay, combining rewards to innovators with diffusion of the gains at a speed that is surprisingly rapid in terms of historical perspective—more rapid than that achieved on a sustained basis by any other economic system.[12]

6. Diffusion of the Gains of Progress

If those responsible for improvements that increase productivity had a perpetual claim to the increased productivity they have created,

[12] The reader will note that this does not include temporary periods of catching up after wartime disruption; and it might properly exclude extra-rapid bursts of imitative growth. As to the Soviet system, the writer has no doubts of the validity of the statement, made as it was in terms of diffusion of benefits. Comparisons of rate of gain in total productivity involve complications of measurement and inter pretation beyond the scope of the present study.

which they could hand down to their heirs, we should all be paying tribute to the heirs of—for example only—Hargreaves, Arkwright, Watt, Eli Whitney, Fulton, Stephenson, Bessemer, and so on. And those lacking ancestors in this class would be no better off than the common man of the early eighteenth century, to go no farther back. Even on the basis of historical contribution, any such allocation would be quite arbitrary, ignoring the contributions of the unsuccessful predecessors on whose work the final successful innovator built. And the reward to the heirs of past innovators would mean that the present generation was deprived of a large part of its current productivity, since the whole present product could be properly imputed to those now engaged in creating it.[13] Historical and current imputation overlap.

The system we accept is one that gives innovators a chance of such reward as they can get out of whatever superiority their innovation can establish in competition with pre-existing processes or products and limited to the time when the innovation is a novelty. By the time it has in turn become part of the generally available "state of the arts," we think it should have passed into the public domain, the resulting gains diffused among the population, and the techniques open to would-be users, including current innovators who, if they make fresh advances, may collect their own differential rewards. If a successful innovator has a monopoly in his innovation, he will still normally find it worth while to share enough of the differential gain with the customers to induce them to buy more of his product. But the full diffusion of his gains occurs when he faces competitors equipped with his innovation or something equally effective—perhaps even superior.

This competitive diffusion may take different forms and is thought of in different ways. Competition may act downward on the prices at which the industry sells, or upward on the prices it pays for the factors of production, or both, in proportions that vary with conditions. The simplest first approximation pictures competition as reducing selling prices. This corresponds to the position of an industry that draws its materials, labor, and capital funds from a large market in which its demands do not take enough of the whole to influence its buying prices materially. This simplified picture reflects some of the key forces and is useful so long as one remembers that it depicts only one way in

[13] This problem in imputation need not detain us. The author has treated the principle involved in *Studies in the Economics of Overhead Costs* (1923), Chap. 23.

which the gains of innovation are diffused. Normally, the results will be to reduce the innovational profits of the industry as a whole, while increasing gross sales. Sometimes, the process may uncover possibilities of profitable sales expansion unanticipated by the more conservative members of the industry. This is most likely to happen when a young product is exploring new potential uses.

If this picture of diffusion via price reduction is extended to the economy as a whole, it has certain attractive features of simplicity, also difficulties that will presumably prevent it from being realized. An attractive feature is that such diffusion benefits everyone, since everyone is a consumer, including persons on pensions or other fixed money incomes. Such gains would go equally to workers in industries where improvements have been made and where they have not, always in their capacity as consumers. Inequalities in the diffusion would result only from the fact that products in which increased productivity has caused more than average decline in prices may play a larger part in some consumer budgets than in others. Meanwhile, money wages would not rise with rising productivity, and this is hardly a thinkable condition. Leaders of organized labor might not be out of a job, but they would lose their most effective talking point. The author knows no economists who advocates this method of diffusion in its completely rigorous form; but some—notably Dr. Edwin G. Nourse—would like to see an important part of the gains of improvement take the shape of a downward trend in the price level.[14]

A larger group would like to see the gains diffused at a stable general price level. This presupposes that average money incomes, including average wages, rise commensurately with the economy-wide average increase in productivity.[15] In this raising of money wages, organized labor will naturally play a part. We may assume that differences in wage increases are less than differences in increased productivity due to industrial innovation, this being in accord with underlying economic forces and with the prevailing sense of equity. This means that, in industries in which productivity has not increased, or has increased much less than the average, wages must rise more than productivity, causing labor costs per unit to rise, while in industries that have exceeded the average rise in productivity, money wages must rise less than productivity, bringing unit labor costs down. Then,

[14] See Edwin G. Nourse, *Price Making in a Democracy* (1944).
[15] The word "commensurately" is intended not to be mathematically precise.

if competition keeps prices in normal relation to costs, the latter class of products becomes cheaper in money terms, and the former more expensive. Holders of fixed incomes get none of the benefits, but at least they do not lose. Evidently, the goal of a stable price level, plus approximate equity in relative wages, requires a complicated and difficult revision of the wage structure, likely to prove not feasible.

What we are likely to get, wages and prices being determined as they are, is a third form of diffusion, in which wages in the more dynamic industries rise as much or more than the better-than-average rate of increase of productivity in these industries, wages elsewhere follow this rate of rise as closely as they can, rising more than productivity in the less dynamic industries, average wages rise more than average productivity, raising average unit costs, and prices rise to offset this, approximately maintaining the proportionate share going to profits. The indicated result is a "creeping inflation," financed by an elastic credit system that is under pressure to furnish the monetary resources to handle the increased dollar volume of business, on penalty of being held responsible for precipitating a recession. Fixed dollar incomes shrink in real value, real interest is less than nominal interest, and conventional depreciation reserves fail to provide funds for full physical replacement.

What competition has to do with all this is not easy to say. It has been suggested that stronger competition between employers might make it harder for them to pass wage increases on to the customer in higher prices, and thus might force them to absorb part of the increased cost resulting from wage increases that would otherwise be inflationary. This might stiffen their resistance to wage increases that exceeded what employers could thus absorb. This clearly raises more questions than it answers. Since we are here asking what we should like, perhaps it is sufficient at this stage to say that we should wish competition to make whatever contribution it can make to a process of diffusing the gains of progress in the most equitable way feasible, which includes keeping inflation to an irreducible minimum. This problem will be discussed in Chapter 18.

7. *Elimination of Inefficient Elements*

One of the more unpleasant services expected of competition is the elimination of inefficient firms, products, and processes by a test more impersonal and, one may assume, more ruthless, than would be likely to be followed by public agencies, if they were charged with this responsibility. Here, as in the case of product differentiation, there is a qualitative and a quantitative criterion. Qualitatively, we want survival to depend on efficiency and serviceability, not on the use of economic power in ways unrelated to these qualities. Quantitatively it is desirable that elimination should take place at a rate that balances the setting-up of new capacity, making room for an inflow of modern and efficient capacity and allowing it a reasonable prospect of return. The corresponding rate of elimination varies according as an industry is expanding or contracting.

Incidentally, selective elimination implies that the remaining concerns have enough capacity, installed or quickly available, to handle the business of the eliminated units without pushing their capacity to a point that raises their marginal cost materially. In that sense, it implies "excess capacity." Another possibility is that more efficient concerns might take over the facilities of the less efficient and operate them more efficiently, perhaps first modernizing them. This can happen when the facilities themselves are not incurably inefficient. Where elimination fails to take place, inefficient facilities may continue in operation, limiting the room for new and more efficient capacity, or may remain closed down but hanging over the market, ready to resume operation if demand revives sufficiently to enable them to earn something more than out-of-pocket expenses. This is likely to occur in a business that has been overbuilt or is contracting, and that faces a fluctuating demand.

Another thing desired is that competition should keep firms vigilant to eliminate inefficiencies of process or product, before losses have so depleted their resources as to make rehabilitation difficult or impossible. The increase of diversification makes this requirement easier to meet, since the resources of the firm are not all tied to one line of products and should not be exhausted if one line proves a failure. But this also makes it possible to continue an unsuccessful line instead of liquidating it promptly.[16]

8. Facilitation of High and Stable Employment

One of the things we should like competition to do is to play whatever role it can most helpfully play in furthering the aim of high and stable economic activity and employment. Regarding what that role should be, questions arise, and few would rate it as the principal reliance. It may be that if the economy were more unmitigatedly competitive than it is, business recessions (insofar as they were encountered) would be more likely to be featured by cuts in dollar values, made in the attempt to maintain physical output, rather than cutting physical output and resisting declines in dollar values. As a means of sustaining employment, this might or might not work better than the behavior we follow—on this, experts would disagree. But competition has some features that are incompatible with thoroughgoing stabilization: primarily the fact that programs of investment and output are planned and carried out by different firms independently, without coordination, always contingent on adequate demand and subject to revision if the demand that materializes is not enough to validate them.

And for maintaining over-all demand, economists prevailingly hold that ruthless competitive slashing of prices is less effective, as well as more disturbing, than well-judged monetary and fiscal policies. Assuming the latter type of policy, what competition can do is to make the economy flexibly responsive to adequate total demand, carrying out the mobilizations that will always be needed to place resources where they are called for by an expanding productive power, and minimizing the pools of unemployment that may persist in an economy where there is not enough of this adaptable mobility. Social security and other security policies need to be so handled as to avoid creat-

[16] But Avco's losses on its line of appliances, beginning in 1953, culminated in 1956 in losses for the company as a whole; and not till this happened was the appliance line liquidated. *Fortune* (February 1957), p. 138.

ing obstacles to proper mobility; as when retirement rights are of a sort that a worker sacrifices if he changes jobs, or when union rules as to job specifications put obstacles in the way of keeping older workers on the payroll by shifting them to jobs with less exacting physical requirements. As I have said elsewhere, the economy would respond better if free from undue rigidities of particular prices and wages, from noncompetitive features of the wage structure that tend to produce what Professor Slichter has called "wage-distortion unemployment," and from obstacles to movement and to entry into particular trades or professions.[17]

The things considered so far bear primarily on stabilization of demand, or rather, mitigation of fluctuations and adaptation to the resulting needs for adjustment. A more basic problem, in which competition plays a more active part, consists in establishing a balance between increased productive power and the uses we find for it, including increased leisure and an increased flow of products. This is a three-way adjustment, in which increased leisure activities help create increased demand for goods and services, into which the American economy appears to put something more than half of its increase in per capita productive power. This fraction appears to have amounted, over a long-run trend, to very nearly 2 per cent a year compounded, or more than 20 per cent per decade. The advance of our level of living may be limited, either by our productive power or by our success in finding forms in which to put it; and it is by no means a foregone conclusion that productive power will be the effective limiting factor.

For the desired balance, the main requirement is that consumers shall spend a large enough fraction of their income so that the remainder, or voluntary savings, will not be more than business will want to spend for investment to carry out the accompanying total volume of production. As an approximate rule of thumb, one might assume that this requirement will be met if we continue to spend for consumption the same fraction of our growing income that has marked the trend of our growth in the recent past. But if real income per capita increases by more than 20 per cent in a decade, it is obvious that consumers will not simply buy 20 per cent more of everything, or 10 per cent more of some things and 30 per cent more of others. If

[17] "Competition and the Objectives of Government Policy," in *Monopoly and Competition and Their Regulation*, E. H. Chamberlin, Ed., p. 334.

production were planned on such a basis, much of the output would fail to find buyers, and industrial contraction would result. To avoid this kind of failure calls for a deal of enterprise, pioneering, and innovation.

It calls for a combination of new products and improvements or elaborations of existing ones, the test being always whether the consumers can be persuaded to pay for the new products or the elaborations. This gives the advertising industry much work to do, because new or altered products do not command acceptance automatically. And this raises the question whether advertising might perform the function that is here in question by merely misleading the consumers into buying what industry offers, regardless of whether it gives them any net increase in service values. To this, the ultimate limit comes when consumers become too disillusioned to respond, but one must regretfully admit that consumers appear capable of absorbing large amounts of misleading salesmanship before reaching the ultimate limit of no-response. Their psychology may be like that of the gambler who was warned that the faro game he was bucking was crooked. He answered: "I know it, but it's the only game in town." Advertising is virtually the only way the consumer has of being made aware of new offerings. He may distrust its dependability, but he has to use it nevertheless.

What we want, of course, is an assortment of offerings that would embody our whole increase in productive power in products and values which, in the light of informed hindsight, we would judge to be worth their cost. This cost includes the cost of research and market exploration and of the selling effort necessary to familiarize the buyers with the new offerings and to popularize them. It includes also the inevitable false starts and failures. Whether some of these should be called "wastes" rather than "costs" is a question hardly susceptible of a proven answer. Another side of the same coin consists in the losses suffered by producers whose products are superseded. Such costs of obsolescence are inevitable features of growth; whether we should judge them wasteful depends mainly on whether the superiority of the successful products represents enduring serviceability or the vagaries of taste or mere novelty. In the latter case, successive displacements might leave no residue of enduring consumer gain.

It could easily be that we should not find ways of using all our increased productive power that would represent such an enduring increase in serviceability. Not that such ways do not exist, but that there may be a limit to the rate at which our machinery for exploring and developing such things can find them and make them marketable. If there is such a limit, and if we reach it before we reach the limit of our productive power, we face an interesting question: Is it better for us to be stimulated into spending the excess of our potential income on wasteful, futile, and frivolous consumption, or not to spend it at all? The question may be adjudged academic, because it is not possible to draw sharp and objective distinctions between serviceable and non-serviceable consumption, even though many cases may be clear beyond reasonable doubt.

Suffice it for the present that the development of new or altered products is, in the aggregate, necessary to the realization of the economy's productive capacity, that it involves heavy costs of trial and error and misdirection, but that if any considerable fraction of the effort so spent yields cumulative improvements in our level of living, this cumulative improvement outweighs whatever fraction of our resources we devote each year to bringing it about. We should like to reduce the wastes and increase the serviceability. But most economic students would prefer an economy actively energizing its productive resources and progressing annually, with an amount of waste motion, to one with less waste motion and less employment of resources or slower economic progress. The former represents the direction in which the institutions of market research and sales promotion are energetically steering the American economy.

Here, having introduced a very large subject, we must leave it for the present. Various phases of it will appear later, when we discuss innovation and product differentiation.

9. Business Freedom Desired for Its Own Sake

Those who uphold competition commonly do so because they regard the status of free private enterprise as a desirable thing in itself. What freedom means in this connection is, of course, not the abolition of regulations of health and safety, hours of labor, and a multitude of other matters of welfare. What is meant is freedom to decide what, if anything, to produce, by what methods, how to sell it, and at what price or prices. It means that in these strategic matters the private business man has a range of discretion within which he can make decisions and take the consequences. It means that there are multiple, decentralized foci of such decisions, mutually controlling one another and limiting one another's discretion without wiping it out. The discretion is part of what freedom means; the limits on it are needed to protect the freedom of the rest of us. We do not want it to be within the individual power of private business to choose to give the economy, or to withhold from it, the benefits discussed in earlier sections; we should like it to be free only to choose in what role and by what methods it shall act in furtherance of those benefits. Society can afford to leave any particular individual free to decide whether or not to supply his services; because if he decides not to supply them, society is not thereby deprived of any product which it wants and is willing to pay for; others will supply it, on terms which no one has power to dictate arbitrarily.

One consequence of this preference is that we seem inclined to give the benefit of the doubt to policies that would tend to protect the existence of numerous competitors, as against a "tough" kind of competition that is likely to eliminate too many and leave an oligopoly. But we show this leaning only where there is a margin of doubt. The American consumer is not likely to patronize the old-fashioned retailer in preference to the supermarket if convinced that the supermarket gives him more for his money.

10. Freedom of Purchasers to Relax Market Vigilance

One benefit which many consumers depend, in varying degree, on receiving from competition is the establishment of a market in which they can do a good deal of their buying, chiefly of the "repeat" variety, without spending the time and effort necessary to compare different sellers' prices and check them against the corresponding qualities, and will still not run any great danger of being grossly exploited on either price or quality. It is one of the facts of life, for consumers, that the task of making sure that on every purchase one is getting the best bargain the market affords is impossible; and any attempt at a close approximation to it carries a human cost that is prohibitive, to a rational consumer. He or she has more rewarding ways of spending his or her time than pursuing perfection in this kind of marketing "rationality." And the consumers' efforts, if carried this far, would impose a burden on the dealer, cutting down the volume of sales a salesman could transact in a day and raising costs the customer would ultimately have to pay. The efficiency of American retail distribution begins with openly marked prices (instead of the old-fashioned cabalistic symbols) on identifiable products. This assures the customer the same price as other customers in the same store. It does not assure equal prices in different stores, but it facilitates the kind of customer comparison that keeps differentials between stores within bounds.

The result reflects a combination of factors and attitudes. The dealer values regular customers who trust him to treat them fairly, and he has an interest in keeping them satisfied that they do as well with him as elsewhere, without the need of keen and constant shopping around. Such customers need to have some awareness of the market, even though their chief competitive safeguard is the assurance of getting as good treatment as others who shop around more actively. (On the other hand, in some trades, special favors are given to attract new customers, while the one who shops around may gain some bargains; he may find different products treated as "leaders" by different dealers.) These conditions define a market in which cross-elasticities of demand, while not "perfect," exert competitive pressures that may be sufficient for the rather modest purpose here considered. Later, after more detailed examination of demand curves and cost curves, it will be argued that the condition known as a "sloping individual-demand curve" can be, quite generally though not invariably and precisely, consistent with effective competition. This depends on the customer's ability to judge offerings, which was stressed in Section 5, above.

11. Conclusion

To sum up the conclusions of this survey of the benefits we want from competition, they include forces of dynamic progress that carry costs. In our prevalent scale of values, the gains are worth what they cost. But a serious look at the costs lends stress to the importance of keeping them close to the minimum that is really unavoidable. This minimum includes the costs of countermeasures, which are less than the costs of neglect. The benefits of competition also include equilibrating effects, necessarily incomplete and best described as reducing disequilibria and limiting them. In a stagnant economy these equilibrating forces could lapse into inertia from disuse; though there would still be need for them, since a literally stationary economy is inconceivable. Thus there is truth in J. B. Clark's position that a dynamic economy will "hover" closer to its "static model" than a sluggish one. Where the two kinds of gain conflict, those of a continuing progressive character outweigh gains that might be initially larger but not progressive.[18]

[18] *Essentials of Economic Theory* (1907), p. 195. Cf. also *The Distribution of Wealth* (1902), p. 404.

CHAPTER 5

Elements of Economic Structure

1. Introduction

The structure of the economy as a whole is so bafflingly varied and complex, that, in order to think about it at all, it is necessary to use simplifying concepts. But in using them, one faces a double difficulty. They defy the kind of definition that tries to draw sharp boundaries separating one from another. This is familiar enough to students who have faced the problem of defining precise boundaries for competition and substitution, the product, and the industry. The other horn of the dilemma is to define pure types; and here the difficulty is that a system of explanation confined to these pure types misses some of the features that are most important for understanding the kinds of competition that actually exist. This is true even of the pure types intermediate between competition and monopoly, in ways already suggested in Chapter 3.[1] Fuller understanding of competition consists largely in a search for these neglected features and their effects.

The central type, which this search takes as a point of departure, is the picture of a firm trying to "maximize its profits"—which in itself is insufficient to define its behavior—by selling a "product," with or without competition from other firms selling the "same" product, or a variant of it. The forces that limit its profits and determine what it must do to "maximize" them are conceived as focusing on the one side in curves of demand—for the "product" of this firm or for that of the whole group of competitors—and on the other side in curves of supply or of cost. In the two chapters that follow, we shall look at the

[1] Since writing the above, I note that it is corroborated by Joe S. Bain, *Barriers to New Competition* (1956), p. 2.

conceptions of demand, supply, and cost curves. But first we need to look at the firm, its motivation, and the conditions of industry and market structure that determine the forms its motivation takes. These will be the subject of the present chapter.

2. The Firm[2]

It is not hard to define a "firm" in principle; it is an independent unit administering operations of production involving purchase, addition of value, and sale of the resulting product or products. But if what we are interested in is the character of the firm, this tells us little. The "firm" may be a single self-employed odd-job man, a one-family farm or retail store, or anything up to Du Pont, General Motors, or U. S. Steel. It may create a single product, but generally it turns out a number of products, often an enormous number, grouped into a "line" or a number of "lines." In such cases, we need to break up the convenient fiction of a firm creating one product, and deal either with a firm creating multiple products or with a product that is only part of the output of a firm. We shall need to use both conceptions, for different purposes. If we look at the firm, prices of single products may be indeterminate; and if we look at the product, it may have no clearly determined cost in a multiproduct firm. And it may or may not be subject to competition from small firms that specialize on this item, and must cover costs from it.

Firms differ widely in the number of functions they perform, and this is not confined to what is ordinarily thought of as vertical integration in which, for example, a manufacturer reaches back and produces his own materials, or reaches forward and does his own marketing. Many manufacturers purchase parts or subassemblies, and the producers of these items are in effect competing with their customer's option to make them himself. The independence of such suppliers hinges on whether they have a varied market which affords them ample alternatives if one customer does not do well by them. If they are

[2] An analysis of the nature and problems of the firm, similar in general character and conclusions to that given below, is made by Neil W. Chamberlain, *General Theory of Economic Process* (1955), Chaps. 10-12.

small, it may be convenient to dispose of their whole output to one buyer; but this generates dependence through loss of touch with a competitive market. The writer has been told that a certain large chain store refuses to take more than a given fraction of the output of small suppliers, wishing to avoid reducing such suppliers to dependence—possibly also wishing to avoid the responsibility for such dependent suppliers. Problems of dependence in the other direction arise when a small dealer distributes the product of a giant supplier, especially if he is that supplier's exclusive agent. The line between such exclusive dealerships and vertical integration can become tenuous.

At a different level of auxiliary service, the public accountant, the efficiency engineer and the advertising agency, all act in the role of independent enterprises, selling their services to numerous firms, often in quite different industries. The standing of Price, Waterhouse or Young and Rubicam is warrant that such special-service enterprises can gain a commanding position. Their product is a service entering into the production of a wide variety of end products. If advertising is an industry—as in reason it seems to be in the sense that it sells a product—it is also a part of most other industries. Functionally, the service rendered by the independent advertising agency is only a part of the service of sales promotion—the part that is farmed out by the client industry. This illustrates the fact that it is not feasible to classify industries by the productive function they perform.

The assumption that a firm pursues maximum profits is an extreme simplification. Indeed, it is a simplification to assume that any unified objective governs all the operations of a firm, especially a large one. This covers up a multitude of divergencies. Theory has a tendency to dispose of these as being either differences of view on what kind of action will maximize profits in a given case, or differences between longer or shorter time perspectives in which profits may be viewed. To this view there are two answers. First, insofar as it is correct, it does not preclude the need of examining these divergencies, but emphasizes that need. Second, there are motivations that this explanation does not cover.

There is recognition of broad community responsibilities, which may be window-dressing in many cases but is also genuine in enough cases to affect the prevalent tone. There is the desire to give the customer a worthwhile product, which may be at war with maximum profit or may be in harmony with it, according to conditions that challenge the most searching analysis. There is an interest in the survival and growth of the firm as such, not viewed exclusively through the spectacles of maximum dividends to the stockholders who are technically the owners. And there is the pervasive fact that things undertaken as means to profit come to command the interest of management in their own right. This is a pervasive psychological trait, underlying Veblen's "instinct of workmanship"; and in the case of a large corporation it is reinforced by putting particular functions in the hands of specialists, who may be chosen because they already are interested in these functions, and some of whom have an interest of a professional sort.

We have seen that competition hinges on efficiency of technical processes, on selection and design of products, on selling effort and pricing. Procurement should also have been included, since it involves much more than simply paying market prices for purchased supplies. It includes much essentially productive work in locating supplies, and in mutual adaptation between supplies and requirements, in which users and suppliers may usefully cooperate. It includes acquiring ownership of sources of materials, and if these are scarce, big firms may acquire so much of the best supplies as to handicap small competitors or new entrants. Or advantages in competition may be gained by getting special price concessions in purchasing supplies. Such bargaining advantages are more controversial than superiorities in the other forms of competitive action, as being monopolistic or "unfair."

Each of these forms of action calls for planning and execution. The planning involves research and experimentation, with gathering and interpretation of information and estimates of the probable results of any new policy or the reception of any new product or selling appeal. The execution is not only the test of the previous planning, it may point to the next problems with which planning will have to deal. For our purposes, one point is that these processes are divided among different departments, to an extent varying with the size of the firm. It is proverbial that production and selling departments do not see eye to eye on catering to customers' differentiated preferences, and there are ample opportunities for similarly divergent views among other departments.

Another point is that these activities involve much that is exploratory, unprecise, and uncertain. This is certainly true of the effect of a change in a price, or in tactics of selling appeal. The "maximization" of profits is a process of trial and error, prevented by changing conditions from reaching any precise result. The firm's reaction to uncertainty is an essential feature of its behavior. The most typical reaction of modern business to uncertainty is to try to reduce it by investigation. By the time the result reaches the executive who is to base a decision on it, it is normally in the form of a simplified picture of a "most probable" condition or outcome. But somewhere in the operation there needs to be room for a recognition of the range of uncertainty, and what will happen if the outcome turns out to be more or less favorable than the "most probable" forecast.[3]

It seems fair to say that in modern business, the firm wants to be in a position to rejoice at an unexpectedly favorable outcome, but is more concerned not to expose its position to serious risks if the outcome is unexpectedly unfavorable. Above all, it does not want to imperil its own survival. As to uncertainties about what the firm's rivals may do, if it follows the suggestion of the theory of games, it will assume that its rivals will make the most formidable competitive move among those they might choose with an eye to their own advantage. Then the firm will plan its counterpolicy in the light of the most difficult conditions it is likely to meet.

As to time perspectives, they vary from that of the fly-by-night concern, which aims to make a killing and move on to fresh hunting grounds before the customers have time to find out they are being victimized, to the concern that plans for indefinite continuance in business. Prevalent policies in major industries are closer to the latter type, so that the fly-by-night firm may be recognized as existing but nontypical, and analysis may concentrate on firms that at least aim at indefinitely continued survival in their existing market. Even here, however, it appears that there is need to distinguish between the planning of specific programs of production and selling, and the more general policies into which the specific programs should properly fit. The relation between these two levels of planning presents an interesting problem. Lloyd G. Reynolds states that: "Production and sales plans are rarely viewed with much confidence for more than three months ahead."[4] The conclusion is that, when firms find it necessary or expedi-

---

[3] Cf. Chamberlain, *ibid.*, pp. 214-20, 240-43.
[4] *The Structure of Labor Markets* (1951), pp. 163-65. Cited by Chamberlain, *op. cit.*, p. 220.

ent to undertake commitments for a longer period, they try to leave themselves a safety margin for unforeseeable changes in conditions. Reynolds was speaking of wage commitments, but the same applies to long-term debts and other forward undertakings of a binding sort. The inference seems warranted that it is only the definiteness implied by the word "plans" that is limited to short horizons; and that objectives and policies adapted and adaptable to meeting uncertainty have a much longer reach, and govern the short-run "plans" more than they are governed by them.

The firm's attitude toward particular products may aim at making a good profit for a limited period, after which, if the product succeeds, competition may be expected to reduce the profit possibilities to a modest level. Then the firm may face a new policy decision whether to continue the product as a low-return staple, and it may lose interest in pushing it, or may even in some cases abandon it. As to the firm's entire line of products, there are further differences in time perspective, according as the firm is in a strong position, with a range of policy open to it, or whether it is hard pressed by competition that forces it to concentrate on the necessities of immediate survival. An industry is likely to include firms in both kinds of position, and its total behavior can be understood only in the light of this diversity. Each type conditions the actions of the other. It should be needless to point out that such interactions are obscured wherever economic analysis represents the firm's motivation—as it typically does—by a single, undifferentiated concept of "profit maximization," pictured as the same for all firms in a given model.

These interactions call for further modification of the list of different time perspectives presented in Chapter 3 as being implied in different theoretical models or in different situations. It was there argued that the models overemphasize tendencies to an oligopoly stalemate and underemphasize variants tending to competitive behavior. Even the stalemate model is modified if it is recognized that different firms have different ideas of the profit level that is best for the industry to aim at; and that the industry tends to be governed by any strong firm or group whose pricing policy expresses the most modest idea of the optimum profit level.

In addition, the conclusion that oligopoly leads to a monopoly type of price reckons without some of the devices available for competition which will not be instantly neutralized—quality competition and price "chiseling" being outstanding categories. These need to be envisaged in the light of the types of firms likely to engage in them, and the reactions of the others, not only to the specific tactics but to the general situation in which these tactics are to be expected. There are small concerns which are often able to do a limited amount of price shading without bringing down the whole price structure to their level; but they are likely to overstep these limits under short-run pressure. If "chiseling" spreads, it may lead other firms to defensive price reductions aimed at regularizing a situation that has become thoroughly disorderly.

But if nobody in the industry is attracted by the gains of competitive undercutting, judging them to be temporary, and if the result is a price policy representing some strong firm's judgment of what is best for the industry, there remains the question of this firm's time perspective. It does not follow that a price will be set that would maximize the industry's profits, say, for the next year or two. Such a policy still involves a degree of shortsightedness, tending to bring its own corrective, through new entries if not through "chiseling." The outcome tends to express longer-run forces and expectations, either through leadership alive to potential competition, or through such competition becoming active. If the major firms held an umbrella over the industry's market and held it too high, the small mavericks in the industry might in the aggregate become the controlling factor.

This condition would hold unless there were a strong seller's market in which all were working at capacity or close to it, and could go on doing so even if they let one large firm or a substantial group underprice the rest. But suppose there is a strong seller's market? Then another level of farsightedness may come into play, of the sort leading to the conception that it is good business policy either not to raise prices or not to raise them as high as demand would temporarily make possible. The various elements back of this idea and policy invite speculation; but for present purposes it may be enough that this kind of policy is sometimes followed, and that it seems to call for the most exacting standard of foresight yet considered, in that it needs to be widespread in the industry. In such a situation the most farsighted member would not be in a position to exert controlling pressure on the rest, because if he quotes a lower price than the market will bear, the others can quote higher prices and still sell all their output.

Another idea that belongs in this context is the drive for growth in volume, which appears to be a coordinate end and not a mere means to maximum profit.[5] There may be no need to decide whether this is really just farsighted pursuit of profit, or whether it stems from an expansionist drive inherent in the management of the corporate type of organization. We have seen that there are critical stages in the growth of a firm, at which increased size calls for a change in its form of organization.[6] This may carry with it some risk to the original source of efficiency that was responsible for the growth. But the dominant firms, in industries where large-scale production is a natural development, are firms that have taken this risk successfully.

There may be something in the idea which could be crudely expressed by saying that profits accrue to stockholders and the advancement in prestige and salary which comes with expansion in gross volume accrues to management. And management is in immediate control. To the extent that such considerations may carry weight, the effect on price-policy and profits is likely to be more indirect than direct, leading to the plowing back of earnings rather than foregoing them. But the resulting productive capacity must find a market, and this militates against a policy of small volume and high profit margins per unit. At any rate, insofar as these considerations may affect policy, it would be a point in favor of the managerial motif in the economy, as against exclusive dominance by the calculus of profit and dividends.

To sum up, we have looked at a half dozen kinds and degrees of foresight or the lack of it, in the pursuit of profit. It appears that the highest degrees of foresight tend to profit policies that are closest to the competitive ideal, if this be construed to allow the more successful concerns what may be called a growth profit rather than a minimum-survival profit. And it appears that there are other motivations characteristic of American business, which tend to reinforce the more farsighted and more moderate policies of price and profit. Profit maximization may be the most nearly dominant motive of the business firm, but it is part of a complex, the whole of which cannot be understood in terms of profit maximization alone.

[5] Cf. Chamberlain, *op. cit.*, pp. 232-40.
[6] See Chap. 4, Sec. 4.

3. Competition Within the Firm

It is, of course, commmonplace that the employees of a business firm, especially the executives, compete for promotion in rank and pay. It is also commonplace that, so far as organized labor is concerned, this competitive element is limited by union rules that standardize hours, working conditions, pay, and promotion by seniority. Such rules tend to eliminate the element of intrafirm competition, so far as they are effective. What remains consists of indirect pressures resulting from the different terms on which different labor groups are available, largely to different employers. Of more interest for the present study are arrangements by which large firms place different units of their organizations on a basis that involves some features similar to the competition of independent business firms.

For this type of quasi-competition there are certain essential requirements. The first, naturally, is that the firm shall be large enough and decentralized enough to include a number of distinct units doing similar things, and therefore susceptible of being placed in a competitive relationship to one another. The second requirement is that units have some independent initiative and discretion on policy or methods of carrying it out. This operates within the ruling purposes of the firm. While the top management needs to reserve an ultimate veto power, it needs to exercise this sparingly enough to leave real substance to the initiative and discretion of the constituent units, if it is to enlist internal competitive forces.

The units may be functionalized departments whose performance can be placed in comparison with that of similar functional units, perhaps in other branches of the same firm; but a closer approach to the competitive model occurs when the performance of the units in the different branches takes the form of objective results in costs and volume of sales. Presumably, the closest approach occurs when the units are formerly independent firms that have become subsidiaries without losing their separate cost and income accounts. Their independent policy may deal with methods of production, personnel policies, selection of minor variants of products to push (insofar as not determined by top policy decisions) and methods of promoting sales (within the same limitation).

As to incentives of the competitive type, the basic one in an independent firm is that of profit and loss. Something corresponding to this can play a part in the accounting of the sections of a consolidated firm, even if accounting deficits in one department are made up out of the firm's total earnings. Here there is, of course, a distinction between sections that are directly productive of income, and those that are not. In the latter case, accounting comparisons are limited to costs, except where a department transfers services or partly finished products to other departments, at transfer prices which can be regarded as the products of the transferring departments and as costs to the recipient departments. Obviously, the accuracy of the resulting showing of accounting profit and loss depends on the validity of these transfer prices, and arbitrariness here will be reflected in the competitive showing of different departments.

Aside from such imputations of profit and loss, systematic comparison of records of performance can itself be a substantial incentive. A more substantial incentive arises from the relative expansion of the size of the different departments or other units. Here it is incumbent on the management of the firm to see to it that departmental expansion is soundly based on performance that contributes to the over-all economy of the firm, and is not a mere example of "Parkinson's law." To sum up, internal competition exists in large firms, takes a wide variety of forms, and can be used by such firms as one antidote to the tendencies to bureaucratic formalization to which large organizations are subject.

4. The Product

The difficulties connected with the concept of "a product" arise from trying to distinguish between monopoly, conceived as unified control of some one product, limited only by the rivalry of different but substitutable products, and competition, conceived as rivalry between different producers of "the same" product. And one of the chief reasons this difference seems important is that if the product is "the same," and competitors have an equal chance to acquire the necessary resources and the techniques to use them, their costs should have a tendency to be generally similar, with differences due to greater or less success in meeting the same basic problems. Within this range of difference would lie the minimum necessary supply price, of which the customer would get the benefit. Where the only rivalry is that of essentially different substitutes, there is no inherently natural tendency to this much standardization of the result and elimination of profits above the necessary supply price. This standardization of the result of competition has, of course, been further stereotyped, in the precision type of theoretical models, into a picture of a completely homogeneous product, a single price, and identical production costs, price and cost being exactly equal. This identifies the difference between competition and monopoly in terms that are unmistakable but also impossible, as we have seen; therefore I have substituted a picture expressing the same elements in less precise and more realistic form. But the central idea of the distinction remains the same, and in this less-precise form it should give the key to the distinction between different but substitute products and variant versions of the "same" product.

It is these variant versions that make the trouble; they are not homogeneous, but neither are they wholly distinct. In the terms that are decisive for theoretical model builders, if a homogeneous product is (more than momentarily) sold for two different prices in the same market, something is out of equilibrium; but "variant versions" can sell indefinitely at different prices, being like substitute products in this respect. Along with this goes the fact that different producers of a homogeneous product face a cross elasticity of demand so high that a producer quoting even a slightly higher price than his rivals will promptly lose to them all the business they can handle. In contrast, producers of "variant versions" can sell, within limits, at different prices, subject to the normal principle that one can sell more at a lower price than at a higher. A moderate change in an existing price differential will not cause the product, the relative price of which has been reduced, to displace the other abruptly. They face a sloping cross-elasticity function—again, like substitute products.

This has led some keen-minded theorists to conclude that there is no way of drawing a definite line between these two categories, and that the only such line that can be drawn is between homogeneous products—which cover a minority of cases—and all others; with the further implication that full competition is confined to homogeneous products, all others being cases of monopoly limited by substitution. The alternative view is that substitution—at least if "close"—is a form of competition, from which some may draw the conclusion that one need not worry about the extinction of competition in a given case, so long as "close substitutes" remain, and that applied science is rapidly multiplying these. Neither of these classifications appears unqualifiedly useful. The first excludes most actual competition. The second offers a temptation to include too much, unless closeness of substitution is rigorously limited. This question will reappear in connection with the scope of markets and the impact of the Cellophane Case. By the time a product reaches the final consumer, some differentiation is pretty sure to have occurred. And the homogeneity of the materials is typically brought about by some kind of grading or conformity to specifications by the competing producers. Finished products may be required to conform to minimum specifications. Where they are made economically homogeneous by the setting up of further optional specifications, this is not usually done for the general market, but for specific contracts on which particular purchasers are inviting bids. Producers of materials tend to be unstandardized in one respect: their costs are likely to differ on account of differences in the quality or accessibility of the ultimate natural resources they utilize, as well as on account of differences in productive efficiency. But if the product is sufficiently homogeneous, and so recognized, a customer will pay no more for it to one supplier than to another (the place of delivery being the same), and in that sense they will command the same price.

There remains the question of products that differ from one another, and the corollary question whether any line can be drawn between situations of product differentiation that are essentially competitive and those that are essentially monopolistic. I would like to try out the hypothesis that there are two lines that can be drawn which, granting unavoidable shortcomings from a precisionist standpoint, still have significance; one as marking the transition from differentiated competition to substitution and the other as marking the transition between effective substitution and the vaguer kind of rivalry in which all products are said to compete for the consumer's dollar, in the sense that if he spends more for one, he will have less to spend for others.

The first category—differentiated competition—includes products that satisfy the same principal want, and in which the producer is free to imitate others as closely as he wishes, using techniques that are not radically different from theirs, and differentiating his product only to the extent that it seems advantageous to him to do so, in order to appeal to some subsidiary want more effectively than other variants do, and thus fit into a gap in the array of variant products. The second category—substitution—includes products that appeal to the same principal want, but which are inherently and inescapably different, due either to different materials or basically different techniques. The third category embraces products that serve independent wants, and are substitutes only in the mathematic sense that spending more for one leaves less to spend on others. This category need not concern us here, since with possible rare exceptions it does not develop inter-product cross-elasticities of demand high enough to have competitive significance.[7] This is still more true of complementary products.

The first category will be looked at in more detail later; for the present we may merely say enough to indicate the grounds for treating it as competition, as distinct from substitution. The decisive consideration may derive from the proposition that no monopoly exists where entry is free and feasible. It follows that the producer of a differentiated product does not have a monopoly of his product if others are free to imitate it as closely as they wish. He faces the potential if not the actual competition of products virtually identical with his own, and the actual competition of variant products freely chosen and designed to attract his customers away from him if they can. Any differential advantage he may gain must be constantly defended and renewed. In the case I have called substitution, the differences between the products cannot be altered at will, and the products can-

[7] A simplified model supporting this conclusion might start with a reduction of the price of one such product. Then the original amount of that product could be bought for less total outlay, the reduction in outlay becoming an addition to available income. This would then normally be distributed among the different available products, like any increase in income. Part of it—but presumably only a small part—would be spent to increase the real purchases of the original product. Therefore, the reduction in price would have resulted in increasing the physical volume of sales by a smaller proportion, reducing total money outlay for the product. This identifies an inelastic demand; but demand has to have elasticity greater than unity in order to stimulate competitive actions. If a product has such an elastic demand, this is almost certainly because it is a substitute for something else in the more definite sense used above. An exception might be the product that engenders a really new want.

not be spaced in a continuous spectrum by the action of rival producers trying to fit their product variants into the most attractive unoccupied spaces. The differentials are persistent. This is a real difference, and I am suggesting that it has enough economic importance
to warrant the kind of distinction indicated by the terms "competition"
and "substitution," though admittedly there is no knife-edge boundary
between them, and admittedly applied science is vastly increasing the
power to multiply and modify substitute products. Iron, steel, and
aluminum are different, and while the differences are reduced by alloys, such as Duralumin and ductile cast iron, they are not wiped out.

The most cogent point seems to be that rivalry between two different metals (aside from competition between different producers of
each) has no necessary tendency to bring the profits of producing
either one down to a normal competitive minimum; while there is such
a tendency in an industry in which the differentiation of the products
can be varied at will. It is true that in both cases the pertinent demand curve has a slope; but in the one case the slope is enduring and
in the other, if the present contention is correct, it tends to flatten out
in a moderate time unless renewed. In the following chapters, it will
be argued that such a slope does not produce the monopoloidal results
that have been attributed to it on the basis of the "tangency theorem."

5. The Industry or the Group

The essence of competition is the fact that the single firm acts in a
setting of other firms that stand in a relation of rivalry which conditions the actions of each. This setting has been thought of as the "industry"; the simplest conception of an industry being a group of firms
producing a single homogeneous product within the same market.[8]
But this simple conception gets farther and farther from the facts as
firms become vertically integrated in different degrees, differentiate

[8] See Joan Robinson, *Economics of Imperfect Competition* (1932), pp. 17-18, 89.
The above is a consolidated paraphrase of her definition as given on pp. 17-18,
except that "market" is not there explicitly defined, and must be derived from
the concept of a perfectly elastic individual-demand curve as the condition of a
"perfect" market.

their products, or diversify their output into unrelated products. Thus single firms operate in a number of industries while some specialized firms, like makers of particular parts or subassemblies, operate in only part of the field of the industry to which they belong. In terms of closeness of rivalry, it has been suggested that, for example, a used Ford may be in closer substitutionary relations with a new coat of paint for the house than with a new Rolls-Royce.

These difficulties have led some theorists to adopt the idea of a "group" that cuts across industry boundaries and includes all those products, and only those products, which are in competition or close substitutionary rivalry with the product that is for the moment the subject of study. This is logical, but presents difficulties of its own. Such groups could only be defined abstractly; it would hardly be feasible to make lists of the firms and products included in each one. If it were, such lists would change from time to time.

Another complication may be expressed in the following way. Suppose that a group of products competitive with product A includes product B. While the group competitive with product B would presumably include A, aside from this the two groups might have quite different coverage, if A and B sell mainly in different areas or different strata of demand, and compete only at the edges of their markets. However, since the only people who would need to identify the products included in a "group" would be investigators engaged in industry studies, this peculiarity can safely be left to them to deal with as they encounter it, estimating the degree of transmission of competitive forces through the chain of groups or subgroups. It need not be regarded as invalidating these concepts for general analysis.

Another suggestion is to forget about industry and group and merely consider the elasticity of demand for a single firm's product. But how is an investigator to judge how elastic a firm's demand curve is? If the firm is a member of a purely competitive industry, this elasticity will be close to infinity; if it is a monopolist or oligopolist, the elasticity will be much smaller, or may have a "kink." I would urge that it is generally easier to observe the objective conditions and structure of the industry and draw conclusions about the probable character of the demand curves, than the other way around. However, the chief point about competition is bound up with the fact that the demand for one firm's product depends on what rival firms are charging, with the resulting difference between what happens when one firm alone changes its price, and when the whole "group" does so. Also, for the purpose in hand, the only elasticities that have competitive significance are not only greater than unity, but very much greater. This rules out not only what has here been called the purely mathematical kind of substitution, but all except the really close degrees of functional substitution.

On the whole, the objections to abandoning such concepts as industry and group seem weightier than the objections to retaining them as orienting conceptions. One would need to recognize that their boundaries are matters of degree, allowing an amount of latitude and remaining to be determined in empirical studies according to the facts of each case.

It may be worth noting that "industries" are of two broad kinds. One kind produces a material or a productive service, which normally goes into a considerable variety of end products; the other produces an end product, and may choose among a variety of technical methods and materials. The steel industry and the advertising industry are examples of the first kind, the automobile industry illustrates the second. This distinction becomes highly active when a new industry is being established. Producers of a new material may need to undertake the task of finding and developing uses for it, thus branching out into numerous other industries of the end-product sort. This kind of integration may be more or less compulsory. Producers of a new end product will experiment with different techniques and existing materials, but are less likely to be driven into developing new materials (though this may happen) while backward integration is likely to come only after firms in the industry have reached great size—that is, after the industry is no longer new.

6. The Market

Given a product produced for sale, it must have channels through which it reaches purchasers, and these channels constitute the market. This may be looked at from a number of standpoints. For the single seller, his market is the area in which he actually sells: from the standpoint of economics, the market for a product is the scene, or scope, of the operations and economic forces that determine the character and amount of the product and the terms on which it is disposed of, including whatever structure of differentials may exist between product variants, localities, or sectors of the market. If one seller has a monopoly, his individual market is coextensive with the whole market for his product, and wide differentials are often possible, especially if obstacles are placed in the way of resale by favored customers. Another kind of resale may take place when, as suggested above, the regular price is kept below the level that supply and demand would permit in time of shortage, as when used cars can be sold for more than new. If the seller is in competition, his individual market is an undivided fraction of the market of his industry or group, or at least of those with whom he is in effective competition.

From the standpoint of the antitrust laws, a competitive market may be defined as an area of trading, unified control of which would deprive the customers of the benefits of effective competition. This trading area may be defined geographically or in terms of degrees of product differentials. Geographically, to deprive customers in a given locality of the benefits of effective competition may require unified control which is virtually nationwide, but commonly control of a much smaller area suffices, an extreme case being morning or evening newspapers in a single town. Cost of transportation, relative to value of product, may restrict markets to local areas or may permit them to be nationwide. As to product differentiation, we have seen (Chapter 3, Sec. 3, above) that the antitrust laws are not concerned because a seller has unified control over his individual product, even if that product is in some respect unique, so long as it is competing with other freely selected variants of what we have classed as "the same product."[9] The antitrust laws are concerned only when such rivalry is limited or obstructed by something other than human inertia or lack of exhaustive knowledge of the available offerings.

This is clearly a much more elastic concept than the one sometimes employed in precisionist theories, of a trading area in which there can be but one price at one time for one product. Some relaxation of this rigorous concept is a necessity, even on its own grounds of precise

[9] They appear to go further, including genuinely close substitutes. Cf. U. S. Attorney-General's National Committee to Study the Antitrust Laws, *Report* (1955), pp. 46-47, 322; cf. also discussion below, of the impact of the Cellophane case.

analysis. In a mercantile type of market, prices could not change by the independent action of individual competitors unless there were room for some price differentials, at least temporarily, as some sellers try experiments, and others decide whether or not to follow.[10] Under the antitrust laws, a market in which there is no such experimenting is suspect as noncompetitive. To take account of product differentiation, there is need for further relaxation to allow for enduring differentials between grades, brands, etc.

Contracts for future delivery introduce further possibilities of differentials between prices governing deliveries made at any given time even by the same seller. In such cases, a change in the current price may affect anything from the whole volume of current deliveries down to a minor fraction of them, if most of the deliveries are being made on contracts made earlier at different prices. Variations in this kind of arrangement include provisions for revising the price for deliveries on standing contracts if the market changes, especially if it changes to the advantage of late buyers. Special provisions of this sort can introduce interesting variations in the competitive incentives to reduce prices or to raise them.

The dynamics of market behavior includes variation not only in amounts produced and consumed, but in inventories. This can be a stabilizing or an unstabilizing factor. When part of an extra-large crop goes into increased carry-over, or when a temporary burst of demand is met by drawing down inventories, this has a stabilizing effect. But when cyclical ups and downs of current sales are accompanied by similar ups and downs of inventories, fluctuations in consumer demand are intensified in being passed on to producers.

Reverting to the scope of market control that is relevant to the antitrust laws, if this relevant market is part of a wider market area, spatially or productwise, control over the wider area tends to be less unified than over particular sectors. Thus it can be an advantage to the defendant to establish the wider area as the relevant one. Here the crucial question is whether unified control of the narrower area substantially impairs effective competition. If it does, it should not be necessary to prove unified control of the wider area. In the Cellophane Case it became an important issue whether the relevant market was

---

[10] While Alfred Marshall does not explicitly recognize this factor, he relaxes his definition of a market enough to make room for it. See his *Principles of Economics*, 5th ed. (1907), pp. 112, 324.

that for cellophane, or the wider market for flexible wrapping materials, which includes various materials that do not have the distinctive service characteristics of cellophane, and some of which have little resemblance to it. Concentration of control in cellophane was extreme, in the wider field much less, and the court took the wider view.[11] It would appear that this involved a dubious widening of the scope of the competitive market into the area designated above as that of inherently different substitute commodities, far from interchangeable.

Subsequent cases appear to accept the principle of the Cellophane Case, holding that rivalry of close substitutes is to be included in the whole market situation which must be weighed in deciding whether a given merger has substantially lessened competition, under the antimerger section of the Clayton Act. But it appears also that these subsequent decisions have limited the application of this principle to genuinely interchangeable products and have not followed the Cellophane Case in its inclusive definition of competing substitutes, which most economists would probably consider unduly wide.[12] Despite the wonders of applied science in creating synthetic substitutes, it has not made all substitutes fully interchangeable, nor rendered substitution in general equivalent to competition as a dependable and effective protection to the buyer. If competition does not exist in a given case, effective substitution helps. But it is not safe to generalize that substitution between products renders unimportant the preservation of competition among versions of the "same" product.

From another standpoint, markets are the scene of those active processes that have long been dismissed with bare mention as the "higgling of the market," by theorists whose main interest lay in the equilibria of demand and supply that were supposed to be reached when this higgling had run its course. A study of competition as an active process needs to pay more attention to this stepchild operation, starting with the adoption of a terminology which brings out its essential features (such a terminology is now lacking). The most promising expedient appears to be to give an enlarged meaning to the term

[11] Cf. George W. Stocking and W. F. Mueller; "The Cellophane Case and the New Competition," *American Economic Review* (March 1955), pp. 29-63.

[12] The recent state of the law on these issues is discussed in Milton Handler's annual review of "Recent Antitrust Developments," in Association of the Bar of the City of New York, *Record*, Vol. 14 (October 1959), pp. 318-58, especially pp. 324 ff.

"bargaining," using it to designate the processes by which terms of exchange are arrived at, whatever these processes may be, and including all the things an exchanger (actual or potential) does to protect his interests in a prospective exchange. This leaves the term "negotiation" to describe the "higgling" process, which takes place only in certain kinds of transactions, and in which each party tries to induce the other to improve the terms of his offer.[13] This terminology will be used in the following classification of types of price-making.

Price-making may be divided into three main types and a larger number of special types, including various hybrids of the three main ones. These three are: supply-and-demand pricing, the quoted price, and the negotiated price.[14] Special forms and hybrids include remainder and disposal sales, sales of second-hand goods (chief example, the used-car market), auctions, buying on sealed bids, negotiated departures from sellers' quoted prices (a hybrid that might be called "fringe negotiation"), and quoted or negotiated prices subject to revision under specified contingencies. The essence of all these forms of dealing consists of buyers and sellers, each trying to get the best terms the market affords. Their basic equipment is market information, their basic weapon is the power to refuse to deal unless the terms are satisfactory, and their most effective protection consists of the availability of competing alternatives to which they may resort. As has already been mentioned, one of the services of competition is to come near enough to standardizing the terms of exchange so that many customers may buy without bargaining or canvassing available alternatives, trusting that they will get approximately the standard terms the market affords.[15] This is reasonably safe only if there are plenty of other customers who are canvassing market alternatives and making it unsafe for any sellers to offer terms notably poorer than others are offering.

The "supply-and-demand" form of pricing is most clearly seen on organized exchanges, and is sometimes spoken of as the "bourse" type. Here bargaining by both buyer and seller is reduced to little more than accepting or rejecting the terms they find available, acting in the

[13] See Chamberlain, op. cit., Chaps. 6-8. Cf. also Carl M. Stevens, "On the Theory of Negotiation," Quarterly Journal of Economics (February 1958), pp. 77-78.

[14] Cf. C. Clive Saxton, The Economics of Price Determination (1942), pp. 12-15. Saxton stresses the fundamental difference between pricing in organized markets and quoted-price selling.

[15] See above, Chap. 4, Sec. 10.

light of their own needs and their judgment of how the market may move in the future. It is crucial that the seller's supply has been produced before being brought to market, in contrast to single producers' current control of their individual supplies in industrial marketing. If the seller rejects the price of the last preceding transaction, some unsupplied buyer may or may not offer more, or the best available offer may be less than the price of the previous transaction. Thus the price may change; but the cause of the change is the total balance of demand and supply, of which the bids and offers that happen to be marginal are symptoms. It is this kind of marketing of which it is appropriate to assume that the individual supplier controls his own supply only with reference to future marketings, and acts in the expectation that other sellers' supplies will be unaffected by his own actions. Since we are not primarily concerned with this kind of pricing, we need not go into the technical forms of transactions, including dealings in futures, or the devices of manipulation. In the case of farm products, it is generally assumed that no single supplier is large enough to affect the price; though on some commodity exchanges there may be single suppliers or buyers large enough to affect the price by the individual supply or demand for which they are responsible.

Under the "quoted-price" system, the seller offers not a supply to be bid for, but a price at which he expects to fill whatever orders come, replenishing his inventory as it is depleted, by production if he is a manufacturer, or by ordering from his suppliers if he is a merchant. For most of the output the force on the supply side is not a literal supply but an amount of productive capacity and the producer's wish to utilize as much of it as he profitably can. Each seller's output is gauged currently in accord with his volume of sales, in a way in which the output of wheat cannot be currently controlled. If sales are disappointing, the producer will seek to increase them, and the remedies may include price-reductions or an attempt to make the sales effort more effective or the product more attractive. In some circumstances he may produce to stock to a limited extent, but only if he expects an ultimate sale that will cover an appropriate reckoning of cost. It is chiefly in clearance sales or in the disposal of remnants that a literal supply is thrown on the market and a price made that will "clear" it. But even here, the price is quoted by the seller, and the intended clearance at that price may or may not be complete.

In the characteristic American one-price system, "bargaining" on the seller's side consists of choosing what offer to make, in the light of his judgment of everything entering into sales possibilities, while bargaining on the buyer's part is reduced to little more than accepting the seller's terms or rejecting them and looking further. If the buyer expresses his reasons for rejecting the terms offered, he does not—in the one-price kind of establishment—do it with the idea of getting better terms from this establishment on his own purchase. Shops exist which practice this kind of negotiation on individual sales of substantial size, but they are not typical in American retailing.

Manufacturers, especially when facing large buyers who threaten to take their business elsewhere, are more likely to make departures from their "list" prices. This shading of quoted prices is widely prevalent, highly important, and may range from an essential means of effective competition to a perversion of competition or an instrument of monopoloidal privilege. It implies terms made between the parties that others do not automatically share (unless they have contracts that provide for such sharing). Such "fringe negotiation" implies a market that is imperfect but may still be competitive. This would mean that it has enough communication and free play to cause these advantages to spread and in a moderate time to become generally available to all whose business has the appropriate characteristics.

The market would then be deciding whether the special terms were economically warranted by the test of whether competitors would imitate them. If the imperfection of the market is greater than this, the special advantages may remain the perquisites of successful negotiators and may give them a controversial kind of advantage over their competitors. Where one side has a monopoly position, the bargaining leverages available to the other side are obviously reduced by the relatively unsatisfactory character of the substitutes that constitute the available alternatives.

The two main forms of negotiated price may be illustrated by the real estate market and collective bargaining by organized labor. The common features are that single transactions are important enough, generally distinctive enough, and occur at sufficiently infrequent intervals, to be worth the trouble of negotiation. The common method is for both parties to quote initial terms better than they expect to get, and to make concessions from these initial terms, which may (or may not) lead to an ultimate agreement. The difference between the two forms centers on the different character of the alternatives that face the bargaining parties in case of nonagreement, and that constitute their bargaining leverage.

In the real estate market, the seller's recourse is to offers from different potential purchasers, or the offers he hopes to get if he waits longer. If he holds out for a higher price than he is currently offered, he is weighing the uncertain chance of getting a higher price against the certain cost of a delayed sale. The buyer's recourse consists of the terms on which he might secure other properties: terms that he typically tests by making an offer below the asking price, for the property that appears to be the most likely prospect. He faces what is on the whole best classified as competition of differentiated products, in an imperfectly organized market. Even here, the growth of large-scale housing developments, with closely standardized units, leads to a close approach to a one-price system within each development. However, since the present study is primarily concerned with problems characteristic of industry and trade, the specific features and variant forms of the real estate market are of only incidental interest. They are mentioned here by way of comparison, and to locate the practices of industry and trade on a wider map of the processes by which terms of exchange are reached.

In contrast to this, wages under collective bargaining are a negotiated price of a sort that is definitely noncompetitive, and presents special features and takes peculiarly stubborn forms, because for either party the alternative of finding someone else to deal with is not part of the *mores*, and neither party resorts to it except in the most extreme and aggravated cases.[16] Normally, agreement is the only ultimate outcome contemplated, each party being dependent on continued relations with the other. (Unions may regard some inefficient employers as expendable, but their pattern-setting agreements are not made with these employers.) Therefore the crucial bargaining weapon is the mutual infliction of loss by the interruption (strike or lockout) of the operations on which both parties depend. The prior negotiation is a complex of poker-playing diplomacy and politics, propaganda, and face-saving.

The ultimate settlement takes place within economic limits that are

---

[16] The long-continued Kohler strike is one of these exceptional cases.

often elastic, set by the ability of the employer to operate—with or without feasible economies or a feasible price increase—and by the willingness of individual workers to work on the terms the collective agreement sets. Insofar as these economic limits figure in negotiations, they are necessarily conjectural, not tested as market bargaining would test them. It is this kind of negotiation under which wages have, over the past twenty years, increased faster than physical productivity, resulting in an increase in the dominant component of monetary costs of production of industrial and commercial products, and setting limits on the flexibility with which prices can be adjusted to changing conditions of supply and demand.

7. *Freedom of Entry and Exit*

Perhaps the fact that freedom of entry is mentioned far more often than freedom of exit is a tribute to the dynamically expanding quality of our economy. New allocations of economic effort can most easily be brought about when investment is expanding vigorously, and changed forms of equipment can be furnished by using uncommitted capital resources. When once committed in specialized form, capital can seldom be transferred into some other branch of production without loss, which may come close to being total. This is an imperfection, but unavoidable. To bring about "perfect competition," free and costless exit as well as free entry is necessary; and the fact that it is impossible is the chief reason why "perfect competition" must always remain imaginary. It is "pure competition" with an escape hatch that does not exist in practice.

Given this escape hatch, competition can exist in its most unmitigated and rigorous form, and still the participants are saved from disaster by the free two-way mobility of resources. If there is overinvestment, the excess resources simply withdraw and the minimum normal competitive return is restored. In practice, pure competition without this safeguard can be quite disastrous. Firms struggle against extinction and may endure protracted losses before succumbing.[17] This

---

[17] Cf. above, Chap. 4. Sec. 7, on elimination of inefficient firms.

may be mitigated by a prosperous condition in other industries, affording good alternative opportunities.

Turning to freedom of entry, it plays a basic part in competitive theory. It is perhaps the most readily understandable check on the charging of prices that would yield excess profits. If the members of a trade are making such profits, it may not be self-evident at a glance why they should take action, each in his own interest, that results in eliminating these excess profits. But it is easy to understand why outsiders who are not making excess profits should want to get into the favored trade and enjoy them. Professor Joe S. Bain has recently expressed the view that the potentialities of free entry have not been given an amount of attention commensurate with their importance.[18] There is something to be said on the other side: theory has a way of assuming that there is an optimum size of firms, and that under free competition they tend to approximate this optimum size, and this assumption gives a certain bias toward picturing expansion of an industry in terms of increased numbers of firms rather than increased size of existing firms.

Perhaps the truth is that both entry-exit and competitive behavior as between existing firms are subjects that could benefit by more realistic analysis. And perhaps the aspect of free entry that is in most need of development is its effect in causing those already in the industry to limit their prices and profits with a view to forestalling excessive entry, by not making the industry so attractive as to invite it. In other words, the effect of potential competition. This is the aspect on which Bain focuses his study.[19]

This becomes an issue where firms have some degree of oligopolistic power. Under active competition of the atomistic sort, firms may be fully occupied in meeting existing rivalry, and if they ignore potential entries, this will make no difference. But where firms are few enough to cause each to gauge its actions with a view to others' probable responses (this being the key feature of oligopoly), it may be natural that the same foresight would extend to considering the effect of their policies on new entries, thus introducing what may be the chief competitive force bearing directly on price in cases where oligopoly is so thoroughgoing that it stalemates direct price competition between

[18] Bain, *op. cit.*, p. 2.
[19] *Ibid.*, pp. v-vi.

the existing sellers.[20] Competitive forces may then depend mainly on whether entry is free or obstructed. In contrast, current theories tend to visualize existing firms as neglecting this potentiality until it materializes and divides the business into shares too small for maximum economy. Bain would appear to be justified in regarding this as a special case—he calls it "bizarre"—rather than normal oligopolistic behavior.[21]

What is "entry"? The answer might seem obvious; but the effects of vertical integration, and especially of diversification, flanked by the achievements of applied science, have given the concept new and additional meanings, the impact of which is worth scrutiny. It is generally conceived as the establishment of a new firm, either creating new physical facilities or adapting existing facilities to an industry in which they had not previously been used.[22] It is quite proper to distinguish it from the mere taking over of existing facilities by a new business unit, replacing a previous one which does not re-enter the business, and continuing to use the facilities in the same branch of production as before. It is true that if the new firm has fresh ideas and capacities, something new has really been added, which may enlarge and transform the effectiveness of the productive unit. However, this is an imponderable and uncertain matter, and the bare fact of new ownership affords no guarantee that it will happen. It is about as likely to happen from a revitalization of an existing management without transfer to a new firm.

The motives to new entry are generally conceived in terms of prospective profits as judged by potential entrants, chiefly by their estimates of profits prevailing in the industry. However, in an economy as dynamic as ours, one hypothesis that appears worth exploring is that an evident technical opening may attract entries, without any close dependence on the profits currently being made by the firms that are bearing the load and taking the risks of pioneering. This often involves false starts and accompanying losses, and succeeding firms may hope to benefit from this expensive exploration by the leaders.

[20] *Ibid.*, p. 27. It will be argued later that small numbers do not inhibit competition in products, whatever they may do to direct competition in price. It is arguable that a lapsing of active price competition tends to transfer the competitive impulse to the field of the product with results that may or may not make for serviceable adaptation of offerings to the range of consumers' desires.

[21] *Ibid.*, pp. 39-40.

[22] Bain is explicit and rigorous in so limiting the concept. *Ibid.*, p. 5.

Examples of conspicuous profits are an added attraction, but may not be necessary. An industry in this pioneering stage may include more firms than it does later, after the less successful ones have been shaken out and the more successful ones have expanded.[23] At a later stage, the established survivors may have a greater advantage over the new entrant, having passed through the lean period which still lies ahead for him, and which may include substantial sales-promotion outlay while he is making his way into a tenable market position.[24] This handicap is mitigated if the new entrant is an established firm, branching out by diversification. It often (though not always) has some resources that it can apply advantageously in the new line.

In more general terms, the motives bearing on entry may be divided into the attraction of prospects in the industry, the counterattraction of alternative openings for the persons and resources involved, and the difficulties encountered in bringing together the necessary capital, know-how, managerial capacity, and trade connections. Abstract theory seems to lean toward concentrating on the first, while Alfred R. Oxenfeldt's significant study tends to stress the last.[25] The most numerous entries—and exits—occur in the very small-scale trades, in which the owner is commonly also manager and worker, and is typically willing to work for a combined return smaller than the sum of the separate returns needed to enlist these functions from distinct persons. Insofar as profits can be distinguished in such cases, they are small, but capital requirements are also small, and know-how appears simple enough to persuade many entrants, rightly or wrongly, that they face no serious handicap on this score. In this reckoning the potential entrant's view, right or wrong, determines his action. Entrants into the very small trades have alternatives that are not generously lucrative, or else they would not enter. Such entries may increase in a recession, indicating that a deterioration of the alternatives is decisive, rather than an improvement in the attractions. At such times, entry may be a refuge from unemployment.

In those kinds of manufacturing in which moderate-sized firms have

[23] Cf. J. K. Galbraith, *American Capitalism: The Concept of Countervailing Power*, 2nd ed. (1956), pp. 32-33.

[24] Galbraith, *ibid.*, lays so much weight on this as to conclude that ". . . As a result, in an established industry, where the scale of production is considerable, there is no such thing as freedom of entry." Bain, in contrast, distinguishes different degrees of obstruction.

[25] Alfred R. Oxenfeldt, *New Firms and Free Enterprise* (1943), *passim.*

a chance, including those that specialize on a limited line of products, entries are likely to be drawn from among fairly well-paid industrial executives, who have managerial know-how and connections. Their ventures into entrepreneurship are still gambles, and may not succeed. Where very large size is really necessary to standard efficiency, new entries may have to choose between cost handicaps due to limited size, and building larger capacity which they may not be able to keep fully occupied. In the latter case, they might be increasing the total capacity of the industry beyond potential demand.

In modern industry, what amounts to new entry may take place without the setting up of new "firms," through the extension of existing firms via vertical integration or diversification.[26] The distinctive feature of this kind of entry is that it is carried out by firms that already command large resources of capital and research that may be turned in the direction of the new product, even if not already of a sort that would be contributory to its production. This kind of entry may not only minimize the difficulties a new firm encounters in building up a large new organization; it may take place for reasons not decisively dependent on an inviting condition of excess profits in the industry entered.

One form that raises special problems is expansion into the field of a substitute product, seeking a hedge against the risk that the substitute may displace the original product or encroach seriously on the demand for it. Where this risk exists, the desire for a hedge is natural. But if some degree of monopoly power also exists, actually or potentially, the absorption of substitutes compounds it. This question appears to admit no simple a priori answer. In general, it appears that entry by integration or diversification of existing large firms increases the force of potential competition in large-scale industries where it is most difficult for a wholly new firm to get started on a viable scale and market status; but it does nothing to ease the difficulties faced by such independent new-firm entrants.

[26] Bain gives this type of entry brief mention, evidently considering that it does not fulfill the requirements he has in mind, since it does not mean the establishment of new enterprise units. Nevertheless, he seems to accord some usefulness to entry by diversification. *Op. cit.*, p. 215. Entry by vertical integration raises further problems as to competition with existing nonintegrated units.

8. Summary

In general, the position taken in this chapter favors latitude and flexibility in the definition of the basic concepts discussed, including a recognition that in some important matters, diversities of situation, size, motivation, and time perspective are of essential importance in determining the result. So far as this is valid, it means that any single, uniform assumption about these matters is inadequate. The distinction is defended between competition of differentiated products and substitution between inherently different ones. A firm may operate in a number of industries or in only part of one. It may sell at a supply-and-demand price, a quoted price or a negotiated price, or by variant or hybrid methods. A new entry in one industry may be an existing firm from another industry, branching out into a new activity. Potential competition arises from the desire to forestall new entries. Firms differ in the force of this desire, but are subject to the general principle that the attitude that leads to the most strongly competitive policy tends to be the controlling one in a given market. This holds good if this policy is followed by a unit or a number of units, the members of which have the capability of expanding to a significant extent at the expense of the others.

CHAPTER 6

The Behavior of Costs

1. Introduction

The purpose of this chapter and the one following is to present those features of the behavior of demand and of cost that seem essential for the broadened treatment this volume undertakes. As an introduction, it seems important to explain, somewhat more fully than has already been done, why this broadened treatment requires correspondingly broad concepts of demand and cost, even at the sacrifice of the expository convenience and precise determinateness that go with an oversimplified picture. Such an explanation needs to show for what purpose these concepts are needed and what kind of difference they make, taking the prevalent form of equilibrium theory as a point of departure.

Equilibrium theory starts with the assumption that firms try to maximize their profits. As we saw in the preceding chapter, this is an oversimplification; but even if it be accepted, it dictates no definite result, but permits a wide range of behavior according to the various controlling conditions. Formal theory secures what purport to be exact results by picturing these controlling conditions as reduced to a simplified framework consisting of curves of demand and of cost, represented as formally (or fictitiously) precise. By the different types and behavior of these curves, this theory analyzes a number of important gradations of business behavior, over the whole range from pure competition to secure monopoly. The more rigorous forms of this analysis, as already contended, lead to the conclusion that all forms of independent action that are feasible in industry and trade share the defective features of monopoly.

The present study argues that this unfavorable judgment is connected with the oversimplified and static character of its basic concepts, especially the curves of demand and of cost already critically analyzed in Chapter 3. As to the reliance on diagrams, the student not only remembers the diagram; unless he is a rare person he objectifies it, visualizing a firm as existing in a world composed of such intersecting curves, instead of insistently reminding himself that the firm is confronted, not with a curve on paper, but with the much more complex economic situation, one aspect of which the curve symbolizes in simplified and over-precise form.

Thus this advantage in exposition is purchased at a heavy price, because the necessary simplification virtually compels neglect of factors that are really important. Outstanding among these are the factor of time and differences between the demand and cost curves applying to different firms in the same industry. And this means excluding precisely the factors that are necessary to effective competition under the conditions of modern industry and trade, where firms are limited in number and differ in efficiency and in size—some being large or ultralarge.

Under such conditions competition is an active process of give-and-take, the character of which hinges on moves and countermoves (involving time), on progressive as well as self-limiting changes, and on diversities between rival firms in their costs and their attitudes toward them, their time-perspectives, their size, and the elasticities of the demand schedules that different firms face or envision. I am firmly convinced that effective competition under modern conditions depends on a healthy kind and degree of diversity in these respects. As to what kinds and degrees are healthy, this raises more problems than the present study can hope to solve. It can at best state some of them, and suggest tentative answers.

The problem for dynamic analysis is to find feasible and effective ways to take account of such factors as these. Can this be done without making the resulting picture unmanageably complicated? One cannot tell until one tries; and there seems to be no escape from trying, if one is to do justice to reality. As to why this is so, it may be worth while to examine briefly a key case, showing why, in the situations actually faced, the conditions favorable to the most effective competition include the much-disparaged condition known as a "sloping individual-demand curve"; and also showing how this conclusion is connected with the dynamic behavior of costs. The case against sloping individual-demand curves grows out of equilibrium theory in its precise form.

In this theory, competition is conceived as requiring that a seller shall not have it in his power to increase his profits by giving less and demanding more—that is, by raising his price as a monopolist can do. He must have no power over price, and no ability to affect it. He must face a market in which he can sell nothing unless he meets the market price, and can sell his whole output if he does meet it. This is the condition described as a "horizontal individual demand curve." We have glanced at its operation in the preceding chapter (Section 6), and we shall look at it more searchingly in the next chapter, stressing the qualifications that are necessary in practice.

Given this market condition, competition will bring price and the seller's marginal cost into equality, and this is held to be the only completely competitive price. In contrast, if, with price at this level, the seller faces a "sloping individual-demand curve"—that is, if he can raise his price and lose only a fraction of his business—he can get a price that is above his marginal cost.[1] In the theory we are examining, this is regarded as an evidence of a monopolistic element. Indeed, it has been proposed as a measure of the degree of monopoly power.

Here the real trouble begins. "Marginal cost" can mean various things.[2] When a productive unit is working at less than its optimum capacity—which under normal conditions means most of the time—its immediate, short-run marginal cost is less than its average cost per unit of product. But unless it also covers its average cost, it is not earning a theoretically normal competitive price.[3] These two conditions cannot both be met unless marginal cost (short-run and long-run) and average cost (total cost per unit) are all equal and equal to the price. This amounts to stipulating that productive capacity, when it is operating at its best rate, shall always be exactly equal to demand at a cost price. To make this a requirement of competition amounts to characterizing any excess capacity as monopolistic.

Taking up these propositions in reverse order, the last one is clearly

---

[1] Of course, if demand is very weak, the seller may be unable to cover his marginal cost, whatever price he charges.

[2] Cf. the present writer's *The Economics of Overhead Costs* (1923), especially Chap. 9, "Different Costs for Different Purposes."

[3] In practice, handicapped firms may, of course, operate for considerable periods without earning a standard return on their long-term investment, which lacks theoretically perfect two-way mobility.

a counsel of impossible "perfection," inconsistent with dynamic conditions. Firms build for future growth, and for handling fluctuations. These are not limited to fluctuations of the total output of an industry. If single producers are making active competitive efforts to get business away from one another, their efforts would be stultified unless they had the capacity to handle, not only their existing business, but the added business that competitive success would bring them. To get more orders than the firm can promptly fill is an embarrassment, though it sometimes happens. Thus the assumption that firms invariably operate at optimum capacity, far from describing a state of competitive activity, is inconsistent with it, describing only an imaginary static terminus in which competition as an activity adjusting outputs, costs, and prices would have ceased to be operative.[4]

It does suggest one criterion of feasible competition: namely, that the drives and pressures of short-run competitive situations shall not be so drastic as to prevent "representative" firms from earning the minimum returns that are economically necessary in the long run to the health of an industry. In other words, competition should not, as a regular thing, have a ruinous or cutthroat character. This is clearly desirable in principle, but it cannot be brought about by never having any excess capacity. Any feasible approximation must take account of fluctuations, of the natural competitive tendency to some "excess capacity" under average conditions and a consequent excess of average cost above marginal cost a large part of the time.

This puts the problem of "pure competition" in a different form. If price cannot cover total cost at all times, can a flexible price achieve this on the average, with losses in slack times offset by profits in times of strong demand? This solution faces at least two serious difficulties. In view of what has just been said about the naturalness of excess capacity as generated by competitive conditions in times of normal demand, the conclusion seems warranted that for most producers a majority of the time short-run marginal cost would be less than average cost, and would equal or exceed it only in considerably shorter periods of extra-strong demand. Only in the latter periods would "pure competition" permit prices to be raised sufficiently to equal or exceed full economic cost. It is decidedly doubtful whether it would be

[4] The writer's view is that competition is consistent with intermittent price adjustments with intervening stable intervals, but hardly with permanent cessation of adjustment.

economically feasible to make profits enough in such periods to offset the losses incurred in normal and subnormal periods. And if it were economically feasible, there might be other serious obstacles and drawbacks in the way of exploiting the profitable periods by raising prices as graspingly as would be necessary to balance the accounts. It would be very bad public relations, in a period when industry needs good public relations very much.

This raises the more general question of the usefulness of short-run flexibility of prices in response to changes in demand, as distinct from longer-run flexibility in response to changes in costs. The usefulness of the latter is unquestioned; but as to the former, it seems as likely to accentuate general fluctuations in economic activity as to stabilize them. The price-fluctuations called for in the case we have been discussing are so extreme as to go far beyond the amount that could render useful service toward stabilizing the economy. And as to maintaining a long-run normal average return under pure competition, the overwhelming probability seems to be that the gains could not offset the losses unless the fluctuations of demand were so mild that for a large part of the time operation would be close enough to capacity to leave producers without incentive to cut prices toward short-run marginal cost in the attempt to reach capacity operation.[5] Otherwise, a long-run normal return might require that excess capacity be limited as only a well-managed combination could limit it. It is not surprising that some hold that self-preservation calls for restriction of this brand of competition.

All this is on the assumption of a kind of competition that drives prices below average cost, with short-run marginal cost as a limit. The resulting dilemma could be mitigated without resort to noncompetitive tactics, if the demand situation faced by each firm were of the "sloping" sort that permits the firm to earn some margin above short-run marginal cost. It may or may not be able to make this margin wide enough to cover total cost—before this point is reached it may be losing business to its competitors at a rate that would reduce its total profits, or threaten to do so if continued, and the same applies to the competitors. The outcome depends on an interrelated complex of "cross-elasticities" of demand, aggressive and defensive, long-run and

---

[5] The question how close this needs to be will be taken up in the following chapter, Sec. 8.

short-run. More basically, it depends on whether this firm can turn out a product that will hold its own with competing products at some price (not necessarily equal to those of the competing products) that will cover costs. If it cannot meet this test in the long run, a "sloping individual-demand curve" will not save it, though it may ease the pressure of short-run competitive situations, and to that extent make survival easier. It gives a firm some range of discretion in price policy, which an unwise firm may misuse at its own risk.

The point of this preliminary discussion is to show how the behavior of costs creates conditions in which the "sloping" type of demand behavior is on the whole favorable, rather than unfavorable, to a desirable and practicable (though inexact) form of competition. This affords a reason for examining cost behavior first and demand behavior afterward. The discussion also points to the need of keeping always in mind the interplay between short-run and long-run behavior, both of cost and of demand.

2. What Cost Curves Are Intended to Show

The intent of the kind of cost curves we are examining is to show the changes in costs due to changes in volume of output, as distinct from other causes of change in costs that are always entering in, and as distinct from the timing of variations in money payments. Thus these cost curves attempt to isolate the effect of output on costs. In doing so, they cover two distinct concepts: the expectations about changes in costs that govern business decisions, and the results which ultimately materialize. Theory commonly merges the two by assuming that expectations are accurate. Actually, the approximations and rules of thumb employed in business decisions are important in their own right, despite their inevitable inaccuracy; especially as there is no way of verifying them with precision, even after the event. Another feature is that the use of costs in making decisions is—or rather should be—always a matter of comparison of available alternatives; and this may determine the scope of costs that is revelant. For example, the decision whether to take on a new product is not bound by prior commitments, as is the decision whether or not to abandon a product, for the production of which specialized investments have been made and cannot be unmade without some sacrifice.

The costs regularly envisaged in cost curves are total economic costs, including those that take shape in amounts of labor and materials used, and of capital used or held available.[6] As to capital, they include the attrition of its value, plus the necessary return which constitutes the supply-price of investment. This last is distinct from the fact that some of the capital is represented by debt calling for interest payments, and some by equity claims to whatever net earnings may remain. The proportion between constant and variable capital costs has little or nothing to do with the proportion of debt to equity financing. And some operating expenses—constant or variable with respect to changes in output—are postponable, so that the timing of incurring the cost does not correspond closely with the timing of the corresponding financial payments. Inventory may be depleted, or maintenance or replacements deferred. The minimum of unpostponable financial outlay is not the same as the amount of constant costs, in the sense of costs independent of output, but it may be an important fact for a hard-pressed firm, which can operate for a time without covering all its costs, constant or variable. The costs are currently accruing, and it is not escaping them, it is disregarding or deferring them.[7]

For purposes of these cost curves, changes in costs due to changes in output are conceived as changes in amounts of labor and materials used, and of capital used or held available, as distinct from changes in the prices paid for them. This corresponds to the situation of a firm which draws its factors of production from a market that is so large, relative to changes in the amounts taken by the firm in question, that these changes are not themselves responsible for changes in the prices of the factors. Such price changes impliedly respond, not only to the demand from the entire industry rather than from the single firm, but to the demand from other industries using factors of production drawn from the same general market.

[6] This matter, and others discussed in this chapter, are analyzed in more detail in National Bureau of Economic Research, Committee on Price Determination, *Cost Behavior and Price Policy* (1943). Here only the general character of cost behavior is considered, insofar as it bears on competitive relationships. A distinctive scheme of cost categories is found in P. J. D. Wiles, *Price, Cost and Output* (1956), Chap. 2.

[7] See *ibid.*, p. 10.

To neglect such price changes is a legitimate simplification, roughly applicable to the situation of many industries and especially to short-run changes of output, but it does not fit all cases. A single large firm may be a heavy factor in the demand for labor in a local, regional, or otherwise specialized market, and long-run changes in its individual demand may be substantial factors in such a market. Something similar may be true where a highly concentrated industry is the sole user, or a very important user, of some raw material. The petroleum-refining industry in California, and tobacco and meat packing are outstanding cases in point. Here there is competition of the few in purchasing the material, and its price can be pushed up by an increase in one user's purchases. In the matter of access to capital, large and strong firms tap a national market of huge size, and secure better terms than do smaller concerns. The latter may also draw from limited local markets, where capital is more expensive. Either way, they pay more for the greater risk involved in small-scale operations.

An example may be cited from the telephone system, which traditionally acts in terms of an unusually long-range perspective. When, nearly forty years ago, it was deliberating whether to make the major shift to dial-operated exchanges, it took account of the fact that it drew its manual exchange operators from a limited sector of the labor market—girls possessing special qualifications—and that its predictable expansion would make such heavy drafts on this limited sector that a substantial increase in its wage scales would be normally expected to result. This factor weighted the decision on the side of the automatic installation. Such future possibilities, while entirely proper material for a long-range executive decision, are too conjectural to be appropriately included in a cost curve that carries some implications of measurability. To treat them in this way would be a rather pronounced example of the kind of pseudo-measurement in which economic theory sometimes indulges when it draws curves for which only hypothetical omniscience could furnish quantitative data.

A different sort of question is afforded by premium rates for overtime. These are in a literal sense changes in wage rates; but they correspond (very roughly) to the increased human costs of overtime work; and they do not represent a change in the terms of the existing wage bargain, but are embodied in it. Also they are definite in amount. For all these reasons it seems appropriate to include this item, where it occurs, as one of the regular and predictable factors in the increase of marginal cost when plant and equipment is used beyond its best capacity. The same would apply, in principle, to wage systems carrying guarantees of minimum employment or to substantial separation pay, together with the further fact that they make the behavior of the wage bill partially irreversible, increasing the financial obligations assumed. in hiring workers who may acquire such rights, and reducing the financial savings an employer can make by laying workers off or discharging them. This is in addition to the incentive the employer has to avoid undue cost of labor turnover and to hold his organization, or at least a nucleus of it, together if forced to accept a temporary curtailment of output.

A further fact is that change in output in itself costs something. While the human factors present complex possibilities, it seems safe to conclude that operation at, for example, 80 per cent of capacity will be more costly if the plant does not operate at this rate long enough for operating conditions to settle down fully, before changing to some other rate of operation.[8] Therefore, if the short-run cost curve represents the cost of operating at different percentages of capacity, the curve should be a zone rather than a sharp line, since the cost of operating at 80 per cent of capacity varies with the length of time the plant operates at that rate. And if the average rate of operation over a considerable period was 80 per cent, this being an average of fluctuations from 50 per cent to 110 per cent, the average cost for the whole period will be higher than the cost of operating steadily at 80 per cent. Thus the long-run curve of the movement of costs with increased "scale" is not only nearly flat through the most important parts of its length, and a zone rather than a sharp line, but it lies above the "envelope curve," intersecting the short-run curves of varying output with fixed capacity instead of being tangent to them.

The behavior of labor costs with varying output is modifiable by contractual arrangements or by governmental requirements; and the net effect in recent years has been to increase the elements of labor cost that cannot be avoided by reducing the rate of operation. This irreducible characteristic can no longer be regarded as confined to costs on account of fixed capital. Indeed, it is conceivable, though

---

[8] This point has been developed inductively by W. W. Cooper and A. Charnes. See "Silhouette Functions of Short-Run Cost Behavior," *Quarterly Journal of Economics* (February 1954), pp. 131-50.

perhaps not likely, that, in the element of cost that is irreducible in short-run fluctuations, labor might at some future time come to play a larger part than capital.

3. Differences in Cost Between Producing Units

Cost data, gathered for various purposes, including price control during two world wars, revealed a substantial spread between lowest-cost and highest-cost firms in the same industry. Also, cost did not vary uniformly with size. In reporting on the World War I results, the so-called "bulk-line" cost curve was used. Here each reporting unit was represented by a rectangle with the horizontal dimension representing output and the vertical dimension representing unit cost, for the period covered. When the rectangles were arranged in order from lowest cost to highest, the tops followed a curve with a relatively flat mid-sector, representing the mode of the figures, and a high-cost tail. The typical prewar condition was that the price was enough or more than enough to cover the cost of all but the high-cost tail, which represented something like 11 to 14 per cent of total output. This much was produced at a loss. (The figures covered operating expenses, not full economic cost, thus avoiding the worst discrepancies in accounting methods.) Naturally, firms in this class must either improve their performance, or be forced out of production ultimately. But a study of retailing by Professor Secrist indicated that the unprofitable tail showed a turnover of membership, but no tendency for the group as a whole to disappear.[9]

This group may include new firms, destined to become well established and profitable, but currently going through an initial lean period when personnel is being built up, production methods shaken down, and clientele and trade connections established. Or it may include older firms that have moved to a new location or tried some other major new departure, either in the hope of notable success or in an attempt to find a remedy for existing difficulties, and are still in the preliminary stages in which the new departure has not shaken

[9] See Horace Secrist, *Expense Levels in Retailing* (1924).

down and shown whether or not it is going to pay off. Or firms may have suffered from fire, flood, or other contingency. Or they may suffer more enduringly from technical handicaps or lack of access to adequate capital, or they may be merely inefficient. In some cases, it may be difficult to distinguish productive inefficiency from bargaining handicaps.

With all due reservations as to the accuracy and relevance of particular figures, and with allowance for differences of industrial structure and conditions of active or dull business, the general "bulk-line" pattern accords with the logic of dynamic industries and trades in which some firms take the lead with innovations, which may or may not succeed, and others follow the successful leads with varying degrees of promptness and success or the opposite. Thus one seems warranted in accepting this pattern as approximately representative for industries or trades in which the number of independent firms is large enough to make it meaningful to speak of a typical pattern or structure.

This is, of course, only the beginning of trying to trace the relative part played by firms in different sectors of the "bulk-line" curve. A priori, one could not say confidently whether the most strategic role would rest with the kind of firm which Alfred Marshall called "representative" or, as seems inherently more likely, with some kind of interaction between firms of different sorts, in different situations and subject to different incentives and pressures to aggressive and defensive action. This includes strong firms, able to follow a "full cost" pricing policy, and weaker firms, unable to cover full cost, but hoping to improve their situation by gaining some added business that will more than cover its added cost, or merely hanging on and trying to defend their existing volume as preferable to elimination.

4. Cost Differences and the Concept of Entry

This picture of typical industry-structure adds something to the concept of entry of new firms into an industry that was discussed in the preceding chapter. It lends emphasis to the idea of net entry as a balance of entries over exits, and to the fact that losses do not bring early and automatic exit. It means also that new entries may encroach on the business of existing firms, or may leave them room to expand, according as the industry is or is not expanding. In an expanding industry, a net balance of new entries may take place while the more efficient existing firms are maintaining their proportionate share of business or even increasing it. And it is self-evident that an expanding industry offers new entrants a better prospect for passing quickly through the probationary stage when they are establishing market contacts and building up their volume of sales to the minimum needed to place them in the range of concerns that can earn at least a modest return under competitive conditions.

In the light of all this, how shall one define the condition of earnings in an industry that invites a balance of entries in excess of exits? This is presumably mainly a matter of the general range of profits and losses in the industry. New entries will not be prevented merely because some firms are losing money; neither will they necessarily be attracted because one or more extra-strong firms are earning liberal profits. The latter condition might, however, be attractive to some entrant who hopes to offer a particular brand of product that would be a close rival of some highly successful variant already in the market. It also appears from Bain's excellent and important study that the general range of profits that can be sustained in an industry of considerable concentration, without being brought down by new entries, varies with varying conditions affecting the difficulties and handicaps new entrants face. These appear to cause differences in the force and effectiveness of potential competition.

This discussion leads to the question of the minimum return, which is part of the economist's conception of cost; and this turns out to cover a considerable range, between the low return necessary to keep a firm in business, once it is committed, the higher prospective average necessary to induce entry, and the still higher return an entrant must expect to make after going through the probationary period, if the leaner returns of this period are to be offset. Back of this there are, of course, numerous questions in the calculation of actual costs; prominent among them the problems involved in the attrition and replacement of capital as a cost. To these we may next turn.

5. *Attrition of Capital as a Cost*

"Full cost," of course, includes a return on investment, representing the necessary supply price of investment of capital and of the entrepreneurial services and uncertainties that are inseparable from it. This is a net return above all operating costs, including as costs all attrition of capital. But this last element involves considerable indefiniteness and uncertainty, in view of two features of the present type of economy. One is technical improvement, the other is the ever-present contingency of price inflation, in an economy in which the prevalent conventions of accountancy still reckon the maintenance of capital investment from the basis of an unchanged dollar value as a stable unit of measurement.

Obviously, if replacing a capital unit costs twice as much as its original cost, accrued depreciation on an original cost basis does not build reserves equal to the cost of identical physical replacement. As against this, it is often pointed out that major units are seldom identically replaced, but rather replaced with improved units that embody more service value than physically identical replacements of the original units would, at present prices. Theoretically, replacement of the original dollar value might exceed or fall short of replacing the original service value, according to which of these opposing factors predominates, though the concept of service value appears necessarily inexact, being compounded of quantity and quality of product and cost of producing it, and dependent on the unavoidably uncertain element of obsolescence. On the average, it appears a foregone conclusion that the wartime and postwar inflation has diluted the buying power of replacement dollars by more than technical improvements could offset. This means that maintenance of the real value of the capital calls for replacement outlays in excess of the original cost of the items replaced; and that the excess must come out of funds identified in the accounts as "surplus" (retained income), part of which becomes really a replacement reserve.

A further complication arises because depreciation is regularly based on the time it takes capital equipment to wear out, while in a dynamic economy it commonly is superseded by something more efficient before it is worn out. The timing of this functional obsolescence is inherently unpredictable, even as an average risk, since it depends on the uncertainties of future progress. Therefore it is not well adapted to being included in accounts of costs as an annual rate of capital attrition, though it clearly needs to be taken into account in making executive decisions. Thus it is natural that it is dealt with in non-accounting terms, typically the rule-of-thumb that an investment must show a prospect of paying for itself in a given number of years to be worth making, this "payoff period" being shorter, the more dynamic the technique involved.

The method of accounting for costs of capital attrition takes effect on the book value of capital assets. From the standpoint of competition it is desirable (though not necessary) that this accounting should be so handled that newly replaced units would be represented by a book value equal to their current cost, and that aging units would have a book value equal to what a well-advised owner would find it worth while to pay for their remaining service life, in competition with up-to-date units of similar capacity. It appears that in practice depreciation accounting can do no more than minimize its departures from such a theoretical standard. Thus the minimum necessary supply price of capital is a matter involving latitude of judgment. This is true, even if all one is asking is whether a given firm is earning this minimum amount.

In that connection, it seems established that the minimum supply price of owners' capital, allowance for risk, and wages of management is smaller if they are furnished in one bundle by one person and register as his personal sacrifices of production, than if they are furnished by different persons, each of whom has to receive dollar compensation for the factor he has contributed. This helps explain how small enterprises continue, with substandard earnings. As will appear later, where such personal supply functions affect market behavior, they behave differently from financial expenses.

6. *The Minimum Necessary Return*

It is evident from the foregoing that a return yielding no profit above cost, or yielding only the minimum necessary supply price of capital and enterprise, is far from an exact quantity; it is rather a species within which wide variations are possible. The result is to call for reconsideration of some ideas based on more simple and exact notions. One idea that needs modification is the seemingly obvious idea that a firm will aways prefer some profit to no profit. From this the conclusion may be drawn, with misleading logic, that a firm will always prefer some profit on a smaller volume to no profit on a larger volume, or will always prefer some profit for a short time to no profit for a longer time. Some of the chief defects that theory attributes to the "competition of the few" stem from this kind of reasoning.

But the logic becomes shaky when it is realized that the line between profit and no-profit is far from exact, that no-profit includes some sort of minimum standard return, and that this minimum is really a range covering substantial variations. As we saw in Section 4, above, it involves a prospect including a substandard return during what I have called the probationary period of a firm's existence, and a higher return after the firm has established itself—if it succeeds in doing so. And of course the minimum necessary return for an entire industry is a composite, including firms in their probationary period, firms in temporary difficulties, firms on the way to an enforced exit, and established firms earning different rates, up to the highest in the industry.

All this has a bearing on the view that the existence of the kind of demand designated as a "sloping individual-demand function" leads necessarily to uneconomically high pricing, attracting a wasteful amount of new entry and leading to restriction of output below the optimum scale, as mentioned in the introduction to this chapter. It appears that an industry may be, as a whole, in a "no-profit" condition that does not invite a balance of entries above exits, while the stronger firms in the industry are earning positive profits. Then, if they are thinking in terms of long-term possibilities of progressive growth, it may be rational for them or some of them, to prefer a larger volume on a thinner margin. But the same kind of calculation may apply also to unprofitable concerns whose poor earnings are due to inadequate volume. If their individual products are sufficiently differentiated to give their (short-run) individual-demand functions a slope that would enable these firms to increase earnings (temporarily) by raising their prices, their basic difficulty would be intensified over a longer future, and the deterioration would be likely to be progressive over time. They are much more likely to try to increase their volume by competitive tactics: that is, to try for larger volume on thinner unit margins.

These particular firms may be assumed to have unused capacity, which means that the added cost of added output is much less than their average cost. But this condition is, in various degrees and guises, general throughout competitive industry; and firms' varying diagnoses of it, attitudes toward it and reactions to it, do much to determine the character of competition. Here the basic distinction is between the cost of added utilization of existing facilities, which occurs in response to fluctuations and is therefore called "short-run" marginal cost, and cost of increased "scale" of facilities and operation, which occurs in response to expectations of enduring growth and is therefore called "long-run" marginal cost. The two are interrelated, in that the kind of long-run facilities a firm builds is dependent on the extent to which it wants to provide for flexibility in handling expected fluctuations as well as growth.

P. J. D. Wiles proposes to substitute "partial adaptation" and "total adaptation" to designate this general distinction and especially objects to calling them "short-run" and long-run" cost adjustments.[10] He notes that short-run adjustments may involve postponing outlays such as maintenance, which will take their toll in the long run. Postponability of outlays is important, but needs to be construed in the light of a clear distinction between the incurring of costs of production and the making of monetary disbursements, which may be timed differently. Depreciation accounting converts the attrition and ultimate exhaustion of an asset into a current charge. Deferred maintenance is, in principle, also an attrition of assets, incurred at the time of deferral, but not so treated in the accounts. Its impact in the shape of monetary outlays may be *disclosed* in the long run. Deferral may occur when the plant is extra busy, in which case reserves to meet the impact are

[10] Wiles, *op. cit.*, pp. 8ff.

likely to be naturally accumulated; or it may occur when output is low and funds are scarce, in which case a return to normal output may solve the problem. In either case, real cost is temporarily greater than the books show.

Such deferred impacts are quite different from the costs involved in altered scale ("total adaptation"). This appears to be the substance of Wiles' objection to the "short-run-long-run" distinction. As between his terminology and that of utilization versus scale, the latter appears to have some advantages of explicitness, while the "short-run versus long-run" distinction appears usable, so long as the underlying facts are understood. We may look first at short-run variations of output.

7. Short-Run Variation of Cost with Varying Output

When a commercial or industrial plant or establishment is set up, it must normally be prepared for some variations in output; either fluctuations in the total output, or fluctuations in output of particular products, including shifts from one product to another. Fluctuations are of different sorts, including daily, weekly, or seasonal cycles of use, or irregular contingencies due to weather, to general business fluctuations or the vicissitudes of particular products. Vicissitudes may occur on the supply side as well as on that of demand. Canning, to take a single example, is highly seasonal, with yearly output contingent on the crop or the catch.

Methods of handling fluctuations vary widely. They include dovetailing output of different products, where a shift between products is more economical than fluctuating total operation. Dovetailing requires adaptability in working force or equipment or both, putting overspecialization at a discount. Working to stock permits production to be steadier than sale, but requires that the product be durable and in dependable demand. It will be convenient to pay chief attention to cases in which total output fluctuates. It is this kind of fluctuation to which the conception of "constant and variable costs" is an appropriate and useful approximation. That is, there are categories of costs dependent on capacity and others that vary with output. The simplest case is one in which the variable costs are, within limits, uniform per unit of output, or near enough to be so regarded.[11]

The point should be stressed that the behavior of business outlays is only partly a natural and inevitable reflection of technical facts. The chief example of this sort would be direct outlay for materials going into the product, a natural "variable" cost. But even here, there are different accounting conventions for giving these materials a dollar value, where their prices have changed since they were acquired. The treatment of administrative salaries as a constant expense and of wages as variable does not have the same kind and degree of natural-ness, as is attested by the move for a "guaranteed annual wage" and by various experiments in putting a floor under a worker's total earn-ings. This behavior of wages and salaries is modifiable by contract. Nevertheless, there is naturalness in the fact that, floor or no floor, wages of direct labor vary at the margin, with ordinary fluctuations of output, and vary roughly in proportion to output up to the point where premium overtime begins; while administrative salaries and much indirect labor are substantially constant, for moderate and tem-porary fluctuations of output. If labor as a whole were to cease being a "variable" cost, it could only be by becoming an equity claimant, as the common stockholder is.

The conventional or arbitrary element in the classification of costs into constant and variable appears clearly in the various methods used in cost accounting to allocate burden. But there is an underlying tech-nical reality that these accounting conventions should not ignore—for example, the extent to which depreciation is or is not a function of wear and thus variable with use—even though the technical fact is hard to estimate quantitatively. The economic consequences may be complicated where functional obsolescence due to technical progress occurs before wearing out. Even here, the point of economic replace-ment is affected by the amount of deterioration due to wear that has occurred.

A form of cooperative is conceivable in which workers would be equity claimants, while machinery was leased and paid for on a basis of use, as under the old United Shoe Machinery leases, and it is sig-

[11] A more accurate statement would be that total cost varies *as if* it were com-posed of two components, constant and uniform variable.

nificant that this would reverse the usual classification of costs, making capital the variable cost and labor the "overhead." There are practical reasons this is not likely to become the prevalent form of organization. But it may serve as a reminder that these cost classifications contain conventional elements subject to modification, though within limits set by the natural elements, technical and human, underlying the conventions.

Reverting to the simple formula of a constant plus a uniform variable component, this approximation is the basis of the familiar "break-even" diagram, in which total cost is represented by a straight line starting at a given amount for zero output and rising at a uniform slope, while gross income is another straight line, starting at zero for zero output and intersecting the cost line at the "break-even" point. This tells, for a given price and selling cost, how much must be sold in order to make a profit. It can be modified to represent situations in which increased sales call for reduced price or increased selling cost, or in which certain classes of sales are more costly or less profitable than others.[12]

Attempts to improve on such rough approximations by accurate measurement of the variation of costs face serious difficulties.[13] The purposes of the present study are less concerned with precise measurement than with the general character of the variation of costs and its relation to the methods used to deal with fluctuations of output; and especially the ideas about these things that guide the policies of business firms. From this last standpoint, even such a rough approximation as the "break-even" diagram is pertinent. Regarding the limits of its applicability, there appear to be two broad types of cases: those in which this cost formula applies (approximately) up to an absolute limit of capacity, beyond which output cannot be increased, and those

[12] One writer has spoken of a "hip-roofed" break-even chart, to deal with this last feature.

[13] This matter has been well reviewed in National Bureau of Economic Research, *Cost Behavior and Price Policy*. Cf. also P. W. S. Andrews, *Manufacturing Business* (1949), especially p. 105. C. Clive Saxton, in *The Economics of Price Determination* (1942), pp. 96-97, finds reported behavior of costs in samples of large and small firms in British industries involving approximately uniform marginal costs for variations of output of 10 per cent to 15 per cent above or below "normal," and higher marginal costs at outputs departing further from normal. (Minimum average costs would be reached at larger outputs than minimum marginal costs.)

in which output can be increased beyond the optimum rate, but with increasing variable costs per unit. The first type appears to consist of continuous-process forms of production, which cannot be substantially speeded up; and the second may be divided into manufacturing and mercantile types, which appear to differ significantly from one another. One way of distinguishing the continuous-process type from the others is that in the others, starting and stopping costs are not large.[14]

Perhaps the chief differences in methods of handling variations of output are that in continuous processes, this is done mainly by varying the number of productive units in operation; in other kinds of manufacturing it can also be done by varying hours of operation, using short-time or overtime or employing extra shifts; while in merchandising the use of extra productive units is exceptional, varying of hours of operation plays a secondary part, minor variations are handled by the standard personnel making varying amounts of sales, and major peaks by adding extra personnel. Each type of variation presents its characteristic problems.

In the continuous-process kind of production, single units need to be shut down occasionally for repairs or overhauling, aside from any variation of demand. The relining of a blast furnace is one of the more regularly recurrent instances. Then, if production is to go on at a steady rate, there must be other units that can be put in service. This calls for multiple units, even in cases where a single giant unit would be most economical, *while operating*. Adjustment to varying output adds the further factor that part of the units are needed only part of the time, and work only a fraction of the time that is technically feasible. And this brings into play the principle that the stage of wear or obsolescence at which a plant unit should be retired and replaced depends on whether it is wanted for full-time or only part-time use. Where techniques have not changed radically, occasional peaks may be most economically handled by retaining stand-by units of less than top efficiency, because the capital costs of replacing them with up-to-date units would outweigh the operating savings secured from the new units under part-time operation.

This principle appears in various forms. In some cases, a firm may construct a big plant, designed for the most efficient handling of the minimum demand it has reason to expect, so that this plant may be

[14] National Bureau of Economic Research, *op. cit.*, p. 112.

kept operating at a uniform rate, while the fluctuating excess is handled by methods that are less economical but more flexible. The big plant would presumably contain enough units to provide for the lay-offs that are technically necessary to continuous uniform production. Where there are enough facilities of substantially equal operating efficiency to handle the maximum expected load, the total cost function may approximate, closely enough for working purposes, the model represented by a constant component plus a uniform variable component, up to a fixed limit of capacity, so that there is always some economy in added output, so long as it can be handled. Average cost exceeds short-run marginal cost throughout, but by a margin that diminishes as capacity is approached.

In the noncontinuous kind of manufacturing, the greatest economy is commonly secured when a single shift can operate for a standard working week; though as the standard week becomes shorter, it may be feasible to arrange a second shift without incurring the added cost that is characteristic of night shifts. Much repair work can be done when the plant is not operating, obviating part of the need for stand-by units for this purpose. Longer hours of plant operation are an obvious economy in terms of plant overhead, but may not be worth purchasing at the cost of poorer hours and working conditions for labor, this latter being more often the decisive consideration. In handling short fluctuations by part time and overtime, the firm maintains its normal working force and avoids the turnover cost of breaking in new workers who may not be continuously needed, unless it has a reserve of workers for whose requirements part-time employment is suitable. If the handling of peak loads involves overdriving the plant, this may cause increased breakdowns, as well as increased spoilage of product. The upshot of these and other conditions is a cost function that can be pushed beyond its optimum, but with increased average and marginal cost, in which premium rates for overtime are likely to be the most conspicuous factor.

The ability to handle fluctuations in some of the indicated ways, without undue increase in cost, also furnishes part of the means of providing for growth, in that an increase in volume, beyond the absolute optimum for existing equipment, can be handled without necessitating an instant enlargement of this equipment. But growth by many small enlargements is unnecessarily expensive; and the method generally preferred is to add sectors of substantial size, which may not be utilized at once up to the optimum or close to it. These sectors may be distinct plants, capable of independent operation. Then each may be specialized to serving a particular area or to particular products in the firm's line, thus gaining added economy, though at the cost of some alteration in the original equipment. But there is a limit to the economy of specialization on single-purpose equipment. It is economical only so long as the product-line does not change, and a balance needs to be struck between this kind of economy and the requirements of flexibility. This the firm has to determine according to the nature of its processes and products, and the stability of demand.

In the case of retailing, the basic equipment consists of space sufficient to display the stock and make it available and to accommodate comfortably the normal number of customers, this being, of course, especially vital under modern self-service methods. With more conventional methods, space is needed also for enough sales personnel to serve the normal flow of customers comfortably; and in either case, space is needed to handle customer peaks without such crowding as would drive customers away or block the transaction of business. As compared with self-service, conventional methods of selling would seem to have more flexibility in this respect, using added sales personnel to handle peaks. At recognized peak times, such as the Christmas rush or special sales, customers expect some delay and inconvenience such as would, if it were habitual at ordinary times, drive them to seek more adequately equipped establishments.

The customer's time is worth something to him—or he thinks it is—and if the ratio of sales force to customers is one that keeps the sales force continuously busy, thus economizing their time to the utmost, too many customers would be kept waiting inordinately. Maximum economy of the combined time of sales force and customers calls for a ratio at which some customers do some waiting at times, and at other times the sales force is not occupied to capacity. A lower ratio of sales force to customers means poor service; high-quality service calls for a considerably higher ratio. In the one case, the customer's wasted time carries less weight than that of the sales force. If the resulting savings in selling expense are passed on to the customer, he—or she—is getting lower prices at the cost of some waiting and other elements of inferior service. A well-organized competitive market would give customers who prefer this kind of saving, at the necessary cost in time and other elements, a chance to express this preference by trading with this kind of outlet; while customers who have the opposite preference pay higher prices for superior service. Such differentials in service would naturally go along with parallel differentials in the range of quality of the goods offered.

For our present purpose, this points to the conclusion that a sales force normally has some unused capacity. In general, it appears that moderate short-run fluctuations in sales volume cause no variation in the cost of the basic sales operation of serving customers; relative to such changes, it appears about as constant as the store overhead itself. This points to the economy of increasing sales volume, either by cutting prices on articles having a demand more elastic than unity in terms not of total price but of the margin above cost of goods sold; or by increasing sales promotion where the response fulfills the same condition, or by securing the handling of products, the producers of which have given them effective sales promotion.

To sum up in the most general terms, this discussion seems to have identified two main types of short-run cost behavior, the limited-capacity type in which marginal cost is less than average unit cost up to the point beyond which output cannot be increased, and the elastic-limits type, including most trade and manufacturing, in which output can be increased beyond the optimum, at increasing average cost. It would seem self-evident that the first type tends to occasion larger percentages of excess capacity for a given need of providing for peak loads, capacity being defined in terms of optimum rate of output. The problems stemming from unused capacity would be expected to be greater and to take a more inflexible form, in industries of this type. It has appeared that in retailing, within moderate ranges of volume, short-run marginal cost of serving customers is close to zero, and it has been suggested that the self-service type of retailing has in addition some resemblance to the limited-capacity type of behavior.

Economies of full utilization, with extremely low short-run marginal costs, tend to intensify the pressures of competition. If it acts on prices, it tends to generate the Marshallian "sentiment against spoiling the market," which may be variously implemented. This pressure may be mitigated by product differentiation, which may be cultivated with this mitigation in view. Thus the emphasis may be on price-cutting or on expenditures for sales promotion or on modification of the product, or on some combination according to the nature and responsiveness of demand.

8. Long-Run Economies of Scale

Long-run economies of scale, as distinct from economies of full utilization, tend to fewness and high concentration. In extreme cases,
they may lead to "natural monopoly," where an industry has room for
no more than one firm of optimum size. More often they tend to natural oligopoly. Or a local market area may support only one plant of
optimum size, resulting in a tendency to spatially separated plants
with competition only from a distance, which raises special problems
where costs of transportation are heavy.

A full examination of the causes of economies of scale and of the
problems and difficulties of measuring them, would be unduly burdensome for the purposes of this study.[15] One pervasive principle may be
mentioned. "Scale" may refer to a single process, a "plant," or a firm
as an organizational unit. Except for single processes, economies of
scale have something to do with advantages derived from combining
related processes in physical juxtaposition (in a "plant") or in administrative correlation, or both. In some processes, very large units are
highly economical (subject to the need for flexibility); and where
complementary processes are as well or better handled by small units,
the number of these may be multiplied without loss of efficiency.
Where the economy of the large units is of dominant importance, and
where these different processes naturally go together within the
bounds of a single plant, the economy of the large units may dictate
the optimum scale for the whole, resulting in a tendency to large
plants. Where small-unit processes are of a sort that can be independently carried on without loss of efficiency (through cost of transport,
need for larger inventories, or other causes), the firm may have the option of farming out such processes to small-scale specialists. But if it
tries to farm out too much, it will reduce the scale of its large-unit
processes, as well as impair its operational coordination. Where the
large-unit processes can be economically segregated in distinct physical

---

[15] The author's discussion of causes, in his *Economics of Overhead Costs*, though
published in 1923, may still have some validity. Problems of measurement are
well treated in National Bureau of Economic Research, *op. cit.*

units (*e.g.*, research, finance, and important features of selling), and where they go beyond the optimum scale of single plants, they tend to multiplant firms. There may be some qualified tendency in such cases for the processes with the largest optimum scale to govern the optimum scale of the whole firm; but fortunately this is no absolute law and is subject to counteracting influences, otherwise concentration would be even greater than it is.[16]

In general, it appears very rare that the economies of scale in a single plant continue to the point of "natural monopoly," with qualification for the element of limited local monopoly characterizing a plant whose only competition comes from a distance, as already mentioned. This is probably best regarded as a problem of spatial competition, rather than of monopoly in the full sense. For most of the relevant market areas, the most probable conclusion seems to be that there is room in the area for a fair number of single plants large enough to be within the range in which economies of plant size are either negligible, or at least too small to be decisive, in the light of the various other factors affecting efficiency. Negatively, there is no clear evidence that cost increases with extreme size of single plants or of firms. Perhaps this means no more than that size has not been pushed past the point at which substantial diseconomies would be incurred. In any case, the attempt at statistical verification collides with the inescapable difficulty that plants or firms of extreme size are necessarily too few to permit their cost experience to be statistically significant; this in addition to the more pervasive difficulties of measuring scale and cost.

The indicated typical curve seems to be one in which the smallest size group shows high costs due to small size, after which the curve flattens out until it shows no clear and material economies traceable to size within the largest size group. One fact that appears clearly in the "envelope" form of cost curve is that the long-run economies of scale are less than the short-run economies of full utilization of a plant of any given scale. In other words, the long-run curve is flatter than the short-run curves to which it is depicted as tangent in the envelope cost curve.[17] If there is an exception to this, it occurs at very small

[16] E. A. G. Robinson gives a very good treatment of this problem: see *The Structure of Competitive Industry* (1932). It seems possible that in the United States, the largest-scale processes may have more tendency to govern the scale of the whole than under English conditions, which afford the setting for Robinson's study.

[17] This has been critically discussed in general terms in Chap. 3, Sec. 10 above.

sizes of plants and is likely to occur where such obstacles as the cost or difficulty of reaching an adequate market or limited access to capital cause plants to be built of a size so small as to incur high costs.

For example, in an empirical study of the costs of cement production in the years 1929 and 1932, in which the number of plants covered was sufficient to derive meaningful regressions, both in terms of size of plant and of percentage utilization, the plants whose size was small enough to give rise to diseconomies comparable to those of small percentage utilization were located in the sparsely populated parts of the West (other than the Pacific coast), where in order to reach a market large enough to absorb the output of a plant of economical size, very heavy transportation costs would have to be incurred. Thus the firm in question might face a choice between the high operating cost of a small plant and the comparably high operating cost of a larger plant operated too far below capacity. Since the larger plant would incur a heavier capital cost, this would tend to decide the choice against it.

As for organized and specialized research, the results apply to multiple plants and multiple products. It is clear that the very small firm cannot afford to do research by itself; and it is equally obvious that, as between two firms, one of which has four times the sales volume of the other, the larger firm can spend half as much per dollar of sales revenue on research and still have twice as large a research budget. While the value of the results of the research may not be doubled—that is, the expenditure may be subject to diminishing returns—the economy of size would seem to be nearly unlimited in the sense that a larger firm can always have some advantage over a smaller firm in the same branch of production.

But that is not the same thing as saying that the one large firm would make a larger contribution to the technique of the industry than two smaller firms which between them spend the same amount on research. Here the advantage of competitive diversity enters in, with multiple independent formulation of problems to work on; and the general judgment appears to be that the competitive system is likely to be more fruitful of results, always assuming that it is not too seriously handicapped by limited financial resources available to the competing units. Where this is the case, cooperative, governmental, or academic research are likely to step in. Otherwise, where the importance of research is great, the accompanying economies of scale appear to tend, not to natural monopoly, but to natural oligopoly.

Other advantages of scale occur in financing procurement and selling; and cutting across the others are advantages in the handling or reduction of risks. Among these sources of advantage, a few selected aspects may be mentioned. Selling has many dimensions, including the size of single sales or the volume covered by single contracts or sales to single customers, volume sold in a given area (intensiveness of coverage) and area covered. For example, advertising in nationwide media is economical coverage if the sales area is nationwide. While every firm must sell its product, there is wide variety in the extent to which manufacturers take active part in the processes of distribution. The more far-reaching forms of participation in selling and procurement may be dealt with under vertical integration.

Risks may be broadly classified into physical and market risks; and economies may be distinguished according as they arise from large numbers of similar risks, or from combining risks of different sorts, which are likely to offset one another. The first type enables the large firm to get the benefits of self-insurance, while the second type comes into play when a firm diversifies so as to hedge its risks with risks of an opposite sort. The clearest case of the latter kind occurs when one product faces the rivalry of a substitute, and the outcome is uncertain. A firm producing one such product can hedge this risk by going into the production of the other. This would be an advantage, even if the firm had no monopolistic position in either industry. If it did have monopolistic power over one of the substitutes, limited or threatened by the substitution of the other, its entry into the substitute field would hedge this risk, but only in a partial way, so long as the substitute product was thoroughly competitive within its own field. For this very reason, the entry of the monopoly into the substitute field would be suspect, because the monopoly would have such a strong incentive to use its position to extinguish effective competition in the substitute field, thus extending and entrenching its monopolistic power. Since in practice the boundaries of monopolistic power, where competitive forces cease to be effective, are imprecise and controversial, diversification into substitute fields, by big firms, is one of the most difficult features of industrial structure on which to draw the line between legitimate practices and those carrying a monopolistic threat.

9. Vertical Integration

There is no inherently natural assortment of productive processes that should logically be included in the operations of a single plant or a single business enterprise or firm. "Integration" refers to the combination within a firm of functions that can be, and customarily are, carried on by separate firms. The extensions of function so spoken of include extension backward into the supplying of materials, parts, and subassemblies, or forward into further processing or distribution. Some of these combinations of functions can quite naturally be carried on within a single plant, which for this purpose may be defined as the material embodiment of a set of processes that are carried on in physical juxtaposition. A plant has many options whether to produce or purchase parts, subassemblies, or partly processed goods, or how far to carry the finishing of its products. On these optional processes it is in potential competition with other producers, who may be relatively small specialists or large specialists supplying plants in many different industries, or may be other units of a single huge industrial combination, the parts of which engage in intrafirm competition.

There is a place for the relatively small, specialized supplier of parts and subassemblies. In fact, this is one of the ways in which a modest-sized firm can offset the economies of great size. But it faces special problems, since it sells in competition with the customer's option of making the thing himself or getting it from another unit of the customer's own combined organization. In the latter case, it becomes a matter of the customer's policy how far his choice is based on an objective reckoning of costs, or what kind of cost-figuring he uses and whether he engages in reciprocal buying. The situation contains elements of potential arbitrariness that may or may not materialize. This feature is increased if the supplier ties himself to a single big customer, as he is often tempted to do, despite the potential danger of allowing other market contacts to lapse.[18] Such a status is feudal rather than competitive.

[18] In the preceding chapter mention was made of a major chain store that reportedly set a limit on the proportion of any supplier's output that it would pur-

The obverse of this is the familiar situation of the specialized fabricator who must buy his supplies from an integrated firm that is also his competitor in fabrication. Granting that integration may be a source of economy, and that the best way to determine whether this is true in any given case is by a competitive test, the terms on which the independent fabricator gets his supplies are obviously crucial to the validity of the test. Absence of formal discrimination in price is not sufficient, if the price itself is not fixed by effectively competitive forces. If the integrated supplier is sufficiently impressed with the importance of keeping on the safe side of the Robinson-Patman Act, he may lean over backward to be fair to the specialized fabricator, both in price and in allocating supplies. But this is hardly a positive guarantee.

Integration raises further problems when the large producer extends his operations into the field of distribution of his products, *via* his own distributing agencies or exclusive arrangements with existing outlets. It is perhaps in this area that the advantages of great size have their greatest extension, and at the same time center in things that can hardly be classified clearly as productive economies, but rather as advantages of market contacts. The size required to set up a nationwide network of exclusive distributing agencies may be much larger than the size required to operate an efficient producing plant. It follows that a relatively small competitor may be an efficient producer, but handicapped in the distribution of his product. Automobile distribution in this country seems to be a clear case in which the established method of distribution calls for much greater size than is needed for efficient production.

This appears peculiarly unfortunate because, as we shall see more fully in the next chapter, effective competition hinges on an industrial structure in which an influential part is played by firms that are strong and efficient, but each of which produces a relatively small fraction of the industry output. This is the modern substitute for the atomistic competition of pure theory. Such firms have ample room for expansion which is large, relative to their existing size (in technical terms, they have a high cross-elasticity of demand), and this is necessary to give them adequate incentives to active competition, both in price and in improvement of products.

---

chase, in order to prevent its suppliers from becoming dependent on it—perhaps also to avoid incurring the responsibility that such dependence generates.

As an example, the introduction of foreign cars into the American market has faced this kind of handicap in distribution. It is interesting and hopeful that, in the face of this difficulty, foreign cars have made their way into our market to an extent that the major American producers could no longer dismiss as not significant. The pattern includes existing dealers adding a foreign small car to their lines, a dealer specializing in a group of foreign cars, or even in one such. It appears that the competitive handicaps in question have not proved insuperable; but this does not make it desirable that such handicaps should exist, as obstacles to experiments in the tapping of neglected sectors of demand.

In smaller ranges of size, the distributional handicap of the smaller firms takes the shape of being forced to sell through wholesalers, in competition with bigger rivals who can push their own sales directly. All in all, this group of advantages of size, arising from vertical integration and concerned with procurement and distribution, may include the most serious obstacles to effective competition by moderate-sized firms. And the most baffling feature of this group is the way in which productive economies are interwoven with strategic advantages in procurement and sales promotion, involving impairment of the impersonal impartiality that is supposed to characterize a competitive market, and to assure relatively small competitors a chance to survive on their economic merits. These features go beyond the scope of the present chapter.

CHAPTER 7

Demand and Supply Functions

1. Basic Conceptions and Their Relevance

The tool of analysis with which demand theory starts is the concept of elasticity of demand, representing the ability and willingness of the market to absorb larger amounts of a product at a lower price than at a higher price, other things being equal. Before our analysis ends, we shall need to extend the concept to include the response of sales volume to varying expenditures on selling effort, and on the product itself. But at the outset we may concentrate on the relation between sales volume and price, and develop some of its often-neglected features.

Elasticity of demand takes two forms that need to be distinguished. In the first, which is appropriate to the produce-exchange type of market, the active variables are the supply that must be marketed and the total state of demand. The price results from the meeting of these two quantities, being the price at which the whole supply will find buyers. In the second, which is appropriate to most of the situations in industry and trade, price becomes an active variable and, in connection with the total state of demand, determines the amount that can be sold. In the main stream of transactions of this second sort, the amount produced or supplied adjusts itself more or less currently to what can be disposed of on terms that producers are willing to accept. Even in the secondary stream where remnants are taken off the market, it is not an imperative "must" that the entire amount should be sold.

For purposes of analyzing the difference between monopoly and competition, the next step is to break the concept into two subgroups on another basis: distinguishing the kinds of demand functions perti-

148

nent to monopoly or concerted or unified action in selling, from those pertinent to various kinds and degrees of competition. At one extreme stands the demand function for an entire product, pertinent to a monopoly; at the competitive extreme stands the demand function faced by a single seller of a homogeneous product, acting independently and ignoring the effect of his actions on his rivals' actions. Most of the cases in industry and trade lie between these two extremes. The earmark of competition is that the second group of demand functions is normally much more elastic than the first, and the possible price for each seller (or the range of possible prices) is limited by the offerings of his competitors. This is why competitors, who face the individual kind of demand function, behave differently from noncompetitive sellers, who face some variant of the aggregative kind of demand. This difference in elasticity and in maximum possible price affords a conceptual means of summing up the strength of competitive forces at work in any given situation.

In the extreme competitive case, elasticity is conceived as infinite—a horizontal demand function—and any slope in the demand function is often identified with an "element of monopoly." But effective competition does not require such extreme elasticity as its mainstay, for reasons indicated in the preceding chapter and hinging on the need for a margin above short-run marginal cost if long-run marginal costs —typically close to average costs—are to be covered.[1] More pertinent to our analysis is the question whether elasticity is greater or less than unity: unit elasticity meaning that a change in price results in an opposite change in volume sold which is exactly proportionate, so that gross dollar volume of sales is unchanged. Obviously, if a competitor is to make money by reducing his price, his volume must increase considerably more than this; his gross dollar volume of sales must increase enough to more than cover the added costs of his added physical output.

In view of this, it seems useful for some purposes to compare the proportionate change in physical volume of sales not only with the proportionate change in price, but also with the resulting proportionate change in the seller's margin above his relevant marginal cost. This may be called "margin elasticity," as distinct from "price elasticity." If it is greater than unity, the seller can increase his net earnings by

[1] See Chap. 6, Sec. 1.

reducing his price. The importance of this for competition is self-evident. So also is the importance of the quantitative relation between margin elasticity and price elasticity. Price will be in theoretical equilibrium at a level at which margin elasticity is equal to unity, and this equilibrium would be stable if a higher price would mean higher elasticity and *vice versa*; that is, if the firm would lose a larger proportion of its customers by raising its unit margin than it would gain by a similar reduction of its margin. A demand curve that is straight or only slightly convex downward would have this characteristic. A monopolist's margin elasticity will normally be less than unity (indicating that a higher price will be more profitable), until it reaches the range at which some substitute becomes a close rival. Under competition, the elasticity of individual demand is likely to show this kind of variation fairly strongly in the neighborhood of the average cost of a strategically situated firm, because prices above this level invite competitors to expand, while lower prices do not.[2]

By way of illustrative example, if a firm is operating substantially below full capacity, this will make short-run marginal cost relevant; and if this is three fourths of average cost, price elasticity at that level must be equal to four, to bring about equilibrium. If it is greater, competition would tend to drive price below average cost. But if the firm is operating close to capacity, long-run marginal cost is relevant and is likely to be, for practical purposes, indistinguishable from average cost. Then the long-run responsiveness of demand becomes relevant, and may involve progressive expansion or shrinkage of sales volume over time. To this, a firm under competition may respond much as theory supposes it to respond to a demand-curve that is close to horizontal, without driving price below average cost or allowing it to rise much higher, except temporarily. This calculus fits the familiar fact that a firm with unused capacity and heavy constant costs is impelled to cut prices deeper than a firm that will have to increase its capacity to handle a substantial increase in its sales volume.

[2] An extreme case of a somewhat different sort is the "kinked" oligopoly demand-curve, in which elasticity shifts abruptly, according as a firm's price moves are or are not met and neutralized by its competitors. This will be taken up later.

2. Monopoloidal Demand Functions

The demand function for an entire product applies in the limiting case of a complete monopoly which is secure against competition both from existing firms and from new entries and is limited only by the closeness of substitutes or the willingness of buyers to do without the product. In such a case the price that yields maximum profit or minimum loss will generally, though not necessarily, yield earnings above the minimum necessary supply price of the product. But such a complete and secure monopoly must be rare in industry and trade, in a country with active antitrust laws. And when economists try to classify American industry and trade into monopolistic and competitive categories, it is safe to conclude that few of the major industries they class as "monopolistic" are of the complete and secure type that is governed by the demand function for the entire product.

These cases are predominantly cases of high concentration, of leadership limited by willingness to follow the leader's policy, or collusion limited by similar willingness to conform; and always limited by two forms of potential competition: potential reactivation of latent competition between existing sellers, and potential new entries. In such cases, the demand function faced by the aggregate of the *existing* sellers is not the total demand for the product, but that fraction of this demand which the existing sellers can expect to keep, and which will diminish progressively if their pricing policy invites a progressive increase of new entries.[3] And the demand faced by a single seller is the fraction of this fraction that the particular seller can expect to keep in the face of possible losses of business to rivals. For this reason, the usual assumption on this score—that a seller in this situation will maintain a uniform percentage of the total sales of the industry—is doubly undependable. And the theory based on this assumption, that such sellers charge prices that would yield maximum profits to a complete and

[3] Cf. Joe S. Bain, "A Note on Pricing in Monopoly and Oligopoly," *American Economic Review* (March 1949), pp. 448-64; reprinted in American Economic Association, *Readings in Industrial Organization and Public Policy* (1958), pp. 220-35. Bain's treatment does not envisage progressive inroads by new entries, this limitation being natural to a diagrammatic analysis.

secure monopoly, needs amending as theory in the light of premises that better reflect the essential realities of such a situation. Such an amended theory would agree better with the observed behavior of such firms.

The amendment may be approached via the question whether a monopoly price tends to be rigid or flexible in response to fluctuations of demand. As we shall see in Section 8, below, an expansion of demand might in theory (depending on its shape) cause an expansion of output with no rise in price, or a rise in price with no expansion of output, or a combination; this last being the most likely case and the one regularly assumed in theoretical diagrams. This is on the assumption that the monopoly was exacting maximum profit, both before and after the change in demand. The generally accepted case, then, calls logically for flexible prices; while the amended theory rationalizes the observed tendency toward rigidity.

Insofar as the monopoloidal firms are limited by the two kinds of potential competition, both these limits are closely related to cost of some sort, thus introducing a stabilizing factor, not responsive to fluctuations of demand. The same is true of the price level at which some important substitute might become closely competitive. The resulting prices would be substantially less than the price that would maximize profits for a firm that can disregard such limitations. Then if the demand shrinks, such a firm would generally be able to minimize the shrinkage in its earnings by maintaining approximately the price it had set in more favorable times, without encountering increased potential competition or substitution. In so doing, it would be pricing closer than before to the (new and reduced) profit-maximizing level. The main conclusion is that the sort of qualified "monopolies" that are pertinent to this study do not price to maximize profit to the utmost extent permitted by the demand for the entire product of the industry. Secondarily, this is the chief reason for their tending toward rigid, rather than flexible, pricing in response to fluctuations of demand.

3. Competitive Demand Functions

In the limiting case that goes by the name of "pure competition," as already noted, the demand for the product of a single seller is supposed to be infinitely elastic—his individual demand curve is horizontal. In the produce-exchange type of market this has a clearly understandable meaning.[4] The active variable is supply, and price results from the balance of supply and demand. If one producer increases his supply, he can sell it all without affecting the volumes sold by the other suppliers. In the purely competitive case, his supply is a small fraction of the total and can be sold without perceptibly affecting either the total supply or the market price.

In the quoted-price type of selling, the idea of an individual demand function, and especially a horizontal one, becomes more involved. In order to dispose of an increased supply, a producer must do something to increase the demand for his individual product. If one starts with "pure" and limiting cases, one must look to a reduction of his individual price as the means of increasing his sales. From this it may seem to follow logically (with a brand of logic that requires scrutiny) that one seller's individual-demand function can be more elastic than the aggregate demand function—thus creating competitive pressure—only if his price differs from those of the other sellers. By the same kind of logic it seems to follow that if the market equalizes different sellers' prices quickly, competitive pressure cannot exist, because no seller can increase his proportionate share of the total business. This contains an element of truth, but is grossly overstated, as further scrutiny will show.

In the first place, one can go astray if one construes too rigorously the idea that a change in price is the *only* thing that can bring about a change in the physical volume sold and that a price differential is the only thing that can change the relative volumes of different sellers and is by itself sufficient to do this. This is about as misleading as the opposite error of assuming that a quoted-price market behaves like the produce-exchange type, with producers first bringing a supply to market and then letting supply make the price at which the market will be "cleared." Realism needs to find some picture intermediate between these two extremes.

In the case of homogeneous products, the smallest feasible price differential may decide who gets the order, as between offerings equally available to the buyer; and if the lower price is widely known and available, it may attract all the business the producer who quotes it can handle, mostly at the expense of his rivals, thus approximating

---

[4] Cf. above, Chap. 5, Sec. 6, and Chap. 6, Sec. 1.

a horizontal individual-demand function, within the limits of the low price producer's unused capacity. But even in this case, it is misleading to ignore the marketing facilities and activities that need to go along with the quoting of a price in order to make it effectively available in increasing a producer's volume of sales.

This leads to a recognition that wider and better marketing facilities may increase sales volume without a change in price. Ordinarily, the tactics used for this purpose include various combinations of price, selling effort, or alterations in the product itself, aimed at making it either more attractive relative to its cost of production or less costly to produce relative to its attractiveness. The same tactics are variously combined in the defensive responses of the competitors whose sales volume is encroached on by the successful competitor—a move in the realm of price may be met by a move in the realm of selling effort, or vice versa. Increased selling effort or increased attractiveness of product tend to increase the whole demand function for the industry, as a mere reduction of price does not. Where a producer is of substantial size, there may be cases in which his efforts to increase demand for his own product may spill over into increased demand for his rivals, though normally some part of his gains are at their expense, unless they meet his moves successfully. Such a case appears to be neither pure output competition nor pure price competition, but a compound.

It is quite conceivable that a firm should decide, after canvassing the market and judging it susceptible of expansion, that it could sell a larger output without reducing its price, by an expanded selling program that would more than repay the increased selling costs, and might even increase sales enough to leave selling costs per unit unchanged, once the new program was well under way. The firm might decide that others would expand, whether it did or not, so that it could not get a higher price by refraining from output competition, but would do better by bidding for as large a share as possible of the increased volume. In that special sense its expected demand function, in terms of selling outlay, might be horizontal. Beyond some point, of course, increased selling effort is bound to encounter diminishing returns, even in an expanding market.

In addition, there are always the innumerable "fringe" items that surround a price and give it more flexibility than appears in the list quotations; and there is always the possibility of surreptitious shading of price, or many ways of dividing one's business into sectors and treating them differently pricewise. The conditions under which a firm may decide to use price as a competitive weapon, the forms its use of that weapon might take, and the complementary weapons that may be used with it—these make up an array of problems such as no student can hope to exhaust. In dealing with such problems, simple concepts of price-elasticity of demand do not carry one very far. The condition symbolized by an (approximately) horizontal individual-demand curve may occur and may have some importance over a limited range of movement of output and price, generally under particular conditions causing rivals' reactions to be disregarded. But, as we have seen, this extreme elasticity is not necessary to effective competition.

Where a product is differentiated, with different sellers offering variant versions, the meaning of the demand function for the aggregate of all their offerings presents difficulties of definition. Chamberlin circumvents this by focusing on what may be called "horizontal" differentiation, in which the different sellers have identical individual demand functions and would, in equilibrium, charge equal prices. Then a general price change would mean an equal change for all. However, some of the problems we shall face are concerned with differences in grades that the market would rate as higher or lower and that command different prices. In this case, an equal percentage change in all the prices would be likely to have different effects at the high and low ends of the price-quality scale. A proportionate reduction might shift demand upward in the scale on account of its "income effect." Thus it might actually reduce the demand for the lowest-priced grades, while a general increase in the whole scale might increase the demand for these grades—as seems to have been happening recently in the case of smaller and "compact" automobiles.

One might try to define a general price change as one that would leave unchanged the relative volumes of sales in the different grades. But if prices were reduced, this might, by shifting demand in favor of the upper grades, put the lower grades in a position in which they could not maintain their relative volume without a more-than-proportionate price reduction. This might not be feasible costwise for some and might drive them to attempt some counteracting shift of their position in the quality scale. Thus it appears likely that a general shift in the price scale tends to lead to opposite shifts in the quality scale. In any case, it is so sure to be accompanied by other changes that the search for precise definition becomes a matter of rather arbitrary abstraction. We may be content with the idea that, for any reasonable conception of a general and more or less harmonious price change, total sales volume would be less elastic than that of any one seller in response to a change in his relative price as compared to the general scale. The same would be true in principle of response to changes in product or in selling effort, the difficulty of defining a harmonious general change being greater. In general, one would expect sales of the lower-priced grades to be more responsive to price, and the higher-priced grades more responsive to quality appeal and selling effort.

4. Importance of Competitive Diversities

The assumption that competing producers all have individual demand functions of equal elasticity is a convenient analytical simplification. As with all such simplifications, the question to ask is whether the things it leaves out are things that make a substantial difference to the result. I shall contend that they do, and that effective competition in industry and trade hinges on diversities between the demand functions that different sellers either face or conceive themselves to be facing, so that they act on the basis of that conception. We shall see these diversities at work in many forms. And we shall be examining a tentative hypothesis to the effect that the force of competitive pressures is peculiarly dependent on those firms whose situation and perspectives give them incentives to the strongest competitive action, coupled with capacity to take substantial amounts of business, thus setting a competitive pace the others have to match, in order to hold their own position, though they might not have initiated such competitive action on their own motion. These pace setters may be small, provided they have ample capacity to expand.

It is revealing, and more than a little baffling, to explore how far it is practicable to represent the force of competitive pressures and incentives by the elasticity of the individual-demand function confronting a firm, as that firm conceives and acts on it. It may act on a preliminary "hunch," or on one revised in the light of experience. Its perspective—short-term or long-term—may be influenced by its position of security or insecurity: a firm in urgent need of cash may not be able to afford the luxury of a long-range policy. Then it is likely to aim at securing some immediate and sizable orders, even on terms that tend to "spoil the market," resulting in the severest form of competition, especially if the product is homogeneous. Looking at quoted-price selling, with the number of sellers limited, we have seen that one could construct a series in these terms.[5] It would begin with the seller who disregards rivals' responses to his moves, go on to the seller who anticipates their reactions but expects to be able to circumvent them or to make enduring gains before they become effective, then to the seller who expects his moves to be neutralized and therefore faces an expected demand function of the aggregative sort, and loses his incentive to act competitively; and finally going on to the seller who, in spite of this loss of competitive incentive, is still alert to compete against the flow of potential new entries, recognizing that this could encroach on the demand function faced by the existing sellers in the industry as a whole.

This series is not only a severe oversimplification, it also reveals the way in which a seller's subjective attitudes affect the demand function as he envisages it and acts on it. For example, to say that he expects to be able to circumvent his rivals' reactions to his competitive moves implies that he wants to circumvent them and is not predisposed to accept the idea that his moves will be neutralized, and to welcome the accompanying release from active competitive pressures on price. Or if price competition becomes ineffective, but the competitive urge remains, it will spill over into some of the other forms of rivalry—whether to the customers' benefit would need to be examined in terms of the conditions of each case, especially the competence of the purchaser to ensure that product rivalry takes the form of increased serviceability. As to price competition, much evidently hinges on those competitively minded firms that hope to circumvent the neutralizing effect of their rivals' responses.

This problem, of neutralization of competitive moves and resulting competitive stalemate, occurs under the quoted-price type of selling, applying mainly to openly quoted price changes on homogeneous products. It does not apply to the produce-exchange type of marketing, since competitive moves consist of bringing larger supplies to market, and when rivals automatically meet the resulting reduced

[5] Cf. above, Chap. 3, Sec. 10.

price, they do not prevent the original sellers from increasing their relative market share. Neutralizing responses must consist either in matching the original sellers' increased supply, thus further reducing prices; or in reducing the rivals' supply to sustain the price, in what would amount to an "umbrella" policy, such as only dominant single producers are in a position to carry out. However, in quoted-price selling of differentiated products, a degree of stalemate might result where the products in question are closely competitive at a stable price-ratio, so that price changes are expected to be met. In the realm of theoretical models, the stalemate is made more likely if the model-builder assumes that individual-demand functions and cost functions are equal, as E. H. Chamberlin does in his most basic theorem.[6] It seems likely that this assumption of equality underlies his further assumption that limited numbers lead to the expectation that price-moves will be met and neutralized, with the competitive stalemate as a result.[7]

Incentives to competitive action can be introduced into such a model by diversities and uncertainties about the demand and cost functions and whether an initial move will be met and if so, how effectively and promptly. Such diversities and uncertainties exist and afford openings for at least temporary competitive gains, with probabilities of an enduring aftermath. They apply to price moves, and perhaps more fully to moves in the areas of produce appeal and selling effort, which cannot be met so precisely or so promptly. Thus they are not mere incidental complications, but are important conditions of an effective competitive outcome, in the kinds of cases we are considering.

5. *"Cross-Elasticity" of Demand*

The reason competitive moves are met by rivals is because the successful competitor encroaches on his rivals' volume of business: that

---

[6] See *The Theory of Monopolistic Competition* (1933). The equality of demand and cost curves, which is referred to on p. 82 as an "heroic assumption," appears to be a necessary part of the conditions referred to by the phrase "in fact" on p. 90.

[7] *Ibid.*, pp. 100-01.

is, because of "cross-elasticity" of demand. This is something that does not exist in the produce-exchange type of marketing, but is crucially important for the type we are considering. It represents the transfer of business between competitors resulting from a change in their relative prices, which is most simply treated as a change by one that is not met and neutralized by the other's response. The formal definition of cross-elasticity, hinging on the response of A's volume of sales to changes in B's prices (his own remaining constant), is a way of isolating this transfer effect from other possible effects; but it might equally well be defined in terms of the amount B gains *at A's expense*, or loses *to A*, as a result of B's price-move. Either definition would exclude gains in volume of business that a reduction of B's price might bring to B, in excess of the resulting reduction of his competitors' volume; or vice versa if B raised his price and lost more business than his competitors gained at his expense.

For our purposes the essential point is, first, that this transfer affects both A and B and, second, as we saw in Chapter 3, Section 9, that the transfer of the same amount of business represents different cross-elasticities for A and B if their existing volumes of business are different. In simpler terms, if B, having a sales-volume of half a million, gains business totaling $100,000 at A's expense, that is a 20 per cent gain for B. But if A's volume is five million, it is only a 2 per cent reduction for A. The same arithmetic applies if instead of A, B's encroachments are evenly distributed among ten firms whose aggregate volume adds up to five million. In an actual case, of course, the encroachments are not likely to be evenly distributed. Some of the ten firms will be closer competitors of B than others; these will lose a larger percentage of their business, and will be more likely to make some defensive response. Thus this diversity in cross-elasticities means that some firms have stronger incentives than others to initiate competitive moves, or to meet them if others initiate them.

Before undertaking to draw conclusions from all this, some other dimensions need to be taken into account. One consists of the limits within which a given elasticity of demand may operate: for example, the amount of business A can lose to B is limited by B's unused capacity. Another is the time pattern involved. How rapidly does a change in price take effect on sales volume, and how long does it require to have its full effect? It may be virtually immediate, chiefly in the case of openly announced changes in single sellers' prices for homogeneous products or in retail sales of perishables. Or, as in the case of reduced electrical rates, the full effect may require years, plus changes in business and housekeeping methods with the popularizing of equipment for new uses of current.

This may serve to illustrate a fact that seems to be insufficiently realized: that any demand-curve representing the different amounts that can be sold at different prices (other things impliedly equal) necessarily holds good for only a fairly short time, if only because in a longer run other things will refuse to remain equal. Costs will change, both one's own and one's competitors', products will be modified, total and per capita income will change and so will the general price level. Thus the original price will lose its meaning, and with it will go the meaning of any demand curve framed in terms of the response of sales volume to that particular price. To assume that business firms maximize their profits as determined by such short-run functions is to assume that they are more short-sighted than well-managed firms are.

What lasts longer than the significance of a particular price may be a pricing policy relative to one's competitors' prices or relative to one's own costs. An example of the first would be the much-publicized policy of Macy's store, to sell 6 per cent below competitors. An example of the second would be the policy inadequately described as "full-cost pricing," which in application leaves room for concessions if necessary to meet competition. This policy might be rationalized as based on recognition that, in the long run, competitive demand for the firm's product will not permit higher pricing than this. In a market where prices tend strongly to equality, the standard set by competition may be the "bulk-line" relation between price and the range of costs in the industry; and the scope for departures from this standard may be quite limited.

To understand a demand function in terms of time perspective, one must ask further questions about it. Will the change in volume of sales be self-limiting or self-reversing as when present sales of durables are in part an anticipation of future demand and to that extent encroach on future volume? Will it represent a finite continuing amount added to sales volume or subtracted from it, or will it be progressive over time? Except for the most immediate cases, these all reach into a future which, at the time a producer makes an initial move, involves unavoidable uncertainty, as to the amount and speed of his gains and accompanying inroads on his competitors, how soon if at all his rivals will make a defensive response, whether this response, if it comes, will be in price, quality, or selling effort, how effective it will be, and how promptly the effect will be felt. Then the competitors have an interval in which they may appraise the threat involved and decide on their response, and in this interval the initiator may make gains, some of which may continue after his competitors respond.

A third factor is the different attitude sellers have toward changes in their sales volume according as they are increases or decreases, either as absolute amounts or as percentage shares of the total volume of the industry. A firm that will not initiate a move to increase its sales volume competitively may react strongly to defend itself against a decrease, especially if the decrease threatens to be progressive, in which case even a moderate initial decline may look serious. And it may cause margin elasticity to be reckoned from short-run marginal cost, rather than from full cost, since it brings about a condition of unused capacity.

6. Diversities of Response in Terms of Quality

If diversity of size creates differences in cross-elasticities of demand in terms of price, does it have a similar effect in terms of competition in quality? Well-balanced competitive pressure in this field clearly hinges on knowledgeable purchasers. Does it also hinge on the existence of competitors which, while large enough to command the resources of applied science and technology, are still small enough, relative to the total sales of a given product, to have ample room to grow if they succeed in tapping some neglected stratum of potential demand, small enough to have a lively interest in even a minority stratum of the market, and sufficiently hard pressed to be less conservative than the giants in taking a chance of this sort? I do not claim to know the answer. All I am sure of is that the question is important, and that there is ground for hypotheses to the effect that competition among giants introduces a bias into the rivalry between economy and luxury models, and that smaller firms may help to correct this bias. This will be taken up more fully in Chapter 10, Section 3.

7. Gains from Which Rival Firms Share in the Benefits

In practice, while in many cases it may be quite clear that one firm's expansion in volume of business is at other firms' expense, the causes of expansion and contraction are often multiple, and complex enough to make it impossible to measure cross-elasticity. And it often happens when one competitor is conspicuously successful in developing market acceptance for his product, perhaps developing new uses for it, that his activities in expanding demand open up expanding markets for his rivals as well as himself. In such cases the emphasis is likely to be on customer persuasion, breaking through the inertia of custom in ways of meeting wants and inducing consumers to meet familiar wants with products that are either new or new to these uses, or using familiar products for new purposes. But also a considerable part may be played by bringing the price of a product down low enough to make it economically feasible for uses for which it had formerly been priced out of reach.

The development of vegetable shortenings appears to illustrate the way in which one firm's business moves may open up sales opportunities for all in the industry. Procter & Gamble pioneered with Crisco, establishing its marketing position and advantages over lard. This gave Lever Brothers an opportunity to build on the resulting experience, and they brought out a rival brand, Spry, in which certain defects of Crisco were remedied, and launched it with a vigorous campaign. Procter & Gamble not wholly unprepared, lost only a little time in countering by resolving difficulties with its product, plus vigorous selling effort. As a result of the combined impact of improved products and vigorous selling, the second year of the active competition (1937) saw combined sales considerably more than doubled, so that Crisco's sales were greatly increased, despite the formidable volume that Spry had built up.[8] In addition, the growing market made

[8] Accounts of this episode are given in "99 44/100% Pure Profit Record," *Fortune* (April 1939), p. 152; and "Mr. Countway Takes the Job," *Fortune* (November 1940), p. 100.

room for a number of new smaller firms. Here, of course, the most favorable condition was present, in the shape of an opportunity to displace an existing product (lard) with a superior substitute. In a more stabilized situation, there might not be room for such spectacular expansion, and competitive encroachments might be a more serious matter.

8. Limits on Amount of Business That May Be Competitively Shifted

Reverting to the question of the limits within which particular elasticities of demand operate, these are especially important where it is a question of some competitors getting business away from others. The seriousness of such encroachments can be viewed as hinging on the total amount of business likely to be lost in whatever time period a competitor's perspective may cover, with further allowance for the likelihood that the shift in business may continue progressively beyond any limited period that may be contemplated. Here the familiar classification of periods is useful, hinging on whether the limit on the amount of business that can be shifted is set by available inventories from which orders can be filled immediately (very short period) or by productive capacity in existence and available to fill orders (moderately short period) or by the prospect of adding more capacity. This last is spoken of as the long period, and for most purposes this may be sufficient to remove any rigid limits on the amount of business one producer can take away from his competitors.

This comes to depend on whether his minimum supply price—mainly determined by costs—is enough lower than theirs. For this purpose, the relevant cost is the cost of added output from added capacity; and the relevant time-period would ordinarily be the time needed to plan, finance, construct, or acquire and equip a substantial addition to existing capacity, plus a probable interval needed to build up demand to a normal rate for the new facilities. A longer period may be relevant in cases where rapidly expanding market opportunities keep ahead of additions to capacity, particularly if expansion of capacity is hampered by limited specialized resources. Then a first round of capital expansion may not be sufficient to supply all the demand that is willing to pay remunerative prices; and it may take a longer time than usual to overcome the limits set by existing capacity.

In the "very short period," special problems occur when the shift in business would cause existing inventories to depart substantially from the normal reserves that producers keep to enable sales to be regularized in the face of vicissitudes of production, or to enable production to be regularized in the face of normal short-time fluctuations of demand. A quick expansion of orders may exhaust a producer's inventories, and thus set a limit on his ability to make deliveries. His customers may submit to delays, thus reducing their own inventories below a desired level; or if they are unwilling to wait, they may shift some or all of their orders to competing suppliers who have larger inventories that enable them to fill orders more promptly. To avoid this, the suppliers who are having the difficulty are likely to operate overtime, incurring high marginal costs which they may be unable to reflect in their prices, since they are trying to hold their customers against competitors who are in a position to make deliveries without resorting to overtime.

If the shortages of inventory are in standard products or materials, producers whose supplies are short may enter the market and bid up the prices of the scarce products.[9] This also raises these producers' marginal costs. Demand for a particular material entering into production tends to be inelastic in proportion as this material forms only a fraction of the cost of production. If this material has many uses, from some of which supplies can be easily diverted, demand for a single use has less effect on price, and the case of absolute limitation does not arise. Or if a substitute material is readily available, demand for the first may become elastic in the neighborhood of the price relation at which the two are closely competitive. But if a shift from one material to a substitute requires a technical change-over, this is likely to take time, and is unlikely to be an available way of overcoming limits set by a strictly temporary shortage of a particular material. If the condition bids fair to continue, causing price to remain within the competitive range of a substitute, then the absolute limit is removed, and demand becomes elastic as producers resort to the substitute.

[9] Producers have been known to arrange with a competitor to procure the competitor's (standardized) product and market it in their own containers.

The demand for a material with few uses and open to substitution is likely to flatten out near such a critical price range, and its price may tend to settle close to such an extra-elastic sector, if forces of demand and cost bring it into that neighborhood, causing substitutes to become a critical factor. For a material with many uses, there are likely to be many humps, or dips, and the amount of business at stake in the rivalry it faces for one particular use may be a minor fraction of its total volume.[10] Just above a "hump," demand is more elastic than just below it, but the inelastic sector is not likely to extend far in the case of a material with many uses of varied sorts, while it may extend quite far in the case of a material with a limited range of uses.

Reverting to the very short-run problem and considering the case of excessive inventories, the substitute material with a limited range of uses faces an especially inelastic demand if the attempt is made to dispose of an excess beyond the amount that existing uses will readily absorb. In general, where inventories are excessive, the excess is normally limited, and its disposal may mean pushing it into a sector of the market in which demand is less elastic than normal, largely because of the limited time within which disposal is sought.

Perhaps the commonest method is that of special disposal sales conducted by retailers, to get rid of remainders, goods that have failed to move or the end-of-season stock when it is time to replace it with goods for the incoming season. In the distribution of automobiles, the used-car market forms a large but limited sector of supply-and-demand pricing in which part of the supply proves unsalable and is scrapped. This affects the sale of new cars, in which the readiest and largest price adjustment occurs, not in the price the dealer nominally charges for the new car he sells, but in the turn-in allowance on the used car he takes in trade, this being regularly regarded as his way of shading the list price of the new car. And it is a method by which the amount of price-shading can vary from buyer to buyer, making each transaction a special act of negotiation. After all, no two used cars are exactly alike.

This turn-in market is divided into two parts: the taking of used cars in trade by the seller of new cars, and the sale of the used cars taken in. This second part is increasingly divided into two stages: the sale of the used car by the new-car dealer to a used-car specialist and

---

[10] Cf. Ross M. Robertson, "The Changing Apparatus of Competition," *American Economic Review* Supplement (May 1954), pp. 51-62, especially pp. 53-58.

the resale by him to a user. The whole used-car market is, along with the real estate market, the largest negotiated-price market of the supply-and-demand sort, for differentiated products. When the market for new cars is weak, dealers expect to take a loss on their turn-ins, and they may do so in more normal times as a method of shading the list price. More questionable is the practice of first "packing" the list price with additions of which the buyer is not a good judge, so that the swollen turn-in allowance becomes fictitious or partly so. The federal price law which went into effect in 1958 was aimed to prevent this price-packing by requiring an itemized disclosure of the price-components; and its first effect was a reduction of turn-in allowances.[11]

Manufacturers may allow their products to go at a discount, un-branded or bearing private brands that do not carry the prestige of the regular brand. In the regular practice of disposing of "seconds" at a discount, one conjectures that at times of slack demand, the definition of "seconds" may become somewhat more elastic than usual. These methods all have one distinctive feature in common: they at-tempt to keep the disposal sales as distinct as feasible from their regular marketing, so as to minimize encroachments on the sales they expect to make at remunerative prices, and minimize the need to curtail regular production as a means of working off excess inventories.

In the case of materials and standard producers' goods, especially if they are sold on organized markets, excess inventories will normally bring about a reduction in the general market price, leading to lower costs to the producers using them. These lowered costs, other things equal, would be reflected in lower prices for the ultimate products, with a promptness that would depend on the prevalence of "last-in, first-out" methods of accounting, or methods of similar effect, and on whether producers following such methods are strategically active price-makers and faced by effective competitive pressures. In general, the effect of special inventory conditions is limited to the amount of abnormal excesses or shortages, and is likely to spend itself in a limited time, whether cross-elasticities of demand are high or relatively low. It also, as indicated, sets in motion the natural corrective by altering the rates of production.

When demand is strong enough to enable producers in general to operate at or near the optimum rate for their existing facilities, the

[11] See *New York Times*, Sept. 20, 1958.

problem of competitive transfer of business obviously does not become acute. No one is in danger of losing a substantial amount of business, because no one else has enough unused capacity to take a substantial amount away from him, without encountering rising costs that would remove the incentive, unless the price is abnormally high to start with, relative to costs. But it has been argued above that unused capacity, in more than negligible amounts, is a normal competitive condition. Then, if the product is one for which cross elasticity of demand is very high, the familiar possibility exists of competition driving prices below full cost (even though they remained above short-run marginal cost), because there is enough unused capacity to enable competitors to gain (or lose) substantial amounts of business, sufficient to offset the small price reduction that is necessary either to get business away from a rival, or to protect one's own volume of business against a rival's price reduction. In the terms suggested above, "margin elasticity" of individual-demand functions is greater than unity, for enough producers to be important marketwise. The actual effect, however, is not simple, as we shall see later.

Here come into play the various elements discussed earlier in this chapter, including the principle that cross elasticities are greater for smaller than for larger competitors, and that some who would not initiate price reductions may be impelled to meet, defensively, those that others make, this being reinforced by the common attitude that attaches more importance to preventing a decline in the volume of a firm's business (absolute or relative to the total of the industry) than to securing an increase.

In the first place, barring special emergency pressures, a producer with very small amounts of excess capacity is not impelled, as he might be in strict theory, to slash prices down to the limit set by short-run marginal cost in order to utilize this capacity, because, if he succeeded, this would bring him to the point at which any further growth would require an enlargement of his capacity, at an added cost approximately equal to full average cost. Thus he would be incurring, in a future so close as to be virtually the present, these full average costs if he enlarged his volume of sales all the way up to his existing capacity. Thus the fact that his temporary "margin elasticity" is greater than unity becomes irrelevant, since if he acts on it successfully, he is brought into a condition in which it is less than unity because his marginal cost has risen, and the reduced price that was profitable is so no longer. This is, of course, especially true of an industry or trade in which a tendency to long-run growth is the normal expectation, and would be expected soon to absorb any small amount of unused capacity. In such a case, a firm may plan for a normal average margin of unused capacity, with the result that it may not wait until unused capacity is reduced to zero before feeling the need to expand its facilities. Then long-run rather than short-run marginal cost becomes relevant, not when unused capacity goes to zero, but when it falls below whatever expansion margin the firm may set for itself. From this standpoint, strategic importance attaches to the group of firms with the largest percentages of unused capacity, rather than to the average for the entire industry.

Assuming that there is enough unused capacity to bring short-run "margin elasticities" into play, then if the previous discussion is valid, we might expect that this would affect the smaller firms first, since their cross elasticities are greater than those of the big firms in the same industry. But if a single small firm cuts prices below full cost, in order to utilize some unused capacity, the amount of business at stake is, by definition, so small that large firms may figure that they can more profitably ignore it than cut prices on their larger volume of business in order to prevent the small firm from taking the small volume involved in its utilizing its unused capacity. This is especially true if the business is growing sufficiently to enable large firms to expand, even if one or more small firms are taking limited amounts by price shading. On the other side, profitable initiatory moves or counter-moves by large firms depend on their ability to localize the price shading, presumably by some form of discrimination, so that their margin elasticity on the segregated sector of their sales would be greater than unity. And this involves obvious legal risks from the Robinson-Patman Act.

If there are a number of small firms, whose total unused capacity adds up to more business than the large firms feel they can afford to lose, the large firms will be impelled to defensive action, and this sets a different kind of limit on the amount the small firms can safely try to take. They may learn by experience, punctuated by occasional re-taliation from the larger firms, to keep within these limits of tolerance. Then the emergence of general active price competition will hinge on the situation of medium-sized firms, small enough to have cross elasticities substantially greater than those of the largest firms, but strong enough not to feel that active competition with the largest firms is suicidally dangerous for them.

9. Residual or Umbrella Demand Functions

When a single firm is large enough to do a substantial fraction of the business in its industry, its individual-demand function may be determined by the demand function for the entire product of the industry, minus the supply functions of all the other producers. If "supply function" means simply the amounts the other producers put on the market and succeed in selling, this expression is a tautology; but it becomes a significant expression of causal factors if the other producers are in a position to sell all they wish, without bringing down the price. This happens when the large firm assumes price leadership and bears the brunt of limiting total supply to what can be sold at the price it has set. This policy of "holding an umbrella" is feasible only for a firm that holds a large fraction of the market, and on condition that the others' "supply functions" do not include an expansion so large as to threaten the leader's position.

The outcome depends on how high the "umbrella" is held, and how much restraint the beneficiaries see an interest in exercising. We have just mentioned the kind of case in which the small firms learn how much business they can take without overstraining the tolerance of the leader. We have also touched on the question whether one of the small firms needs to undercut the leader's price in order to increase its relative share of the business, or whether it can expand while at least ostensibly meeting the leader's price. In the latter case, the effective limit on their increase in sales appears to be a hybrid, partaking more of the nature of a demand function than of a supply function. But it seems likely that an umbrella holder must expect that other firms will do some price shading, in one form or another.

We may examine how the supply of the "other" firms might behave via three simplified possibilities. (1) They may meet the leader's price and sell their former proportion of the total volume of the industry. Then their individual-demand functions have the same elasticity as that for the industry as a whole, indicating a monopoly price as the result. The trouble is that if a price were set that exploited this possibility fully, the behavior on which it rested would break down: the beneficiaries would enlarge their shares at the leader's expense, in one way or another. (2) They may be allowed to work at full capacity and may not attempt to expand further. Then (momentarily disregarding growth) they take a fixed amount of business and the leader gets the rest. His elasticity of demand will be greater than in case (1). If, for example, he does half the business, his demand will be twice as elastic as that of the industry as a whole. But here again, if the terms he is protecting are really inviting, the others will enlarge their capacity, and case (2) will transform itself into case (3) in which the other producers expand or contract their relative share of the business, according as the terms the umbrella allows them are inviting or forbidding.

This last is the assumption made by Dean A. Worcester, Jr., in a recent article in which he argues that the "umbrella" policy contains an inherent tendency to break down.[12] On this assumption, the long-run effect depends on whether the leader's price is above full cost for the more efficient of the other firms. If it is, they will expand and dislodge the leader from his position of leadership. On this basis, he must stay within the limits set by the potential expansion of the other existing producers or lose his market position. His power would be limited to preventing the price from going below "full cost"—possibly down to short-run marginal cost, as it might under unrestricted competition. He could not enduringly sustain it above a "full-cost" level. Unless he had ways of restricting the expansion of the other firms, his power would be limited by competitive forces of the long-run variety. The limit could hardly be expected to operate precisely. If the leader protects its own full cost, and if its average efficiency is below that of the best of its rivals, its proportionate share of the business might naturally show a gradual decline. This might be made up for by an occasional acquisition of a competitor. Needless to say, this highly natural outcome has been observed in practice.

[12] Dean A. Worcester, Jr., "Why 'Dominant Firms' Decline," *Journal of Political Economy* (August 1957), pp. 338-46.

10. Supply Functions: Basic Conceptions

The conception of a supply function has almost disappeared from economic analysis of problems relevant to industry and trade, cost functions having taken its place. This is partly because it was formulated in terms of the response of supply to a price that was conceived as fixed by the market independently of anything a single seller could do about it. This does not fit situations in which the single seller has a range of choice of price and can charge more if he is willing to sell correspondingly less, or vice versa. Secondly, the behavior of the seller in response to different prices was conceived in an uncritically a priori fashion, typically assuming that a higher price would always elicit a larger supply so that the supply schedule must always have an upward slope. There are important ranges of fact to which this simple picture fails to correspond. A supply schedule turns out to take a number of different forms, with different behavior, and some of these differences will be important for our study of competition.

We have just been looking at the "umbrella" form of price leadership, in which the supply furnished by a group of producers was their response to a price that they accepted and followed; but this was true of them precisely because the price leader determined his output in a quite different way: he limited it to the amount the demand would take at a desired price. The typical short-run supply function in industry and trade is simply a willingness to take all the orders that come, at the price that is being charged; but back of this lie the longer-run forces, which set limits based on cost of production. As we have seen, this long-run supply price is not necessarily equal to any particular producer's cost, since at any one time some of the output will be produced at a profit and some at a loss. Also, since increased output may bring reduced costs, it is entirely possible for a long-run supply function to have a downward slope. This does not mean that a larger output is produced *because* the price is lower, but that if the demand will take the enlarged output at a price that will cover the reduced costs of quantity production, the enlarged output can be supplied at a lower price than would be needed if the demand were smaller.

That is, supply in the long run is a reaction, not to price alone, but to the whole state of demand of which price is a part.[13] The bearing of this comes out clearly if one asks how the supply function of a monopoly behaves. If a monopoly raises its price, it does not produce more because the price has risen; it produces less because the demand will take less at the higher price. If the state of demand expands, the effect may be different according to the nature of the expansion. For analytical purposes, one may distinguish what may be called a horizontal expansion of demand from a vertical expansion.[14] The first would happen if the population grew, while its wants and per capita purchasing power remained unchanged. The highest price the market would stand would be unchanged, and so would the elasticity of demand at any given price. The monopoly would naturally expand its output; and if its unit cost were unchanged, the presumption is that its price would remain the same.

A purely vertical expansion of demand might take place if population and wants remained unchanged, but purchasing power increased. Then the output that would satiate demand would be unchanged, and so would the elasticity of demand for any given output (but at different prices). Then if the monopoly were pricing for maximum profit, and if its unit costs were either zero or rose proportionately with rising purchasing power, it would sell the same output as before, but at a higher price. Only if the expansion of demand had a mixed character—both horizontal and vertical—would the monopoly increase both its output and its price.[15] This appears the most probable case, and it is interesting that theoretical models habitually assume it, though without formulating the underlying rationale. On this basis, as we have seen, a profit-maximizing model indicates that monopoly prices should normally be flexible in response to fluctuations of demand; while a model in which profits are not fully maximized in the short run yields results that better reflect observed tendencies toward price rigidity.

When short-run relations of supply and demand are out of long-run

[13] Cf. Joan Robinson, *Economics of Imperfect Competition* (1932), pp. 85-86.
[14] *Ibid.*, pp. 70, 87. Cf. above, Sec. 2 of this chapter.
[15] Strictly speaking, this might happen in lesser degree if demand moved vertically and cost remained constant or increased less than demand did.

equilibrium—that is, when the price that will "clear the market" is substantially above or below a long-run supply price—the resulting adjustment takes different forms according as supply can be altered currently, or as either production or demand is seasonal. Seasonal production occurs mainly in agriculture; and here special tendencies to overcorrection have been observed, notably the familiar corn-hog cycle. A generalized theoretical explanation of such tendencies to overcorrection is attempted in the ingenious "cobweb theorem," in which next season's supply is a function of this season's price, and tends to be excessive if this season's price is extra-high, and vice versa. This contains truth as indicating how such overcorrections *can* happen. But it reaches the erroneous conclusion that the series will be convergent, approaching equilibrium, only if the demand schedule is more elastic than the supply schedule; while if the opposite is the case, the successive cycles will depart progressively farther from equilibrium.

This proves too much. Where a farmer can vary the proportions of different products in his output, the supply of any one product is, to a virtual certainty, more elastic than the demand; but cycles do not depart progressively farther from equilibrium. The key to the puzzle is that next season's supply responds, not simply to this season's price, but to the price expected to prevail next season, in the light of all the conditions. This expectation is affected by this season's price, but does not assume that it will be exactly repeated. This case may serve as a warning of the trickiness of the concept of a supply schedule, when construed simply as a function of the current price.[16] Furthermore, the supply that a given price would call forth, if continued, may not materialize fully in a single season. Hence there is no sufficient reason for expecting progressively wider cycles of overcorrection.

The corresponding problems of industry and trade have been briefly touched on above, under excesses and shortages of inventories, and of productive capacity. Here there seems to be no systematic tendency to cycles of overcorrection of supply, such as results from the seasonal character of agriculture. Current control of supply leads to a different result.

---

[16] The article by Gustav Akerman, "The Cobweb Theorem: a Reconsideration," *Quarterly Journal of Economics* (February 1957), pp. 151-60, appears to come close to being a definitive disposal of this theoretical model.

11. *Two Major Kinds of Supply Function*

There are two major kinds of limitation on production from the supply side, which behave differently, and the differences are of decisive importance for the understanding of the behavior of different kinds of production in response to competitive pressures. In one kind, the resistances to production are dominated by monetary expenses, or the supply prices of factors of production, figured in monetary terms, as they would appear in the reckonings of a business corporation. In the other kind, the decisive limiting factor is the ability and willingness of an individual to devote varying amounts of his own time, effort, and resources, as in the case of a one-family farm, or a small one-family shop, or in the case of a laborer, as represented by the effect of an increase in his hourly wages on the number of hours per week he is willing to work. In the businesslike type, the minimum supply price is more definite, though in each case, some production will go on at less than fully "normal" returns. The most important difference is that in the business type, the necessary out-of-pocket expenses cover wages and the rewards of management, on a contractual basis. In contrast, if a one-family farm or shop cannot get a price that will yield the owner-operators the equivalent of standard wages for the grade of work done, including management, and a standard return for personally owned capital, it will go on working for what it can get. The owner-operators' labor and management are not on a basis of contractual remuneraton, but are equity claimants in the residual income, if any.

The reactions of supply to changes in remuneration are different. If a business firm finds that the market affords an increased price, its normal reaction is to produce more. If workers receive an increase in their standard scale of real hourly wages, their normal and rational reaction is to work fewer hours per week, taking part of their gain in more goods and part in more leisure.[17] Some observers have thought

---

[17] An exception may occur if the increase is due to temporary causes and it is rational for the workers to make the most of it while it lasts. But even in a defense emergency, extra wages have in some cases stimulated absenteeism. A more

they saw traces of a similar reaction in the other direction when prices of farm products have fallen, and farmers tried to make up for the loss by planting larger crops. Whether or not this backward-sloping supply schedule is demonstrable in agriculture, it is proverbial that supply is at least highly unresponsive to high or low prices for the products that make up a farm's entire output.

It remains true, of course, that particular crops will respond to high or low prices, relative to the prices of other crops that might be grown on the same farm; and this would appear to be one of the advantages of diversified agriculture, as against an unduly inflexible one-crop system. In the same way, labor will move from a lower-paying job to a higher-paying one (though with some sluggishness) and differential incentives (as distinct from a general increase in hourly rates) can elicit extra time and effort. And an employer offering superior terms and conditions may be able to select his workers more carefully and secure premium quality in return for premium compensation.

12. Elastic Meeting of Demand and Supply

The equating of demand and supply is seldom, if ever, a precise matter. In the first place, supply viewed as stock may mean various inventories at various stages of production and distribution, and they do not all have the same meaning. Under some conditions they may represent confident buying, while under other conditions, they may represent inability to sell what has been bought. Under some conditions, a customer may count unfilled orders given to his supplier as part of his available supplies—if he is confident that delivery will be made on a schedule that fits his requirements. Under other conditions, if delivery is uncertain, he may duplicate his orders, creating fictitious statistics of demand. Aside from such occurrences, the backlog of unfilled orders gives the producer a prospective demand

genuine exception may occur if workers who have had a low and inelastic standard of living receive wage increases great enough to arouse hope and ambition to gain a substantially higher level, qualitatively different and sufficient to command their imagination. This might call forth more work.

against which he can plan his schedules of production and delivery.

Both for the producer and the customer, inventories afford a margin to enable operations to go on if the regular flow is temporarily interfered with. The considerations bearing on the amount of inventories carried and the timing of orders for replenishment might be described as technical requirements, modified by market expectations. If the market is favorable and the chief likelihood of change in demand or price appears to be upward, that may point toward carrying heavier inventories than mere technical requirements would indicate. The opposite case might point toward hand-to-mouth buying or buying with guarantee against price decline. In the absence of such special expectations, formulae may be used to indicate when to reorder.

Where production is seasonal and demand more nearly continuous, or where demand is seasonal and production can advantageously be spread out, these discrepancies in timing give rise to distinctive types of inventory. There is the carry-over of staple crops such as wheat or the seasonal pack of canned salmon, and there is the accumulation of cans to be used in the short canning season, or of toys for the Christmas trade. Here there are two kinds of purposes for which inventories are needed. There is the coordination of production with consumption as it would be if the amount and timing of both were accurately predictable and all that had to be done was, for example, to distribute the use of the season's wheat crop so that it would last until the next crop came in, and would then be used up. But there is the further possibility that the next crop may be late or small. This gives additional occasion for carry-over to ensure regularized consumption. This is especially important in a case like wheat, in proportion as wheat is more of a basic necessity than canned salmon.

The market incentive—when it is in command—is partly to regularize milling operations, and partly to buy when price is low and realize later when price may be higher. Such carry-over operations mitigate price-fluctuations due to irregular supply. This adds an element of elasticity to a demand that is inherently highly inelastic. Price supports, of course, introduce a different kind of carry-over, not limited to the amounts private traders would accumulate on market principles. Instead, government holds its own kind of umbrella over prices and absorbs whatever the market will not take at the support prices, without expecting to be able to dispose of the surplus at a commercial profit. This of course severs the normal connection among supply, demand, and price.

To sum up, the flexible adjustment between demand and supply is an indispensable feature of our economic system; but the system can work with a minimum of disturbance and interruption precisely because the adjustments between demand and supply do not have to be made with hair-trigger timing and exact precision. And it may bear reiteration that, in the main stream of transactions, the force that operates on the supply side of the market is not supply in the literal sense of an amount of goods, but the producers' capacity and willingness to produce the goods for sale. Productive capacity is one of the two decisive factors on the supply side of the market, but it is not supply. That requires also the conditions that make it economically feasible to operate the capacity and turn out goods. The "law of supply and demand" is not violated merely because some productive capacity is not working. And this law does not impose on the price the obligation to make such adjustments as would keep all productive capacity operating all the time. The problem of the desirable and feasible behavior of price is less simple than that. It is full of perplexities, and at many points it is probably not susceptible of a confident and definite answer.

CHAPTER 8

Innovation

1. Changing Conditions of Innovation

Innovation involves two stages: the invention of something new and its industrial or commercial introduction and exploitation. The inventor may be a separate individual or a specialized firm, or the two stages may be combined within a single firm's organization. Inventions are multitudinous, and most of them never reach the stage of exploitation, while many attempted exploitations fail to achieve economic success. A crucial phase is the process of selecting inventions that appear to have promise of economic value, developing them to the point of feasible application, and testing their value in practice. Realized innovations are the end-results of this process of selection and development. The whole series of processes absorbs great amounts of economic effort and resources in the promotion of accelerating economic change.

In a thoroughly dynamic economy, utilizing applied science as ours does, innovation is not only basic; it takes on new forms, does new kinds of things, with new organizational sponsorship, new enabling conditions, and new needs for watchfulness regarding its human and social consequences. In the Middle Ages, industrial techniques were the "mysteries" of the handicrafts in the custody of the masters. With the mechanical revolution that got under way in the eighteenth century, techniques started on their way toward domination by a new set of mysteries—those of applied science, back of which lies basic research, both being in the custody of research laboratories, some of which are becoming gigantic. In the earliest stages, the ingenious mechanic, or at least the individual inventor, appeared sufficient; but the need for a background of scientific understanding soon emerged. James Watt had to work out for himself the physics of the pressures, volumes, and expansions of gases, on his way to creating an efficient steam engine.

178

The early inventions were more efficient processes for turning out familiar end products—textile fabrics, coal, and iron—and such changes as took place in products were incidental results of the new processes. Now, new materials and new or altered end products pour out from the massive research and testing laboratories and into use, at a rate calculated to overwhelm the consumer, faced with the task of making reasonably intelligent choices between them. And the enormous scale of laboratory research and testing raises disquieting thoughts whether we are reaching a stage of technology in which only a few giants can survive.[1]

Conditions have changed drastically since the time when Alfred Marshall could take the position, in his presidential address of 1890, that the efficiency of large combinations consisted mainly in turning to account existing knowledge and that, despite the hiring of specialists to make experiments, which their resources permitted,

> . . . these advantages count for little in the long run in comparison with the superior inventive force of a multitude of small undertakers. There are but few exceptions to the rule, that large private firms, though far superior to public departments, are yet, in proportion to their size, no less inferior to private businesses of a moderate size in that energy and resource, that restlessness and inventive power, which lead to the striking out of new paths.[2]

Admitting dependence on scientific knowledge, he held that nearly all of it becomes available to the able small enterprisers, "as soon as it is achieved," and that he can make freer use of it than a laboratory scientist working under direction.[3]

This statement by a profound observer of economic processes appears worth citing partly—but only partly—as a record of conditions that are past. In Marshall's later writings, notably his *Industry and Trade*, published 29 years after the address just cited, one does not find this extreme view of the superiority of a "multitude of small undertakers." Schumpeter, in his *Theory of Economic Development*,

---

[1] On this problem, and on the related problems of incentives and of the diffusion of resulting benefits, see the valuable articles by Henry H. Villard, "Competition, Oligopoly and Research," *Journal of Political Economy* (December 1958), pp. 483-97; and "The Social Cost of Monopoly Profits," *Political Science Quarterly* (September 1957), pp. 380-87.

[2] "Some Aspects of Competition, 1890," in *Memorials of Alfred Marshall*, A. C. Pigou, Ed. (1925), pp. 279-81.

[3] *Ibid.*

found innovations that displace older processes to be generally carried out by new firms, but envisaged a new era of great combines, in which innovation would increasingly become the internal concern of a continuing economic body.[4] And in his *Capitalism, Socialism and Democracy* (1942), the emphasis has shifted entirely to huge organizations that can maintain a monopoly position only so long as they do not restrict output and raise prices, as monopolies are conventionally supposed to do. They save the wastes of competition, making economies from consolidation; and are driven by the dynamism of their position to give the public some part of the benefit.

> Motivation is quite immaterial. Even if the opportunity to set monopolist prices were the sole object, the pressure of the improved methods or of a huge apparatus would in general tend to shift the point of the monopolist's optimum toward or beyond the competitive cost price in the above sense, thus doing the work—partly, wholly, or more than wholly—of the competitive mechanism, *even if restriction is practiced and excess capacity is in evidence all along. . . .*[5]

These somewhat cryptic hints about motivation suggest questions that may be as well worth following up as Schumpeter's more explicit thesis. The question at issue, one should remember, is not the survival or elimination of small firms, but the importance of the part they can play in innovations. As to that, it seems clear that both the facts of economic organization and our mental pictures of them have swung so far from Marshall's early dictum that that dictum is worth pondering as a reminder that there may still be virtue in numbers of moderate-sized enterprises; and that we could profit much if we could gain understanding of the kinds of service to progress that the relatively small firm can best render, and the ways in which it can best be fitted into an industrial structure in which the resources available to a giant firm count for vastly more than they did in the England of 1890.

From the standpoint of this volume, the crucial question is: What is the proper place of competitive forces in promoting innovation or dealing with it, and how may they take their proper place and render effective service? As to this, there is probably no problem area in which monopolistic and competitive features are so inseparably interwoven. These include patents and their expiration, uniqueness and efforts to imitate it, differential advantages and the competitive erosion

---

[4] First German ed. (1906); English translation by R. Opie (1934), pp. 66-67.
[5] Pp. 101-02.

of them. One may make a beginning of bringing order into this complex by noting that the monopolistic factors or the delayed action of competition act to give the innovator incentives to make an innovation, while the competitive features have a dual character. They operate to diffuse the benefits of past innovations, bringing them into the public domain. Under favorable conditions this puts the innovator under pressure to make further innovations if he is to maintain a competitive advantage and the better-than-minimum profits that go with it. This effect of competition in adding to the stimuli to innovation depends on its action in eroding innovators' profits, though only provided that action is "imperfect," delayed, but ultimately effective. This is an oversimplified picture, but it will do as a starting point for inquiry. One should not hope for a formula that will precisely define an optimum balance between these complementary but opposing elements.

Even from the single standpoint of conditions favorable to bringing innovations about and testing them for serviceability, there is an involved complex, in which conditions that are favorable from an enabling standpoint do not correspond neatly with those affording incentives or with the tests of the serviceability of an innovation to the innovator, the customers, or the general public. An innovation that creates a wholly new product creates an industry, and as a result a monopoly position in the innovation may involve monopoly in the industry created. In contrast, in minor product variants or improvements in processes, a monopoly in the innovation may mean merely a competitive advantage in the industry; but it may need to be introduced on a large scale to afford the innovator gains commensurate with the costs of innovation or the benefits ultimately resulting for the industry. For a new end product, demand must be created, generally starting on a small scale, by methods that reach the ultimate consumer. For a new material, the immediate market consists of fabricators, and the methods of sales promotion are correspondingly different. However, the need to develop demand in this case may lead the innovator into fabrication as a way of demonstrating purposes for which the novel material is peculiarly suited. This was conspicuously the case with aluminum; and as independent fabrication developed, it raised problems of competition between a supplier and its own customers. Where the conditions of a product innovation lead to high concentration in the resulting industry or subindustry, this may have different effects on price competition and on quality competition and on competitive incentives to develop different kinds of quality. These problems will be examined in the next two chapters.

2. A Series of Overlapping Revolutions

Any act of innovation is, in its essence, an alteration of previous practice or a departure from it made with the facilities available in the existing environment and under conditioning influences and limitations imposed by it. Thus, innovation is a joint resultant of the existing and the novel. But since successive waves of innovation shift the point of departure and alter the conditioning environment, each such wave becomes historically unique. Therefore any attempt at general statements in this field faces special hazards and needs to start by making distinctions, beyond those already made between process, material, and end-product. In the changes of the past two centuries and more, one can distinguish a mechanical revolution (prepared for by major improvements in agriculture and transport), a power revolution, a revolution in materials, brought to full fruition by chemical, electronic, and nuclear revolutions, and bringing on a revolution in end-products.

In the economic application of these technical factors, revolutions have been brought about by the factory system, the business corporation and its functionally departmentalized administrative organization, new forms of credit and sales promotion—this last being only one area in which the resources of incipiently scientific psychology have been applied.[6] Last, but not least, come the new forms of adaptive social action that become necessary to deal with the less desirable consequences of businesslike innovation—the material and social debris that it brings in its train and that, if not controlled and constructively handled, can threaten the health of a civilization.

The earliest eighteenth-century textile inventions used wood as material in their mechanisms and could be operated by man power. For later ones, local water powers were sufficient, and these remained the

---

[6] These last present some of the most disturbing implications. One hopes, as a lesser evil, that the psychology underlying many current sales appeals is inaccurate, because if it is accurate in its low estimate of the level of intelligence it appeals to, this means that the American people are not fit for self-government.

main power source through the first quarter of the nineteenth century, though the first steam cotton mill was built in 1785. Iron plentiful enough for a mechanical age became available with the solving of the problem of replacing charcoal with coal in smelting—a long struggle that reached a turning point in 1760 and culminated in 1790 with the use of steam to power blast furnaces.[1] Thus machine production, coal, iron, and steam collaborated. Compared to the multitudinous variety of modern techniques, their characteristic ultimate sources of power have remained few: falling water, coal, and oil, with solar radiation a relatively minor source, and explosives, jet and rocket fuels of more military than industrial importance—so far. Thus nuclear power, now on the threshold, is a major addition to a limited list. Proximate or derived power sources include steam, electric-magnetic, and electronic energy.

The transmission needed to apply power exhibits much more variety, including the conversion of power from one form to another. In the simplest steam engine, a chemical process—combustion of coal—is converted into steam under pressure, this to reciprocal motion of a piston and this to rotary motion. In a turbine, the rotary motion is produced from the velocity of the steam, on the principle of the inclined plane, streamlined to utilize the dynamics of moving gases. The conversions of power in transmission include reduction—as when deadly high voltages are stepped down for household use—and amplification —as when minute energies of radio waves are amplified in a loudspeaker. Constant use is made of the principle by which large energy is triggered by a control requiring little energy. In such a primitive mechanism as a bow, the energy of human muscles is transmitted to the string and through it, by a complex geometrical relation, to the tips of the bow, where it is stored in the form of spring tension. It is released at speeds impossible for human muscles, further multiplied as a movement of no more than six inches of the bow tips is translated into a movement of roughly twenty inches in the arrow, the ratio increasing until the primitive ballistic missile leaves the propelling string.

Key qualities of mechanical processing are speed, precision, uniformity, and regularity. The latter qualities made possible the system of interchangeable parts and its fruition in the assembly-line technique. Uniform speed of steam engines was secured by the centrifugal gov-

[1] See W. Cunningham, *Growth of English Industry and Commerce In Modern Times*, Pt. 1 (1921), p. 524.

ernor, primitive ancestor of the multitude of "feedback" controls that have played such a part in "automation" and "cybernetics"; backed by electronic computers, which in solving problems of multiple variables far surpass the capacity and accuracy of the human brain for this class of work and appear to possess surprising capacity for adaptation, which is still being investigated.

The revolution in materials began in ways that illustrate the principle that something existing in nature becomes a "material" when people find out how to use it. They also illustrate the fact that stages of processing intervene between a primary material as found in nature (e.g., iron ore) and a secondary material in form for fabrication into ultimate products. The same is true of nitrates and rubber. Synthetics introduce a third stage in which the primary material is chemically transformed into something with wholly new properties, revealed only in the laboratory, and by virtue of which it may perform industrial miracles. Hardness, toughness, and temperature resistance are multiplied, and resistance to various corrosive chemicals is increased, while tungsten-armed cutting tools deal with otherwise impossible materials. If speeds of rotation are wanted at which ordinary materials would fly apart, special alloys resist the enormous centrifugal force. New building materials free the builder from the constraints of form imposed by wood, brick, and stone; and as a result we may witness a rash of architectural atrocities before the new freedom finds acceptable shapes in which to embody itself.

The impact on the character of human activity at work is presumably no less important to welfare than an increase of consumer's goods, and certainly more important than the luxury fringes of our standard of living—which is expanding but not in all respects improving. This work impact has gone through an evolution, in which tasks were first subdivided and made stultifyingly monotonous, then handed over to machines over which the workers exercise a supervisory control that has regained qualities of skill and discretion, of a different sort from those of the handicraft worker. In the organizational field the revolution of responsible and departmentalized industry has included employing professional specialists to deal with the human conditions and relations involved, applying the principles of sound human relations insofar as these are understood. One hesitates to class this as "applied science," especially after the doubts just expressed about the scientific validity of the applied psychology observable in the field of advertising.

3. Grades of Innovation

"Innovation," as the term is commonly used, means putting something novel into economic use. It does not include unused inventions, but may build on what was learned from them. Innovations are of all degrees of importance and of narrow or wide application. A major one normally requires a series of contributory enabling devices and is followed by a series of further improvements or new applications. Watt's steam engine illustrates this, while the cotton gin may be the proverbial exception—a quick mechanical breakthrough, creating a machine ready to go into widespread use, to satisfy a major existing demand, and simple enough to be produced by many local mechanics (making Eli Whitney's patent largely useless). It enabled the expansion of American cotton growing, of English and American cotton manufacture, and industries utilizing cottonseed. Thus the economic effects ramified, whether or not the mechanical principle involved had multiple applications, as did Whitney's greater and more enduring innovation—the principle of interchangeable parts.[8] The greatest innovations ramify, in one or both of these two ways, while lesser ones may have narrow application.

An innovation generally displaces something, and sooner or later the specific device embodying it will be displaced in turn, though the principle employed may survive. This raises the question whether the gain from the innovation covers the loss from the displacement; and whether successive replacements are cumulative gains, each starting where the preceding one left off, or are noncumulative, each starting where the preceding one started. Cumulative, or additive, innovations include those in which superiority is a matter of objective performance, by standards that have some fixed meaning, while nonadditive ones are to be found where standards are subjective and may be relative and shifting, valuing the novel thing because it is novel, and then devaluing it as it becomes familiar. But the realm of subjective preferences also includes cases in which the trying out of new things results in discarding

[8] The mechanical principle of the cotton gin was that of fine spikes on a revolving drum, pulling the fibres through openings in a comb-like structure, too narrow to let the seeds through.

the old for something which, by the best standards available, would be judged to represent a progressive improvement, which is cumulative. In such cases (if those concerned can ever agree on them) and in the first kind, there is a gain sufficient to offset the loss involved in the displacement of the obsolete process or product. In such cases this loss has already occurred when the superior product or process becomes available and would not be avoided, but rather increased, by keeping obsolete equipment in service. It would be reduced, not increased, by well-timed replacement. And successive replacements are cumulative gains.

In contrast, in style changes, it is logically possible to go through a series in which *a* is displaced by *b*, *b* by *c*, and so on, until finally *n* is displaced by a return to something essentially similar to *a*. Things like this happen, especially in the more extreme styles. Shall one say then that the sum of the seasonal gains, as registered by preference for the new style over last year's, adds up to zero? That answer would contain much truth, though the complex of values in the case is not so simple. The people affected include more than a half dozen distinguishable groups, from those who enjoy leading styles (at some risk, if the styles refuse to follow a particular attempted lead) to those who cannot afford to keep in style, but suffer from not doing so; and no psychic summation is possible. All one can be sure of is that the net resultant, whatever it is, has no relation to the sum of the successive market preferences for the new style over the old.

If such a series yields a positive net result, it depends heavily on the group of consumers who are looking for values more positive than novelty as such. They are likely to express preference for the more moderate among the initial offerings—these being the ones less likely to do violence to the standards expressed in the secular trend of consumer preferences, from which seasonal style changes are variations. This group may reject a violent style, setting limits on the potential dictation of the designers. They may fall back on what is thought of as the non-style sector of the market; meaning the conservative sector in which change is very slow. With luck, the net resultant may bring an increased tolerance of variety that loosens the tyranny of style, is favorable to comfort and to allowing those who have common sense or good taste to express these qualities.

There is little evidence on how many consumers prefer an annual style change (some undoubtedly do), but there is much evidence that it is convenient and presumably economical for producers to concentrate a season's production on a limited list of types and models, after satisfying themselves that the market will accept them. The logic or illogic of this last was illustrated in a different form when my wife and I were choosing wallpapers and were told, of a certain book of samples: "You wouldn't want those, they're last year's patterns"; the patterns in question being reproductions of colonial papers. The class of interest for which this salesman was speaking is a legitimate interest, making for economies some of which might be passed on to the purchasers in general; but the market clearly does not have sensitive and accurate ways of offering customers a choice of fewer varieties at lower cost or a wider variety at a higher price registering the resulting higher cost, and testing just how much added variety customers are willing to pay for, at prices registering its added cost. In such things as clothing and furnishings, an adequate selection is an element of quality of service, for which the customer may pay a price, either in money or in the effort of reaching a well-stocked outlet; but the connection between cost and price is far from close.

When a machine is displaced by one that does the same thing more economically, the general presumption is that a reproduction of the original model would be as economical as it was originally. There are exceptions: for example, if the character of available materials has changed, necessitating alterations in the equipment if equally good results are to be secured. If the old machine has reached the end of its normal life, it will be replaced by a new model if the new model shows lower total unit cost than a reproduction of the old model would do. Complications arise when improvements raise the issue of scrapping a machine that still has years of mechanical serviceability, and the firm has to reckon with the added cost on capital account from earlier versus later replacement. A further complication (which does not change the essential principle) occurs in the case of a set of machines, with units of different ages but which need to be of uniform type for effective operation.

The most speculative item in such a decision is the speed of functional obsolescence to be expected on the new equipment that replaces the old, and which will cause the new equipment to be replaced in its turn. It is this factor that managements take roughly into account, when, instead of reckoning return on new investment above accounting costs, they use the rule-of-thumb concept of the "payoff period," within which, according to available estimates, the investment would return its whole cost. In an industry with rapidly changing techniques, a period as short as five years is often used in such calculations.[9] This does not mean that the management thinks five years is the most probable economic life of the investment in question; it is a simplified equivalent for an expectation including a possibility that the investment would never fully pay for itself, and a probability that it would take considerably more than five years to do so, as its earning power dwindles toward an ultimate vanishing point. The payoff formula seems likely to include an attempted margin of safety against over optimism in the estimates, either of the duration of the investment's economic serviceability or the amount of expected economies, with avoidance of loss given greater weight than an equal chance of profit. Such a weighting is in general harmony with the attitude toward uncertainties expressed in the "minimax" principle, and is warranted in all but exceptional circumstances.

The point at which the investment loses all value and replacement is called for is not reached as soon as superior new equipment is available. The choice is to modernize now or later; and Schumpeter has pointed out that it may be too costly to modernize at every link in a chain of improvements.[10] It may be economical to scrap and replace new equipment, but only if there is an improvement so decisive that, in competition with it, the existing equipment could not earn even depreciation, since if it could, it would be economical to allow it to do so as long as it can.[11] In such a case, postponement of replacement does not avoid the loss of value of the existing equipment, most of which has taken place regardless of the amount of deprecia-

[9] It should be noted that this is a guide to a policy decision, and has no necessary implication whether the firm would wish, or would be allowed, to charge accelerated depreciation in its accounts on the basis of a five-year life. This privilege has been used as an inducement for investments to meet emergency needs of peculiar public importance. We are here considering an attempt at a prudent business judgment on the value that competition and technical progress will allow a proposed investment to realize.

[10] *Capitalism, Socialism and Democracy*, p. 98. This is true even under competitive conditions, though Schumpeter mentions it in connection with monopoly.

[11] J. B. Clark, in classroom lectures, cited a case in which new equipment was replaced before it had begun to operate. The moral was that, while the point at which replacement becomes economical might be the same for a monopolist or a competitor, the competitive firm is under more compelling pressure to write off the functional depreciation and take the consequences.

tion accrued on the books; but a continued policy of this sort may result in a longer prospective working life for the new equipment when the replacement is finally made, with allowance for the likelihood, inevitably uncertain, that its economic life may, through further functional obsolescence, be shorter than its physical life.[12] This likelihood needs to be taken into the reckoning bearing on replacement; otherwise the competitive comparison would be biased against the old equipment, and might result in economically premature modernizations. Incidentally, such a decisive improvement as is here considered is unlikely to be followed quickly by another equally decisive, as a minor improvement may be followed by another, also minor. An opposite error occurs when equipment is kept in service past its term of usefulness, to avoid the capital loss (on the books) from abandoning it, and writing off its remaining book value. This book value may have little to do with the remaining economic value, or with the economically correct time for retirement and replacement.

4. Stages of Innovation

As already indicated, the life history of a successful innovation is a cycle. It is developed, profitably utilized, and ultimately loses its value as a source of special profit in one of two ways. It may be superseded by something better, or it may simply become standard practice, available to all competitors and its benefits diffused, through competition, perhaps to the customers in general and perhaps to the workers.[13] Meanwhile it serves as a point of departure for the further innovations that follow. We have already discussed the kinds of cases in which there is a cumulative benefit to be passed on, and the kinds in

[12] "Physical life" is a misleading term. If it is to be strictly distinguished from functional obsolescence, it might be defined as the point beyond which, due to inferior performance and increased cost of maintenance, its net earning capacity before depreciation would have a present worth less than salvage value, in hypothetical competition with new equipment of identical sort, assuming such equipment to be still available as a standard product. Actually, major replacements are unlikely to be made with identical equipment, thus blurring the line between physical depreciation and functional obsolescence.

[13] As to diffusion, see above, Chap. 4, Sec. 6.

which the existence of such cumulative gain is dubious. The latter kind may find its justification in the general principle of the producer's freedom to offer appeals to the consumer; but the kind that yields cumulative gains is the mainstay of economic progress.

We may look first at the process of developing and utilizing an innovation. This may be regarded as typically going through six stages: a problem, an idea for its solution, a feasible solution on the laboratory or workshop scale, at which stage a patent may be taken out on any patentable elements, an investigation of commercial potentialities, a pilot plant or other modest-scale tryout, and full-scale application in the hope of commercial success. The first two stages create an invention, the last three apply it as an innovation. The first four stages are stages of outgo, and only in the last stage, if at all, is full reimbursement ordinarily to be expected. The series may take months in the case of a minor improvement, or decades in the case of a major change, in which case the total outlay, before reimbursement, may run well up in the millions.

During the process, the sponsorship or custodianship will shift, construing the term broadly to include shifts within the personnel and departmental structure of a large corporation. If it starts with an individual inventor, the resulting patent will ordinarily be transferred to the business firm that will apply the device or develop and market the product.[14] The classical method, in which the inventor formed a partnership with a capitalist, is giving way to development by some existing firm, which has largely taken the place of the "new firms" featured in Schumpeter's earlier conception. If it all takes place within a large company, there are shifts from originating personnel to research department and to operating department. As sponsorship shifts, there may be corresponding shifts in the complex of motives, incentives, and criteria of the current sponsor. These cluster around the central search for profit, but are not all to be explained in terms of the pure calculus of profit maximization. Innovations may be adopted— say in the realm of employee relations—for which a quantitative test of profitability may or may not be possible. If not, the decision that they are "good business" rests on a faith in the business value of imponderables.

[14] The author knows an individual inventor who developed a device on the workshop scale and found that the great corporation which would be a logical user preferred not to acquire the patent, but to purchase the device from him. This presumably reflects antitrust attitudes unfriendly to excessive massing of patents.

The original problem may start with a want and a search for means of gratifying it; or with a substance and a search for uses, or wider uses, to which it can be put. The substance may have been discovered virtually by accident, while looking for something else, as in the case of nylon.[15] Or a substance may strongly suggest a use, but may need analysis and synthesis before its main uses are achieved—as was the case with the development of caoutchouc into the rubber that has become such a mainstay of industry, especially transport. The story of Charles Goodyear's determined efforts, his contribution, and his failure to reap financial reward, is an epic of the heroic (and risky) age of the individual inventor. The problem with which an innovation starts may be conceived and attacked by an independent inventor, or may be assigned to a research staff by a business manager, or the staff may be allowed enough scope to take it up on their own initiative.

Given a problem, an idea for its solution *may* come with the "flash of genius" mentioned by Schumpeter; but there is more evidence of the kind of genius consisting of technical competence plus persistent work on the succession of problems of which the original problem turns out to be composed. The key may lie in recognizing the occasion for the application of some earlier result of basic research. Or knowledge may be needed that only fresh basic research can supply; in which case no one can foretell whether the answer will be favorable or unfavorable. However, there are an increasing number of problems about which it is possible to predict, roughly of course, the time it will take to solve them.

In case of a new product, at some early stage there may be a canvass of demand possibilities, necessarily tentative, which may give an inkling whether the prospects warrant going further. Where an innovation deals with productive processes and does not substantially affect the product, the exploration of demand is limited to sounding out the response to reduced prices that may result from reduced costs. Naturally, this has a major impact only if the innovation in question brings about a major reduction of costs. But the substantial testing of demand comes with the setting-up of a "pilot plant" or other small-scale venture in production for sale. Here technical difficulties that were not revealed at the laboratory stage are uncovered and dealt with, and costs may be judged, though the full economies of large-scale exploitation may not be available.

[15] Richard R. Nelson, "The Simple Economics of Basic Scientific Research," *Journal of Political Economy* (June 1959), pp. 297, 301, 303.

With full-scale exploitation comes the final test whether the gains to the innovator are large enough and last long enough to recompense the earlier investments and shortages of net income in the developmental stages. This is the stage during which the innovation ceases to be a novelty and becomes a target for efforts to imitate, to reduce its special value by finding a different, but equivalent, substitute, or to supersede it with something better. In this period any original patents will presumably expire, and the question will remain whether patent advantage can be prolonged by supplementary patents, or whether, aside from such added patent protection, the "know-how" gained from taking the lead will enable the original innovator to keep ahead, affording sufficient continuing advantage to offset the costs of pioneering. For that purpose, costs of pioneering need to be continued, on a defensive if not an aggressive basis. It is in the light of all this that the successful innovator must decide on its policy for exploiting its position, once it has reached the stage of full-scale commercial operation.

The innovating firm has available a range of policies, in which immediate and long-run advantage and aggressive and defensive considerations may be variously combined. At one extreme, it may aim at maximum short-run profit and meet competition when it arises. Or if it succeeds in recompensing its original outlays while it still holds a competitive advantage, it may then use its advantage, or part of it, to increase volume and build up a stronger market position against the time when its original advantage will have lapsed. Or it may begin the building up of market position earlier, accepting more moderate returns and taking longer to recover its original outlays. And it will be trying to prolong or renew its advantage, installing fresh improvements and preparing to make others.

This picture is like Schumpeter's view of innovation in being especially appropriate to major innovations, occurring at substantial intervals. In this setting, minor improvements, occurring at shorter intervals, appear as incidental and subsidiary features. By way of recognizing innovations of less basic character and shorter time period, we might consider the annual model, as seen notably in automobiles, or the less regular but frequent model-changes that prevail in various durable products. The annual model change occurs where the generic product is well-established, and each producer is planning the demotion or devaluation of his own last year's model as well as those of his competitors. All are making innovations simultaneously, and it is only the market's reception that discloses whether any one has gained an advantage over his rivals. If he has, he can enjoy the benefit for at least a season. Subsequent models will stress successful features, unsuccessful ones will tend to disappear, but the process is a ponderous one.

The creation of a new model of automobile is said to take three years, and substantial mechanical changes appear nowadays to come at intervals of two years or more, with minor changes of styling intervening. The place of the pilot-plant stage is taken partly by a course of rigorous and punishing testing under service conditions or worse—and even then defects may slip through. In another way, the purpose of limited-scale testing of market acceptance may be fulfilled by introducing special experimental models, without changing the producer's whole line at once. This, however, runs counter to the current tendency to standardize major subassemblies for use in as many models as possible, for the sake of the economies of mass production. Though all the competitors are working all the time on the problems of innovation and of meeting others' innovations, the most crucial part of this work at any one time may be preparatory for models of several years later. The upshot is that, even where the trade brings out annual models, the cycle of innovation and competitive devaluation is considerably longer.

The process of meeting a competitor's innovation begins before his innovation is introduced, with defensive preparedness in the departments of research, design, and engineering, to be ready to meet whatever improvements may be made by one's rivals. A firm cannot afford to omit this; and if it carries it on efficiently, there is always the chance that something would be developed that would have more than merely defensive value and would give the firm a positive advantage over its competitors. Thus, moves may change their character, from defensive to aggressive or in the other direction.

So far we have been discussing the stages of innovation on the assumption that competition exists. There is always the chance that a new product will become the basis of a monopoly covering the industry that produces this product. This will not happen often merely on the basis of a patent covering the new product, unless it is supplemented and its effect prolonged by other preclusive tactics. It is the function of effective antitrust policy to prevent such extensions of the limited monopoly of the patent. If nevertheless an outright innovation monopoly arises, the public interest demands that a transition to effective competition be somehow brought about if in any way possible, thus filling the policy of keeping innovational monopolies temporary, embodied in the patent laws. A significant reaction to such a situation is Judge Learned Hand's holding in the Alcoa case of 1945.

Alcoa was an outright monopoly based on aggregation of patents (which expired in 1909) and fortified for the subsequent period by superior ore holdings and some preclusive practices that were enjoined in a consent decree of 1911 and were not at issue in the 1945 case. The latter case hinged on the perpetuation of the monopoly for three decades after the expiration of its original patent basis, by other means than "unfair" preclusive tactics. On these facts it was held that mere persistent expansion, occupying the field as fast as growing demand affords room, and ahead of potential competitors, may evidence monopolistic intent and may constitute monopolistic preclusion, and cannot be defended as the automatic and inevitable result of business efficiency.[16] Judge Hand inserted a caveat to the effect that this doctrine does not apply to successful competitors in general. "The successful competitor, having been urged to compete, must not be turned upon when he wins."[17] The apparent harshness of the ruling appears to arise from grappling with the peculiar difficulties of this problem of transition from temporary innovational monopoly to competition. It may be a warning that firms in this position do well to lean over backward in affording opportunity for competition to establish itself. As for remedies, the substitution of a big two or big three may be better than complete monopoly and may bring highly effective rivalry in improving technical processes but falls short of a structure conducive to fully effective competition in giving customers the benefit, via price or quality.

At this point we may leave the discussion of the stages of innovation, having completed the cycle on which we started. If we went on, we should be discussing, not the process of innovation but the results, which take the shape of "competition of the few," competition between firms with different costs of production (mentioned in Chapter 6, Section 3) or competition with differentiated products, which will be taken up in the two chapters that follow.

[16] *U.S.* vs. *Aluminum Company of America,* 148 F. (2d) 416, especially pp. 429-32 (1945).

[17] *Ibid.,* p. 430.

5. Enabling Conditions for Innovation

Conditions conducive to innovation may be roughly divided into underlying or background conditions, direct enabling conditions and incentives—the last mainly centering in ability of the innovating firm to collect a sufficient fraction of the resulting gains, but not limited to this. The underlying conditions include the character of the people and their culture. A people and a culture conducive to innovation are interested in material means and apt at material contrivances. They have a bent toward the comprehension of mechanisms. It is no accident that Newton, Darwin, and James Watt were of the same civilization. Newton did not discover and record either the force of gravity or the movements of the planets; what he gave us was an understandable and verifiable mechanism connecting the two. Darwin did not discover the fact of evolution, though he filled in our picture of its stages with systematic observations. But his revolutionary contribution was a mechanism explaining how evolution came about. Where the best minds deal with the cosmic mechanisms, other high-grade minds will focus on mechanisms nearer home.

It is perhaps only self-evident that a culture adapted to innovation is one in which departure from traditional ways of doing and thinking is tolerated or even regarded as creditable. The Protestant Reformation made a germinal contribution to this attitude; a contribution that has a much wider reach than the application of Calvinistic doctrine to the ethic of capitalism, as set forth by Max Weber. It does not stop with the crude notions of early capitalism, but moves on to social innovations that may be needed to make private business serviceable to community welfare. What is needed is that a highly able part of the population should have a strong problem-solving bent in the material realm, and that they should operate under a secular government and religious attitudes that are hospitable to its exercise. An initial condition is some surplus of energy above the demands of a struggle for bare existence, and capital resources that people are willing to venture in pioneering.

Allied with this are the existence and availability of complementary techniques and devices. Industrialization means that an economy in which a majority of the population is agricultural is transformed into one in which an increasing majority is found in industrial and commercial towns. To feed these towns and supply them with such materials as agriculture still produces, the efficiency of agriculture and transport must increase comparably to that of industry. In the United States, less than 8 per cent of the population on the farms are producing troublesome agricultural surpluses; while in Soviet Russia, farm efficiency is its most stubborn bottleneck. Thus, it was a necessity rather than an accident that the British textile revolution of the eighteenth century was prepared for by a great increase in agricultural productivity and the improved roads brought about by Telford and McAdam.

Watt's steam engine needed cylinders accurate enough to hold compression, and Wilkinson, a maker of cannon, bored them. As metals and other materials are multiplied and diversified, as tool-making and machine-making industries stand ready to supply equipment and financial mechanisms to make capital accessible, and above all, as scientific knowledge and the means of its application multiply, innovation is speeded up cumulatively. A final enabling condition is that organized labor should accept innovation and cooperate in the necessary adjustment of working rules and job ratings. In the United States this requirement is, in general, met; as the main labor organizations understand the dependence of high and advancing real wages on high and advancing productivity. Such obsolete practices as exist have probably, on balance, more effect in increasing dollar costs than in reducing productivity.[18] The upshot is that innovation has become, paradoxically, the accepted way of life. Ponderables and imponderables are geared to facilitate it. It has become an established institution.

Coming down to more specific enabling conditions and viewing them from the standpoint of the maintenance of competition, we face

[18] Such practices, including the technically obsolete hundred-mile rule for reckoning a day's run on railroads, undoubtedly play some part in the manifold causes of the crisis that faces American railroads. This rule and others date back to the time when the railroads were considered monopolies, and when the economies of increasing traffic density furnished a source of gains in which organized labor could demand, and secure, its share. These rules have survived into a period in which traffic density causes diseconomies as well as economies, while the roads face really threatening competition from highway and air. It seems that, in the light of inescapable economic requirements, such rules are in need of reconsideration.

the problem of the relative capacities and roles of large and small firms under modern conditions in which mass production plays such a dominant part. Do the advantages of the huge firm weaken the position of small firms to an extent that threatens the continuance of healthy competitive conditions? This way of putting the problem is an extreme oversimplification and only a first step toward envisioning the complex of interrelated factors involved. The agencies at work include not only producing firms of all sizes, but specialized functional agencies operating on a business or a nonbusiness basis, with governmental agencies of research and information playing an increasingly important part.

The enabling conditions for invention differ from those for application and exploitation of inventions. The requirements for mechanical improvements differ from those for chemical improvements or others calling for massive use of the resources of laboratory science, and these again differ from those for improvements in business organization or industrial relations. The functional specialist is on a different basis from the firm engaged in creating an end product and devoting what skills and resources it can to trying to improve the product and to produce it effectively. Meaningful questions must be concerned with what kinds of contributions, in what phases of the process, different kinds of agencies are qualified to make, and how they may be afforded the necessary enabling conditions and most effectively coordinated.

The originality necessary to invention may be widespread and found in a wide variety of forms. It is here that the advantage of really large numbers counts, along with a free and independent position for creative individuals to follow their bent in furnishing pregnant ideas, from among which successful innovations may be developed. In some cases this may be done by the originators, but more often there is a transfer to some business firm, unless the originators are already employed by such an organization. The developing firm may be of any size. At this stage, the advantages of the giant firm count heavily in some kinds of innovation, while for other kinds, firms of medium or moderate size may be able to combine the advantage of numbers and independence—though not a Marshallian "multitude"—with size enough to be able to afford a department of research, engineering, and design, or may be able to secure these services from specialized agencies. It may be, as Jewkes and others have contended, that a majority of useful ideas still germinate with units that could be classed as small or relatively so; but in application and exploitation a potent advantage rests with units of at least moderate size.

For very small units, a distinction needs to be made between a small minority that start with a pregnant idea and develop it, and the great majority that is found where very small units prevail in the actual work of production, such as the one-family farm or the small store or service establishment. From the former group, pregnant innovations arise in significant numbers, despite the relatively small size of this group. But for the great majority of very small productive units, efficiency and progress depend heavily on specialized services made available to such units. The state experimental farm and the county agent devise and disseminate improved methods and adapt them to the special conditions of particular farms. Efficiency in very small-scale retailing needs the help of expertly devised systems of accounting and stock layout, adapted to the needs and limitations of such enterprises, for which highly formalized systems would be prohibitively burdensome. In manufacturing, enterprises that are too small to be able to afford a permanent research department are likely to need to have access to independent specialized services, including those of research laboratories and engineering firms, for particular jobs and to meet particular needs.

Of the very small enterprise that starts with a germinal idea, two instances may be cited. Pepperidge Farm bread, a successful and much-imitated product innovation, grew from the smallest conceivable beginnings, but it originated, not in a small commercial bakery, but in a consumption hobby of an upper-class housewife, which turned out to meet a large potential demand of a specialized sort. Another instance originated with a young designer of firearms, who had ideas about postwar openings in the market for pistols and got ahead of the dominant firms in exploiting them. Starting in a tiny shop, and aided by the expansion of the pistol-shooting hobby, his business has grown phenomenally, making its competition strongly felt in the industry. Such instances of success require special abilities, but in the aggregate they are highly important as an offset to the standardizing tendencies of mass production.

6. Incentives and Inducements[19]

Given the enabling conditions for innovation, the stimuli or inducements become important. The ones more obviously derived from business self-interest are concerned with the opportunity of the innovator
to acquire for himself an adequate fraction of the gain resulting from
his innovation. In the areas of objective and additive contributions,
the innovator's gain is almost inevitably no more than a fraction of
the whole, unless the whole effect includes unusually heavy losses
inflicted on others than the parties directly concerned. Such diffused
losses can conceivably exceed diffused gains. In the over-all picture,
the community must at least think that there are large gains that
innovators do not absorb to themselves, or the community would have
no interest in providing the facilitating conditions that the modern
community furnishes—and which the medieval community, for example,
did not. But it is in the nature of things that at the time a particular
innovation is made, no one can be sure of the amount of the gains or
of the incident burdens, or how they will be apportioned.

We may focus our discussion around initiatory or aggressive innovations made in the hope of increased profits, with the understanding
that the inducement to defensive innovations on the part of competitors seeking to avoid a reduction of profits or to minimize deficits
acts with even more compelling force. Larger profits per unit may
come from a reduction of costs, either from more economical processes
of producing the same commodity or from cost-reducing alterations in
the product that either do not reduce its salability or reduce it less
than they reduce its cost. This includes economy in the use of scarce
materials or the substitution of more suitable materials. It also includes changes that would be classed as adulteration or deterioration,
the outcome depending on the ability of the customer to judge what

[19] The problems treated in this section are epitomized in a verse by Kenneth E.
Boulding:

> We all agree that innovation
> Will benefit both world and nation.
> The question we must answer later
> Is, will it help the innovator?

he is offered, with whatever aids are available to him, and to make deterioration unprofitable by his sales resistance. In matters beyond his immediate competence, his sales resistance may be of the delayed-action sort celebrated in Lincoln's familiar dictum about fooling the people all of the time. Here the results may depend on the producer's integrity, his long-run or short-run perspective, this in turn being affected by the pressures, competitive and otherwise, to which he is subjected. We shall encounter these problems again in the following chapters on competition with product differentiation.

The second major method of increasing a firm's total profits is to increase its dollar volume of sales, either by price reductions, which may be made possible by reduced costs, or by making its product attractive to more buyers, or through increased total selling effort, including entering new geographical market areas or tapping new strata of demand.[20] This might be done through new differentiations in a line of products, appealing to different income levels among consumers, or by a better guess where the most lucrative demand is located. These ways of utilizing an innovation to increase profits may be employed in almost any kind of combination.

The limiting case at one extreme is the firm that reduces its unit costs and absorbs the whole saving in increased unit profit, making no effort to use its reduced cost as a basis for enlarging its output. Its scope for increased profits is measured by its existing sales volume.[21] The larger the sales, the greater the inducement to innovate. A complete monopoly can absorb the entire saving its improvement has created, thus having maximum inducement to innovate, lacking only the pressure of competitive necessity. It is more likely, however, to share the gain to some extent with customers, in an effort to take part of its gains in increased volume. At the opposite extreme is the producer of a wholly new product, who must get all his gain from new sales volume, under various possible policies in regard to quick profits versus sustained growth at a more moderate profit rate per unit.

Between these extremes lie the innovations in which the product keeps its identity, even though modified, and the innovator hopes for

[20] As indicated in the preceding chapter, this presupposes a demand with margin elasticity greater than one, or equivalent responsiveness to outlays on nonprice competition.

[21] More precisely, since its volume may change for other reasons, the measure is the volume it would have had, aside from its improvement.

an increase in his existing sales volume. Here the effects of existing large size on the inducements to innovate, on the kind of change in the product that is preferred, and on the form in which the gain is taken, all become complex and will need to be further examined. The large existing volume of sales may, under favorable over-all conditions, afford a base from which a large absolute increase in volume can be secured more easily than if the starting point were a smaller volume. But if the increase in volume depends on a reduction in unit price or other selling action reducing the margin per unit, the decisive thing is not the absolute increase in volume. What is needed is a percentage increase sufficient to offset the reduction in margin per unit, and from this standpoint an initial volume that is already large, relative to the total volume of the industry, may leave too little room for an adequate percentage increase. The relatively small firm, if it makes a cost-reducing innovation at all, has a larger interest in using part of the resulting economies in ways that will increase its total sales volume because, as already seen, its cross-elasticity of demand is greater. Such a firm cannot hope to collect all the gains that result from its innovations; and it may be only by increasing its volume that it can collect a large enough fraction to make the innovation pay. Thus monopoly favors innovation, qualifiedly, while competition creates positive pressure to share the gains with customers.

It would be possible to construct a theoretical case in which, assuming impossibly perfect foresight, the total benefits of an innovation to the industry are just enough to outweigh its cost; in which case it would be a paying matter for the innovator only if he could collect the whole benefit. This may imply making the innovation the basis of an industry-wide monopoly and leaving the rest of the community without an interest in it. Actual cases involve uncertainty; and if the inducements of a well-organized patent system are insufficient, there can seldom be a social interest warranting further extension of the privilege of innovational monopoly. The over-all interest in preventing the setting up of enduring industrial monopolies outweighs the conjectural loss from failing to induce the adoption of a few innovations that, by the terms of the problem, would have limited prospective value.

In terms of the effect of size, as distinct from monopoly power, on inducements to innovation, one may hazard a few tentative conclusions that appear inherently logical. One is that opportunities to widen the firm's profit margin per unit of sales or to increase its existing sales volume without narrowing the profit margin per unit offer the largest absolute gain to firms with a large existing volume of sales. Another is that opportunities to increase a firm's volume of sales by methods that involve a narrowing of the profit margin per unit—for example, by reducing prices—appeal most strongly to firms that are vigorous but relatively small, hence with high cross-elasticity of demand and ample room to grow. For a wholly new product, the prize of successful introduction may appeal most strongly to the vigorous but relatively small firm, but for such a firm the risks of a long unprofitable introductory period are more serious than for a larger firm. This difficulty may be resolved most naturally by a firm large enough to practice diversification and thus combine its risks. However, the tax laws complicate this picture, affording incentives both to independent exploitation and to mergers. One incentive is the possibility of converting the profits of innovation into capital gains, with a resulting tax advantage. A firm that has not enough profits against which it can charge off past losses may have a value for merger with a more prosperous firm, the merged firm being able to charge off the losses against its more ample profits.

Finally, as to different kinds of quality innovation, we have seen that there are opportunities for both improvement and deterioration, as judged by what customers would choose if they knew what they were getting, with due regard to differences in the kind of service desired by different groups of customers, as affected by their price-paying ability or disposition. Anticipating the findings of the following chapter, we shall encounter problems of production for majority demand versus adaptation to the differentiated desires of minority groups, problems of durability versus planned obsolescence and problems of luxury grades, standard grades, economy grades, and inferior grades, the last defined as low priced but rendering disproportionately poor service.[22] We shall find ground for the tentative conclusion that, in addition to the kinds of innovation for which very large concerns have the greatest inducement, they may be lukewarm or worse toward the introduction of economy grades and may have reason for positive resistance to sudden and large increases in durability.

[22] This classification is used by Stanislaw H. Wellisz, "The Coexistence of Large and Small Firms: a Study of the Italian Mechanical Industries," *Quarterly Journal of Economics* (February 1957), pp. 116, 118-19.

The most general conclusion is that from the standpoint both of enabling factors and inducements to innovation, the optimum condition calls for adjusting a variety of requirements. It may include some very large firms, whose volume of production permits large gains to be made; but other considerations require that they be surrounded by the largest number of competing firms that is compatible with these smaller firms being strong and large enough to command the necessary enabling resources for effective innovation.[23] This might include firms that concentrate in specialized sectors of the industry, provided market conditions are such that their limited coverage does not expose them to competitive tactics that would reduce them to the status of dependent satellites. In most industries this need not mean that the actively innovating firms must be very numerous: the essential thing is that they should set a pace that competitors are under defensive pressure to follow, because their competitive standing depends on their relative success in keeping up with, or close to, the advancing "state of the art" as led by the active innovators. The industry might include a number of firms that avoid the costs of initiatory pioneering and, by acting as ready followers, maintain a competitive position and help to keep the more active innovators on their mettle. But for the purpose in hand—competitive stimulus to innovation—the total number in any given market could be moderate: far smaller than the number called for by the atomistic competition of theory.

Lastly, as an inducement to innovation, comes the prospect of an interval of time during which the innovator can enjoy an advantage and recover his costs of pioneering before his advantage is dissipated. This dissipation may occur by imitation, by the development of equivalent alternatives, or by new innovations that render the first one obsolete. In either way, the generally available "state of the arts" approaches or catches up with the innovations and sets a new competitive level, the benefit of which is diffused over the economy. Then the first innovator is challenged in turn to renew his advantage—if he can—as the only way to go on earning the liberal profits that successful innovation brings. This completes the cycle of "creative destruction" stressed by Schumpeter and continues the "race between innovation and imputation."

The principle involved has well-nigh universal application; but it

[23] Cf. Willard D. Arant, "Competition of the Few Among the Many," *Quarterly Journal of Economics* (August 1956), pp. 327-45.

takes a variety of forms, and the time interval within which the innovator can keep his advantage and reap his reward varies greatly, so also does the amount of uncertainty involved. The outcome varies according to the nature of the innovator's advantage, the methods he uses to realize his gains from it, the extent to which competitors are equipped with defensive preparedness to enable them to respond promptly and effectively, and the kinds of countermoves they employ. As to the durability of the advantage in process or product, it goes almost without saying that it is increased if protected by patent rights —almost but not quite, since patents involve disclosure, and this invites imitations or substitutes that attempt to stop short of legal infringement. Patents will be separately discussed below.

If the advantage consists of a more economical process, it may tend to last longer if it is not used as a basis of pressure for increased sales volume, since such use of it would put added pressure on competitors to achieve countervailing economies. However, even in the absence of such pressure, it is not safe for the innovator to act as if his advantage would last forever; and when rivals do catch up, he may be in a stronger position if he has in the meantime increased his volume. The most obvious method is a simple price reduction, but this is also the easiest method to imitate quickly; and it will be imitated, especially if the product is standardized. But a firm wishing to exploit a newly gained low-cost position may hope to increase total demand and discourage higher-cost rivals from expanding their capacity, perhaps even forcing out some of the weakest firms, while it expands its own capacity in hope of securing all or most of the increased volume resulting from the price reduction.[24] If the product is differentiated, there is more possibility of price reductions that will not be instantly met; also more room for nonprice methods of increasing sales, to which the response of competitors is less quick and precise than to a simple reduction of the generally quoted list price.

As for the effect of competitors' research and preparedness, it is obvious in general that it must tend to shorten the time they would

---

[24] The reader may note that this departs from the usual assumption that when a price reduction is met, each seller retains his former proportional share of total sales. The reason for the departure is indicated in the text. The result is closer to the Cournot duopoly model, in which A lowers his price, expecting B's output to remain unchanged; but it takes a special condition to warrant such an (approximate) expectation.

need to meet a rival's innovation. As to specific defensive responses they might make to his improvement, it may teach them something that they could put to use more promptly because of the "know-how" gained from their own research. Or it may put pressure on them to put into earlier use something on which they are working and which they would otherwise have subjected to more deliberate and thorough testing. If a competitor has a thoroughly tested improvement available, of a sort that may widen profit margins or increase sales volume, it is not often that he will hold it in reserve, waiting for someone else to make the first move. To do so habitually would stultify his research department. The chief circumstance in which something like this might be expected to happen would be if the improvement called for considerable capital, and especially if several firms were known to have similar improvements ready to introduce. This mutual readiness might act as a deterrent; but if there are a fair number of competing firms, it is not likely to be long before some one of them breaks the deadlock and puts competitive pressure on the others. Before this happens, the prospect might be represented by an extra-short payoff period; but this would become irrelevant after one large producer had taken the lead and forced the issue on the others.

But while the fact that the various competitors are working simultaneously on devising and testing improvements may shorten the interval between one firm's innovation and its rivals' countervailing moves, the interval is bound to be longer in the case of improvements in process or modifications of existing products than in the case of new moves in selling tactics, while response to simple price reductions will always be the quickest of all. What may be called the "innovational interval" is threefold: the interval before the innovator's gains are felt by his competitors and put pressure on them, the interval before the competitor makes an effective response, and the interval before the response wipes out the competitive aftermath of the gains made by the first innovator during the first two intervals, when he held an advantage. One test of an adequate innovational interval might be whether an efficient and progressive firm can hope to make a fresh step ahead before the competitive advantage of the last one has been completely eroded, so that it may hope to go on earning something more than the minimum competitive return. The converse is that a laggard firm will cease to earn even this the minimum rate.

If major innovations are intermittent, there may be intervening periods in an industry in which imitation is followed by intervals of approximate equilibrium. But the more usual trend involves a fairly continuous series of minor innovations intervening between major ones. If a firm follows a major innovation with a series of minor improvements, this helps it to keep a step or two ahead of imitators, and so prolong its advantage. This raises obvious problems whether the diffusion of the benefits of the original innovation is being unduly delayed, and the spread between the best available and the generally available made unduly wide. Such problems play a large part in connection with patents.

7. General Role of Patents

The patent system is a public policy, adopted to promote the interests the public has in invention and its utilization, in the setting of a system of primarily private business enterprise. It plays a major part in four distinguishable functions: the stimulation (and rewarding) of invention and its utilization, the selection of inventions for adoption and for receipt of rewards, the determination of the amount and character of rewards to individual inventors and to industrial developers, and the ultimate general diffusion of the resulting benefits. Needless to say, this final function is crucial. From one standpoint, the method followed may be regarded as a grant to the inventor of property rights in the thing he has created, with a recognition that in such cases the thing created is not only a physical object but—since it is unique and novel—the whole class of objects following this model. This means that in such cases property—the essence of which is rights to exclude others from one's property—implies monopoly. But since monopoly is an exception to the general property system, it does not carry, in this case, all the rights regularly attached to physical property "in fee simple." It is, in essence, property qualified by a public interest of a rather special sort, conditioned on the fulfillment of the four functions just mentioned.[25] The first qualifying requirement is

[25] Cf. U.S. Attorney General's National Committee to Study the Antitrust Laws, *Report* (1955), pp. 224-25, 231-32, 249-50. Page 225 presents a lawyer's view (which I do not share) that a patent is like other forms of property. Qualifications on this idea will be mentioned below.

that of making public disclosure of the invention; but further needs arise for avoiding abuses as they appear in practice.

The patent system is a way of affording an incentive to the individual inventor who works on a problem of his own choosing, at the same time imposing on him the task of enlisting capital and enterprise to exploit any promising invention he may succeed in making. In contrast, many inventors work on the payrolls of business firms or public agencies, but they generally work on problems chosen by the organization that employs them, and resulting patents are likely to be assigned to the employing organization. If it is a business firm, the patent fortifies its profit incentive. Inventions made on the public payroll are mostly made for public purposes other than financial profit and are likely to be left in the public domain for maximum utilization, unless they are kept secret for military reasons. It is, however, quite conceivable that a publicly held patent could be made to serve a useful purpose in maintaining the quality, for example, of an important drug the government has developed, and preventing abuses in its distribution. In the absence of patents, business firms would still make and promote inventions, but they would use secrecy to protect their profits, and the social advantage of disclosure would be sacrificed.

As an alternative, it may be worth while to examine the idea of putting inventors on the public payroll as the standard method of promoting the kinds of inventions that would be exploited by private business. The public payroll is used where public procurement creates a joint interest between the government and its suppliers. How would it work if it became the general reliance for promoting economic progress? The key problems here are: What would happen to the multitude of personal inventors who choose the problems they want to work on? How would the government choose the problems on which it would pay chosen inventors to work for the benefit, in the first instance, of private business? The mere posing of these questions may indicate the inappropriateness of such a method. There are more would-be private inventors than could be put on salary, and a minority have ideas that ultimately prove useful. Strong private enterprise will want to do its own selecting of projects and will still want protection for the costly work of development.

The public payroll will serve for inventions in which the public interest is dominant—especially in the field of safety and health—or in areas where private productive units are too small to be effective innovators—agriculture being the outstanding example, but not the only one. Selection via experimental development, under any system, will be a matter of competitive comparison of some sort with existing practice. This is the first competition an innovation has to meet, and it determines whether the patent protection has any value, by market standards. Most inventions fail to pass this test. The possession of a patent—if it operates as it is supposed to do—means that during its term the rewards of the innovator are determined by the competitive superiority of his innovation to existing practice, not by such superiority, if any, as he may be able to maintain in a free-for-all scramble with imitators. This second level of competition is, in theory, deferred until the expiration of the patent, and this deferment increases the inducement of the innovator to incur the expenses and risks of development.

Actually, an innovation that has proved its value will normally give rise to near imitations or substitute devices, and will have to meet their competition, even if it is protected against literal infringements. The growing practice of licensing proved patents may reduce the incentive to this kind of counter-innovation. But in theory and intent, a patent formalizes the "innovational interval" at seventeen years, thus increasing the inducement to innovate and allowing the innovator to meet competition in two stages, the first confined to his competition with existing practice and the second a free-for-all. In this sense it involves the maximum reliance on competition consistent with allowing the rewards of innovation to be determined by its proved economic value. The many defects of the system in operation do not extinguish this basic feature, for which any radically different system would have to find a substitute of a less automatic sort.

If inventions were not patentable, would competition be increased? It is an interesting subject for speculation. It might make little difference in cases in which patents are already freely interchanged. In other cases it might mean that the inventor or his assignee could not get a return by charging royalties to competing users, but only from his own direct use of the innovation. This might increase the incentive to attempt to establish a monopoly. Also, as already suggested, the public disclosure required as a condition of a patent might be replaced by attempted secrecy, leading to considerable misdirected effort and doing no good to the morale of industry. It is far from clear that the abolishing of patents would increase effective competition.

However, patents can be used in ways that extend restriction of competition beyond the scope of the thing patented, and then the antitrust laws become applicable. Indeed, under modern business conditions, it appears to be of the inherent nature of a patent that the boundary delimiting permissible ways of using it requires a rule of reason to determine and limits the patent as a form of private property.[26] These limitations may be chiefly in evidence in the remedies embodied in particular antitrust orders, including consent decrees; but they may become generalized as other firms try to put their practices beyond danger of attack.[27] These border-line practices include accumulation of patents by assignment, nonuse of patents, grant-back of subsequent improvements to licensor or their use to extend the term of the patent monopoly, price-fixing of the patented article, limits on the field of use, tying clauses, restrictions on patentee, package licensing, cross-licensing or interchange (which has different significance according as the patents interchanged are complementary or competing), and blackmail of competitors by unwarranted infringement actions or—in reverse—defense against warranted infringement actions by unwarranted allegations of antitrust violation.[28] Where cross-licensing operates monopolistically, the remedy may require licensing all comers at reasonable royalties.[29] Border-line questions include licensing without royalty, also fuller disclosure of "know-how" than the patent itself requires. It seems evident that patents as a form of property are subject to a large and distinctive array of qualifications.

8. Remaining Problems

If this discussion has run largely in terms of how it is ideally desirable that innovation should act, the foregoing list of dilemmas in practice should bring it down to earth and to the realization that it can never be a simple matter to maintain the proper function of

[26] Cf. *ibid.*
[27] *Ibid.*, p. 228.
[28] *Ibid.*, pp. 226-49.
[29] *Ibid.*, pp. 255-56. One member of the committee, following the property theory of patents, objected that this subjects patents to partial confiscation, such as is not applied to other forms of property in seeking remedies for antitrust violations.

innovation in a competitive economy. The interest of the community, in maintaining as much competition as feasible among innovators, does not coincide with the interest of the innovator himself; and the community interest cannot be embodied in specific rules. If an improved process is introduced into an existing competitive industry, the continuance of competition implies either that the improvement is not so decisive as to preclude competition, that competitors can imitate it or find substitute processes that will keep them in the running, or that the innovator licenses his improvement at royalties that permit licensees to survive in competition. In the case of variants on existing products (mostly not patentable) the problem is hardly serious. But in the case of new products, it may assume a stubborn character.

There is probably a general difference between new materials, such as aluminum, magnesium, cellophane, and nylon, and new fabricated products, such as safety razors and vacuum cleaners. With fabricated products, competition among innovators appears to present no very difficult problem. The expiration of the Gillette patent was followed by lively competition of rival brands of safety razors. But in the case of new materials, if patents are backed up by massive control of sources of materials and power, as in the case of aluminum, for which power in great units is needed, the conditions are present for a new-product monopoly that may outlast the original patents and be hard to convert into competition, especially under a legal system that is geared to combat identifiable monopolistic actions, rather than to bring about or maintain whatever conditions may be needed for effective competition. Might this be an occasion for employing the principle of anticipatory and preventive action, already embodied in a rudimentary way in the 1950 amendment to Section 7 of the Clayton Act, dealing with mergers? This would mean preventing the acquisition of sources of materials and power from going to such lengths that its natural and probable effect would be to preclude the entry of competitors. If an innovational monopoly or near monopoly is established, a merger with a close substitute (e.g., aluminum and magnesium) would appear contrary to public policy. This is complicated by the fact that aluminum and magnesium are combined in some alloys.[30] But if effective competition exists in the production of each substitute, such

[30] See Charlotte F. Muller, *Light Metals Monopoly* (1946), p. 23.

a merger would be a hedging of the risk that one substitute might displace the other, without creating a monopoly.

Where the production of a new major material involves extensive processing that cannot be economical except on a very large scale, it may be that "competition of the few" is all that can be expected. This poses the familiar question how effective such competition can be expected to be. The problem of its effect on competition in price and in quality will have to be deferred to later chapters. But as to rivalry in efficiency of productive processes, there appears to be no reason for supposing that it is rendered ineffective by the mere fact of small numbers. The optimum number, from this single standpoint, presumably depends on the nature of the techniques used. If techniques are advancing, there is a strong presumption that the benefits that find their way to the customer will be advancing also, even under highly imperfect competition, even if at any given time he is not getting the benefit of prices that yield only a minimum competitive rate of return on the existing range of costs, or even if the level of costs of which he gets the benefit lags behind the best techniques that are known and available. A few years' further advance will normally more than wipe out this lag, if the economy remains dynamic. This is the paramount consideration.

At this point we may leave this necessarily incomplete discussion of innovation in its relation to competition. In the next two chapters we shall take up differentiated products, and competition among them.

CHAPTER 9

Product Differentiation

1. Introduction

While product differentiation is treated in theory as a special case, it is actually the most general case, or the most comprehensive class of cases, since nearly all the products and services in industry and trade involve some differentiation between competing sellers, in the product itself, in services connected with it, including transport, or in the "image" it presents to the mind of the buyer.[1] It follows that most of the defects of competition, as well as most of its virtues, are to be found in competition of this sort. It is an inseparable feature of the most essential operation of a freely progressive economy: the operation of constantly finding new products in which to embody its constantly increasing productive power, and products that consumers will take. The free economy allows private enterprise to draw on the resources of applied science to devise offerings and present them to the ultimate consumer in the most persuasive form their advertising agencies can devise and at freely chosen prices, and the consumer makes his choice; under powerful persuasion, to be sure, but persuasion that stops short of compulsion—either positive compulsion to choose a particular product, or negative compulsion that excludes all alternatives but the one the authorities have preselected.

The efficacy of this process presents plenty of problems, starting with those of customer choosing and ramifying out from there. How good are the tests of quality that determine into what products our

[1] As to the importance of this last, see Kenneth E. Boulding, *The Image* (1956). Cases in which substantive differences in the product are essentially pretexts for a differentiated image shade into cases in which the only difference is in the image. The distinction may be recognized "in principle," but in practice no sharp line can easily be drawn.

economic resources shall be directed? How many customers get the benefit of available tests? Is the range of choice wide enough but not too wide to enable him—in the light of his own limitations—to register his preferences effectively? There are quantitative problems of economy and waste in the creation of the products and in the guidance of customers' choices. Of course there are wastes. Progress is unavoidably wasteful, but must be accepted as worth its cost. The problem here is to identify avoidable "wastes" and minimize them; but this process is itself a form of progress involving time, exploration, and error. Thus the boundary between avoidable waste and unavoidable costs of progress is a movable one; what are now unavoidable costs may become avoidable waste as we learn more about ways of avoiding them. Coordinate with all these is the problem—with which economists feel more at home—of prices that yield reasonable returns on production conducted with reasonable efficiency and economy, in the conditions inseparable from progress.

Competition is a joint resultant of activities and adjustments in the fields of processes, products, selling efforts, and prices and can be understood only in terms of this joint character. This imposes well-nigh insuperable difficulties for the methods of analysis regularly employed by economic theory, of building models which isolate a single variable, leaving all others constant. The results of such models are not only incomplete but likely to be misleading. As other variables are added, the models not only become too unwieldy for effective aid to understanding, but involve more complicated calculations than business men do or can employ.[2] As a result, simpler interpretations, closer to actual behavior, become more serviceable, as we shall see.

The defects of the competitive process include, at one extreme, inefficiencies due to the uneconomically small size of some units and, at the other extreme, impairments of the qualitative direction and the quantitative effectiveness of competitive forces, some of which are due to the overgrown size and insufficient number of competing firms, while others are inherent in product differentiation. In this field the problem of the number of firms necessary to effective competition takes a special form, for which models drawn from "pure competition"

[2] Chamberlin's solution requires the business man to know the optimum price for every combination of product and selling appeal, the optimum product for every combination of selling appeal and price, and the optimum selling appeal for every combination of product and price. The resulting optimum of optima clearly overtaxes the analytical capacities of business decision-makers.

are of little use. As to the force of competitive pressures, cases of product differentiation range from situations of near monopoly to those of uneconomically severe (cutthroat) competition. Among the virtues of competition of differentiated products, the foremost is the incentive it affords for product innovation, and next to this, perhaps, is the quality of generating strong competitive pressures in situations where the number of competitors is smaller than formal theory regards as necessary. This does not mean that numbers may be disregarded, but it alters the problem and points to a different answer. Virtues and defects are perhaps most closely combined in the business methods of guiding customers' choices, which are highly effective in promoting ends, some of which are social necessities, while others cannot fail to be viewed with disgust, tinctured with alarm, by all right-thinking citizens. This is true despite controls aimed at requiring factual disclosure and preventing outright false statements. Means of improvement exist, but early elimination of evils is not to be anticipated.

It seems that this type of competition covers such a wide range of conditions that no single simplified model can possibly tell the essential story about it. It seems further that the prevalent forms of theoretical analysis concentrate on the defects to the neglect of the virtues and judge the defects by a standard of comparison (what *would supposedly* happen under pure or perfect competition) which is not only not feasible but is, in terms of a present-day economy, meaningless.[3] A question testing this proposition would be: Would "perfect competition" in the automobile industry require that, at every point where Ford cars are produced, there should be an indefinitely large number of competing producers of Ford cars, each large enough to attain maximum economies of large-scale production; or would it require that at every such point the existing volume of production of Ford cars should be divided among an indefinitely large number of producers which, despite their necessarily small size, would be as efficient in production as the existing Ford plant? Either answer is meaningless: the first implies an astronomically vast total demand, the second implies efficiency with impossibly small size. Yet one or the other is necessary if price at each point of production is to be determined by

---

[3] E. H. Chamberlin, "Monopolistic Competition Revisited," *Economica* (November 1951), pp. 343, 349, admits this meaninglessness, adding (footnote 2): "I must plead guilty myself to having done what is here held to be 'meaningless.' . . ." His plea in extenuation implies that this comparison was not intended to be used as a normative standard. It has been widely so construed and used.

pure competition. An alternative, which might be relevant so far as it went, but would be insufficient as well as undesirable, would be the standardization of all automobile production on a single make and model.

Instead of using such an arbitrarily imaginary standard, it seems that a useful analysis would leave room for a wide variety of actual conditions, while an appraisal would ask what conditions, consistent with the requirements of modern industry and trade, are also consistent with a healthy kind and degree of competition, by the tests already suggested.

2. Material Already Covered and Remaining Problems

The discussion in this chapter will build on materials that have been brought out in earlier chapters; and it may be worth while to review some relevant points in the background materials and to indicate the problems that remain. In the first place, I have chosen to reject the conception of the line between competition and monopoly derived from the requirements of precision in theoretical analysis, in which the (nonexistent) condition of "pure and perfect" competition is the only unqualifiedly competitive condition, and to subscribe rather to the conception that appears pertinent to the antitrust laws, which, as we have seen, find no monopolistic quality in product differentiation *per se,* but are concerned about obstructions to freedom of rivalry in this field.[4]

Along with this goes the principle that the condition described as a sloping demand function for the product of an individual producer can be consistent with the fullest degree of price competition (as well as competition in production, in selling effort, and in the design and selection of the product itself).[5] A contributory point is that demand

[4] See above, Chap. 3, Sec. 3.

[5] See above, Chap. 6, Sec. 1, and Chap. 8, Sec. 1. In place of the theoretical requirement of an infinitely elastic individual-demand function, the above analysis assigns a strategic position to whether the individual-demand function has a "margin elasticity" of more or less than unity, as determining whether it pays a firm to raise its price or to reduce it.

curves, drawn to represent the relation of volume of sales to price as a sole variable, necessarily neglect the vitally important factor of time, and their relevance is limited to fairly short-time adjustments.[6] Progressive changes over time are more important, especially the necessity of taking defensive competitive action against a threatened progressive decline in a firm's volume of business. It has also been brought out that cross-elasticities are larger for smaller firms, and that this difference is important as affecting the incentives to competitive action.[7]

A further point in support of the usefulness of finite elasticity is that it is generally necessary for a firm to earn some return above short-run marginal cost if its long-run returns are to cover either average cost or long-run marginal cost—the two being generally close to one another in the long run.[8] This should presumably be taken to refer to a representative firm: individual firms may make either profits or losses. There remains the problem whether the short-run margin above marginal cost, and the individual demand elasticity that generates it, have any inherent tendency to lead to economically sound cost-price adjustments, in which the short-run forces are in reasonable harmony with sound long-run behavior and adjustments. The fact that it is economically correct for a demand curve to have some slope proves nothing about what the economically correct slope is or whether it is purely a matter of chance that actual slopes are reasonably near the correct standard.

We have also looked at some of the differences in time perspectives of firms, which affect their competitive behavior; indicating that firms whose situation or perspective tend toward the lowest prices have a natural tendency to set limits on the prices available to their competitors. In these terms, the tangency theorem is seen as assuming that firms are shortsighted enough to injure their own interests by making profits that invite an excess of new entries: something that obviously may happen, but is not an inevitable result of product differentiation, if some firms have different perspectives.[9]

We have seen that competitive advantages gained by successful product innovation present a peculiarly difficult problem in trying to

---

[6] See above, Chap. 3, Sec. 9, and Chap. 7, Sec. 3. Cf. "The Uses of Diversity," *American Economic Review, Proceedings* (May 1958), pp. 474, 476.

[7] See above, Chap. 7, Secs. 2 and 3.

[8] See above, Chap. 6, especially Secs. 7 and 8.

[9] See above, Chap. 3, Sec. 10, and Chap. 5, Secs. 2 and 6.

appraise the extent to which such advantages represent net gains or improvements in the country's level of living and the extent to which they are purely relative, displacing one another in a repeated process of induced obsolescence, in which each novelty wipes out the novelty value of its predecessor without necessarily making any net addition to economic welfare.[10] In the aggregate, product innovations do leave a residue of gain by standards—such as that of physical health—with which no one could quarrel. But the residue effect on mental and social health is a more dubious matter, and authoritative standards are lacking. Consumers' preferences, under the conditions in which they are generated and expressed, are certainly not authoritative standards of welfare, and to accept them as such—as theoretical "welfare economics" does—is to abdicate the problem. If no authoritative yardstick is available in a free and democratic society, it is at least possible to examine the conditions necessary to successful choosing, and to compare them with the conditions that exist in the current American economy. It may be easier to identify conditions necessary and favorable for successful choosing than to define the choices that should result. At any rate, that easier task is one this chapter will undertake.

3. Types of Differentiation

On types of differentiation, volumes could be written, even if the discussion were strictly limited to matters bearing on the efficacy of competition and the discipline it enables the customer to exercise over the producer; and the kinds of complementary agencies that are needed to make up a system that can handle these functions with reasonable success. At the outset, the meaning of differentiation and homogeneity will stand some clarification. The homogeneity of a product, marketwise, has little to do with whether the product as it comes from the producers—say, the wheat farmers—is physically uniform: emphatically, it is not. Uniformity for marketing purposes is attained by a system of grading. If wheat, as traded in on the exchanges, conforms accurately to these grades, this is not because of the shape in which it comes from farms, but because of subsequent mixing operations by

[10] See above, Chap. 7, Sec. 3.

traders, upgrading a lot to bring it up to standard or downgrading a lot that has an excess of quality.

In contrast, if a manufacturer wants to establish a distinctively differentiated character for his product, one prerequisite is to see that it is uniform within itself. This uniformity is (imperfectly) secured by "quality control," including inspection and rejection of "seconds," which may be separately disposed of; also by guarantees and privileges of return, or free service where necessary to put the product in standard working condition. If the buyer cannot depend on the quality of the producer's product being the same in successive purchases (and he generally cannot), that undependability is in itself an inferiority from the standpoint of market acceptance.[11] Contrariwise, if a retailer wants to be homogeneous with other retailers in his class, he must not confine himself to one make of a given product, but must carry all the principal brands, or at least a selection enough like that of the other retailers so that the likelihood of some customer missing a favorite brand is negligible, and substantially all the buyers to whom his location is most accessible or convenient will trade with him on a convenience basis. If some of the other dealers offer substantial concessions in price, then convenience will have to compete against a price differential, and the lower prices will capture some of the most price-sensitive buyers, especially if it is not too inconvenient for them to buy from the price-cutting dealer less often and in larger lots than they would from the most conveniently located dealer.

This brings us to the distinction between purchases made in small units and frequently repeated, and those made in large units and at considerable intervals. In the latter case, advance study on the customer's part is called for, and many buyers will "shop around" before buying, if they can do it without too great inconvenience. For small and frequent purchases, the method of "trial and error" has a chance to work reasonably well, since little is risked and the chance for a second trial comes quickly. This, be it noted, does not mean that the buyer will always know if he has made a relatively poor choice, or will always be satisfied if he has made a relatively good one. His short-

---

[11] The kind of exception that illustrates the rule was described in Alvin S. Johnson's novel, *The Professor and the Petticoat* (1914), in which a newcomer to Texas was introduced to the local variety of cigars. He was told that in the same lot, one might be the best he had ever smoked, another the worst. If he picked a bad one, he was supposed to throw it away and try again. The market for a modern manufactured product would not be so tolerant of variability.

run experience in the use of a "repeat" product is far from an infalli-
ble guide to its quality, let alone its rating as compared to alternative
products. Experience will lead him to eliminate brands with which he
is definitely dissatisfied; beyond this, its operation is uncertain.

Frequency of purchase is related to the fact that some products
render their service in the act of being consumed, like food and fuel;
some render it by existing with as little change from time and wear as
possible, like a house or furniture or, on a level of less durability, a suit
of clothes; and some render their service by performing mechanical
operations which necessarily involve wear and tear, but in which this
is a thing to be minimized. The kind of knowledge needed for judgment of quality, before or after experience with the product in use,
varies with the kind of service rendered: nutritional, physiological,
structural, mechanical, or decorative—and the last is not to be rated
as nonessential, since beauty and harmony can be such vital elements
in the quality of living, while the opposite can be subtly and unconsciously destructive. But at least these qualities are visible, while many
of the others are invisible: inaccessible to mere inspection by the ordinary buyer. These invisible qualities affect safety and health, as well
as dependability and durability in performance, while the values involved in style and appearance include beauty, prestige, and social
acceptability, including the contrary desires for distinction (e.g., the
style leader) or personal individuality and for conformity.

These superficially contrary values may be integrated in a way of
living that maintains its basis in the cultural values of the past, while
experimenting with the instrumentalities of the present. Ideally, values
of the past should be modified or discarded only consciously and if
they deserve it in the light of altered ways of thinking, while experimenting should be guided by an awareness of its impact on the values
the individual holds. It is this enormously difficult and unstandardized
ideal, basic to a free and democratic society, which conventional
theoretical economics lumps under the belittling and myopic label
of "taste," misleadingly assumed to cover all elements in consumer
choosing and to be a purely individual matter about which no argument is possible, at least on the part of economists. We shall return
to this question in a moment. For the present it is clear from the foregoing that safety and health, including psychological health in the light
of growingly scientific knowledge, are not mere matters of "taste," and
cannot properly be left to the individual choice that is either unguided

or guided only by commercial agencies acting under strictly "business" motives. The idea that they are in fact so left is one of the fictions of individualist mythology.

The forms these types of value differentiation take vary widely as between houses, domestic appliances, automobiles, furniture, clothes, other textiles, foodstuffs, medicaments, and cosmetics. In a house, the customer judges its size, convenience, and appearance; he takes for granted that concealed wiring is not a fire hazard and that the floors have a margin of strength beyond the requirements of any load he may put on them. This sort of minimum standard is backed by legal standards, but beyond this there is much room for difference between well-built and jerry-built structures; and it is a fortunate purchaser who is personally qualified to detect these differences by inspection, or has qualified and disinterested advice at his disposal.

As to textiles, accumulated experience should enable the housewife to become a judge of staple types; but the ever-changing variety of synthetics presents problems beyond the reach of this kind of unaided judgment. To aid or supplement it, two kinds of information are available: more complete disclosure of content than is now required, and certifications based on tests of performance. As this is written, a bill is pending, calling for more complete disclosure of percentages of constituents, and is being opposed by the Textile Fabrics Association and other textile interests; the chief argument being that such information would be of little help to the consumer in judging whether the fabric "is durable, shrinkproof, colorfast, and will give adequate service."[12] The alternative is illustrated by the "Sanforized" label, certifying tested performance in resisting shrinkage and sponsored by a private firm. This is clearly a legitimate method, as far as it goes, for dealing with one feature of performance for which objective tests are badly needed. It does not fill all the needs that disclosure of content is designed to meet, and does not mean that all well-advertised brands are dependable warranties of good performance. In the current advertising it is being used as counterpropaganda against proposals to extend requirements of disclosure of content, and used with essentially the same type of appeal that has been used to promote uncritical reliance on

[12] Letter to the Editor of the *New York Times*, May 21, 1958, by A. M. Klurfeld, Executive Director, Textile Fabrics Association. Cf. reply by Representative Frank E. Smith, *ibid.*, May 28, 1958.

brands, rather than the vigilantly critical attitude that is called for.[13]

As to foodstuffs, we rely on public controls for assurance that milk does not come from tubercular cows, nor meat from diseased animals. As to preservation, there are packaging, canning, ordinary refrigeration, deep-freeze and chemical preservatives, all competing with one another. Since preservatives have multiplied beyond the government's capacity to test all of them, even with larger budgets than it has available, a real question has arisen as to the location of legal responsibility for their safety. In any case it seems to be rightly taken for granted that the unaided consumer is in no position to detect harmful elements and protect himself against them. Medicines are a clear case in which the doctor's professional advice is called for, while the "proprietary remedies" occupy one of the most dubious areas of consumer free choice. As to perfumes, they might appear to be clearly in the unstandardizable realm of "taste"; though the ad men may have gone beyond this with claims implying that the decisive key to quality is the capacity of acting as an erotic stimulant to the opposite sex. Is it conceivable that such claims might be susceptible to testing?

Products differ not only physically but in terms of services rendered in connection with them, and in all the ways in which they are presented as stimuli to purchase and the things that go to form the image of the product in the potential consumer's mind. In this matter packaging has come to be a major factor, aside from its effect in protecting the product. Important factors are the convenience and accessibility of distributors' facilities, the method and effectiveness of display, and information, demonstration, or persuasion offered by the salesman. Methods of distribution include the retail store that carries a selection of competing brands of a given product, or the store that is a distributing agent, nonexclusive or exclusive, for this particular product or for all or a major part of its business. The exclusive agency obviously means that the customer must shop around at a number of such agencies to make a comparative choice, instead of finding competing brands behind one counter.

A more serious effect, as the system of exclusive agencies spreads,

[13] *Ibid.*, May 21, 1958, p. 20. In a full-page spread, the real reason for confidence in the label is stated in a detached line of fine print, while the eye-catching appeal is to irrelevant flattery—"Let your woman's intuition guide you"—to depend on the brand. The net effect is to divert attention away from tests in general, including those that give this particular brand its rational claim to confidence.

is in making it more difficult for a young and small firm to introduce a new brand. The firm may need to be able to offer a well-rounded line before it can break into the market effectively. Or the producers of a new product, sales of which have not grown large enough to support exclusive agencies in every town, may have to choose between the resulting lack of accessibility and the use of existing retailers, who may not make effective demonstrators for a specialized product. In this way size affords a distributional advantage. This reaches its highest development in the system of exclusive agencies for the sale of automobiles, which requires giant size to enable one make of car to have in each town an exclusive agent to whom that make of car is his sole or principal business.

4. Reasons for Homogeneity or Differentiation

If, as already seen, the homogeneous or differentiated character of a product requires deliberate action to bring it about, the reasons for different action in different cases are to be found partly in the character of the producer and the productive process and partly in the character of the market and the type of customer. Extractive producers can create homogeneity within their own product or with others, by selecting and grading; but the small farmer can in this way establish distinctive character for his individual product only for a small local market. It takes a very large grower or a cooperative to give meaning to brands in a regional or national market. Where grading is used to make different producers' products homogeneous in regional or national markets, this is to be understood in the light of the fact that the commodity is a material and purchasers are traders or processors, not ultimate consumers. They may want to turn the material into a product that will be distinctive in its appeal to consumers' tastes; but what they want to know about the material is how it will perform in the productive process, and, for this purpose, physical uniformity is a prime requisite. It is cheaper for them if the market certifies this; otherwise, they must stand the cost of making their own tests. Finished products constitute the main market in which product differentiation can be an asset and not a liability—always assuming that it can be made to appear attractive to a substantial number of customers.

The seller of a differentiated product may attempt either to minimize or to maximize the difference between his product and its closest rivals, physically or in terms of the "image" it presents to the mind of the buyer. At the two extremes, physically different products may be made to appear identical, or products identical in the physical essentials may be differentiated by branding and packaging, or superficial alterations in appearance, with accompanying aid from sales appeal.[14] Such tactics, it may be needless to say, are beamed at the individual consumer, directly or via persuading dealers that the product will attract consumers. The more logical case, and perhaps the more normal one, is one in which differences in selling appeal are based on genuine differences in the product—whether these differences are important or superficial.

Imitation may be used aggressively by a firm trying to get a share of the demand that has been built up by a successful variety or brand; or it may be used defensively by a firm whose sales are being encroached on by a rival's successful variant, if the defensive firm accepts its rival's success as representing the market's preference, to which it is prudent to conform. However, the alternative method, of a counter-differentiation, is always open, provided the research department has something in readiness. This is, of course, the stronger reaction, and also involves the greater uncertainty. A firm that is relatively weak, especially in research on product design, may be unlikely to try it. Otherwise, there seems to be no rule determining which reaction will be followed.

The homogeneity of a product may, it seems, become a talking point in the market for opposite reasons. The cut-rate seller has an interest in demonstrating that his product is "just as good"; and if he can cite the fact that all brands meet the same governmental specifications, that may be an effective way of making his price differential efficient in promoting sales. Cut-rate sellers of vitamins are a case in point, suggesting that this may be a stage in the bringing down of brand prices. Discount houses get the same effect by selling standard brands at reduced margins, economizing on their own service rather than on the

---

[14] As to the former, "adulteration" is a case in point, with the proviso that it may be an economically desirable economizing of scarce components, without deterioration of the service value of the product.

quality of the product. Mail-order houses face a special problem, in that they sometimes buy producers' standard grades at a discount, without the standard brand, and are unable overtly to advertise the identity of their offering with the brand the producer is selling at a higher price. Their own brands carry less prestige. On the other hand, in the cement industry, selling in a different market structure and to dealers or contractors, producers have stressed the uniformity of their standard grade, welcoming a market for this grade in which, despite minor variations above minimum required standards, no producer could or would use his brand name as a basis for a premium price, or for a premium-quality appeal that might cause competitors to feel that they could not compete without establishing a price differential below that of the superior brand.[15]

5. *Convenience of Dealers' Locations*

In terms of convenience of dealers' location, differences of location are compounded with product differentials and with different types of dealers, to create a variety of patterns that cannot be derived from theoretical models which neglect this compounding and deal with one variable at a time. Students of marketing have long recognized the distinction between products for which buyers will want to shop around and compare offerings and those of which single purchases are made on a basis of convenience. The first case occurs where dealers' offerings are differentiated, single purchases are large, and the buyer makes them infrequently. Then, once the first dealer in an area is reasonably well located, if there is trade enough in the area to support a second dealer, who will have his connections still to establish, his best location is near the first, where customers can inspect and compare his offerings with maximum convenience. The same consideration holds more strongly for a third or fourth dealer, and the trade tends to cluster. A wholesale produce market clusters for essentially the same reason. In towns of moderate size, the buyer's automobile makes this clustering tendency more elastic, without eliminating it. Parking space becomes

[15] The basing-point pricing structure, of which the cement industry afforded a conspicuous example, will be discussed later.

important, and supermarkets need more space than is available in built-up centers. The advantage of making the maximum use of a single act of parking tends to the diversifying of establishments that have good parking facilities, or to the clustering found in suburban shopping centers. This also emphasizes the fact that convenience of location is relative to the customer's common orbit of movement and is not uniquely measured by distance from his or her residence.

In the "convenience" type of trade, single purchases are small, and the different dealers will generally have minimized the differences between their offerings in the way already suggested, so that few customers will take the trouble to shop around. Then dealers will tend to scatter (within limits set by physical conditions and zoning restrictions), each seeking a location that will be most convenient for a particular constituency of customers. Discount houses, being necessarily fewer than "regular" dealers and competing in terms of cheapness rather than convenience, face a different set of conditions in their choice of location.

6. Hotelling's Model and Others

This problem has been explored theoretically, notably by Hotelling in his well-known early article.[16] In it he built a model of a linear market with buyers evenly spaced and transportation costs uniform with distance, in which there are two sellers of a homogeneous product, each selling at a uniform price at his establishment, while the buyers pay the transport costs. The sellers are initially located near the opposite ends of the market, and each seeks his most profitable price, assuming the other's price will not change in response.[17] Under these combined conditions, each seller would have (ex ante) a sloping in-

[16] See H. Hotelling, "Stability in Competition," *Economic Journal* (March 1929), pp. 41-57. The title indicates that his first interest is in finding a determinate solution for a case of duopoly, escaping from the instability stressed especially by Francis Y. Edgeworth (*Papers Relating to Political Economy*, 1925, Vol. 1, pp. 400-07). The second theme—the tendency to locate too close together—appears to conflict with the first. The article illustrates the pitfalls of reasoning by analogy and of dealing with variables in isolation, which act jointly in practice. The present writer will indicate his dissents in the following pages.

[17] Hotelling, *op. cit.*, p. 46.

dividual curve, leading to a determinate equilibrium price above marginal cost (assumed as zero). Hotelling then makes the sellers' locations adjustable, concluding that they "will crowd together as closely as possible."[18] He then qualifies this conclusion (for reasons discussed below) but continues to hold that they locate closer than is economically correct. He then extends this principle by analogy to sellers of differentiated products located side by side and concludes that such products are made too much like one another.

As to location, the problem hinges on a competitive buffer zone between the sellers, and the backyard of each, which each holds securely so long as it is small, relative to the buffer zone, because its volume would not repay the price cut necessary to invade it. Using Hotelling's basic figures and assumptions, one finds a critical point where the buffer zone occupies the central half of the market, each seller having one quarter as his backyard. When the buffer zone gets smaller than this, although neither seller can increase his profit by a small price reduction from the former equilibrium level, he can do so by a reduction large enough to capture his rival's backyard. (This sudden discontinuity is a peculiarity of Hotelling's spatial model and does not correspond to conditions of differentiated products.) Then it pays the rival to respond, defeating the invasion but leaving both parties worse off than before. Hotelling mentions this as a danger threatening to upset the equilibrium, but does not mention that it comes into effect if the sellers get closer to one another than the quartile adjustment which he considers correct as minimizing total transport cost.[19] Any closer approach would change the equilibrium into a war unless the sellers refrain because of the certainty that such a price slash would be met, while continuing to make smaller price adjustments, A changing his price on the assumption that B's price will not be changed in response, in the face of the fact that B always does change his price in the light of his new individual-demand function resulting from A's price change. This double standard of expectations may not be wholly nonsensical, but if so, it is for reasons outside the model. And the scope for small competitive adjustments would in any case approach zero as the sellers' locations approached one another.

But the above analysis carries the logic of the model further than is warranted by its oversimplification of reality. Hotelling considered

[18] *Ibid.*, pp. 51, 53.
[19] *Ibid.*, p. 53.

the adding of more variables, but made clear that this would vastly complicate the analysis. And in his closing remarks about product differentiation, he appears to have been guided about as much by observation and insight as by deduction from his spatial model.[20] Thus he recognized the fact (not derivable from his model) that it takes more than a minimal product difference to establish a customer preference that will lead to a sloping individual-demand function, which he requires. Nevertheless, his analysis misses the essentially simple reason (already discussed) why the "shopping" type of trade tends to cluster and the "convenience" type to scatter. Perhaps the chief moral consists of the limitations and pitfalls of rigorous mathematical analysis in this field.

Using spatial analogy in a different way, Lawrence Abbott reaches a conclusion opposite to that of Hotelling: namely, that a producer selecting a product to sell in a quality spectrum occupied by quality competitors will try to locate as far as he can from his nearest competitor, not as close as he can.[21] Chamberlin, starting with a model like Hotelling's but confining it to its original spatial meaning, comes closer to the scattering tendency than to the clustering tendency when the number of sellers is larger than two.[22]

7. Horizontal and Vertical Differentiation

As already indicated, product differentiation can be within a given range of price and quality, and between higher or lower ranges of price and of presumptive quality appeal.[23] (The question of the extent to which actual quality agrees with relative price must be left open for later discussion. One is not warranted in assuming that they correspond exactly, or even closely.) These two types of differentiation may for convenience be called horizontal and vertical. They are worth dis-

[20] *Ibid.*, pp. 54, 56.
[21] Lawrence Abbot, *Quality and Competition* (1955), pp. 140–60, especially p. 147.
[22] E. H. Chamberlin, *The Theory of Monopolistic Competition* (1933), Appendix C. Chamberlin distinguishes clearly the "shopping" type of trade and the reasons why it tends to cluster, spatially.
[23] See above, Chap. 7, Sec. 1.

tinguishing because they can sometimes lead to different types of behavior; as, for example, a general strengthening of demand may actually reduce demand for the lowest grades, as the center of gravity of demand moves upward in the vertical scale.

This distinction is well illustrated in the case of goods that sell in "price lines," as women's ready-made garments do. There are differences between dresses within the same price line, and differences between dresses selling at higher or lower price lines. Incidentally, this is a case in which the price is made before the product. In the same way, though with less formalized precision, there are these two kinds of difference between automobiles: those in the same price class and those in higher or lower price classes. In the one case, producers are exploring the differences (and similarities) of taste and preference among buyers of similar price-paying willingness and ability; in the other they are also comparing the preferences of buyers in their own price bracket with those in the next higher and next lower price-paying groups, who together constitute the marginal buying group for whose trade they are in active competition. Having designed their car, the producers hope to be able to persuade buyers that it is the best car in its price range or the cheapest car in its quality range; that as compared to the next cheaper car it is enough better to be worth the existing price differential; and that as compared to the next most expensive car it is, if not equally good at least near enough to make the difference in quality less than the difference in price.

One very meaningful way of looking at this kind of rivalry is to say that what the individual producer is offering as his individual product, and what the customer is valuing to see if it is worth what is charged for it, is not the car as a physical whole, but the differences between this car and its closest competitors.[24] This, I believe, affords a truer ap-

[24] This is an altered way of expressing and applying J. B. Clark's principle that commodities are "bundles of utilities," and that different buyers are marginal for different units in the bundle. (See his *Distribution of Wealth*, 1899, pp. 234-42.) In this passage he stressed what I have here called vertical differentiation, tracing the chain of qualities that constituted his "bundle" all the way up from the crudest and most imperfect substitute to the highest grade in the market, and regarding this highest grade as simultaneously embodying all the utilities added by the successive steps in the series. In his independent formulation of marginal utility theory, this was his uniquely distinctive contribution. In applying it, his emphasis was on an aggregate of consumers' surpluses arising from the whole series, and the general abandonment of the idea of consumers' surplus may have led to undeserved neglect of the "bundles" principle itself. My present use of this prin-

proach than the proposition so often encountered, that where product differentiation exists, each producer has a monopoly of his own product. This appears open to objection on the ground that mere uniqueness does not carry the unified control that is the essence of monopoly unless others are precluded or obstructed from imitating the unique features of the thing in question. The marginal buyer is comparing this car with another designed for success in just this comparison, and he is appraising the difference between the two offerings.

The vertical scale of quality gradations may be broadly divided into luxury, standard, economy, and inferior grades, with the proviso that these gradations are relative to the market and change with time, as well as differing from country to country. For example, standard grades of durable appliances in this country would be in the luxury grades in Italy.[25] There are gradations within these broad divisions, and even more in the market for turn-in and resale of used durables, since these vary with the age of the item and the grade it had when new, and an older Buick may compete with a younger Ford. "Inferior substitutes" are defined by Wellisz as:

> Goods which have a lower initial price than the "standard" products, but which over their lifetime have a higher cost per unit service than the latter. Shoddy clothes and cheap mechanical products which are subject to high maintenance costs and which give unreliable service are familiar examples. . . . Such goods find a market because the purchasers are unaware of the eventual expense, or because they cannot mobilize the necessary funds to purchase the higher priced "standard" goods. . . . The demand for inferior substitutes is largely explainable through the inadequacy of credit facilities available to small firms and to consumers. The production of "shoddy goods" is largely confined to countries in which time-payment schemes are nonexistent or carry a prohibitive cost."[26]

Needless to add, the cost of time-payment methods needs to be in-

---

ciple is not concerned with consumer surplus, but with the way in which the market objectifies the difference between two variants of a product, attaching a price rating to it in the course of the horizontal and vertical competitive rivalry to which one variant is subject. It may be noted that Chamberlin's analysis accords primary position to horizontal differentiation, assuming that the different producers have identical individual-demand curves.

[25] See Stanislaw H. Wellisz, "The Coexistence of Large and Small Firms: A Study of the Italian Mechanical Industries," *Quarterly Journal of Economics* (February 1957), pp. 116, 118-20.

[26] *Ibid.*, p. 119.

cluded in reckoning whether the cheaper product is more expensive in terms of ultimate service value.

Wellisz defines "economy models" as those "which render poorer service but which are in fact cheaper than the standard products," using a hand sewing machine as an example.[27] In the American market, it seems that there is room for a kind of economy model which renders essentially standard service in terms of performance, but lacks what by simpler standards would be rated as luxury features of gadgets, push-button automaticity, styling, and superperformance, which are embodied in the models that have become standard in the prosperous American market. The above definition of inferior substitutes would include many second-hand articles, sales of which have not been eliminated by the availability of relatively cheap time-payment plans. Thus, while Wellisz points to a seldom-mentioned service of time-payment plans in eliminating shoddy goods, this is not the whole story and needs also to be balanced against the shifting of purchases upward toward luxury grades, both in the new market and among the choices available in the market for used articles. One feature might be enabling producers to establish luxury features as standard, in the market created by time-payment selling.

8. The Customer as Limited Sovereign

Starting with the principle that the effectiveness of competition is limited by the customer's ability to judge what he is getting, we have seen that the rule of *caveat emptor* is replaced by minimum standards, publicly set, in an increasing number of cases in which the buyer's mistakes could endanger safety and health—his own or that of others. In the case of automobiles, this principle is extended to continued operation, covering periodic checks on the safety of the vehicle and on the driver's own competence to operate it. In some cases the controls extend from minimum standards to prohibition, including sale of liquor to minors, or to anyone in prohibition areas, and sale or possession of weapons or narcotics. Freedom *not* to consume is limited, as in the case of children whose parents neglect their nutrition or medical care.

[27] *Ibid.*, p. 120.

Beyond these essentials lie the unstandardized values which can more or less appropriately be treated as matters of "taste" and the proper field of consumer free choice. Here particular individual vagaries are presumably more important to the individual than to society, while in the aggregate the freedom to pursue them is part of the way of life of a free society. This extends beyond such matters as taste in foods, and into matters having a bearing on health, which are not regarded as appropriate for regulation, such as the application of the modern science of nutrition to the choice of a well-balanced diet. Here education, rather than control, is relied on. Food for the mind is not less important than food for the body; and here also most of the choices of adult consumers are treated as matters of "taste."

However, in this realm compulsory education for minors is a major limitation on the freedom not to consume, the responsibility extending to the parents. But in the selection of mental nourishment, negative controls are limited by the principle of free speech and press, and positive religious indoctrination is limited by the separation of church and state, which in excluding sectarian instruction from the schools, may go too far toward minimizing recognition of the importance of religion itself as a basis of the ethical standards on which western civilization has been built. Negative controls in the mental realms exist, but are limited. They cover libel, obscenity, and propaganda tending to subversive action (especially in time of public danger), as distinct from revolutionary philosophizing.

It might seem that in the physical realm, some things are too important to be left at the mercy of the vagaries of consumer sovereignty, while freedom of thought and expression is regarded as too important *not* to be so left, even though the permitted degrees of freedom carry recognized dangers. This double standard may be reconciled by the idea that everyone—or nearly everyone—wants physical safety and health, and that in this realm objective standards are possible, to supplement the average consumer's limited ability to judge what he is getting; while in the mental realm the question what people want is precisely the thing that must be left open for debate. We may not nowadays hold the full optimistic faith of Jefferson or of Milton, that truth can never in the end be worsted if it is left free to combat error, and we are confronted with propaganda that deliberately renounces the open and honest advocacy they envisaged and systematically disguises its real aims, but we still hold that authoritative thought control is the greater danger, and that other countermeasures are to be sought. As to the question whether modern massive advertising is a form of thought control, subtle or not-so-subtle, our answers must be sought in the same spirit.

This leads to the next major question: that of implementing and guiding customer choosing, in which under modern conditions some kind of advertising plays an indispensable part, but only a part, other agencies being essential to an effective system of guidance and safeguards. And such a system needs to be differentiated, to fit the needs and capabilities of different kinds of customers. These include the giant firm, with the resources and the interest to acquire full knowledge of what it is getting; the small firm with the interest but not the resources, which needs and will use the services of outside specialists on occasion; the merchant who is a specialist or who handles a varied line; and the consumer. Consumers may be broadly divided into adults buying for themselves, adults selecting and budgeting for the requirements of a household, adolescents, and children, with some allowance for the increasing extent to which parental guidance fails to control minors. Among consumers, some are careful buyers, others careless; some more price conscious and others less; some trustful of advertising claims and some skeptical. We may pay primary attention to consumers, whose capacities and facilities are most sketchy relative to the requirements of their exacting task as purchasers.[28]

Among reasons for this sketchiness is the fact that the process of selective elimination of the least efficient, which operates among business firms, has little or no application to consumers. We are all consumers, and we are not bankrupted out of this role by inefficiency. Our mistakes are not easily proved, and those who suffer from them are seldom in a position to marshal the pertinent evidence. A consumer may become a connoisseur in some field that commands his or her special interest, and in this field may know more than those from whom he or she buys; but such fields of connoisseurship are very unlikely to cover the kinds of products on which the bulk of consumer outlay is spent; and the cost of becoming a connoisseur in everything one

[28] See W. C. Mitchell, "The Backward Art of Spending Money," *American Economic Review* (June 1912), pp. 269-81, reprinted in volume of same title (1937), pp. 3-19. It is difficult to imagine a more distinguished analysis of this theme, and remarkably few allowances need to be made for the passage of forty-nine years since it was written.

buys is prohibitive. The typical American consumer is supplied with income that gives him means of occupying his leisure time as well as his working time and raises the "opportunity-cost" of time spent in becoming an expert buyer, to a point such that relatively few American consumers seriously attempt it, because, in terms of "psychic income," the prospective gains—always uncertain—lose out in the contest with more immediate demands and attractions. But he—or she—does to some extent judge by comparative performance on "repeat" purchases and by the advice of acquaintances on more important ones.

9. Selling Activities

Selling activities are commonly thought of as occasioned by product differentiation, though actually they are necessary in disposing of any product that is not sold on an organized market. That is, they arise from the quoted-price type of selling. But their most characteristic forms stem from product differentiation. These forms are almost innumerable, and this study must select a few for discussion, hoping that they will prove typical. Different forms of selling bring out different methods; methods appropriate to selling materials or equipment to a manufacturer would clearly not be appropriate to selling tooth paste or cosmetics to an ultimate consumer. Basic forms include sale through independent dealers who handle rival makes, sale through nonexclusive or exclusive agencies, or direct. The mail-order house met a special need in a distinctive way, and is adapting to new conditions, especially the automobile, which enables customers to reach its branch stores. The discount house seems also to have become a distinct type. But occasional mail orders taken by regular-type dealers do not appear to constitute a successful type.

Methods include personal visits from salesmen, advertising to eye and ear, display of product, demonstration of product, servicing of product, gratuities to purchasing officials, and reciprocal buying. Salesmen's visits are hardly economic except in selling to producers or to some kinds of dealers. Advertising, with all its wastes, is a more economical way to reach large numbers. Advertising in newspapers and

magazines, and in mailed circulars, is perhaps best adapted to convey-
ing information. It is subsidized by the pertinent sectors of the postal
deficit. Advertising by radio and television have their distinctive capacities and limitations. Taking up advertising as a representative form
of selling effort, it is a means of sales promotion that incidentally
serves as a chief agency of consumer guidance; and this dual character
raises awkward questions how much these two functions have in common, and at what points and how seriously they conflict.

The first and basic service of advertising is to make potential buyers aware that certain goods are offered. With this goes necessarily
some information about the product: the irreducible minimum being
enough to identify the product—by brand or otherwise—and the want
it claims to satisfy. Almost equally necessary, unless the customer is
expected to buy out of curiosity, is identification of the particular
want-satisfying properties that distinguish this make or brand. This
rule may be varied where, in order to arouse curiosity, a series of ad-
vertisements starts without identification, leaving this to come later,
after interested attention has been enlisted. An outstanding example
was the original introduction of the Gillette safety razor, and a resi-
dential enterprise in the New York district recently employed the
same device. Advertising generally includes further information, which
is selective in the light of the kind of sales appeal that accompanies
it. This information is of use, quite aside from the confidence the
buyer may or may not have in the claims that are made for the product; and it overlaps the more controversial role of suggestion and
persuasion, which can neither be wholly segregated nor dismissed
wholesale as illegitimate or valueless. It is part of the modification of
buyers' wants, which may be usefully educational or pernicious. Here
social appraisal cannot avoid qualitative judgments.

The basic method of appeal is to enlist some strong existing interest
(ranging from highest to lowest) and to connect it (correctly or in-
correctly) with the product being promoted. The interests appealed to
include health, security, family affection, beauty, social acceptability,
sex, recreation, restlessness and the desire for new experience, prestige,
economy or cupidity, humor and vanity (shrewdly used to disarm skepticism). A recent variant is self-spoofing by advertisers, apparently an
attempt to enlist humor in the disarming of buyers' skepticism and resistance to inanities by going part way with them. But if the script-
writer shares these reactions, he may go too far for the tolerance of

his agency or his medium. The stimulation of such attitudes can be a threat to the vulnerable points of interested propaganda.

This brings us to the role of the advertising agency, which sells to the producer its generalized *expertise* in the arts and applied sciences of salesmanship, to which it will add a study of the particular features of his product and its market, combining them in its selling program. The intervention of this specialized middleman cannot fail to have a profound and pervasive effect on the character of advertising guidance —and misguidance. Much depends on the standards of the reputable agency. Agencies of various sorts are presumably responsible for some of the best and most serviceable features of advertising and some of the worst and most disserviceable. These latter are found in advertising beamed at consumers of whose scale of values and level of critical intelligence the advertising specialist has obviously formed a very low opinion. Can it be that these specialists have developed a bent of workmanship which gives them a bias toward overemphasizing, in their picture of consumers, just those traits which the specialists best know how to manipulate? And do the surveys of market response to different appeals, on which the advertising specialist relies, give disproportionate weight to short-run responses, and too little to the longer-run reactions in which the lessons of experience have a chance to register?

10. Objective Guidance, Including Testing of Products

Against definitely false statements, the consumer has legal protection, plus some limited requirements of disclosure of content. As to the arts of psychological manipulation and misleading implication, his often-dormant critical faculties might well be activated and exercised on this kind of material. He has, if he will use it, a splendid opportunity to practice applied logic in appraising implications that stop short of definite statement, and asking why they stop short. Instead of merely resenting the more misleading devices of this sort, it would be more useful if educators would use them as examples for analysis in appropriate courses, selecting both political and economic examples and, in each area, appeals that will stand critical examination and others that will not.[29]

The outcry which such a course would create would afford a fair index of the need for it, and of the groups who have a vested interest in techniques of persuasion that might suffer from such scrutiny. If the outcry prevented the course from being given—as it probably would—an alternative would be a course which explains the techniques of advertising to those who might want to use them, but is also available to some who might be helped as consumers by understanding the advertising tactics they would confront. The defect of such a course might be that, being given by a reputable school of business, it would probably concentrate on expounding serviceable techniques and fail to include sufficient exposure of the other kinds. Courses in consumer economics offer another approach. Such exposure, in one form or another, is an important feature of education for life in the modern community.

Objective guidance for consumers is available from a variety of sources, starting with courses in household economics. But objective guidance may come from a source that has an economic interest in the result. Life insurance companies have an economic interest in promoting health, and they make objective advice available; other insurance companies have the same kind of interest in reducing risks of fire and accident. It may be a nice question whether a mutual savings bank is a disinterested agency in its competition with the attractions of installment buying; in any case its urging to receive interest rather than pay it faces an uphill contest.

More specific aids to consumers consist in making available the benefits of technically competent testing of products. This may be done in various ways and by various agencies, starting with the testing of their own products done by reputable firms with a long-run interest in maintaining the standing of any products with which the firm's name is identified. In this case the consumer judges the firm rather than the specific product, in the first instance, subject to such comparison of performance as he is in a position to make, with the chance to change if performance is definitely unsatisfactory. This is in addition to legal requirements of disclosure and of truthful statement, already mentioned. Further tests may be made privately or publicly.

[29] The writer's pet series of questions would be: "What impression is this statement intended to convey? Does it state this explicitly? If it could state it explicitly would it not do so? If it does not, why not?"

Public testing of consumer products in general is not a live issue, since, as we have seen, present budgetary resources are insufficient for testing of all new products for harmful effects on health alone. Rating of products on grounds of general performance would raise stubborn questions of the impact on the interest of producers who might get an inferior rating. Questions would be raised about the adequacy of sampling, or claims would be made that the product had been improved since a given rating was made. A product might rank differently on different items of performance, making an over-all rating inappropriate, especially if it were decided that gradings should be reported only by listing products that were satisfactory. In the latter case, producers whose product was just below a critical line might have even more grievance, as compared to those just above, than if the ratings were reported in detail.

How much consideration should be given to the interests, or rights, of the producer of a product that is rated by competent tests as inferior? We need not waste time arguing whether such ratings violate a producer's "right" to sell his product if he can find buyers. The hidden premise here is that this "right" covers buyers who would not buy if they knew what they were getting; and the buyers' right to that kind of knowledge takes precedence, being in harmony with the social interest in a market that is well informed. But here, as in other cases of changing the rules while the game is going on, there are questions of equity in the speed or abruptness of the change. One might imagine a case in which consumers' demand is suddenly converted to 100 per cent reliance on test ratings of products, and that these ratings are in strong disagreement with relative prices. It might be apprehended that firms whose products show a low rating would face a disastrous slump in sales, creating local unemployment which might not be made up for by increases in the sales of other firms. There might be fear of a loss of confidence in the quality of consumers' goods in general, resulting from the disparities between quality and price and leading to a general reduction of the willingness of consumers to buy.

Actually, no such sudden shift in the basis of consumer buying is likely. What might be expected, at most, would be a more gradual pressure in which firms whose products had good ratings would get an increased share of the natural growth of demand, while others might face a moderate decline in sales that would put them under competitive pressure to price their products at a differential below the higher-rated ones, to make up for the lower product rating in the minds of those consumers who are sensitive to such considerations, and avoid losing their trade. The price reduction might be regarded as a short-run makeshift policy, to be followed up by a move to improve the quality of the product and its test rating: something that would naturally take longer than a price reduction. The net effect in a longer run should be to make the scale of prices, relative to qualities, correspond more closely with the realities of the products; and the further effect of this should be an improvement in consumers' confidence that they would get their money's worth if they bought goods. This should take the place of any decline of confidence that might occur in the short run.

Since the government is unlikely to occupy this field of general test rating of products, the field is left for private agencies, certifying certain products as of satisfactory quality, or rendering their services and issuing their reports to subscribers. The number of subscribers to such services is growing, but is not large enough to have a decisive effect on the market. If the growth continues, as it seems likely to do, its effect will probably still be limited because there will presumably always be a considerable fraction of the consuming public who will not be interested enough to subscribe, or to spend the time and effort necessary to study the reports and brief themselves for every substantial purchase. If we should suffer a combination of prolonged dull times and price inflation, this might make consumers attach more importance to getting the greatest possible value out of their spending, and therefore make them more willing to make substantial use of such services of guidance.

The private testing agency operates, of course, subject to the legal remedies available to producers who may be injured by its reports; and therefore must be scrupulous in confining them to the objective facts and findings of the sample tests, indicating the character and limitations of the evidence and not generalizing beyond it. What it may accomplish, despite the caution with which it has to operate, is to enlarge the quality-sensitive and price-sensitive sector of consumers, this being the sector from which come the most effective competitive pressures. More than this, it arms its special quota of consumers with a basis for choice that takes in the whole array of offerings in the market and is not limited to the brands with which the individual consumer has had experience. Such consumers might be expected, on "repeat" purchases, to show less tendency to go on buying the same brand merely because one has bought it before, so long as it is not positively unsatisfactory.

As to this, reported figures of "repeat" sales in the automobile market seem significant. "Nearly 70 per cent of the drivers of low-priced brands will buy the same brand again. About half the owners of medium-priced makes will remain loyal to their brands. Owner loyalty in the high-priced field is high. Cadillac's great strength is due to the fact that nearly 95 per cent of the owners come back for another Cadillac."[30] These differences in percentages invite reflection and interpretation; but for our present purpose the most striking thing is that in spite of these high percentages of repeat sales, indicating brand loyalty, there is intense competition for the replacement purchasers who do not buy their former brand, plus the new sales that represent a net increase in the number of cars, plus some uncertain fraction of the repeat sales which are not unalterably committed, but would shift to some other make if the present one showed a decline in the attractiveness of its offering, relative to those of its competitors. Allowing for these factors, one might roughly estimate that, where 70 per cent of car owners buy the same make again, fully half of current sales have to be competed for, aggressively or defensively. And this competition is strenuous, for the firms that have not succeeded in maintaining their percentage share of total sales.

As to the effect on this competition of a possible growth in the use of professional test ratings, it is subject to a heavy discount because the factors of style and appearance count for so much in this market and are matters of taste. And while flashy performance can be measured, its value is also mainly a matter of taste. By and large, the effect of competent test ratings might be to increase some buyers' awareness and knowledge of features of performance, including dependability and durability, and to give these features somewhat more weight than they would otherwise have, as against style and appearance. It does not appear likely that this would increase the danger of disaster to firms that are having difficulties in this competition of giants. For example, the difficulties that have beset Chrysler in the past decade appear to have stemmed more from guessing wrong as to what style features would find favor with the market, than to any technical inferiorities that technical tests might reveal. In industries in which style

[30] See "Chrysler's Private Depression," *Fortune* (June 1958), pp. 129, 184.

features are less important, relative to performance, the immediate impact might be greater, but unlikely to be revolutionary; and the long-run effect could hardly fail to be salutary.

11. Position of Producers and Dealers

These various methods of improving the basis of consumers' choice cannot be expected to produce perfect results; and much will continue to depend on the care and integrity with which producers themselves safeguard the quality and performance of their products. Wherever performance is traceable to the product that is responsible, the firm that looks to the long-run stability of its position has a strong incentive to safeguard quality; since if it does not, consumer dissatisfaction will become serious in time, even if the majority of consumers are relatively inefficient choosers. Firms with shorter perspectives tend to be less dependable; and the worst situations seem likely to arise in the case of new products or products that are newly finding an enlarged market, in which satisfactory standards have not been established, and numerous firms of varied character are competing. Some are too small for adequate research and testing of their products, some are unscrupulous; and the weeding out of unsatisfactory brands has not yet done its work. In one such case, where fraud and misrepresentation were reported as rampant, it was suggested by a member of the industry that the industry's trade association might assume responsibility. Such an association would have an interest in preventing the whole industry from being discredited by the practices of its least dependable members. In this respect, competitive pressures work in both directions, and the problem is to strengthen those working upward, and weaken the others.

If the individual consumer lacks the help of comprehensive test ratings of products, the number of brands he can effectively compare is narrowly limited. In the case of many products, there are vastly more brands than he can compare, and more than a retailer can afford to keep on his shelves. This is true, even after allowing for local preferences that may reduce the number offered for choice in any one area. Then the selecting is done in the first instance by dealers, in the light of their judgment as to what brands are likely to move in good volume, at margins profitable to the dealer and giving reasonable satisfaction to his customers. If one brand does not move well, his normal course is to drop it and try another. Insofar as national advertising has built up demand, the dealer's selling task is made easier; and insofar as the dealer is allowed a liberal margin, the producer may enlist the dealer's interest in pushing his particular brand, subject always to its capacity to give reasonable satisfaction, and to the check exercised by some fraction of his customers who may have access to product ratings, and to other dealers who compete more definitely in price. The widening of the effect of consumer selection beyond the few brands between which effective choice can be made in this way, depends on a species of chain effect in which dealers are in competition with others who carry selections that are different, at least in part, and these with still others. Otherwise the multitude of brands, especially in some prepared foodstuffs, could not all be marketed because single dealers could not carry all of them. This chain effect is reinforced by the consumers' grapevine: the comparing of notes between consumers who deal at different shops, and whose combined experience covers a wider range than that of any one.

12. Some Conclusions

For effective competition, it is necessary that the total number of producers and brands, between which some kind of competitive selection operates, should be substantially larger than the limited number between which any one consumer can make successful choice. Otherwise, numbers would be too few for effective competition among established firms, and there would not be room for new firms, with new product variants, to enter the market and have a chance to survive on their merits. It follows that great importance attaches to anything that extends the scope of effective choosing beyond the range of the individual's direct experience. This includes rating tests (or failing these, the consumers' grapevine) and the chain effect of competition between dealers who carry partially different selections of products.

This process of consumer choice is necessarily a decidedly imperfect mechanism for selecting those producers who best serve the consumers' interests; nevertheless it is a good deal more effective than might be thought, from an analysis that concentrates on its weakest links. To sum up, the consumer needs protection against his own mistakes, where safety and health are threatened; and he needs better guidance than he would get under the unmitigated rule of *caveat emptor*—let the buyer look out for himself if he can. There is room for prohibition of some products, where harmfulness is great and unquestioned and public opinion backs the prohibition, for minimum standards of health and safety, for requirements that statements voluntarily made in advertising shall be truthful, and for further requirements that labels disclose content, where that is essential to consumer judgment. At the level of voluntary action, there is a useful and growing place for agencies that distribute the results of tests to consumers who subscribe to the services. And none of these safeguards can obviate the need for responsibility on the part of the producer himself for the quality of his product.

As to the relationship between such responsibility and farsighted business interest, there is no point in the kind of reasoning that derives the whole complex from "profit maximization," or assumes that if responsibility has any independent force, this implies that "altruism" displaces the profit motive.[31] The relationship is two-way; and things done originally as means to some ulterior end come to command the doer's interest in their own right. If a man's main motive is to turn out a good product, either from pride in it, or from the "instinct of workmanship," or from a desire to be of service, he cannot fully achieve his end unless he makes his business self-sustaining. And if his first aim is to establish a long-run paying business, he cannot do this unless he safeguards the reputation of his product. These elements are combined in the various existing patterns of sound business practice. The long-run perspective is, of course, especially important with respect to the less visible features of content and structure that make for enduringly dependable performance; since the consumers' reaction to these features is at best delayed, and while it may be progressive over time if the product maintains the identity of its quality features

[31] The present writer has discussed this more fully in "The Ethical Basis of Economic Freedom," Kazanjian Foundation, Westport, Conn., 1955; reprinted in *Economic Institutions and Human Welfare* (1957), pp. 171-225.

sufficiently to cause current sales to be affected by the satisfaction or dissatisfaction of earlier buyers, this effect may be weakened or confused by changes in the product.

So much for the conditioning factors underlying the creation, marketing, and selective acceptance of differentiated products, with some reference to the simplifying devices used by theorists. In the next chapter we turn to some key problems of the effect of all these factors on competition.

CHAPTER 10

Competition Under Product
Differentiation

1. Introduction

In the following discussion of this many-sided array of problems, the effect of competitive pressures on efficient and economical methods of production will be taken for granted. The analysis will fall under two main heads: the qualitative problems involved in the impact of competitive pressures on the product, and the quantitative problems, with which economics is more accustomed to dealing, centering in costs and cost-price relationships. Selling effort as a means of competition has both a qualitative and a quantitative impact, and therefore its relevant aspects will be discussed separately in each of the two main divisions.

In accordance with the position taken earlier, that competition is a joint operation on product, price, and selling effort, this division of the discussion does not mean attempting, for analytical simplicity, to isolate competition in price from competition in product and selling: where such isolation occurs in practice, it must be viewed as an imperfection. What is attempted is the more complicated task of discussing each in the light of the others. Their relation may be illustrated by a few preliminary simplified statements. For elements of quality which the customer cannot judge, competition in price tends to deterioration of these elements through enforced skimping on the cost of producing them (though this pressure is not compulsory on producers substantially above the margin). On the opposite side, one can imagine situations (rather special ones) in which price competition is inactive while quality competition continues to act on those elements of quality that appeal to customers, with the result that customers tend to lose the option of paying less and economizing on these elements of quality. In balanced price-quality competition, they retain the option of getting such elements and degrees of quality as they are willing to pay for. These principles work themselves out with many variations in the less pure cases that occur in practice.

2. The Impact of Competition on the Product

In the light of the foregoing, what can one say about the impact of competition on the product and its quality? It appears clear at the start that whatever one can say will be neither simple nor precise. Not only can competition act toward improving quality or deteriorating it; it can focus strongly on some kinds of quality and neglect others; it can concentrate on adapting its offerings to the modal preferences of a mass market and can reinforce these modal preferences by its propaganda, or it can cultivate, in varying degree, the variant preferences of minority groups. And so the answer must start with the proviso "it depends." It depends on how effective "consumers' sovereignty" is; and this in turn depends on whether it is limited to tasks that are within its powers, and how well it is implemented by aids to the judgment of the qualities of products.

The effect of competition on the quality of products *would be* calamitously bad in its net balance if all elements of quality were left to its unrestricted action. But that is an imaginary condition, just as much as is the attempt to imagine what "pure competition" would mean in the production of automobiles. The effect of competition on the character and quality of products operates within limitations which—in their general character and not, of course, in their detailed specifications—are inevitable in any enlightened society. They aim to deny the satisfaction of some wants, held by the appropriate authority to be inherently and seriously harmful or corrupting to the society (the harm in such cases generally extends to others besides those seeking the satisfactions) or to forbid the choice of means proved to be harmful or dangerous. Thus general sale and use of certain products is prohibited—dangerous drugs being in charge of the medical profession—and minimum standards of safety and health are set for others.

The careful reader may note—and others may need to be reminded —that the writer is not here presuming to substitute his personal subjective "tastes" for those of consumers in deciding what they want, or what they ought to want.[1] The issue is different. Only fanatics propose direct control of the qualities of products in what are genuinely matters of taste as distinct from more essential interests and those having a public aspect. But we do want the consumer to know what he is getting, to the end that he may be a not-too-ineffective and misguided sovereign and may put informed pressure on the suppliers. The critic of the economy need not pass judgment on the quality of wants, but rather on the suitability of different kinds of agencies (including the consumer himself) operating under- different conditions, for registering judgments on what consumers want and what they are offered. This carries recognition that some features of product quality can be better judged by a research agency than by the uninstructed consumer. Agencies of voluntary guidance can go further than authoritative controls, their best service being that of information and education. The commercial agencies of voluntary guidance—advertising and salesmanship—have been touched on in the preceding chapter. Such judgments about agencies are clearly within a social scientist's bailiwick, though neither he nor anyone else can claim infallibility. The upshot is that some scheme of division of labor and of checks and balances between agencies, including individual market choices—all fallible—can work better, with all its defects, than any one agency would if made supreme.

From this standpoint, one of the chief differences between different elements of quality is whether they are visible or invisible. The bear-

---

[1] This is hardly the place for an exhaustive discussion of the issues between the position taken here and that of the kind of "welfare economics," which implies that welfare is exclusively a matter of "taste," not subject to argument or evidence, and which takes market-made choices as final indices of the effects of consumer goods on welfare, abstracting away from the favorable or unfavorable conditions of knowledge or ignorance under which these choices are made. This brand of "welfare economics" bypasses the real issues of "consumer sovereignty" with which this study attempts to deal. The alternative view, which attaches similar finality to any *de facto* decision of government, appears equally unwarranted. Both seem to bespeak a search for finality or infallibility, which is out of place in social science. It is surely not out of order for the social scientist to examine the objective evidence whether, for example, under unrestrained competition, medically harmful foods and medicines will be bought and sold, or houses sold in which inferior wiring constitutes a fire hazard.

ing of this on the consumers' ability to judge is obvious. Features of style, finish, and appearance are clearly visible. They are also most clearly matters of "taste." Less visible qualities reveal themselves in the performance of a product; and here a critical factor is whether the consumer who experiences good or bad performance is in a position to trace it to the product that is responsible. On this score, performance is, in general, easier to trace in the case of durative goods than in the case of consumables; but another distinction which overlaps this one may be even more important, namely, the distinction between performance which is external and mechanical and that which has physiological effects. Mechanical performance is easier to trace and diagnose—the suit wears out too quickly, the roof leaks, the machine breaks down. In contrast, the consumer is not in a position to judge for himself whether the hidden constituents of his diet or his medicines are making for health or sickness, and even apart from hidden constituents, few consumers are competent in the modern science of nutritional values. They may know they are not as well as they would like, but may be at sea as to the cause or the remedy.

In the light of the above, it is interesting to note the characteristics of the cases cited by Chamberlin as examples of adulteration compelled by the pressure of competition. One is the case of commercial mayonnaise adulterated with gum arabic.[2] Accepting the case as stated, this comes under the heading of invisible adulterants, and it is applied to an article of diet that is not a nutritional staple, but a flavoring sauce. It is presumably not physiologically harmful, but dilutes whatever incidental dietetic function the components perform, and debases the flavor so that, to the discriminating housewife, it is not the same product as the dressing she makes for her own table. Chamberlin's other case is the adulteration of sole leather. Here again the adulterant is invisible, and it takes effect, presumably, in reduced durability—a quality that presents special problems which will be discussed presently.

Even where performance is traceable, there is the further question whether defects reveal themselves soon enough to enable the consumer

[2] See E. H. Chamberlin, "The Product as an Economic Variable," *Quarterly Journal of Economics* (February 1953), pp. 1, 24, 26. Chamberlin speaks of a "Gresham's Law" of quality deterioration. This law, it will be remembered, applied when currencies of different worth were accepted at the same value. Obviously, the application to consumer goods occurs only where the consumer accepts better and worse quality without distinction.

to protect his interests by repairing or replacing poor products, or rejecting them on the basis of the experience of fellow consumers. The defects of "jerry-building" are integral to the structure and not easy to remedy without drastic reconstruction. And when defective wiring has caused the house to burn down, it is too late for remedy. For the ordinary consumer, things taken into the body afford a wide area of opportunity for the marketing of frauds or products whose usefulness is sheer and demonstrable delusion, however sincerely it may be believed in. Some of these may be relatively harmless, some are dangerous to health. To the extent that this realm is left to unrestricted competition, such disutilities will be assured a wide market. But to the extent that dangerous products are forbidden, along with misleading claims for other products that may not be harmful, and with requirements of disclosure of content, the level of competitive appeal will be raised. And to the extent that scientifically dependable guidance is not only made available but positively promoted in the public interest, the more enlightened sector of consumers will follow such guidance and will constitute a fraction of the market in which competitive pressures will work toward improvement of quality rather than deterioration.

This leads to the question of the effect of competition on the extent to which products are differentiated to suit the varying preferences of the different groups into which, on the basis of such preferences, the market is divided. This has long been noted as a source of dissension within a firm, between the sales department, interested in adapting the product to local pecularities of demand which it encounters in the field, and the production department, interested in keeping costs down by avoiding an undue multiplication of differentiated types or models. This becomes a competitive matter if some rival or rivals are catering to these local peculiarities. Such peculiarities may be diminishing as a factor in the demand for products, under the influence of nationwide advertising, including mail-order selling, and the effect of the automobile, movies, and television in assimilating hitherto segregated areas to a national pattern. But personal preferences remain, and they combine with the vertical differences represented in the range from luxury models to economy models. Does competition tend toward seeking maximum sales by giving each group the particular product it prefers, or does it tend toward minimizing cost by adapting its product to the preferences of the largest group and relatively neglecting the special wants of small groups which would call for small runs and increase average costs? As one might expect, the answer is that competitive pressures act in both directions, and some kind of a balance has to be struck, according to conditions.

These conditions include the number and size of the producers in the market: a subject the relation of which to differentiated-product competition has not been systematically investigated. On the basis of observation, it appears clear that small numbers—say even three or four dominant firms in an industry—are enough to generate extremely vigorous competition in adapting the product to bid for the purchaser's favor. The competition is all the more vigorous because each firm may be vitally affected by what a single rival does and must be prepared for a defensive response. And in product competition, the prospect of rivals' response does not normally nullify a firm's incentive to initiate a move, because rivals' responses are not instantaneous—as they can be in the realm of price—and they regularly involve some uncertainty. The response may fall short of fully counteracting the original move or may more than counteract it and perhaps elicit some counterresponse.[3] In such a case, some form of the "instinct of workmanship" may play a part, in that, if the research department works on the development of improvements, too many of which are put to sleep, the resulting sense of futility may be harmful to morale.

But if product competition is vigorous, even where numbers are small, this does not settle all questions about it. There are reasons for thinking that a considerably larger number is called for in order that competition may be directed into the healthiest combination of rivalry in quality and price, well-balanced as between luxury and economy models, with an incentive to promote durability where the consumer's interest calls for it, and with an adequate readiness to serve the demands of minority groups of consumers.

Competition in quality is seen in the purest form where a product is designed to sell at a given price, and the product is the active variable. The system of classifying goods into "price lines" is adapted to

[3] The writer was told that about 1925 each of the leading automobile producers had in readiness a similar list of several improvements, but adoption was delayed because each knew that the others were fully prepared to follow suit, making it doubtful whether the competitive gain to the leader would be worth the cost involved. But one company did take the lead, and the improvements became standard. This suggests the hypothesis that such stalemates in product competition can occur, but are unlikely to last long if the improvement is one that will appeal definitely to the customer.

trades in which there are many firms. Where firms are large, relative to the market, a single model by one firm is important enough to receive more individual treatment; but it may still start with an idea of the customer level it will appeal to, and the price range that is appropriate, after which the designers may pack into the product as many attractive features as are consistent with the firm's cost-price policy. This kind of competition can go to a "cutthroat" degree, in which the product costs more than it brings in, as Chamberlin notes.[4] This appears most likely to occur if the volume of sales disappoints the firm's expectations. A more common result would be some approximation to a "full-cost" relationship. Or if the product is a substantial innovation, it may pass through the stages, already mentioned, of an introductory phase of modest volume and substantial margin above unit cost, followed by larger volume at thinner margins, as competitors respond with products of similar or equivalent appeal. Substantial innovations in quality may begin at the luxury level, which serves as a tryout area from which, if successful, they may work down to the standard grades.

F. H. Giddings, in an essay published two years before the Sherman Act of 1890, cited a case of price agreement in the brass industry which did not control production, with the result that competition— which was vigorous—shifted to quality and created notable improvements.[5] One would like to know more about this case; but it seems safe to infer certain characteristics which it must have had. If the firms were under competitive pressure, their customers must have been knowledgeable as to the quality of the product. The product must have been near enough to homogeneity to make agreement on a scale of prices meaningful, yet the grades and varieties could not have been defined with utter precision—there must have been substantial latitude within which a grade or type could be improved—for example, in uniformity of content—while remaining under the former definition and taking the former price under the agreement.

[4] See Chamberlin, *op. cit.*, pp. 4-5. It may be noted that this tendency appears incompatible with Chamberlin's "tangency theorem," which hinges on the proposition that product differentiation leads to prices above cost, inviting new entries which bring cost and price together by increasing unit costs.

[5] See "The Persistence of Competition," in J. B. Clark and F. H. Giddings, *The Modern Distributive Process* (1888), pp. 18, 30-34. Cf. Chamberlin's list of factors working against product deterioration, including the attempts of producers to avoid price competition, insofar as these represent attempts to avoid deteriorating pressure on products. See Chamberlin, *op. cit.*, p. 27.

These requirements fit the case of a processed material, sold to fabricators under customary trade categories. One can only speculate how widely the necessary conditions might be found, especially with modern multiplication of alloys, with uniformity and precision of content, which are part of this same improvement of quality. Giddings, citing John Ruskin's "Unto This Last," judged this form of competition better than the cutthroat price competition that was prevalent at the time; estimating on the basis of current experience that free entry afforded sufficient price protection for the customer. This, however, does not represent fully balanced price-quality competition as defined above, nor solve all the problems that would be raised by legalizing price agreements.

Product differentiation requires substantial selling effort in some form, and if a nationwide market is to be developed, it calls for nationwide advertising. Chamberlin notes that advertising and quality may vary in the same direction—"it doesn't pay to advertise a poor product"—but also that advertising may be used to make up for deficiencies in the product, this being facilitated if, in addition to its deficient features, the product has some effective talking points to which the advertiser can divert the buyer's attention.[6] This double relationship is a challenge to economists, calling for both fact-finding and analysis. A priori, it seems safe to conclude that the greatest scope for using more advertising to make up for less quality occurs where the inferiority is of the sort the consumer will not identify and trace to its source, so as to be alienated by finding he has been sold expensive advertising copy to which the product does not measure up. And in proportion as the quality in the case is of the sort that will be effectively appraised by a sufficient number of consumers, the product will be under pressure to live up to its advertising. Naturally also, the character and motivation of the producer are important determining factors, in ways to which the mere phrase "profit-maximization" affords little guidance. Some producers, following the business rule of believing in their product, may be to some extent self-deceived about its comparative standing. But the stable firm must be on its guard against identifying itself, by heavy advertising, with a product so inferior as to damage the firm's reputation.

[6] *Ibid.*, p. 7, cf. also p. 26. This double relationship occurs wherever two complementary factors can be used in varying proportions, so that the marginal contribution of an increment of one can be balanced against the alternative contribution of an increment of the other.

3. Economy and Durability: Two Special Cases

Increase of "economy models" or economy grades of goods and increases in the durability of products have this in common: by themselves each in a different way has a tendency to reduce sales volume in dollar terms, though this tendency may be outweighed by other tendencies making for expansion. Therefore, competitive incentives to promote these two kinds of quality of products present a special problem for industries that are highly concentrated, so that a leading part is played by "competition among the few." Such competition may be biased against these values; and fair representation for them in terms of competitive pressures appears to depend on competitive action by vigorous and efficient firms, which are small enough, relative to the size of the total market, to have room for large expansion, percentage-wise. To use a different term, in their competition with the bigger firms, their cross-elasticity of demand is higher, increasing their chance to gain through competitive tactics.

Another aspect of this situation is that the giant firm may be seeking to reduce its unit costs by concentrating on mass demand, and neglecting minority sectors of the market, which call for a product variant that would necessarily sell in smaller volume. Where this occurs, it gives the smaller competitor his chance since, for him, the minority demand is relatively a larger matter. On both accounts, the position of the relatively small competitor appears to be of special strategic importance, as affording positive incentives to develop sectors of demand that might be neglected by an industry of a few giants. Otherwise, the development of production to serve these special sectors of demand would seem to depend too much on the "instinct of workmanship," operating within the organizations of the great industrial leaders. Not that this "instinct" is to be dismissed as meaningless—it probably has an increasing place in the complex that makes up industrial motivation—but people do not like to feel that they are completely dependent on it.

The economy model has its best chance to bring a profitable increase in sales to its producer where it can tap an unexploited level of demand which has been prevented, by low price-paying ability, from being satisfied by the existing models, and where the economy model will not—or not to any substantial extent—take sales away from existing higher-priced models produced by the same firm. The outstanding example, in which both these favorable conditions were present, was the original Model T Ford, which put the automobile for the first time within reach of mass demand. It is worth noting that the first Henry Ford did not confine his interest to this model; but in carrying out his companion ambition for an outstanding achievement in the high-grade field, with the Lincoln car, he set up a model far enough removed from the Model T to be noncompetitive with it. He had no established line, with the sales of which the Model T would interfere. The result is history. It is also history that the Ford Company having become a giant in a changed kind of market is no longer producing a car filling a place corresponding to that filled by the Model T. Such a car would now have the used car to compete with.

To illustrate conditions less favorable for the economy model and probably more typical of a mature industry, let us suppose a firm that has been producing a standard model introduces an economy model selling for 20 per cent less. We may suppose also that some of the firm's customers shift from the standard model to the economy one. On sales so shifted, the firm's gross sales volume is reduced 20 per cent, and it must find new sales of its economy model equal to 25 per cent of the number so shifted, in order to maintain its gross sales-volume undiminished. Or if the economy model replaces the former standard model, it must increase its total number of units sold by 25 per cent in order to prevent its gross dollar volume from shrinking. If it is one of a "big three," each vigilant to maintain its proportionate share of the market, such a substantial increase in the number of units sold may not appear probable. A vigorous competitor of smaller relative size might find the prospect promising, and if it makes inroads on the sales of the biggest firms which threaten to be progressive over time, the latter may be impelled, after an interval, to make a defensive response. But in the absence of such a challenge, the giant firm may envision a better prospect of increased dollar sales in packing more "utilities" into each unit, provided total demand permits. This might go far enough to deserve the name "product inflation."

While the above has general validity, it has special application to the recent history of the American automobile industry.[7] Among the factors conditioning this recent history are: the transition from the youthful market which gave the Model T its opportunity to the mature market dominated by replacement, with its cultivated obsolescence; the accompanying abandonment of the low-cost demand to the used-car market (though used cars are not economical to operate) and to the foreign small car (though it is not adapted to the American family-car demand); increased per capita income which reduced the demand for economy models to a minority factor in the market; and the reduction of producers to a "big three" and two struggling competitors. Under these conditions the big three engaged in product inflation, creating monstrosities of size, power, fuel consumption, gadgetry, and nightmare styling, dreamed up by design engineers under the categorical imperative to produce something strikingly different, which will identify the owner of the latest model. More economical six-cylinder engines and manual controls have merely been offered as variants of the overlarge and heavy standard models. All this despite the interest in economy models evinced by the increased sales of small foreign cars, in the face of heavy handicaps.

The creation of economy models adapted to the American family-car market was left to be initiated by the smaller, more struggling competitors, while the big three engaged in defensive preparedness and delayed their final commitment to enter production with their "compact" models until the success of the economy model had been demonstrated by a competitor, who scored a notable increase in sales. This episode appears, as far as it goes, to bear out the hypothesis that competition in quality tends to be biased toward luxury models and against economy models in an industry with too few and too large competitors, especially when demand has reached something like maturity. It also corroborates the hypothesis that a firm that has not enough incentive to initiate a competitive move will respond defensively to a successful move initiated by a competitor.

[7] The writer is here incorporating in revised form material from his paper: "The Uses of Diversity," *American Economic Review, Proceedings* (May 1958), pp. 474, 481-82. E. S. Mason, writing in 1938, analyzed the transition of the industry from the Model T stage to the stage of replacement and induced obsolescence. See "Price and Production Policies of Large-Scale Enterprise," *American Economic Review,* Supplement (1939), pp. 61-74, reprinted in American Economic Association, *Readings in Industrial Organization and Public Policy* (1958), pp. 190, 199-200.

These principles may apply with peculiar force to improvements which increase the durability of the product, since this kind of improvement can result in decreasing the total volume of sales because of the slower rate of replacement.[8] This effect is, of course, delayed by an interval equal to the normal service life of the previous, less durable products, which may be a single season or a substantial term of years. But by the same token, some part of this delay applies to the consumer's benefit from getting a more durable product, except as its greater durability is incidental to better appearance and more dependable performance even in the early stages of its wearing life. Of course, this whole problem is irrelevant to products subject to an annual style turnover, except for that quota of consumers who are economical enough or eccentric enough to wear last season's styles through several seasons, and except for the fact that clothes that are well enough made to look well at the end of one season can be worn longer without getting to look badly. Aside from seasonal-style products, durables differ greatly in the extent to which a reasonably competent consumer can judge by inspection how well they are likely to stand up in service. And this, plus advertising claims and such other guidance as he may get, constitutes the chief basis on which a producer might expect to be able to increase his sales as a result of making his product more durable. Or perhaps the quality of material and workmanship that makes for durability lends the product a better appearance and finish when new, to a sufficient extent to attract buyers.

If one disregards these factors, one could formulate a discouraging model, in which the producer who has suddenly increased the durability of his product by, let us say 50 per cent, pays the penalty of going through some seasons of low replacement demand, before reaping his reward when satisfied customers come back for replacements and bring their friends with them. Meanwhile, the improvement would be likely to have become standard, depriving the innovator of much of his competitive advantage. Here the principle of the oligopoly stalemate might operate, not because competitors respond instantly, but because the customers respond so slowly. When one weighs all these considerations, one is tempted to wonder why, in a highly concentrated industry, improvements of this sort are ever made, unless

[8] *Ibid.*, p. 482. Cf. Chamberlin, *op. cit.*, pp. 23-24, and Hans Brems, *Product Equilibrium and Monopolistic Competition* (1951).

by technically minded mavericks who take the lead and put pressure on the others to meet the standard they have set.

If one falls back on observation, it is clear that some notable improvements of this sort have been made, the increased durability of automobile tires being a conspicuous instance. Here the incentive is strong; durability is the heart of the product, and the lack of it begins to make trouble for the user in a very short time. Thus the case is a favorable one. It is not so easy to get evidence on economically feasible increases in durability that have not been adopted, and the reasons for nonadoption. It is equally difficult to test the impression, often encountered, that there is a fairly general tendency to reduce the sturdiness and durability of products—"they don't make them with such good stuff any more." This sort of deterioration undoubtedly happens, and happens for reasons traceable to the drive of competition toward cheapness in the less visible and identifiable features of a product. But there is little one can say about the more important question how much effect such tendencies have, as compared to the opposite tendencies toward improvement. This kind of criticism has been made of automobiles—yet the service life of automobiles is longer today than it used to be.

Any such deliberate economies in production, which incidentally result in reduced durability, should be distinguished from "cultivated obsolescence" where the obsolescence is the end in view, looking toward making room for replacement sales of new products. For a producer pursuing this end, it would be very bad policy to make a product that will wear out sooner than those of his competitors. In that case the replacement purchases are likely to be made from the competitors, not from the producer who has chosen this method of cultivating obsolescence. Instead, the approved method is to promote replacement by offering the consumer a new and improved article, making the existing one lose its up-to-dateness while it is still as serviceable, let us say, as competing articles of its own vintage. The effective appeal is to the superiority of the new, not the deterioration of the old.

The above analysis suggests that as to durability, competition is likely to act toward maintaining prevalent levels, turning out a product that is as durable as those of competitors, avoiding identifiable deterioration and economizing where the results are not easily identified, while the competitive incentives to improve durability appear to be uncertain, varying with the conditions of the case. One of these conditions is the character of the market for used articles, if such a market exists. A well-organized market of this sort is obviously a favorable factor. It helps to sell a new car if that make has a reputation for holding a good turn-in value; and this is effective in proportion as users have a habit of turning in their cars for new ones at an early stage in their total working lives. On the other hand, if increased durability causes an appreciable number of users to use their cars longer before turning them in, the existence and activity of the used-car market causes the postponing of replacement sales, which is the main deterrent to increased durability, to take place much sooner than it would if there were no used-car market, and no custom of early turn-in. It is to the producer's interest that the period before the first turn-in should not get longer, even if the total life of the car is increased.

Sudden and great increases in durability have such a marked effect in reducing replacement purchases that it is logical to assume that the only kind of firm that has a sufficient interest in making such improvements is a firm so small, relative to the entire industry, that it has much to gain from increased original sales and little to lose from reduced replacement sales. An oligopolist would not be expected to make such an improvement: for example, the razor-blade that lasts a lifetime, or soles and heels that outlast the rest of the shoe. The kind of increase in durability that seems to have some chance, in the competition of large units and limited numbers, is a smaller increase, which has no spectacular effect but may serve as one among various points of sales appeal.

4. Summary as to Quality

To sum up, the response of sales volume to variations in the quality of the product is extremely diverse, varying with the kind of quality element in question, and varying also with the size of the firm's output, relative to the total output of the industry. As a result, the competitive incentive to embody different kinds of quality elements in the product varies widely. Moderate fewness of producers helps the consumer to identify the brands and choose among them and is consistent with strong competition, but unduly limited numbers seem to distort the competition as between different kinds of quality. Especially the kinds of quality that represent economy for the user— economy models and models which at one step bring about a large increase in durability—seem to face peculiar difficulties in showing a profitable sales response for the producer who initiates these kinds of quality improvements, and particularly if his sales volume is already a substantial fraction of the total in his industry. The "big three" type of firm has ample competitive incentive to make its product more attractive in the more immediate, visible, and obvious ways; but for these economy-oriented features of quality, it appears that adequate competitive incentives hinge on the situation of the smaller firm which has room for a radical increase in its sales volume.

This is a different form of the same principle which shows that in competition between firms of different sizes, the cross-elasticity of demand is greater for the smaller firm; also that the incentive to a competitive reduction of price requires a "margin elasticity" greater than unity, implying a price elasticity that exceeds unity in the same proportion by which the price exceeds the margin earned above marginal cost. The conclusion is that healthy competition in this field hinges on the existence of strong but relatively small firms, which between them account for a substantial part of the output of the industry. What remains is the question of the conditions necessary to such competition, and how they may be maintained.

5. Impact on Costs and Cost-Price Relationships

When we take up the question of the effect of product differentiation on costs and on cost-price relationships, we reach at long last the problem in which economists are supposed to be mainly interested. It is also a problem on which one must attempt to generalize while doing justice to the fact that a wide variety of things can happen—and generally do. There can be no guarantee that all the possible outcomes will be consistent with healthy and effective competition; therefore the inquiry tends naturally to turn into a search for the conditions that are consistent with healthy and effective (not "perfect") competition, including the maintenance of an adequate number of firms strong enough to be effective competitors, but whose output of a given product is small, relative to the total output of the competing variants.

By way of comparison one may cite the most widely held theoretical doctrine in the field: namely, the Chamberlinian "tangency theorem," with the conclusions drawn from it, and Joe S. Bain's highly significant study of the obstacles to free entry.[9] Aside from the fact that Chamberlin's is a deductive theorem, while Bain's study is inductive, the outstanding difference between the two is that Bain's study centers on collusive or quasi-collusive oligopoly, limited by potential competition and pricing to forestall the entry of new firms, while the tangency theorem assumes that prospective entry is disregarded until it materializes. In Bain's study, product differentiation fortifies the position of existing firms and is thus on the whole the chief single obstacle to entry, while in the tangency theorem it leads to profits that attract entry. In the tangency theorem, prices are raised until the resulting limitation of scale of production raises costs above the optimum. Bain envisions no single optimum scale, but a range of size above which neither economies nor diseconomies are significant.

Obstacles to entry include the need the new entry has of incurring the extra selling costs incident to building up demand for its product to a large enough scale to be competitively viable, in addition to the costs necessary to maintain a demand once established. But this obstacle is compounded with others arising where the scale of production necessary to standard efficiency is so large as to imply a limited number of firms having fully efficient scale. This accounts for the "percentage effect"—the entry of a single such large firm creates substantial excess capacity, while smaller entries suffer some handicap—though this may not be decisive. These difficulties are minimized if the entrant is an existing large firm which diversifies its output and enters a new line of production. Bain does not count this as a new entry, but comes ultimately to concede it some place among the forces limiting oligopoly pricing.[10] The differences in rates of return in different industries which Bain finds pose a problem that challenges further study. As for the

---

[9] Joe S. Bain, *Barriers to New Competition* (1956). Cf. also Franco Modigliani, "New Developments on the Oligopoly Front," *Journal of Political Economy* (June 1958), pp. 215-32.

[10] Bain, *op. cit.*, pp. 5, 215.

tangency theorem, reasons have been given earlier for regarding it as a rather exceptional case—Bain calls it "bizarre"—in which each seller enjoys a strong brand preference among his own customers—it has to be strong or it would not enable all of them to make short-run profits —and makes shortsighted use of it, ignoring potential competition with the result that the profits are wiped out by new entries.

The contribution attempted in the present study will be an analysis that assumes that firms act without collusion, but not without regard to what others are likely to do, and subject to a mixture of short-run and long-run considerations. They differ in size and in the corresponding cross-elasticity of demand; also in cost. But the chief emphasis is on the difference between short-run and long-run behavior of costs and of sales volume in response to the competitive tactics a firm may employ. The majority of the output comes from firms that are large enough so that differences in cost due to differences in scale of output are not important and may not be clearly distinguishable, being outweighed by differences due to other causes. But part of the output comes from smaller firms, some of which may have dealt successfully with the special cost problems that go with limited output, while others may have higher-than-standard costs. The big firms achieve large output and low manufacturing costs, with the aid of the heavy advertising that accompanies product differentiation and that attains economy, compared to resulting sales, by mass coverage of the firm's entire market. However, competitive pressures may result in carrying the intensiveness of the coverage past the point of diminishing return. As we have seen, economies of mass distribution, plus bargaining advantages, may build up the size of firms beyond that needed for efficient production, and smaller firms may be more handicapped in distribution than in production.

In the short run, under conditions of normal but not boom activity, some firms will ordinarily be working close enough to capacity to disregard the fact that their short-run marginal cost is less than average cost; and to be under no incentive to try to increase their sales volume by cutting their yield with short-run marginal cost as the limiting minimum. But other firms will commonly be working far enough short of capacity to make it logical for them to regard increased sales as a gain if the "marginal revenue" they produce is more than short-run marginal cost. If these firms, competing on this basis, start taking business away from the first group of firms (those working close to capacity), this first group may be impelled to meet the challenge defensively and thus may be drawn into competition based on short-run marginal cost as a minimum. Thus the conditions for cutthroat competition may be present, even in fairly normal times, depending on how elastic the demand functions of the various individual firms are. The more fluctuations the industry is subject to, the more excess capacity will it tend to have, on the average of good and bad times, and the more of the time will short-run marginal cost, rather than full average cost, figure as the minimum limit on competitive tactics, whether in price or selling effort or any variation of product or service which might conceivably bring in added sales in a short enough time to be relevant.

In general, in industries with differentiated products, competitive moves do not face the prospect of being promptly and precisely met and neutralized. In the first place, there is delay and uncertainty as to the customers' response. Only if it turns out, after a waiting period, that the new move is attracting customers strongly, will competitors feel the kind of pressure that leads them to respond; and then their response may be delayed and may take the form of a more attractive product, more selling effort, or a reduced price, or some combination. Then there is the same kind of delay and uncertainty about finding out how effective the response is.

In the long run, unless the industry is a declining one, the added cost of added output will generally come near enough to full average cost so that any discrepancies will not be ascertainable and will not figure in business decisions, which will be shaped in terms of full average cost. It is fair to assume that if the industry earns more, it will expand, and if it earns materially less, it will tend to contract. The long-run responses of demand to the inducements offered by producers present more of a problem. If one seller makes his offerings more attractive and his competitors do nothing in response, it is natural to expect that his gains will be progressive over time. There might, of course, be a natural limit if the added attraction consists of some characteristic of the product or the sales method which is less than universal in its appeal, so that after it has captured all the customers who are susceptible, there will still be others who prefer the different offerings of rival firms. However, if the inducements include price reductions, which can be regarded as universal in their appeal, and if these are not met, it is fair to assume that the long-run response of sales volume would be progressive, equivalent in effect to a very high elasticity of demand.

This is complicated by the expectation that rival firms will respond with countermoves. These firms, we assume, are not naive enough to think that they can make large gains at their competitors' expense without provoking a response. But the expectation of response does not paralyze their competitive incentives; a significant number of firms expect that a successful competitive move, after the rivals have responded, will leave an aftermath of increased sales volume and improved market standing. It is, of course, not a matter of price alone, but of price in connection with product and selling effort, uniting to offer the customer an attractive bargain. And the reputation of offering a good bargain needs to be maintained as a matter of consistent policy. As to the price feature of the bargain, it comes into play when there is some change in the other features. Thus where there is an annual model change or other fairly frequent change in models, the price will be adjusted with corresponding frequency. Between times, changes in price may take place in response to some substantial change in costs or other market conditions. If a change in price accompanies a change in models, and if competing models sell at somewhat different prices, this removes the basis for the expectation that any change in the openly quoted price will be precisely met by one's competitors, as in the case of a homogeneous product. It leaves the firm in the position of exploring ways of improving the effectiveness of its total offering, knowing that its competitors are doing the same thing and that the competitive relationship, whether of cost or of product, has not reached any precise parity.

In this situation, the responsiveness of a single seller's sales to the inducements he offers the buyer, including the relation of his price to cost of production, defies expression in the kind of simple two-dimensional relation of sales to price that is embodied in the kind of "demand curve" used in economic theory. If the responsiveness is high, prices may get below a normal relation to full cost, even though the "sloping individual-demand curves" may mitigate the tendency to cutthroat competition and prevent price from getting dangerously close to short-run marginal cost. If the responsiveness is sluggish, meaning that brand preferences are strong enough to give the typical producer a fairly strong defensive position, the range of return may be above a normal relation to full cost, especially if the existing strong brand preferences are an obstacle to new entries. However, if the competition is between a substantial number of competitors of unequal size but not-too-unequal strength, their rivalry is likely to generate a cross-elasticity of demand that will prevent quasi-monopoly profits from arising. Where a few giant firms are really dominant, there is little in the way of economic law that can be relied on to control their actions. One earmark of such a situation might be that the smaller firms have costs enough higher than the giants so that, even by cutting their margins above short-run marginal costs thin, they cannot make the kind of inroads on the business of the big few that would drive the latter to defensive competitive action.

One of the situations in which cutthroat competition is most likely to develop is one in which a difference between two competing products is recognized, but there is no consensus on what price relationship will equalize their standing with customers. One rival may be convinced that its product needs a price differential to enable it to compete, while the other may insist that price equality is necessary. So the second wipes out differentials as fast as the first sets them up—always downward, of course. Such a struggle can drive prices below cost. This appears to be one of the features that has made competition between rail and truck transport take on a cutthroat character. This is an unstable variant on the duopoly situation with a homogeneous product on which (in the oversimplified model) neither one cuts the price because a cut is sure to be met.

6. May Competition Stagnate?

While product differentiation generally tends to prevent this stalemate from arising, it is worth inquiring whether something like it might come about if the relation between the different firms' products settles down into a kind of stability in which the firms tend to accept and maintain whatever scheme of price differentials has come to prevail. Then a reduction in price by one important seller might be so sure to be promptly met by its principal rivals that the chance to make a competitive gain in sales volume would be minimized, and active price competition might lapse. This may be accentuated by the fact, noted by Chamberlin, that producers interested in maintaining a good product do not like price competition, with its pressure toward cheapening the product.[11] This outcome appears possible, but it carries certain implications. One is that the more successful and profitable firms accept their existing relative share of the market and do not try to disturb it by seeking to increase their share at their rivals' relative expense.

But this raises the question what they will do with their accumulating profits. These give them a chance for growth, and, as Edith T. Penrose has shown, such firms have internal resources of enterprise and management available for growth and have a corresponding drive toward utilizing these resources.[12] If these are not fully utilized in the normal growth that is required to maintain their relative position in the industry, they may be impelled to expand via diversification. But this means injecting new competition into the product fields into which they move; and it also suggests the possibility that other successful firms may be moving into the first firm's field in the same way. Thus the stable status is likely to be disturbed.

Another source of disturbance can arise if one producer develops an important new product variant which changes the relative status of the existing array of products, and with it the basis of the prevailing range of price differentials. Thus, while the static phase of product differentiation may run counter to active price competition, the dynamic phase may tend to restore it, keeping the existing status stirred up. A further factor, of course, would be the existence of numerous relatively small but active and efficient firms, ambitious to improve their competitive standing. The persistence of active price competition may hinge on this combination of dynamic elements.

7. Does Advertising Increase Costs?

One further question which must not be ignored is whether advertising, while tending to keep production cost down by maintaining an efficiently large scale of production, may increase total cost by the

[11] See Chamberlin, op. cit., p. 27. Chamberlin indicates some tolerance toward this tendency, as a possible aid in maintaining the quality of the product.

[12] This thesis was developed by Mrs. Penrose in an unpublished manuscript which the present writer had the opportunity to examine in August 1957; published in 1959 with the title The Theory of the Growth of the Firm.

addition of the cost of the advertising itself. To this question no simple and certain answer can be given. But there is a strong case for the conclusion that, if there is such an increase in total cost, it is outweighed by the residuum of net gain resulting from the dynamics of new-product development, which is necessary to a rising standard of living, plus the progress in productive efficiency made possible by the large-scale production, which in turn is made possible by advertising.

In trying to pursue this question, one faces the difficulty: increased costs compared to what? Not compared to absence of advertising; on that basis producers could not grow to efficient size, and even a wasteful system of advertising could be defended—as ours often is—on the ground that it reduces total costs. It might have some meaning to ask whether competition introduces increased costs, as compared to a system devoted to promoting the sales of the whole group or industry. Such advertising actually is sponsored by trade associations, but it does not take the place of the advertising of single firms, aimed at getting customers away from each other; and it is not easy to imagine how it could do so. When I try to imagine an efficient monopoly, promoting its total sales in the most far-sighted way, I am forced to conceive it as organized into autonomous departments, competing with one another in developing individual product variants. And in that case, each department would want the chance to present to the customers, through its own advertising, the particular strong points of its own particular product variant, as it sees them and as it wants buyers to see them. And this imaginary far-sighted monopoly would give its departments this opportunity. It would presumably see that the departments did not run down one another's products; in that respect it would probably accomplish what current codes of advertising ethics, or etiquette, purport to accomplish, but do not always succeed.

Perhaps it would be able, by budgeting the departments' advertising outlays, to eliminate the purely competitive pressure that results because one firm, by increasing its advertising, reduces the effectiveness of its competitors' advertising and forces them to increase their budgets in order to maintain the same relative position in the group, without any necessary corresponding improvement in the position of the group as a whole. In principle, this might be regarded as an element of increased cost definable as a waste of competition. In practice, such a rationing of advertising budgets would probably have to be flexible, because a department which is introducing something new would press for a building-up budget, larger than the quota allowed as a maintenance budget. The question is, of course, academic, since this country is not going to repeal the antitrust laws for the sake of a conjectural saving in advertising outlays. A less radical method would be to set limits on the amount of such outlays that could be deducted for tax purposes, but this is not much more likely than a repeal of the antitrust laws. This despite the fact that under the present system extravagant advertising by the biggest and most prosperous firms is, in effect, subsidized, because a substantial part of its cost is offset by a reduction of business income taxes, as well as by part of the postal deficit.

Of course, any move tending to reduce total advertising outlays would encounter the solid opposition, not only of the advertising industry but of the newspapers, magazines, radio, and television industries, which derive so much of their support from advertising budgets. They use this support to finance essential public services of information, together with entertainment of high cultural value, plus other entertainment that ranges all the way down to the most powerful degrading influences now operating on what remains of the very high intellectual and cultural level which this country inherited from its "founding fathers." To anyone aware of the American cultural heritage and the degenerative influences to which it is today exposed, the qualitative effects of modern advertising must be vastly more important than any conjectural quantitative effects which it may or may not have in increasing the total costs of products.

One disquieting bit of evidence is the fact that even good products are too often advertised by methods calculated to persuade any intelligently discriminating buyer that their claims are specious, and the most disquieting feature of this is its testimony that the advertising industry believes that intelligently discriminating buyers are a negligible minority in the market for consumer goods. Some improvement might be hoped for if firms with products to advertise, which serve some genuine human purpose, should succeed in emancipating themselves from subservience to the real or supposed superior psychological knowledge of the advertising specialists and their techniques of cynically misusing this supposed knowledge to appeal to the most susceptible weaknesses of human nature. This misuse threatens to dwarf their more serviceable appeals to those faculties of discriminating judgment on which rests the possibility of success in the unavoidably dangerous experiment of a free and self-governing society.

Perhaps one's most serious complaint is against those producers whose products can be promoted by appeals to the degenerative traits of human nature, and the readiness of the advertising specialists to adapt the character of their appeals to the character of the products they are promoting. It seems that one may dismiss the question whether advertising increases total costs as not proven, and in any case secondary to the more serious qualitative problems involved.

8. Discrepancies in the Strength of Competitive Forces

To return to our main inquiry, it appears that the long-run competitive forces have a widespread restraining and disciplinary effect, but one that operates unevenly between different industries. The short-run pressures may show even more variation, not only between times of strong and weak demand—that is to be expected—but between different industries in terms of the kind and degree of their variation between better and worse times. This is chiefly because industries differ in the elasticities of the demand functions which prevail under different kinds and degrees of product differentiation. If the elasticities are high, the tendency to excessively severe competition in dull times may be insufficiently mitigated, while if the elasticities are only moderate, the mitigation of tendencies to such competition may be more than sufficient. This poses an awkward question: Is it a matter of chance whether competitive forces act with a correct and desirable degree of strength, or are there some equalizing forces at work in the direction of an economically correct result?

One such force consists of the reactions of businessmen to the general conception of a sound and fair return or the lack of it. They are not worried if inefficient firms are incurring operating deficits, especially if the deficits lead to the elimination of productive capacity which is both excessive and inefficient. They may be uneasy if the productive capacity in question is merely shut down and remains hanging over the market, ready to resume production if demand revives, and to prevent revival from bringing real prosperity. However, this appears more likely to happen in the case of mass-produced homogeneous materials like cement, than in the case of differentiated end products, subject to more rapid change which tends to cause idle equipment of a specialized sort to become obsolete rather rapidly. Unprofitable capacity may change management without changing owners; and I was told of one inferior and unprofitable plant which changed owners without changing management.[13]

Such things, business men regard as normal; but when efficient firms incur operating deficits, they feel the condition is unsound, and that it is unsound practice to be drawn into a level of competition that will bring this condition about. What Alfred Marshall called a "sentiment against spoiling the market" is widespread and has some restraining effect, especially where product differentiation affords each producer some margin of policy. But informal sentiments are not likely to be sufficient by themselves when the pressures to cutthroat competition are really strong. This may be fortunate, since if a mere feeling in favor of "soft competition" were effective enough to relieve the pressure on representative firms, it would stand in the way of the more painful but necessary corrective—the elimination of some producers by bankruptcy.

If short-run competitive pressures are not strong enough to keep returns normal, action guided by longer-run perspectives may furnish the chief corrective, in the shape of a policy on the part of the stronger firms of not pricing above "full cost," on the average, while quoting lower prices where that may be necessary to meet competition. This last reservation in favor of competitive flexibility is regularly a part of "full-cost pricing," though generally neglected by its critics. This reservation implies that some firms, in some parts of the market, will be setting prices that do not yield them as much as "full cost"; and that firms whose costs are not among the lowest will be unable to make that much in the aggregate. The firms that take the lead in such a policy may be presumed to be acting on the judgment that this is as much as they can get in the long run. Such a policy obviously does not guarantee a "perfect" cost-price adjustment, but it may bring about a reasonably satisfactory one under favorable conditions. This matter will be gone into more fully in Chapter 15, Section 2.

[13] My informant was a highly efficient producer, who was invited to inspect this plant with a view to possible purchase. He was interested, because the plant had habitually undercut his prices, causing him to conjecture that it was superefficient. Discovering the contrary, he did not buy the plant.

9. Conditions Favorable to a Satisfactory Result

What do these conditions include? They appear to include some variety in size and character among competing firms, but not such great difference that all but a few strong firms in a given market are impotent satellites, existing on sufferance of a few giants. The conditions necessary to adequate strength on the part of firms of moderate size include availability of credit on reasonable terms and of technical and organizational research by specialized organizations on a part-time basis, for firms whose limited size makes it too costly to maintain such full-time services in their own organizations. There is needed a balance between exits and entries, allowing for the weeding-out of the unfit without putting the bulk of the firms under ruinous pressures, such as might drive too many of the moderate-sized firms to accept absorption until the remaining independents become too few to exert the competitive pressures which, as we have seen, are so dependent on the existence of substantial numbers of such firms.

The present anti-merger provisions of the Clayton Act, as amended in 1950, present perplexing problems, chiefly where differences in strength between existing firms are unduly great and rest on other factors than productive efficiency, or where numbers have already become too small for a healthy competitive condition. But the principle which the act attempts to embody, of anticipatory action to forestall such concentration as would tend unduly to reduce competition, is both valid and important. There is need for a balance among new entries, internal growth of existing firms (including growth by merger where this will increase competition by strengthening the position of hard-pressed firms), and entry by diversification on the part of existing strong firms. The superior flexibility of smaller firms, often mentioned as an offset to the low costs of larger, mass-producing firms, implies that the smaller firms also practice some kind and degree of diversification. Where the small firm follows the alternative policy of specializing on a sub-product, which it can produce on an efficient scale, there is need that the larger firms which constitute its customers should be numerous enough to give it the benefit of competitive outlets, so that it may not be reduced to the status of a dependent satellite.

These conditions present plenty of problems; and the health of competition under product differentiation hinges on the degree of success attained in dealing with these problems. By comparison with them, the problems emphasized by formal abstract theory appear either nonexistent (existing only in the realms of oversimplified diagrammatic models) or special cases of relatively small importance in the total picture. The defects are serious, and the continuance of healthy competitive forces cannot be guaranteed. But if the conditions of progress are maintained, in products and productive methods and including decentralized initiative and competitive incentives, we can absorb many defects and still have a basis for the judgment that the imperfect and "monopolistic" competition we have is better than the "pure and perfect" competition of theory.

CHAPTER **11**

Competition With Homogeneous Products

1. The Meaning of Homogeneity

In the analysis of competition and of competitive forces, the position of the homogeneous product has suffered a reversal. In the early days of the formulation of precise ideas about competition, the homogeneous product was taken as the general case. Then, with an increase in the importance of the products of industry and trade and a relative decline in the importance of extractive industry, there came an increase in the relative importance of cases in which products are differentiated. Finally, with recognition that such differences as location and promptness of delivery are economically significant, a product might be physically homogeneous and still be differentiated as a marketable item. As a result, products that can be regarded as homogeneous for purposes of economic analysis are becoming a diminishing minority.[1]

For purposes of economic analysis, we may at least start with the idea that the crucial test of homogeneity is that two units or portions of a product are enough alike in the mind of the buyer—preferably a well-informed buyer—so that he will, and can safely, treat them as interchangeable and be guided in his buying by price as the decisive factor, outweighing any differences that may exist. This characteristic can lead to the most widely different results, according to the conditions in connection with which it operates. These conditions include large numbers, small numbers, or intermediate numbers; sale at prices

[1] Some consider them nonexistent when all differences, including services, are taken into account. To the writer, the essential question seems to be whether there are differences that would offset or outweigh a difference in price. If not, this identifies a class of transactions with distinctive economic characteristics as indicated in the following paragraph.

271

made by supply and demand or at "quoted" or negotiated prices; current control by the producer of his individual output or exposure to the contingencies of seasonal production. In terms of theoretical models, homogeneity with large numbers spells "pure competition," while with small numbers it spells "pure oligopoly." The nearest approach to pure competition in practice occurs in agriculture and is generally recognized as unduly severe, calling for some measures of relief. Pure oligopoly, in the models, is construed as the most thoroughgoing departure from competitive standards, short of complete monopoly—in some versions, it is equivalent to monopoly in its effect on price. The effects in practice, as we shall see, are not so simple or so extreme as this; and while they raise substantial problems, these are largely of a different sort.

The requirements of homogeneity, while definable in basically similar terms, take different form in at least three kinds of selling: the organized exchange, the price quoted by the seller or negotiated between the seller and the buyer, and the goods produced to order to meet specifications set by the buyer, who thus sets his own test of homogeneity, at least in the form of a minimum requirement. The purest case of this last sort is the one in which the supplier firms competing for the order submit sealed bids, and the lowest bidder gets the order. Or qualitative considerations other than price may affect the award. This is so distinctive a form of pricing that it will be deferred to a later chapter. For the organized market, the test of homogeneity is that it is sufficient to enable the buyer to bid with confidence on an offer of a given quantity of a given grade and to accept the lowest-priced offer on the basis of price alone. Then changes in prices reflect changes in the balance of amounts offered and demanded.

In quoted-price selling, homogeneity takes effect in a different way, first because the active variable is price, rather than amounts offered and demanded; second because the price normally applies to a continuing flow or succession of sales instead of a single transaction; and third, because of the drastic inroads a price differential between two sellers will normally make on the continuing sales of the seller quoting the higher price, resulting in strong pressure toward ironing out the price differential. The force of this pressure varies with market conditions and practices; indeed, it is inviting error to construe any one of these three characteristics as an unqualified absolute. But with this caution in mind, one might define the criterion of effective homogeneity in this setting in terms of a product uniform enough so that the smallest feasible difference between the prices at which two sellers make it available to a buyer will cause the business at stake—whether single order or continuing flow—to go to the seller quoting the lower price.[2]

Two features of this definition call for notice. The product must be available, and the test of uniformity is the attitude of the purchaser. Two sellers may be offering physically identical products, but if the buyer does not know this, the products may not be effectively homogeneous as inducements to purchase. In quoted-price selling, it is natural that effective homogeneity occurs primarily in sales to business purchasers, who may be supposed to know the products they buy. Or two products may be different; but if the buyers who constitute the market agree in thinking them perfectly interchangeable for their purposes, they have the essential quality of homogeneity.

There may be products which differ only in location; and these can be made fully homogeneous if the sellers offer delivery at the same place, or absorb costs of transport—provided the time of transport does not constitute a difficulty. There may also be products that are differentiated in the minds of the buyers, but fulfill part of the conditions of our problem, in that they may be accepted by the market at equal prices so consistently that a price reduction for one will be met by the other, even though the other could be sold—presumably in reduced relative volume—without meeting the price reduction. Or the market may have established a customary price differential between the two products which is accepted as placing them on an equal competitive basis, and is so stable that it will be restored if altered by a change in one of the prices. This would naturally apply only where the products themselves are substantially static.

So far, the statement has been avoided that homogeneity allows only one price at one time in a single competitive market. Construed strictly, this applies only to an imaginary "perfect market"—an abstraction so far from any feasible and relevant reality as to be of little use to the present study. The more pertinent concept appears to be a chain of transactions, within which equalizing tendencies contend with tendencies toward differences. The equalizing tendencies are limited, chiefly by costs of transference (transport and arbitrage), by limited knowledge of actual transactions, and by the time it takes for fuller knowledge to

[2] The above, plus what follows, is an elaboration of the similar proposition in Chap. 7, Sec. 1.

percolate. The tendency toward one price needs to be understood in terms of the market forces that give it whatever truth it may have, and the conditions and limitations under which these forces operate. Aside from costs of transference, one need only mention forward contracts and irregular departures from published prices, initially secret, knowledge of which percolates imperfectly and at varying speeds.

Under forward contracts, deliveries may be made simultaneously at different prices, even in dealings carried out on organized exchanges, where simultaneous prices for current and future delivery may differ. A producer may be paying different prices if transactions made at one price have not filled all his requirements, or he may sell at different prices if one price has not disposed of a volume of output close enough to capacity to eliminate pressures resulting from short-run marginal cost being below average cost. Or sellers may have the commodity in one assortment of places, and buyers may want it at a different assortment of destinations. If costs of transport are substantial, this at once introduces some of the most baffling complexities of pricing theory and practice. These will need a pair of chapters to themselves. And we have already raised the question how precise homogeneity needs to be in order to bring about its characteristic economic effects.

2. Selling on Organized Exchanges

The organized exchange may be discussed first, as being the simpler case and also as embodying most fully the principle of prices determined by the meeting of supply and demand in markets. This was long treated by economists as the general case and the one consistent with thoroughgoing competition. As already indicated, if products are not homogeneous as they come to such markets, they are graded for purposes of trading. There are also, of course, local produce markets in which the produce is not graded, and prices may differ according to buyers' estimates of its quality and condition. Or growers may operate on a scale enabling them to establish branded grades (*e.g.*, Del Monte and Sunkist) sold through regular channels of distribution. Or smaller growers may deliver to local retailers at negotiated prices, or sell direct at roadside stands. These methods involve product differentiation, and they are mentioned here only because it is convenient to treat the marketing of agricultural products in connection with organized exchanges, which play such a dominant part in the pricing of the staple products.

In these fully organized markets, the ultimate consumer does not appear: the demand that figures is that of processors, traders, and dealers, and the supply is that of some raw material or intermediate product not in shape for final consumption. The system of grading is suited to enable buyers to bid on a basis of price, with confidence in the product they will receive. Where accurate grading is not feasible, as in the cases of leaf tobacco or livestock on the hoof, organized markets take other forms, but are still marked by the fact that prices are determined by the meeting of supply and demand, not quoted or administered by the sellers. The most characteristic markets of this sort are those for basic agricultural products, though there are also metal exchanges, and a variety of other products are thus dealt in, including some grades of lumber.

Farm products thus dealt in can fairly be regarded as fulfilling the condition that any one producer's supply and his influence on price are negligible parts of the whole. In the case of metals, there are larger as well as smaller suppliers, the supply that passes through an exchange may be only a fraction of the whole and may be affected by the actions of single large producers. Such cases shade off from those in which prices are still made by supply and demand, and have some corresponding flexibility, to cases in which prices are directly quoted or administered, as evidenced, for example, by the steadiness of basic steel quotations.

In the case typical of agriculture, each seller is virtually limited to accepting or refusing the price he finds offered in the market and has little effective option to refuse. He might hold his supply off the market temporarily, at some cost and risk to himself, or in extreme cases he may leave it unharvested, but as an individual he does no distinguishable price-making. However, he does not necessarily, or typically, get the same price as all other producers of the same product. Strictly, the market records one transaction at a time, and the next one may be at a different price, since the prices are constantly changing. The market price may govern transactions made off the exchange, but because of its fluctuations, farmers who are neighbors may receive different prices according to the time when their sales were recorded, and purchasers may pay different prices on the same basis.

On the supply side, the element of competition involves no conscious rivalry between producers, and certainly no attempt by one to take customers away from the others. Each assumes the others' supply will be unaffected by his actions. Competition comes in by virtue of the fact that the supply brought by each producer is the outcome of his individual decision to produce, in the light of his appraisal of the prospects, based on the experience and evidence available at the time he makes the decisions that commit him to production. He acts on his own supply, but of course he does not "control" it in the same sense in which a manufacturer does, being subject to the uncertainties of weather and crop pests. And he commits himself a season in advance. If last year's crop was extra plentiful, and last year's price correspondingly low, he does not, if he is sensible, assume that next year's price will be equally low. On that basis the supply of this particular product might drop close to zero in the next season, and the price might soar, setting the stage for a disastrous oversupply in the season next following.

There are evidences that producers do tend to overweight last season's price in making their commitments for the current season, with resulting tendencies to overcorrection of discrepancies between supply and demand, but nothing like what would occur if growers produced all they would be willing to supply on the assumption that they could sell it all at the price that prevailed last season. This last is the basis of the invalid form of the "cobweb theorem," in which the departures from equilibrium of supply and demand become progressively larger if the supply function is more elastic than the demand function, as would normally be the case with an agricultural product.[3] There is no evidence of such a tendency to progressively increasing departure from equilibrium, and it is not reasonable to expect it. This is an example of the pitfalls, already mentioned, of treating a supply curve as determined solely by the existing price, instead of by a reasonable forecast of next season's conditions, including other producers' reactions to last season's market. A more elaborate instance of such departures from equilibrium is the familiar corn-hog cycle, in which the ratio between the prices of corn and hogs alternately stimulates and restrains the conversion of corn into pork products by putting hogs in the feed-lot.

These tendencies to departure from equilibrium appear to be less important than the tendencies working in the other direction. On an

[3] This has been commented on above, Chap. 7, p. 173.

organized exchange, the balance of supply and demand includes the carry-over. When such a market is operating freely, a seasonal shortage may be mitigated by withdrawals from the carry-over, and vice versa in case of a seasonal excess. Normally, of course, the carry-over merely shares the impact of fluctuations of supply, it does not absorb them entirely. It substantially reduces the fluctuations of price that would otherwise result from fluctuations of the balance between current production and consumption. Withdrawals of current supplies into the carry-over as part of a public program of price supports are a different matter. These policies of price support have made their way into use, in the face of strong initial resistance from the individualistic attitudes of American farmers, as a result of the severity of competition in agriculture, which is so much greater than in industry and trade.

3. Competition in Agricultural Staples

This disadvantage to agriculture appears to be, in different forms, a world-wide phenomenon. The form it takes in this country can be described in a variety of ways. Agricultural competition can be classed as "pure but imperfect," and the imperfections are of the sort that make the competition more severe than "perfect competition" is supposed to be, rather than less so. Improvements in production—mechanical, chemical, and biological—have caused output per man-hour to increase at a rate roughly corresponding to that in manufacture and transport, thus falsifying the predictions of nineteenth-century economists, based on the idea of an inevitable historical trend toward "diminishing returns" in agriculture. Meanwhile, demand for agricultural products has been less expansible and less elastic than demand for "utilities of form, time and place" and especially those classed nowadays as tertiary. The resulting inequality of pressure has been accentuated by the high rate of natural increase of population in rural areas, while large cities do not maintain their populations by natural increase.

This results, in some backward and isolated areas, in crowding farm families onto farms too small and too poor in soil and situation to be capable of adequate productivity. With this naturally goes a low standard of cultivation, with the result that these areas are hardly touched by the general increase in productivity. One of the serious pathological features of American agriculture is inequality—not merely or primarily inequality between one-family farms and large-scale farming enterprises, including corporate farms, but inequality between the efficient one-family farm and substandard units, including those on which sharecroppers eke out a meager and pinched existence. There are, of course, also the subarid areas in which rainfall may be insufficient for considerable periods, and which create a dustbowl problem if put under plow. Here the problem of seasonal uncertainty, which affects agriculture in general and tends to make agricultural competition particularly severe, is extended and intensified.

To sum up, we have seen a variety of features of agricultural production that tend toward a relation of supply and demand that is unbalanced to the disadvantage of the producers; while a market in which supply is first created and then encounters an inelastic demand, ensures that conditions of unbalance take strong effect on price. What of the producers' natural remedy of restricting output if the price does not yield him a normal return? Obviously, in any given marketing season, such power of restriction is so severely limited as to be ineffective. To withhold from market crops already produced means that the costs of production, already "sunk," become a total loss; and this will hardly be done unless the price is so low as to fail to cover the final costs of harvesting the crop and sending it to market. The remedy rests with the next season's production, and here the seasonal uncertainties prevent any accurate adjustment, because there is always the strong probability that the next season will not be so unfavorable as the last; hence withdrawals that would be indicated, if the future were expected to reproduce last season's experience, may not occur.

Shifts between different crops are possible, though they may not be easy in areas where production is geared to a one-crop specialization. This difficulty may be mitigated by diversification, which is more needed in agriculture than in industry and trade, because of the lack of current control of input and output, making an oversupply of a single crop a more serious matter in terms of its impact on price. In general, diversification is presumably easier in agriculture than in manufacturing or mining, though not so easy as in mercantile trade. Land and the basic farm buildings and equipment appear on the whole less specialized than manufacturing equipment, though large-scale, one-crop farming does call for expensive specialized equipment; and specialized areas such as the wheat belt can hardly find alternative products for which there is sufficient demand to make thoroughgoing diversification a feasible resource.

Where it is a question, not of selection between different crops but of inadequacy of the farm's total income, the problem is more difficult, because the "natural" adjustment on the supply side calls for the withdrawal of the least suitable land from cultivation, and withdrawal of persons or families from the occupation to which they have committed their personal talents and resources. The expression that "farming is a way of life" expresses the idea that this kind of withdrawal, with the necessity of finding an occupation of a radically different sort, faces more resistance than a shift between different industries or different branches of trade; and will not be so readily made in response to a degree of financial incentive or economic pressure that would be sufficient in the latter case.

From another angle, in the case of the one-family farm there is the kind of supply function, already discussed, in which a large part is played by the personal efforts of the family itself, together with capital already committed.[4] As we have seen, this kind of supply function is highly inelastic and may even have the reverse kind of elasticity in which a lower return per unit of output makes people work harder and produce more. The shift out of agriculture into industry and trade is largely made by the younger generation, but it does not appear to have been sufficient to eliminate the special pressure on those that remain. This pressure falls, naturally, most heavily on producers of less-than-average efficiency. One way of describing it is to say that whereas, in the kind of "bulk-line" array of costs that is typical of an industry or a branch of trade, there is at any given time a small high-cost "tail" of output produced at an operating deficit by producers who will be forced to drop out unless they can improve their performance, in the one-family farm type of agriculture there is typically a much larger fraction of total output that yields subnormal returns on the capital and effort invested by the farm family, but without driving these resources out of production. Such farms often suffer from insufficient capital for the requirements of modern efficient methods. This means that the farm has presumably stretched its capital-raising capacity, and that the

[4] See Chap. 7, pp. 174-75.

capital burden already assumed is encroaching on the net yield available for the farm family itself. Such a hardship condition may not carry its own natural corrective. A wage-earner whose product is not worth a standard wage would be laid off or discharged; a farmer in a corresponding position does not discharge himself.

To sum up, competition in agriculture appears to be subject to tendencies to go to hardship lengths, on account of a combination of conditions, including increased supply impinging on inelastic demand of limited expansibility, under conditions of marked seasonal uncertainty and affecting producers whose response is to accept less return rather than to produce less if some minimum return is not earned. The difficulty does not seem to be primarily due to the homogeneity of staple agricultural products, though the existence of an organized market, which establishes this homogeneity, may possibly have some influence in promoting one-crop farming and increasing the readiness of farmers to undertake production without having a specific market in prospect, as commercial or industrial producers are more likely to do. On the whole, the special severity of agricultural competition appears to result, not so much from any one feature as from the way in which a combination of features works together.

One final difficulty has been left to the last, though many would probably put it first: namely, the fact that farmers' purchases, which enter into their costs, are made at prices some of which may have monopolistic features and most of which afford the producers and dealers more protection from the extremes of competitive pressure than the farmer enjoys in selling his product. The concept of "parity," based on the ratio between the prices farmers pay and those they receive, is used as a basis for policies aiming to protect the farmer from unfavorable changes in this ratio, measured from a base date when it was favorable to the farmer. While this factor cannot be ignored, the weight that should be given it appears to present an insoluble problem, the chief reason being that the conditions governing the prices at which farmers buy do not in themselves explain why the prices at which farmers sell do not adjust themselves to cover farmers' costs, whatever economic forces these costs may embody. This throws us back on the other factors, determining the character of farmers' competition in production and selling. We turn next to the pricing of homogeneous products in industry and trade.

4. Homogeneous Products Sold at Quoted Prices

As a first move in analyzing this problem, it seems that one may leave out of account the theoretical case of homogeneous products sold under the quoted-price system by sufficiently large numbers of small producers to bring about "pure competition." If such industries exist, their problems are different from those with which this book is mainly concerned. And it appears probable that one could not find significant cases in which atomistically small producers produce products meeting pertinent tests of homogeneity, except as their products are graded on organized exchanges. If there are cases in which government or other large buyers set precise specifications, which are more than mere minima, and which are met by atomistic producers, these must be very special cases. It will be assumed here that the prevalent types are those in which the number of firms actively impinging on one another's sales volume is small or moderate, or involves a limited number of large firms plus a larger number of firms that are relatively small, though they may be of substantial absolute size.

We have seen that where products are differentiated, moderate numbers are sufficient to generate vigorous four-dimensional competition in which, though price may not be the most active dimension and may in some cases be the least active, it is complementary to competition in product design, selling effort, and efficient production. It remains to inquire whether competitive forces may be effective without large numbers in the three-dimensional competition appropriate to homogeneous products, in which competition in product design is, by definition, inactive. This is a substantial task, in view of the fact that prevalent theoretical models virtually deny the effectiveness of competition wherever numbers are small enough to cause each firm to recognize that its actions will occasion responses by its rivals. Hence these models need first to be dealt with.

Before doing so, one word of caution is pertinent. Since these models concentrate so completely on price, one is tempted to accept the idea that competition of homogeneous products is confined to price. But this is about as misleading as it would be in the case of differentiated products to assume that, because product design and selling effort are the most active dimensions of the competitive complex, the dimension of price plays no part. The idea of a price that automatically sells the goods is a fallacy that might fairly be regarded as brother to the fallacy of the better mousetrap that sells itself.

Economists are in no danger of forgetting that the selling of mousetraps (in quantity) requires selling effort of some sort; but they may tend to forget that when a homogeneous product is sold in the absence of an organized exchange to serve as a market, the seller must do something to supply the deficiency, to bring his selling offers to the attention of potential customers and to establish active contact for the soliciting and taking of orders. Such sellers do not expatiate on the qualities of their products after the fashion of consumer advertising, but they have active selling departments, and have been known to worry over the amount these departments cost them. The seller of a material frequently or typically renders services of guidance in its use; and the quality of these services may count as a selling point, even if it would not outweigh the smallest feasible price differential and thus would not take the product out of the "homogeneous" class, as we are defining it.

The models we are about to examine mark the most recent stage of a development in which four phases can be broadly identified: recognition of tendencies to destructively severe competition, leading to a search on the part of business for shelters from the rigors of such competition; passage of the Sherman Act, aiming to prevent shelters that took collusive or monopolistic forms; discovery that in fact industrial competition was in general no longer destructively severe; and formulation of theories explaining how noncompetitive results can come about without the kind of collusive or monopolistic tactics at which the Sherman Act was aimed—these theories centering in the models of pure oligopoly. They have had a sequel: a more or less successful move to expand the mandate of the antitrust laws to cover actions having the intent and effect of implementing a condition of "pure oligopoly" and thus impairing competition.

The theory of pure oligopoly starts from the premise that in industries where firms are few, the actions of one will generate reactions from the others, and that firms learn to act in anticipation of these reactions, as producers under pure competition do not. This is reasonable, if the premise is not made too mechanical. More questionable is the assumption that acting in anticipation of rivals' reactions means assuming that one's competitive moves will always be met so promptly and precisely as to eliminate competitive gains in volume, bringing competition to a stalemate. This is mainly applicable to homogeneous products, and even here, as already suggested, it does less than justice to the persistence and ingenuity of American business men in devising ways of circumventing obstacles, including their rivals' reactions. If taken at full face value, it becomes the basis for what may be called the unreasonably rigorous interpretation of the theory.

This interpretation prejudges precisely the questions a discriminating critic should ask about the kinds of responses that do or do not defeat the initiator's purpose, the conditions under which such responses will or will not be expected, the methods of circumventing them and the limits of circumvention, the reactions to uncertainty about all these things, and the varieties of behavior that may result under different conditions. What we may call the reasonable or flexible interpretation of the theory leaves room for these questions, merely assuming that the stalemate pictured in the rigorous model is one of a variety of things that can happen under varying conditions. The most probable outcome it envisages is an alternation between phases of active adjustment and of passive stability. And the phases of active adjustment may include competitive forces.

The rigorous model takes two forms. One, in which a firm expects either its price increases or its price reductions to be followed, brings about what may be called a leadership price. The other, assuming that firms expect price reductions but not price increases to be met, and represented by a "kinked" individual-demand curve, leads to a price which, so long as this expectation holds, remains rigid at any level it may have assumed between some firm's marginal cost as a minimum and a leadership price—possibly that of a different firm—as a maximum.

"Leadership," in a noncollusive model like this one, does not imply any one consistent leader. It implies rather that any important firm can lead a price downward or attempt to lead it upward, subject to veto in the latter case by any other important firm that refuses to follow. The "leadership price" then becomes the price which, in the view of a strategic seller, would bring optimum profits to him if the others duplicated his price moves. The strategic seller should logically be the one with the lowest standard of leadership price, whether because his costs are low, or because he is most concerned about long-run possibilities of progressive increase or decrease in the industry's sales volume, including the effect of attracting or forestalling new entries, or because he is most optimistic about his ability to increase his share of total sales volume at prices equal to his rivals', or because of the combined effect of all these factors.

The result might perhaps be called a "quasi-monopoly" price—that may be a matter of semantics. But it should be obvious that this price is not identical with a "monopoly price" as usually interpreted—one that would yield maximum profits on the entire output of the monopolized product—nor with the price that would yield maximum total profits to all the *existing* members of the industry, considered as a unit and omitting the earnings of new entries.[5] Nevertheless, as presented in the rigorous model, it is close enough to these ideas to have been identified with one or the other of them by eminent theorists. It does not represent effective competition, but belongs to the family of ideas based on the pursuit of business gain under conditions dominated by some kind of concurrent action by the producers in an industry, not by the independent attempts of each firm to increase its business gains, largely at the expense of the others, by individual and competitive pricing tactics. Thus it forms a telling count in the indictment of the competition of the few as inherently and inescapably monopoloidal. An important variant is Fellner's theory of quasi-agreement; while the most significant recent study of a basic conditioning factor is Bain's study of barriers to free entry and their bearing on the force of potential competition. (Bain finds the most formidable barriers, however, in the field of product differentiation.)

The leadership model pictures firms as expecting that both their price reductions and their price increases will be followed. That a price reduction should be met is natural enough; that a price increase should be followed without collusion takes some explaining. The logic runs as follows. If A raises his price, the others could maintain their former prices and scoop A's business. But they could make more by raising their prices to a point just under A's new price, and still scoop his business. However, this would force A to come down to their level. Then,

[5] Cf. especially Joe S. Bain, "A Note on Pricing in Monopoly and Oligopoly," *American Economic Review* (March 1949), pp. 448-64; reprinted in American Economic Association, *Readings in Industrial Organization and Public Policy* (1958), pp. 220-35.

since they would wind up with prices equal to A's in any case, they would profit more by going all the way with him than by going only part way.[6] So they would go all the way, unless some one of them—call him B—thought A had raised the price above what B conceived as the best leadership level, in which case, he would refuse to follow A above that level. Similarly with price reductions, since they will be met, no firm has an incentive to initiate them unless the existing price is above its idea of the best quasi-monopoly level. This model, then, tends to equilibrium at what is often miscalled a monopoly price, but is logically the level set by the lowest idea of the best quasi-monopoly price which is held by any of the important firms.

More familiar, perhaps, is the rigidity model, based on the "kinked" individual-demand function, in which the seller expects any price reduction to be met and neutralized, but not his price increases. The asymmetry of this case—which makes some theorists uncomfortable—is only apparent, since it reduces to the assumption that the lowest price governs in either case. In this model, a price reduction, being met, yields no competitive gains, but a price increase, not being followed, normally brings prohibitive competitive losses of business. The chief gap in this model is the lack of any explanation of what determines the level at which prices remain rigid. So far as the model goes, they are completely indeterminate between quasi-monopolistic and ruinously competitive limits.

Actual prices are not as haphazard as this model would imply, and they must have got where they are by some process that the model does not cover. While prices of this sort are, as a group, in the sticky rather than the flexible class, they do move from time to time; and when they move, it must be because at such times the conditions of the model do not hold and other forces have taken over. The explanation of the level

[6] E. H. Chamberlin (*The Theory of Monopolistic Competition*, 1933, pp. 47, 50) concludes that where firms are few enough to envisage others' reactions, price will reach equilibrium at the monopoly level (this is later qualified for such things as time-lags and uncertainties), but he did not explain how price would be raised up to that level if it were below. I had mentally noted that such an explanation could be furnished; and Chamberlin has recently furnished it ("On the Origin of Oligopoly," *Economic Journal*, June 1957, pp. 211, 218) in the guise of a rendering of Stackelberg's analysis, to the effect indicated in the text. One may accept the proof that a price increase *may* be followed without collusion. Whether it will always be followed, under all conditions, is another matter, into which we shall have to inquire later.

prices reach must lie in these other forces, plus the conditions that cause them to take command and break up the stalemate of the rigidity model. If prices ever rise, without collusion, there must be times when a price increase by one firm will be followed. If they fail to rise when they are clearly below a leadership level, it must be because firms expect an increase will not be followed. If they ever fall, one or more firms must have thought they had a chance to make a competitive gain which would not be fully neutralized, or else must have thought prices were above their preferred leadership level.

This implies that there must be times when firms are uncertain what reactions to expect, and then they may either avoid the risk of disturbing the status quo or if that status is unsatisfactory, some may make exploratory moves, preferably of a sort that can be withdrawn if the results prove unfavorable. Through such moves the rigidity stalemate may give way either to leadership or to active competition. Between times, the stalemate may prevail and may help explain why prices do not move more often. The rigidity phase, being passive, is less important than the active phases that determine the levels at which prices stand at times of rigidity. But I am convinced, on the basis of cases with which I have had contact, that there are situations in which the rigid phase prevails. The "reasonable" interpretation of the theory includes rigid, leadership, and competitive phases, plus a challenge to explain how one turns into another.

One final note: if, in the rigid phase, the industry is merely prolonging a price reached in an earlier active phase, the character of this price depends on the character of the forces that shaped it in that earlier phase. If these forces were effectively competitive, and if such forces, though latent during the passive phase, will resume action at any time when the existing price is no longer in line with substantially altered market conditions and competitive pressures, then the price can be fairly called a competitive price, whether or not any active competitive price movements are going on at the time. This may be obvious, but one encounters attitudes that contradict it, implying that there is no competition unless firms are undercutting one another's prices, thus forcing prices continually downward. The competitive mechanism for raising prices, if they have got below a normal competitive level, is not so obvious. It seems to be thought of, by such critics, in terms of "supply and demand" which are generally inapplicable to quoted-price trading. Thus the principle, obvious or not, may be worth stating.

5. Stigler's Criticism of the Rigidity Model

Probably the most thorough criticism of the model is George J. Stigler's.[7] He has marshaled argument and evidence in a weighty attack on what we have called the unreasonable interpretation of the theory. He has shown that the prices in question do not have the extreme and unique rigidity that this form of the theory calls for, and that they do not differ from other prices so greatly as this form of the theory calls for; and he has cited various instances of kinds of behavior different from what this form of the theory calls for. All this is useful and welcome. Less useful is the sweepingly negative character of his critique, which rests content with discrediting an unreasonable form of theory and shows no concern for fitting his enlightening material constructively into what is here called the reasonable form of the theory.

Taking as a point of attack the assumption that firms (always) expect price reductions to be met and price increases not to be met, Stigler asks whether the results of price changes agree with this expectation and finds that they do not.[8] The trouble with this method of testing the model is that according to the model, price changes will occur only at times when firms do not expect this kind of reaction; hence Stigler's negative results are not only quite to be expected, they are irrelevant as tests of the model—unless any change of prices is to be regarded as a refutation, and that seems a bit too unreasonable an interpretation. The pertinent question seems to be whether *there are times* when firms expect the "kink" type of reaction, and whether *at such times* they do *not* change their prices. This calls for a different kind of evidence, such as might be yielded by an inquisitive following up of the testimony given by business men in regard to their expectations in the Hall and Hitch study.[9]

[7] "The Kinky Oligopoly Demand Curve and Rigid Prices," *Journal of Political Economy* (October 1947), pp. 432-49. Stigler refers to the treatments of Hall and Hitch, Sweezy, Bronfenbrenner and others. Cf. also C. W. Effroymson, "The Kinked Oligopoly Curve Reconsidered," *Quarterly Journal of Economics* (February 1955), pp. 119-36.

[8] Stigler, *op. cit.*, pp. 438-41.

[9] R. L. Hall and C. J. Hitch, "Price Theory and Business Behavior," *Oxford Economic Papers*, No. 2 (May 1939).

Stigler does find a case in which the American Tobacco Company raised a price, was not followed, and rescinded the increase after a severe decline in sales, after which prices declined further for several months.[10] This is an example of the kind of exploratory price change just mentioned as part of a reasonable picture. The case which Stigler considers "the most striking case of contradiction of the assumptions of the theory," but which actually illustrates something different, rather than contradictory, is an attempt made in 1934 by the American Potash and Chemical Corporation to lead the price of potash downward, which was given up when the other firms did not follow.[11] This move was made, not to increase profits but to reduce them, by a firm which judged that this would be desirable for the (three) producers as a group, at a time when both an antitrust action and a projected new entry were in the offing (both later materialized). Thus this case fits the picture of conditions under which downward leadership is logical. And evidently the company *expected* or hoped that the reduction would be followed.

Stigler compares the price flexibility of oligopoly groups successively with groups exemplifying monopoly, collusion, price leadership, and product differentiation, always on the assumption that according to the "kink" theory the oligopoly group should in each case show less flexibility, and finds that it does not.[12] This seems to be a case of testing an unreasonably rigorous form of the model. Stigler had himself given reasons why collusive prices should show high rigidity, and we have seen earlier that the theory of the flexible monopoly price is an error. There are reasons for inflexibility in these other kinds of cases which do not all apply, or not equally, to noncollusive oligopoly. In the light of what we have called the reasonable interpretation of oligopoly theory, there seems to be no reason for expecting it to show greater rigidity than these other types. Perhaps Stigler's most consistent finding is that price flexibility increases with the number of firms in an industry—as is natural, there being more selling units that might develop ideas leading them to want to try out departures from the status quo, some of which, in some part of the market, might succeed.

Stigler closes on a pregnant note. "The kink is a barrier to changes in prices that will increase profits, and business is the collection of devices

[10] Stigler, *op. cit.*, p. 438.
[11] *Ibid.*, pp. 440-41.
[12] *Ibid.*

for circumventing barriers to profits."[13] Thus he expects the kink to be circumvented, whether by collusion, by price leadership of the umbrella type, or of the barometric type which succeeds only by accurately reflecting market forces, or by the kinds of maneuvers contemplated in the "theory of games." Some of the latter might have competitive effect; and it is clearly of enormous importance whether these circumventing devices make effective competition possible by circumventing obstacles that stand in the way of seeking profits by competitive methods, or whether they circumvent competition itself. After all, competition is one of the chief "barriers to profits."

6. A More Positive Analysis

It is time to attack the question under what conditions firms will have opportunities for gain by competitive methods, affording incentives that will not be wiped out by the defensive measures the other firms are driven to take, but will work themselves out in a balance which, however imperfect, will permit aggressive and defensive competition to exist together instead of being mutually inhibited and canceling each other out. The answer depends both on pricing practices used and on the state of the market. As to pricing practices, one of the weak spots in the entire body of theory that has just been examined is its assumption that the published price and the actual price charged are the same. In practice this is rarely the case, and a reasonable theory of this kind of pricing begins with this fact. The discrepancy may play a larger part in the pricing of homogenous products than elsewhere, because the price charged is such a decisive factor, and this accentuates the need of circumventing rivals' reactions to one's own price moves. One of the functions salesmen may exercise, in varying degree, is discretion in the matter of shading the "list" price. Even where such departures, or major ones, are left to high administrative officers for decision, the selling department maintains the contacts and channels the information about the general state of the market, as well as particular situations, in the light of which special pricing decisions may be made.

[13] *Ibid.,* p. 447.

One obvious fact may be worth noting because of its consequences: the actual price may be below the published price, but not, under normal conditions, above it. Hence if a seller's actual price is above a rival's published price, he knows he is being undersold; while if his actual price is below the rival's published price, that proves nothing, one way or the other. When a firm raises its published price, one can be fairly sure that it intends to raise its actual price above its former published price; then if its increase is not followed, it knows it is being undercut, while if a reduction of the published price is not followed, that proves nothing in regard to the actual price. This may explain certain cases cited by Stigler, in which price increases were followed more promptly than price reductions.[14] A secret price increase above the published level occurs only when shortages are being rationed otherwise than by raising the published price, and a "gray market" results.

If a firm wants to gain business by a competitive price move and prevent the move from being neutralized, the first requirement is not to publicize it. Real secrecy is not likely to last long in the kind of business being discussed, in which sellers are alert to track such things down, but some degree of secrecy, with accompanying uncertainty, may last long enough to make the special arrangements appear to afford some prospect of advantage. Along with this, temporary concealment may be helped by not making the concession uniform and general, since such a concession would be quickly known. Large orders, carrying an assurance of a substantial flow of future business, may appear worth while on special terms. Thus the incentive to special pricing is related to what may be called the discontinuity of markets of this type, as distinct from the continuous stream of generally similar transactions which is commonly conceived in theoretical models. As we have seen, the impetus to price-shading may come from large and powerful customers who have, or claim to have, better offers elsewhere or who might produce for themselves, and who use the bargaining leverage afforded by these alternative possibilities, in combination with the importance of the volume of business they represent.

Such large forward orders may be especially attractive if they enable the producer to adjust his rate of production on these orders so as to fit in with the filling of other orders that may call for some irregularity of production and thus make the total flow of production more regular

---

[14] *Ibid.*, p. 440.

while avoiding the risks involved in producing to stock without advance assurance of being able to dispose of the stock on advantageous terms. Some portion of such an order may turn out to be, in effect, off-peak business, though the amount that has this character is necessarily uncertain. A very large order of this sort, if it carries a substantial margin above direct or "out-of-pocket" expenses, even if less than "full cost" including a "normal" return, may be regarded by the producer as guaranteeing its ability to meet those parts of its overhead that call for contractual payments. This might be regarded as warranting some concession from "full cost" if necessary to secure the order, though it would not warrant a price close to short-run marginal cost.

The initiative may also come from a seller who can secure an order only if he makes a price concession. In either case, there is a special segment of sales on which the seller's individual demand curve is, in effect, horizontal at the level necessary to secure the order, so long as the reduction does not spread. But if it spreads to customers the firm could otherwise have kept without needing to give them a concession, there is a reduction of net revenue from their business to be charged against the net gain on the business that the concession secured. The result is something between the horizontal demand function of pure competition and the "leadership" type of demand function which assumes that competitive gains from price reductions will be canceled.

With regard to the tendency of such concessions to spread, there are a wide variety of conditions and a correspondingly wide variety of expectations on the part of firms giving differential treatment. In the most favorable case, the firm may expect that the rest of its business will be unaffected. Then the business it gains by the concession (which we assume it could not get otherwise) becomes an isolated sector of demand with infinite elasticity and affords a gain at any price above marginal cost. Such complete isolation must be quite exceptional. One important case might be that of a large customer who is a strong bargainer and has secured price concessions that are recognized and acquiesced in by the market, and on the basis of which the suppliers who give these regular concessions secure their shares of the large customer's patronage, with the result that any one seller does not, by giving such price concessions, disturb an existing market adjustment in a way that invites fresh departures from the existing and recognized differential structure.

All this means discrimination, with all the possibilities it brings with it of perverting the normal service of competition as between different customers and injuring their competition with one another, since the concession a customer secures has no dependable relation to the cost of serving him. To compensate, if competition between sellers has become inactive, the sharp bargaining of buyers may serve to activate it, though not in an ideal form. From this standpoint, discriminations that tend to spread are the least objectionable. Concessions to some customers are subject to limitations imposed by the need of keeping one's other customers satisfied. When competitive pressures are strong, such concessions tend to arise and to spread, until they may eventually lead to a downward revision of list prices for the purpose of regularizing the price structure. Or if the publicized structure has been raised in an attempt to make it more adequate, without the support of sufficient demand, this may lead to an increase in irregular concessions. The upshot is that the conception of a homogeneous product as one that does not permit differences of price must be qualified to admit a persistent, though fluctuating, amount of differential pricing, even though most of the single differentials may be temporary. The Marshallian tendency of prices to equality exists, but is qualified by the opposite tendency, in degrees that vary with market conditions.

So far we have been speaking of aggressive competitive moves— those aimed at getting rivals' customers away from them. Defensive responses face a choice of methods. One is to meet the competitor's irregular pricing wherever one finds it, confining one's own special concessions to sectors of the market where they are needed to meet the competitor's concessions. The other method is to reduce one's published price, thus eliminating in one move any higher-priced areas that might be inviting targets for the competitor's price-shading tactics, and forcing him to cut deeper if he is to continue his inroads. Where the market has become chaotic, such a general reduction may be aimed at restoring it to regularity. It may also gain good will with business customers, who care less about the absolute price they pay than about paying the same price as their competitors.

Perhaps the most typical situation is one in which different sellers have mental pictures, which may diverge somewhat, of the prevalent state of price concessions, including possibly a recognition of a rough classification of customers into sharper and less sharp bargainers, the latter tending to receive only the minimum concessions that have become recognized as general. Sellers are aware of greater concessions made to sharper bargainers, but may not be sure how widespread these are. If existing demand is substantially short of capacity, the larger concessions will tend to spread, and different sellers, according to their generally aggressive or defensive attitudes, may aim to lead or to follow.

If demand is close enough to capacity so that only a limited quota of sellers are under strong pressure to get added orders to utilize unused capacity, the tendency of concessions to spread may become limited or may disappear. Then, when a seller becomes aware of a particular concession below the general level, or when he is confronted by one of the sharp-bargaining buyers who claims to have a better offer available, assuming he decides to treat the claim as genuine, he has still to decide whether it is a sporadic case, which he can neglect without losing more than one order, or whether it is a symptom of a trend, which he had better not ignore or fall too far behind. It is in this kind of form that the balance of "supply and demand" (more correctly, demand and unused capacity) often makes itself felt on pricing in the kind of imperfect market we are considering. The seller has to balance the gain from securing a particular order at a concession, against his conjecture as to the effect, if any, which his own concession may have in stimulating the spread of similar concessions, and the same applies if he adopts a policy involving repeated concessions; and these conjectural effects are likely to be influenced by the amount of unused capacity and by whether it is increasing, diminishing, or remaining stable.

If a substantial amount of idle capacity exists, it does not promptly result in a reduction of prices to an extent calculated to equate demand with supply at a normal rate of output. It might be that no feasible price reduction would bring this about. A firm does not underbid its rivals by more than enough to secure the business in question—or if it does, this is a symptom of price warfare occurring after price-shading has become extensive and aimed at softening up price cutters and persuading them that it will be more advantageous to return to a closer adherence to list prices. Short of this, if excess capacity persists, and if competition is strong enough to bring about a downward movement of prices, it is likely to proceed by a series of small concessions, which spread and are followed by slightly larger ones, and so on, in a progressive movement which takes time and is not likely to go to the logical limit at which "representative firms" sell at prices that approach short-run marginal cost.

Dickson Reck, in his study of purchasing under sealed bids, finds competition acting in this downward-nibbling way, with the low bid tending to no normal level, merely a little lower than on the preceding letting.[15] There is, of course, a special reason for this in the case of secret bidding, where the bidder does not know what bid he has to beat, but has reason to think that, in the absence of some change in the market, a bid materially higher than the previous low would have little chance of securing the contract. The kind of imperfect market discussed is one in which a seller may know exactly what he has to beat and either just meets it or just beats it; or he may have to depend on imperfect information, which may be slightly out of date by the time it is verified. These features may have some of the same tendency to a downward-nibbling movement, if substantial idle capacity persists.

Turning to the question whether an increase in price will be met, there is a very simple device, in common use, for removing uncertainty: a firm announces an increase in advance and withdraws it if it becomes evident that the others are not following. This reduces the uncertainty to a matter of whether the increase, if it is nominally followed, will act as a point of departure for an increased amount of price-shading. It will naturally have this effect if price is increased to a level affording the kind of profits commonly associated with monopoly pricing; and will also offer an attractive invitation to new entries (including entry by large customers) unless substantial obstacles stand in the way. Thus price increases, even if nominally followed, are not likely to go to the level of short-run profit maximization, but rather to some level belonging to the general family of "full-cost pricing."

One condition in which a price increase is most commonly followed is one in which there has been a general increase of costs in the industry, and the price increase offsets the whole or a substantial part of the increase in costs, the amount being influenced by whether demand appears strong enough to stand the increase in price without serious shrinkage in volume. Another condition in which a price increase may be followed, at least nominally, is one in which a weak market and price-shading have brought prices to a seriously inadequate level relative to costs, causing the industry to welcome a price increase, and possibly to refrain, at least temporarily, from the former amount of price-shading. But a weak demand may prevent such an increase from being followed.

[15] See Dickson Reck, *Government Purchasing and Competition* (1954), especially Chaps. 6-8.

An increase in irregular prices, when they are below the publicized level, is naturally unlikely to be followed in the same precise way as an increase in published prices. But if demand is becoming stronger, there is likely to be a shift toward suspension of irregular price-concessions, and this may spread. In such a condition, the discrepancy between list prices and those actually charged is commonly reduced, resulting in a fairly general increase in actual prices, even in the absence of an increase in list prices. To sum up, this analysis has indicated ways in which prices may be raised, which are not included in the strict oligopoly model, opening up more possibilities of flexibility, depending on varying conditions determining whether an increase will or will not be followed.

7. Summary on Quoted-Price Selling

The sector of the economy at which we have been looking is strategically important; and is perhaps the most difficult sector about which to reach clear and reasonably simple conclusions on the requirements of effective competition and the extent to which those requirements are or are not approximated. It is the sphere of industry about which it is most difficult to give a definite answer to the condemnatory judgments expressed or implied in existing theories. And while our analysis may have been successful in combating the extreme conclusions of the doctrinaire models, the picture it puts in their place may appear uncertain, even confused. It is a picture in which almost anything might happen, between extremes of destructively severe competition on one side, and prices as high as those of monopoly on the other. The possibility has even been suggested of prices getting set above an optimum monopoly level and sticking there, because firms feared what might happen if one broke away from the status quo. And it is impossible to deny that such an uneconomic adjustment might, temporarily, occur. One may be sure it is nontypical, even extremely unlikely; but one is for the most part reduced to speaking of what is likely or unlikely, rather than of what is bound to happen. And our picture of the typical or likely behavior is not one of a tendency to a closely defined equilibrium. With respect to published prices, it is a picture of alternate change and passivity, with pressures accumulating in the passive periods until they bring about a movement, upward or downward. Change in actual prices is more frequent or even continuous.

If one wants to compare the results with some theoretical standard, there is little point in using the standard of "perfect competition," in which excesses and shortages of capacity, relative to demand, cure themselves promptly and automatically, without creating large profits or losses. An alternative is what might be called—disregarding logic— "perfect competition, grade B" in which periods of excess capacity are offset by periods of shortage, in their effects on earnings. In shortages, prices rise until demand equals the limited supply, and when capacity is in excess, prices fall to short-run marginal cost, and the losses of one period are equal to the profits of the other. Since the demands in question are strongly inelastic, this would mean price fluctuations, more violent than would be serviceable toward stabilizing the economy, and without any reason for expecting periods of profits and losses to balance out in a healthy average supply price for productive resources.

Lesser fluctuations of prices and profits would render whatever service can be rendered by prices and profits toward economic stability. They cannot properly be expected, by themselves, to bring stability about, but can be useful in connection with other policies that promote stability in consumer demand and investment outlays. Such moderate price flexibility fits better than more extreme price fluctuation with the growing tendency of firms in these industries to schedule their investment outlays on a basis of extrapolations of long-term trends. Such extrapolations may lean to the optimistic side, and the resulting programs may be curtailed in recessions; but in more normal times, firms are willing to build ahead of the growth of demand, thus spreading the expansion out more than if they were more afraid of a temporary excess of capacity, and therefore crowded their capital expansion into times of boom, thus rendering the booms more hectic.

The kind of price behavior that tends to come about in such cases appears to be subject to forces making in general for a restrained degree of flexibility which is at least not inconsistent with the modest standard just described, and healthier than the extreme flexibility of "perfect competition, grade B"; though few would be bold enough to define optimum flexibility or to claim that it is regularly attained. There are some nonferrous metals, produced by large units but affected by world-wide market conditions of supply and demand, which have in recent years been subject to extreme fluctuations of prices. If the general tendency is toward undue rigidity, published prices exaggerate this, and the evidence of actual prices is virtually unobtainable. The prices in question appear to be more closely influenced by costs than prevailing oligopoly theories indicate.

In general, actual prices tend to decrease when excess capacity becomes substantial enough to make short-run marginal cost relevant to a firm's calculations, by an irregular series of small unpublicized competitive reductions, which are likely to bring prices below average cost, but not all the way down to short-run marginal cost. They are also likely to decrease if they are above average cost, even if there is no substantial excess capacity, so long as output can be increased without encountering marginal costs that are substantially above average costs. Prices are likely to rise above average cost when demand is pushing against the limits of economical capacity. If they have fallen below average cost, they may rise—which means that one firm's increase may be followed—if there is a hopeful revival of demand, or if persistent failure to cover average costs has caused firms to get tired of the results of price-shading, and induced a mood in which some firm thinks its rivals may be ready to follow an upward lead. However, if there is still much unused capacity, an increase of this sort is likely to be unstable, subject to a resumption of the process of price-shading. Or prices may rise less precariously if demand becomes strong enough to reduce unused capacity to such a point that firms can properly and safely reckon from a basis of average costs, rather than from short-run marginal costs. (We have discussed earlier this question of degree in the matter of unused capacity.)

If the immediate state of supply and demand permits a price substantially above average cost, there is the further limit exercised by the two kinds of potential competition already mentioned: the restraint of firms farsighted enough to visualize the likelihood of making price-shading too inviting for some of the existing producers, and the further likelihood of making the industry inviting to new entries. Both these forms of potential competition set limits on the amount by which prices can enduringly exceed average costs. This force of potential competition deserves more attention than it appears to have received in the past forty years and more. Prior to that, its effectiveness may have been overestimated. It can set limits on prices when the active forces are such as to push them too far above costs; but it needs to be accompanied by active competition to furnish more positive price-reducing forces, and to keep producers reminded vigorously and frequently of the standards which active competition sets and from which an industry cannot depart too far without incurring instability. To sum up, under favorable conditions there are forces in this class of industries that act to keep prices in a flexible but effective connection with the costs of a representative firm; higher or lower according to the state of demand relative to capacity.

This of course presupposes that the producers do not act collusively to put an end to the independent action on price and production, which is the essence of competition; and that they do not exert coercive pressures to exclude competitors from the market or from access to the requisites of production. Both "collusion" and exclusion raise difficult and delicate problems, which are not to be resolved by any mere form of words. "Collusion" is a colored term implying concerted action for an illegitimate purpose. Competition itself requires some forms of concerted or quasi-concerted action, to maintain the trade practices of orderly rivalry, but it also needs room for flexibility and adaptation in these practices, or producers may get to know too well what to expect of one another. The point is that these practices must be of the sort that furnish a framework within which active rivalry can go on, without doing anything to determine the terms of the competitive offers in which the rivalry itself consists. The larger the number of competitors, the less likely is their rivalry to stagnate or stalemate. Hence one of the conditions favorable to effective competition is the largest number of competitors consistent with efficiency and with absence of serious or fatal inequalities in efficiency or competing power. It remains true here, as in other sectors of the economy, that effective competition is on an insecure basis unless there are efficient and strong competitors whose percentage of the total sales of a given product is relatively small, and who are not reduced to impotence by the overshadowing power of some giant firm.

CHAPTER 12

Competition Over Distance: Extractive Production

1. Difficulties of the Subject

As if the theory and practice of competition were not complicated enough without it, distance not only adds to the other complications, it compounds them. In an optimistic mood, it seems that the best one can say is that organized thinking about the subject is in a primitive state, or in its infancy. In a less optimistic mood one is led to doubt whether it is possible to construct a theory that will be at once simple and compact enough to be widely understood and realistic enough to be useful in interpreting the seemingly endless variety of situations encountered. They include not only various degrees of homogeneity and differentiation of the product, but also varying degrees of durability, which in turn have an effect on the feasibility or nonfeasibility of resale or arbitrage dealings, and these in turn bear on the amount of difference possible between prices in different locations. Costs of transport, relative to the value of the product, range from costs so heavy as to keep production and sale local, to costs so light that they can reasonably be disregarded. The most characteristic problems arise in the intermediate ranges, in which costs are substantial enough to determine the marketing areas that can be reached from particular locations of production and the prices that can be charged, but not too heavy to permit producers in different locations to compete for the same or overlapping market areas.

Both producers and purchasers may be either diffused or concentrated area-wise, and they may be numerous and small or few and large. Producers may sell on a supply-and-demand basis, in well-organized or unorganized markets, or on a quoted-price basis under regular or irregular marketing conditions, with results ranging from those approximating pure competition to those of oligopoly. Some of the most stubborn problems deal with producers whose only competition comes from a distance, giving them, in dealing with nearby customers, a differential advantage which could be termed a monopoly of location. This is limited by direct competition of distant competitors and by the indirect competition resulting from their desire not only to hold a preferential advantage in sales to nearby customers, but to foster their growth in their competition with similar customers elsewhere, thus increasing the demand in respect to which the nearby producer has this preferential advantage. Thus arises the problem of the division of the resulting "advantages of location" (an undefined term) between producers and their nearby customers.

The result is to add problems of local "discrimination" to the forms of discrimination arising from other causes.[1] With respect to these problems, the meaning of "discrimination" contains undefined areas, including differences between legal concepts and those preferred by most economists. As to discrimination arising from competitive and nonconcerted action, economic theory has not dealt satisfactorily with the problems of analysis involved, while regulatory action has explored the field, but quite naturally without succeeding in drawing precise and definitive boundaries between the kinds and degrees of discrimination and accompanying interpenetration of selling areas that are useful and those that are injurious from the standpoint of effective (not "perfect") competition.[2]

[1] The general subject of price differentials on homogeneous products is briefly discussed above, Chap. 11, Sec. 6; cf. Chap. 5, Sec. 4. Economics and law are in substantial accord on monopoly-building discriminations of the sort that featured the Standard Oil case of 1911. Under the 1914 and 1936 legislation, the pertinent legal concept is "discrimination *in price*," construed to involve differences in price, leaving problems as to what differences are or are not discriminatory, plus further problems of standards of legality for discrimination.

[2] The law strikes at restrictions of the competitive activities and opportunities of individual competitors, as well as of competition in general in a relevant market area. Since the former is easier to prove than the latter, cases have tended to hinge on it, without searching analysis of the latter problem, which is more difficult but more basically important. Regulatory action has tended to assume injury to *competition* as implied in hardship to *competitors* resulting from discriminations. But it is possible for protection of competitors to lessen the force of competition. And injury to competition has in some cases been held to exist where the disfavor to competitors was not shown to have amounted to hardship. These points, and the exploratory character of regulatory action, appear in Corwin D. Edwards, *The Price Discrimination Law* (1959), especially pp. 15, 417, 432-38, 442-61, 518, 523, 528-30, 533-45.

Distance calls for readjustments of some basic economic concepts, and these prove to be unexpectedly troublesome. Instead of a single "market" in which, if it is perfectly competitive, there can be only one price at one time for one product, one is confronted with a *market area* in which, even under similarly perfect conditions, there can be different prices. The differences are limited by cost of transportation, plus the added amount needed to induce traders to move supplies from point to point in the area when the discrepancy in prices exceeds the bare cost of transport. Even more basic is the transformation of the concept of "price," which economic theorists find it so convenient to conceive as a single-valued fact. Sales involving distance break it in two—price paid at destination and net amount received at point of origin. These are best regarded as two dimensions of a single price transaction; but the assumption that price is a single-valued fact has given occasion to seemingly endless argument about which is "the" price—the argument arising mainly out of disputes over the construction of the phrase "discrimination in price" in the Robinson-Patman Act.

My own firm conviction is that this act cannot be rationally construed without taking account of both dimensions of price and that both are implied in its language. Even if sale is at a delivered price, in determining whether a difference in price between localities is discriminatory, key evidence would bear on whether it corresponded with cost of transport, and whether the net yield at point of origin was different. But when the act permits discriminatory prices to be defended on the ground that they were made in good faith to meet an equally low price of a competitor, the "equally low price" could only refer to the price at destination, where the competition was encountered. And if a producer sells F.O.B. mill and shades this price to meet competition at a distance, what he is trying to equalize is the destination cost to the purchaser, whether this is technically called "the price" or not. Any other construction makes nonsense of the defense based on meeting competition.[3] In this light, the battles that have been fought

---

[3] This would be clear under the original language of the Clayton Act, which spoke merely of meeting competition. The phrase "equally low price," introduced by the Robinson-Patman Act, might reduce this provision to the kind of nonsense indicated, wherever sales are made F.O.B. mill, under the kind of verbal construction which insists that "price" must mean one thing *or* the other. Defining it as mill net would, under guise of making the term "discrimination" economically meaningful, wipe out what little remains of the defense based on meeting competition "in good faith." If sales are made at delivered prices with local differentials, the mill net would appear to an economist relevant to the decision whether these differentials constitute discrimination or not.

over the question whether "price" meant price at destination or net yield at origin cannot avoid an air of irrelevance to the substantive issues hinging on the phrase: "discrimination in price." And it is hard to believe that even legal formalities really necessitate these verbal irrelevancies as a means of construing a phrase of an act, the intent of which is not open to doubt. But we are running ahead of our story.

2. The Main Theoretical Models

Although traditional economic theory has allowed its predilection for one price to come near submerging the problems of distance, it has not ignored them completely. It has employed two main models: one in which production is diffused in space and carried on by many small units, while purchase is concentrated; and another in which production is concentrated at one or more localities—but impliedly with competition at each locality—while purchasers are diffused. These types are the basis for Frank A. Fetter's distinction between afferent and efferent markets. The first is exemplified by staple agricultural products, in which producers get prices related to those made in central markets, minus the cost of getting their crops to market. Differentials due to accessibility are combined with those due to fertility and are conceived as capitalized in the rental value of the land.[4]

The second type appears in discussions of industrial production, and here the habitual assumption of general theory is that the producer charges one price at his plant, to which cost of transport is added to get the price paid by variously located customers. I am not aware of any real attempt to explain why pricing was assumed to be on this uniform mill-net yield basis, prior to the time when the matter became a focus of controversy over basing-point pricing. It seems to have been taken for granted as natural.[5] Hotelling, for instance, in his spatial model already discussed, takes it thus for granted without question, and without supplying the conditions necessary to bring it about.[6]

[4] The quality of cultivation also affects the quality of the land, while it pays a superior cultivator to farm superior land.

[5] This follows Cournot's treatment; cf. above, Chap. 2, Sec. 2.

[6] See Chap. 9, Sec. 6.

These conditions would seem to be that at each point of production there should be pure competition, or at least competition effective enough to bring mill prices down to the competitive minimum; and this must be conceived as the same as the minimum at which it would be worthwhile to take on added units of sales. It appears fair to say that economic theorists assumed this result without clearly visualizing the conditions necessary to bring it about.

Thus Fetter appealed to "the principle of indifference" as creating a single price in a competitive market and defined manufacturing centers as markets, without scrutinizing this scheme of terminology to verify whether the conditions necessary to its operation are present in centers of large-scale manufacturing, subject to competition from a distance.[7] And Vernon A. Mund appealed to the competitive type of spatial price structure, using as his examples various agricultural products in which atomistic competition existed in the area of origin and applying this standard to judge the competitiveness of the spatial pricing structure of one of the more isolated manufacturing plants, subject to competition only from a distance.[8] He apparently did not realize the gap that was jumped in assuming that the second kind of competition, if genuinely engaged in, should be expected to bring about the same kind of spatial price structure as the first. There is no sufficient reason why this result should be expected.

If the space devoted to this problem in the present study appears disproportionate, the justification is that this is perhaps the largest area of unfortunate immaturity in competitive pricing theory. Any realistic study of competition over distance, between large-scale industrial units, needs to make a fresh start with the problems of spatial price structures, free of prejudgments that do not grow out of study of the conditions of this kind of competition. In this field it is peculiarly necessary to distinguish two questions. (1) What kind of pricing behavior tends to result from the independent efforts of such industrial units to secure profitable business in competition with one another—competition of the sort to which they are exposed? (2) Since this pricing behavior reacts in turn on the kinds of competitive pressures that result, what is the effect of these reactions? Do they tend to a healthy and effective competitive outcome, and if not, what can be done about it?

[7] See F. A. Fetter, *The Masquerade of Monopoly* (1931), pp. 270-72, 279.
[8] See "Prices Under Competition and Monopoly," *Quarterly Journal of Economics* (February 1934), pp. 288-303.

These questions are, of course, in addition to collaborative action on trade practices (which may or may not be salutary) and action enforced by public orders (which may or may not define permitted conduct and the effects of which are generally shrouded in uncertainty). The need of keeping these questions distinct may seem too obvious to mention; but in this highly controversial field the obvious is often forgotten or brushed aside.

3. The Purely Competitive Agricultural Model

The international market for wheat requires differentials sufficient to generate a prevailing movement from areas of excess production—notably the American wheat belt—to areas of excess consumption in Europe and elsewhere, the movement being consistent and quite stable, and much of it passing through bottlenecks where central markets exist. This has been the basis of the oversimplified model in which the Chicago price is that of Liverpool minus cost of transport from Chicago, and the farm price is that of Chicago minus cost of getting wheat from the farm to Chicago and disposing of it there. Departures from this pattern occur because movements may bypass both Chicago and Liverpool, wheat may be bought in this country below the Chicago-based prices, and actual costs of transport may be below the openly-quoted freight rates. Studies by Holbrook Working and Miss Snodgrass indicate that quoted price differentials vary and are often less than the Liverpool-minus model would indicate, though inducements to movement must exist, because wheat does move.

Less durable produce is distributed in form for consumption to many local markets, in which it is priced on a supply-and-demand basis but without the benefit of systematic grading—impracticable for perishable products. The possibility of reshipment from a temporarily oversupplied market to others offering better opportunities of sale is also severely limited or precluded by the perishability of the products. Therefore prices in different local markets vary according to temporary conditions of supply and differ from one another unsystematically and unpredictably, and can differ by more than costs of transport from one to another.

Where they are still shipped substantial distances from areas of excess production to areas of excess consumption, the producer or shipper naturally directs his shipments to markets where possibilities of sale appear most promising, on the basis of information available at the time of shipment. But individual shippers cannot keep pace with the simultaneous reactions of other shippers to the same (or slightly divergent) market information. As a result, conditions of surplus or shortage in particular consuming centers tend to be overcorrected by the uncoordinated actions of different suppliers, and the supply is not distributed in the most effective fashion. Whether this results in consumers paying more or producers receiving less, in the aggregate, is an arguable question. Consumers in general are unlikely to be alert enough shoppers and bargainers to get the best results out of the resulting market fluctuations. But the economic interest that seems most likely to suffer is that of the small producer, much of whose income may depend on the chance contingencies of the price realized in one or a few particular markets to which his produce has been shipped.

4. A Variant: Citrus Fruits

It was this kind of difficulty that led to the marketing of citrus fruits by cooperative marketing agencies, which could follow up their shipments and divert them in transit in the light of the latest market reports, thus distributing supply in more even relation to demand. They could also compensate the grower according to his contribution to the joint supply, rather than according to the relatively high or low price at which his particular oranges happened to be sold. Such arrangements have obvious monopolistic potentialities, unless the total supply marketed is beyond the control of any one such organization. The picture is varied by large private growers establishing their own private brands, for which they undertake to build up consumer preference by the regular tactics of sales promotion.

There has been a great shift of products from perishable to durable categories as a result of the modern extension of the arts of canning and freezing, resulting not only in a year-round market for seasonal products, but in qualities that in many cases bear no stamp of inferiority to the fresh products. As to the resulting price structure, it seems to have a hybrid character: a branded product sold at a quoted price that must maintain some sort of competitive or comparative relation to the fresh product, even for the purpose of building a really ample off-season demand, and must similarly maintain some competitive relation between frozen and canned products. While these competitive relations include any area differentials that may be encountered, it would appear that the contest between differentiated products has become the more important factor. This development has applied to citrus fruits, modifying the spatial competition to which they are subject.

At an earlier stage, an extremely interesting problem of spatial price structure arose when competition occurred between two producing areas distant from one another—specifically, oranges from California and Florida, marketed by cooperative agencies. This instance of competition over distance brought about a spatial pricing structure that exhibited the essential features of freight absorption to meet competition; all the more instructive because the form of pricing practice is necessarily altogether different from the industrial quoted prices in connection with which freight absorption ordinarily occurs. There is, of course, no question of a single price set by the seller at the point of origin, nor does the seller set a delivered price at the destination; the local market does that, and net yield remaining to the selling agency is subject to the contingencies of local supply and demand. However, it appears that the California marketing agency *aimed at* a uniform net yield, directing its shipments with that in view, sending more to markets where prospective prices promised a higher-than-average net yield at origin and less to markets where the reverse was the case. As a result, prices tended to approximate equality in markets equally distant freightwise from the California growing area.

This meant that when oranges from Florida met the competition of the California product, they encountered an area price structure that would afford the Florida sellers high average net yields on sales in the nearby southern markets, and lower average net yields on sales in the more densely peopled areas of the north and northeast, since they had to pay higher freight costs to reach these northern markets, without realizing commensurately higher prices. If the Florida oranges had been marketed under pure competition, single growers could have disposed of their whole output in nearby southern markets where the average net yield was high, and thereby they would have brought it down, making these areas less profitable for shipments from California. What sort of adjustment might have resulted from this hypothetical competition is necessarily conjectural. What happened in this duopoly of marketing agencies was that the Florida marketing agency divided its shipments between southern and northern markets, allocating them in such a way as to continue the general spatial price structure which afforded them higher net yields on southern sales than in the more populous north. In this modified and approximate sense, they did the equivalent of absorbing freight to reach the northern markets. This occurred because the competition governing sales was not atomistic competition among individual Florida growers, but competition from a distance, with fruit coming from California. Where the governing competition came from a distance, methodical differences in sellers' net receipts appeared, naturally and to all appearance inevitably.

The case is, of course, complicated by the difference between California and Florida oranges, which makes an overlapping of marketing areas natural. In any case, the principle of the free market would include letting the local markets register their collective judgment of the relative values of different lots of fruit, whether from different growing areas or from the same area; and this judgment is probably not wholly separable from valuations that register shifts in the balance of supply and demand. If the total supply is the resultant of free choice by a multitude of individual growers, the total net yield will, on the average of seasons, reflect the minimum necessary supply price of the amount produced, with qualifications as to subnormal returns, connected with sunk costs and seasonal uncertainties, discussed in the preceding chapter. And if there is some restraint on supply, there is still the question whether it is capable of doing more than neutralize these tendencies to subnormal returns, without exceeding the limits of regimentation which our society is prepared to tolerate. There is probably no verifiable criterion of a minimum necessary supply price by which an answer to this question could be proved. And whatever the answer may be, it presumably is not substantially affected, one way or the other, by the spatial pricing practice that is here described as a modified equivalent for freight absorption.

5. *Another Variant: Crude Petroleum*

Another instance of production by many producing units, under controls of supply affecting price and exercised by a number of units small enough to be called oligopolistic, is the production of crude petroleum in the United States. Here the units controlling supply include the regulatory authorities of the principal producing states, plus a limited number of large producing and importing companies. The case is similar to that of citrus fruits in that multiple producers, in different areas, are subject to controls which operate by areas as units. It is different in at least two outstanding respects. One is that demand comes, not from a series of local markets of the supply-and-demand type, but from a highly concentrated group of refiners, possessing a considerable degree of oligopsonistic power and in a position to take considerable initiative in quoting strategically important buying offers. Another difference is that these large purchasers are integrated, owning their own large reserves of crude, though they also purchase part of their supplies. Part of this country's crude supply is imported, under quasi-"voluntary" restrictions, from South America and the Middle East, by organizations in which the great American refiners are represented in varying proportions.

Numerous American independents are moving increasingly into the field of foreign production, though handicapped in the matter of established marketing outlets, creating increasing competitive pressure in an otherwise oligopolistic market. In these major foreign producing areas, costs of extraction are far lower than in this country, while reserves, relative to output, are much larger. The difference in costs of extraction exceeds the costs of transport and would make importation into this country highly profitable if it were unrestricted, since American refiners with interests in low-cost foreign oil can gain by importing it. Costs of transport to the west European market are lower from Western Hemisphere sources than from the Middle East. Needless to say, the resulting geographical price structure is a complicated picture, and it appears to be in transition.

The explanation of the American structure might begin with the depression of the thirties which coincided with the striking of big new supplies, and in which posted prices of crude, which had been $2.00 a barrel in 1926, fell to 50 cents, while actual prices in many areas are said to have dropped to 10 cents.[9] This violent price behavior is consistent with the prevalent view that elasticity of demand for crude is low. This would mean that if a discrepancy arose between supply and demand at previous prices, whether due to excess or shortage of supply or to sharp expansion or contraction in the demand function, and if the price were determined by equating demand and supply, price would change strongly or violently, since moderate changes in price would not suffice to restore the balance of supply and demand. It appears that such potential price fluctuations are nowadays moderated in part by the policies of the big refiners, with their strategic position on both the supply and demand sides of the market. But in the collapse of the thirties such stabilizing forces were either not in evidence or were insufficient.

The result was the setting up of what may fairly be called unacknowledged price supports through control of output, with the aim of adjusting supply to estimated demand and under the aegis of conservation of a limited natural resource. The estimate of demand is made by the United States Bureau of Mines and does not take the shape of estimates of different amounts that would be demanded at different prices. It must be construed as presupposing prices not substantially different from those prevailing, with the further presupposition of low elasticity, so that minor changes in prices would make no substantial difference in the amount demanded. The adjustment of output is made, somewhat imperfectly, by controlling authorities in the different producing states, who assign production quotas to individual producers, aimed at a total state output presumed to be consistent with the state's share of the national output that would balance supply and demand.

The guiding concept from the standpoint of conservation is an engineering concept of the rate of extraction of crude that will result, given efficient techniques, in maximum feasible recovery of the oil under-

[9] See Maurice Byé, *Revue d'Economie Politique* (June 1957), paper translated under title "Self-Financed Multiterritorial Units and Their Time Horizon," *International Economic Papers No. 8* (1958), pp. 147-78, 163. Also Gilbert Burck, "World Oil: the Game Gets Rough," *Fortune* (May 1958), pp. 125, 127. This precipitous decline was reflected in prices paid by Gulf refiners, which are higher than prices in the field. See D. C. Hamilton, *Competition in Oil* (1957).

ground.[10] Beyond this limited objective the conservation concept does not appear to have been carried. One wonders what would happen if the rate of output indicated by this standard should differ from that required to balance supply and demand. Logically, such a discrepancy might be adjusted by altering the permitted amount of imports, but I am not aware of such changes having been made for this reason. It is also possible that the maximum-total-recovery concept has some effect on the calculations that result in bringing new wells into production. It is clear that unrestricted competition in the production of crude oil would lead to an unduly rapid rate of extraction, which would result in leaving in the ground some oil that should be recovered. Therefore restraint on the competitive rate of extraction is at least in the direction of the maximum-recovery standard; and if one is optimistic, one may assume that the rate of production resulting from the quotas is not clearly inconsistent with the range—necessarily an estimate—within which maximum total extraction would fall.

But the effect most clearly attributable to the conservation concept would appear to be the role it played in avoiding judicial condemnation of a system of price supports through limitation of output. It is interesting to note that crude oil quotas became effective in 1934, and two years later the Agricultural Adjustment Administration, following an adverse decision of the Supreme Court in the Hoosac-Mills case (also following drought and dust-bowl conditions) shifted its emphasis to soil conservation, and since then has always included this validating objective in its scheme of things, though it has reverted to placing principal emphasis on the support of farm prices and income.[11] It is only natural to infer that the crude oil controls helped suggest the use

[10] See Wayne A. Leeman, "Crude Oil Prices in the United States at the Gulf Coast," *Journal of Industrial Economics* (July 1957), pp. 180-91. For the California situation, the authoritative work is Joe S. Bain, *Economics of the Pacific Coast Petroleum Industry* (Pts. 1, 2, and 3, 1944-47). Bain's findings are summarized in a review article by Arthur R. Burns, *Journal of Political Economy* (February 1948), pp. 35-53. Cf. also Edmund P. Learned, "Pricing of Gasoline: a Case Study," *Harvard Business Review* (November 1948), pp. 723-56; also Spencer Klaw, "Standard of California," *Fortune* (November 1958), pp. 113 ff.; also works referred to in note 9 above, by Byé and by Burck. For the over-all and international picture, see Federal Trade Commission, *The International Petroleum Cartel*, Staff Report to the Senate Select Committee on Small Business, 82 Cong. 2 sess. (1952) (cited hereafter as Federal Trade Commission, Staff Report); also Economic Commission for Europe, *The Price of Oil in Western Europe* (1955).

[11] Cf. Theodore W. Schultz, *Agriculture in an Unstable Economy* (1945), p. 170.

of the conservation *motif* to validate controls of farm output. The element of conservation bulks larger in the case of oil, and appears to be more clearly incompatible with unrestricted competition.

While the publicly sponsored valorization of American crude oil is proof against the antitrust laws, refining and marketing have no such exemption. It is interesting that D. C. Hamilton's findings, presented with scrupulous caution, point to a degree of effective competition in the Gulf Coast refining industry such as obviously does not apply to the quota-governed output of crude.[12] While prices of refinery products do not fluctuate as continually as prices of crude did before the establishment of the quota system and show short periods of fixity, they appear more flexible than prices of crude have been from 1934 to the present. The only long period of fixity is accounted for by wartime price controls.

As to the area price structure for crude, in this country its general character is dominated by the fact that Texas, Louisiana, and Oklahoma are dominant sources of supply, while the greatest concentration of consumption is in the north and east. The Gulf price of crude is taken as strategic, and the major importing companies quote prices delivered at the Atlantic coast. California is semi-segregated, though prices there cannot go above a level that would bring oil in from Texas. Crude oil is produced in the Los Angeles area and in the San Joaquin Valley, nearer to San Francisco, and the oligopolistic position of the big refiners as buyers of crude evidently permits some latitude of policy in the area price structure. Before 1925, a zone structure was used; later the price in the San Joaquin Valley was based on Los Angeles minus a transportation allowance, though the San Joaquin Valley producers would have realized more from a price similarly based on San Francisco.

Bain found persistent exporting of crude oil and products from California at lower yields than those realized on domestic sales; during the thirties a large proportion of these low-yield sales were made by Standard Oil of California. Hamilton concluded that this did not happen in the rest of the country. In 1929-30, an export association was formed which tried to sustain Gulf Coast export prices above the domestic level. Its membership included less than half of the export volume from its area, and its attempt was a failure.[13]

[12] See Hamilton, *op. cit., passim,* especially p. 120.
[13] Cf. Bain, *op. cit.,* Pt. 2 (1945), p. 204; Hamilton, *op. cit.,* pp. 131-32; and Federal Trade Commission, Staff Report, *op. cit.,* pp. 220-26.

6. Petroleum and Oligopoly Models

The petroleum market structure in the United States in general suggests a question not covered by the usual theories. Here is an industry in which production is controlled by a few authorities—those of the oil-producing states—few enough to act in anticipation of one another's responses to their actions, but who act in terms of output rather than in terms of quoted prices. Does this fact make the anticipation of responses work differently from the stalemate in which the fact that a price reduction will be promptly met eliminates the competitive incentive to make it? There is reason for thinking that it does: that competition of the few works more normally and is less likely to be stalemated if the active variable is supply, and supply and demand make the price.

The situation in crude oil does not correspond to the usual theoretical model of oligopoly in that the model assumes that there is no outright collusion, and it is not realistic to assume this about the controlling authorities of the different oil-producing states. They confer, and it is clear that the outcome includes fairly definite ideas about the proper share of each in the restriction of the country's output. But neither is it realistic to assume joint control of output that works perfectly. The states watch each other, with eyes alert to see if some one of them is not doing its proper part; and this apprehension appears to have enough basis to make it meaningful to ask the hypothetical question: If one state acts independently in its individual interest (that is, in the aggregate interest of its own producers), how will it act? And if another state responds to protect its individual interest, how will it respond? And if the first state learns to act in expectation of the other states' responses, what effect will that have on its actions?

In this kind of an oligopoly model, the first move is an increase in output on the part of one controlling unit, and the first effect—until others respond—is a reduction in price, governed by an individual-demand function of the sort analyzed in Cournot's duopoly model, having an elasticity greater than that for the industry as a whole, in a ratio that varies inversely with the size of the first unit's output as a fraction of that of the industry. If it produces a small fraction of the industry's total, its individual demand function will be highly elastic; while if it produces, for example, four fifths of the total, its individual demand function will have an elasticity only one fourth greater than that of the industry as a whole. The smaller producing units, then, have the strongest incentive to enlarge output, if they do not expect their move to be met; and for one such small unit, any feasible increase in the rate of extraction from existing wells would be so limited as to have little effect on the price. Hence it would be certain to be profitable. (Whether it would leave enough margin to stimulate further exploration and development is a different question, but we may assume that the initial move does not go far enough to eliminate this incentive.) The other producing units suffer by selling their existing output at a lower price. The maverick is reducing their profits, but he is not taking away any of their physical volume of business, as he does when he undercuts their prices in a market of the quoted-price type.

Now suppose that one or more of the other producing units decide to protect their interest, not by collusive action, since that has, by assumption, failed, but by independent economic action of the sort at their command—namely, alteration of their own output. What will they do? Where price is the active variable and the product is homogeneous, the answer usually given is: they will meet the maverick's price-reduction and restore their former share of total sales. Even here, however, as indicated in the preceding chapter, there are variant possibilities. They may undercut the maverick's reduced price, either thinking that this is necessary to get back the business they have lost, or seeking to convince him that price-cutting does not pay. Or if the maverick is small and his inroads limited, they may adopt the umbrella policy, maintaining their former prices and letting him increase his share, so long as he keeps within the limits of their tolerance.

Where the active variable is output, the case is much less clear. If the other producers respond by matching the maverick's increase in output, so as to maintain their former percentage share of the total, they drive the price lower than he drove it; and since their output is presumably larger than his, the further reduction resulting from their response is substantially greater than the reduction his original move occasioned. One might construct a rough arithmetical model, focusing on two units, which for this purpose we may call "firms," one producing 5 per cent and the other 50 per cent of a total output of 1,000. The smaller firm increases its output by 10 per cent, thus increasing total industry output one half of one per cent. For illustrative purposes, it may be assumed that the elasticity of demand for the industry as a whole is one third, in accordance with the idea that elasticity is low, and for this special case, marginal cost of production may perhaps be ignored. Incidentally, the low elasticity of demand means that output has not been limited or price raised to the point of maximum profit. The price is reduced, let us say from $3.00 to $2.95½, and firm A, which enlarged its output, has thereby increased its income from $150.00 to approximately $162.50, while firm B's income has been reduced from $1,500.00 to $1,477.50. What will be firm B's response?

Aside from accepting its reduced profit, it can be conceived as taking action to restore either the former price or its former proportionate share of output. If none of the other firms has taken any action, firm B can match firm A's 10 per cent increase of output and restore its former 50 per cent with a 1 per cent increase of its own, being ten times as large as A. The price is now reduced to $2.91, and B's income is $1,469.55, or less than before he made his response. As a partial consolation B's response has reduced A's income to $160.05, but A is still better off than when he started. However, the producers of the other 45 per cent of total output are still to be heard from. If they respond as B did, then a series of increases starts, as the ultimate result of which B, in order to restore his 50 per cent share of total output, must increase his output 10 per cent; total output will be increased 10 per cent, and the price reduced, let us say, approximately 26 per cent from its original $3.00, and everyone's income will have shrunk about 18½ per cent.

If B elects instead to restore the former price, by reducing his output as much as A has increased his, leaving the total unchanged, his total income will be $1,485.00. This could be supplemented if he were able to dump a corresponding amount on some separate market at any price above marginal cost, and the effect on the original market would be the same. The immediate effect of this will be to increase his income slightly from what it was after A's action and before his own response. This appears to be the most favorable response he can make, in its first effect. The trouble with this method of holding an umbrella over the market is that it virtually serves notice on A, and on other potential mavericks, that they can continue to enlarge their output without suffering any penalty in the form of lower price. The ultimate effects of this, in encouraging further maverick actions, might well give B pause. The response of doing nothing has the same drawback, merely in less degree.

It seems, then, that B has available one retaliatory or punitive response and two grades of umbrella response, including the response of doing nothing. As to the retaliatory response, B and the others may be willing to punish themselves in order to punish A, reckoning that it is worth a temporary reduction of profits to discourage mavericks from further tactics of the same sort, checking their inroads before these become really serious. As to such calculations, economic theory can have little to offer except conjectures of an inexact sort. To sum up, it seems that where output is the active variable, no response is available for countering a competitive move by one of the oligopolists, which would not be more expensive and less attractive than the simple meeting of a rival's price reduction, which is the available response where price is the active variable.

This leads to the next question: If A acts in anticipation of B's response, what response will he anticipate? To this the only sure answer seems to be that he cannot be sure—like the only sure answer of the Grand Inquisitor in "The Gondoliers": ". . . of that there is no manner of doubt." His guess at the probable response depends on the responding firm's guess regarding how far his maverick tactics are likely to be carried, including possible imitation by other mavericks. In such a situation, the theory of games seems to be applicable, dealing with A's adjustment to an uncertain prospect of various possible responses on the part of B. In the "minimax" theory, A is governed by the most damaging response B might be conceived as making, and seeks the least unfavorable outcome for himself, *if* that most damaging response materializes. In the model we have been considering, the most damaging response is the one in which other "firms" attempt to restore their former proportionate share of total output. But this is also very expensive to the other firms, and they are not likely to undertake it if A's conduct affords a fair prospect that he will stay within the limits that will not force the others to their most drastic, and most expensive, responses. If they were sure to adopt this most drastic response, A might be deterred from any initial competitive move; but if A practices moderation, he may hope that really drastic responses may not ensue. So A may start moderately; but this brings into being a fresh (and unstable) status quo, subject to being disturbed by further moves, each of which operates via increased supply and takes effect in reduced price.

Therefore, while the model seems to lead to no precisely definable result, the most probable conclusion appears to be that competition of the few is more likely to be effective where supply is the active variable and supply and demand make the price. In such a case, sustaining price and profits above a competitive level seems to require outright collusion more definitely than where price is the active variable. And if collusion breaks down or proves undependable, or is encroached on by fringes of uncontrolled supply, it seems that these imperfections of control are likely to exert stronger competitive pressure in an industry where supply and not price is the active variable. This conclusion may be applicable to the imperfections of production control in the extraction of crude oil, including the increasing fringe of independent action.

Prices of refinery products are, of course, in the class of quoted prices, in which area differentials reflecting prices of crude are combined with other factors and are not dominant. More important is the factor of joint cost, including cracking to alter the proportions of different end products; also methods of marketing, including the occasional price wars among gasoline distributors. These matters would be out of place here. Something may be said, however, about the world-wide structure of oil prices.

7. World Structure of Oil Prices

The world situation differs from that in the United States in two conspicuous ways.[14] In the first place, there is no such sharp bifurcation of control, between output of crude, publicly controlled by quotas, and the refining and marketing processes, subject in this country to the antitrust laws. Elsewhere it would appear that whatever difference there is runs in the other direction, the competitive shading of prices being more marked in the markets for crude. While some independents have refining capacity without commensurate supplies of crude, a more disturbing element seems to consist of independents

[14] This refers, of course, to international markets outside the Iron Curtain.

with small amounts of crude that they must dispose of in the markets, but lacking refining facilities or established marketing channels.[15] One is tempted to speculate that in this case the principle of the greater competitiveness of the small producer is compounded with a situation that does not afford him the benefits of an umbrella policy, partly because the independents are growing beyond the limits that make such a policy feasible for the umbrella holder, partly because, owing to marketing integration, only part of the supply is marketed, so that the added supply takes effect on a fraction of the total—a "thin market"—and partly because the market is one in which established connections do not yield the maverick a place without some substantial chiseling on his part—merely meeting the current price does not serve his needs. Aside from such conjectures, both crude and refined products are handled by the same cartel-type agencies.

In the second place, there is no such unifying homogeneity of output control in the world market as has been achieved by the oil-producing states of this country and has made possible the approximate effectiveness of our quota system. The consortium of producing companies and their jointly owned subsidiaries is marked by cleavages of interest, including the interests of consuming countries that have no oil, and countries granting oil concessions and having—at least for the time being—only secondary interests as consumers. Even the American antitrust laws have played a part in generating diversity of attitudes between American and foreign companies, causing the Standard Oil Company of New Jersey to renounce various agreements of the consortium on the ground that they might be contrary to the antitrust laws.[16] However, Burck quotes an American competitor as complaining that the British Petroleum Company (formerly Anglo-Iranian) "behaves more like an American company than the American companies do."[17] The international consortium has led an unstable existence, has changed its rules in response to changing conditions of supply and de-

---

[15] See Burck, *op. cit.*, p. 126.

[16] Cf. Federal Trade Commission, Staff Report, *op. cit.*, pp. 57, 104-05, 109-10, 269-74. The company's caution on antitrust grounds became much more pronounced in 1942. Burck, *op. cit.*, pp. 126, 193, mentions a consent decree against the company, secured by the Department of Justice in that year. The antitrust laws would apply to agreements restrictive of United States exports and imports. The F. T. C. Staff Report does not mention this consent decree. To this extent the antitrust laws have a force abroad which they do not have, as to crude, in this country.

[17] Burck, *op. cit.*, p. 186.

mand (under the prevailing partially effective controls) and appears at present to be facing increasing competition, including potential competition from the states in which its concessions lie, and to be increasingly uncertain of being able to maintain a stabilized market. Whether this is in the long-run interest of the world, in terms of an enduring future supply of essential fuels, no one can confidently say, especially in the present state of our ignorance about the potentialities and dangers of atomic sources of power.

The price structure within the area of this consortium has been of the basing-point type, and has gone through a number of stages and appears to be subject to an increasing amount of price-shading or equivalent irregular concessions.[18] In the twenties, when American exports were growing and were a dominant factor in world markets, while Mid-East output was insignificant in comparison, world prices were governed by the prices at United States Gulf ports, plus freight to destination. This structure was formalized by the consortium, and was naturally highly profitable for the growing Mid-East production, because of its low cost and despite the fact that the freight from Gulf ports, included in the price paid in western European markets, was somewhat less than that from the Mid-East, resulting in the equivalent of some freight absorption. Mediterranean buyers of Mid-East oil paid higher prices than western Europe, and on sales to the eastern Mediterranean, the Mid-East producers got "phantom freight." The Venezuela price of Venezuela crude was substantially the Gulf price minus an American import duty of 10½ cents per barrel.

During World War II, increased sales of Mid-East oil in the Mediterranean and for bunker fuel caused phantom freight to become an issue, and the outcome was the establishment of a second base price at the Persian Gulf, equal to the American Gulf base price. Later, Persian Gulf prices did not fully follow increases in American prices, and a differential was established by which delivered prices from the two sources were equalized in the United Kingdom, followed by a shift to a Caribbean base involving a slight reduction. Meanwhile, limited amounts of Mid-East crude began moving to American affiliated refineries at net realizations below the Persian Gulf Price. In 1949, the latter price was reduced to a level that, with an accompanying reduction in the freight component, would equalize delivered prices of

[18] See especially Federal Trade Commission, Staff Report, *op. cit.*, Chap. 10.

Mid-East crude at Atlantic ports of the United States; but the reduced realization on sales to the United States soon reappeared, as the Persian Gulf base price was not reduced with increases in freight rates. Other adjustments were made on refined products, which need not be traced in detail. At present, as already noted, the formalized price structure appears to be subject to increasing erosion from price-shading competition by independents.

The situation with respect to oil is distinctive in that, at the American base, prices of crude are governed by publicly sponsored controls of output and refiners' margins are not; while prices of both kinds at the Mid-East base are governed cartel-wise, but with a view to meeting the competition of Western Hemisphere sources. Objections have included the use of a system of reporting of American Gulf prices, which does not include irregular shaded prices, and freight rate applications differing at times from rates actually available; and especially the fact that, insofar as the system is adhered to, delivered prices are known and can be precisely met, with or without freight absorption as the case may require.

8. Another Variant: Bituminous Coal

The pricing of bituminous coal affords a particularly instructive case, partly because both production and consumption are decentralized, partly because it is not only clearly competitive, but to a degree that has made it a "sick industry," and especially because its pricing structure was briefly controlled by a federal commission, charged with establishing minimum prices, with the result that the differential features of the pricing structure they prescribed bore the stamp of public approval, or at least of acceptance as in the public interest. The aim was to establish prices affording yields at the mines that would cover average mine costs. But it became necessary to allow competitive coals from different points of origin to meet one another's prices at different destinations, with the result that (1) mines at different locations secured different mine yields on sales to a given destination, and (2) the same mine secured different mine yields on sales to different destinations.[19] Presumably a given mine would sell by preference to the destination affording it the highest yield; but if it could not dispose of its full output at this destination, it would naturally seek further sales at destinations affording lower yields. Thus two mines at different locations might both sell in two markets, market X affording mine A a higher yield than mine B, while market Y afforded mine B a higher yield than mine A. This interpenetration presumably reflected features of the previous unregulated, competitive pricing structure and was an equivalent of freight absorption, in a different form. And it illustrates the naturalness of different net yields at point of origin, in an industry far from monopolistic.

These brief and oversimplified sketches cover cases in which supply is typically, but not always, the active variable, bituminous coal being an exception in form, if not in substance. These cases may serve as an introduction to the problems of freight equalization and basing-point pricing in industry, which will be dealt with in the chapters that follow.

[19] See Waldo E. Fisher and Charles M. James, *Minimum Price Fixing in the Bituminous Coal Industry* (1955), Chap. 8, especially pp. 178, 188, 205-07, and Chap. 10, pp. 329-30. This regulation took place under the Bituminous Coal Act of 1937, and the resulting price schedules were in effect from Oct. 1, 1940, for two years, by which time increased demand resulting from the defense drive had improved the condition of the industry. A dominant aim of the act was to enable the industry to pay the labor costs established by collective bargaining. *Ibid.*, p. 39.

CHAPTER 13

Industrial Competition Over Distance: The Problem and Its Development

1. Where Transportation Costs Are Not Decisively Important

Before moving on to the tough problems arising where transportation costs decisively condition the features of an area price structure, brief mention may be made of cases that are not thus decisively conditioned because transportation costs are an unimportant part of total value. These are largely concerned with finished products, typically differentiated, though they also include some special raw materials of high value in proportion to weight, and which may be homogeneous. One feasible method of selling in such cases is to charge a uniform delivered price covering the entire country or a considerable section of it and disregarding differences in costs of transport within this area. If the product is nationally advertised, it may be a convenient feature of the marketing system if price is uniform over the area covered by the advertising. If the product is homogeneous, a uniform area-wide price is a convenient basis on which all the producers involved can sell in competition with one another throughout the area.

An economic theorist might think of the disregard of differences in transport cost as discriminatory between destinations, but if it is a minor and incidental matter, he would ignore it. Legally, a dictum by Chief Justice Stone in the Staley case in 1945 stated that such an area-wide uniform price is not a "discrimination in price" within the meaning of the Robinson-Patman Act. The whole area then fulfills the one-price condition associated by economic theorists with a "perfect competitive market," though this complete uniformity is not dictated by market forces (which would permit moderate differences) but by a trade practice. Whether the existence of such a trade practice constitutes the kind of "conscious parallelism" that is regarded as equivalent to collusion is a question unlikely to arise in such cases. Does the uniformity tend to lessen competition through the regular meeting of rivals' prices? A counteracting factor is the effect of bringing a maximum feasible number of competitors into rivalry throughout the "market." The importance of this in promoting competition is often neglected, but it is important in bringing every buyer within reach of the most competitively minded sellers in the industry.

As an alternative to an area-wide uniform price, there may be local differences if sellers meet competition where they find it and in accordance with its differing local force. This may include temporary local price wars or attempts to discourage or extinguish local competitors; but such irregularities are likely to be limited in time, if they much exceed the narrow limits set by transportation costs. If the product is differentiated, the price structure may include differentials between brands or other variants, and these differentials may or may not have acquired a fixed character market-wise. If not, variant products can meet one another's competition over wide areas, whether or not each is offered at a uniform price, the same for all destinations. In such cases, the area structure is not a decisive matter for the meeting of competition.

2. Problems Arising Where Transportation Costs Are Decisive

This brings us to the class of cases in which there is an area price structure with differentiation based on, or limited by, differing costs of transportation (these being substantial) and in which the character of the product permits little or no difference to persist—aside from temporary discrepancies—between prices charged by different sellers to buyers at a given destination, with the result that the area price structure is decisive for the meeting of competition between producers in different locations.[1] The structure may be regular or irregular and

[1] A somewhat similar result, but less absolute, may occur where habitual price differentials are persistent. Cf. above, Chap. 11, p. 273.

may employ delivered pricing or pricing F.O.B. point of origin or various combinations; it may include freight equalization or freight absorption or so-called "phantom freight," also zones with uniform delivered prices within each zone. These practices may be combined in various ways, including (before modification by legal action) single or multiple basing-point structures.

As the latter term is used, it implies that some mills base their prices on points other than their own locations. These basing points are generally points of production, but may not be. Base mills may sell F.O.B. mill and may also quote delivered prices equal to a base price at the mill plus freight—usually rail freight—to destination, up to the point at which the price from some other base offers a lower delivered cost to the buyer. If they choose to sell beyond such points, they must make delivered prices, "absorbing freight" to meet competitors' offerings. Nonbase mills, having no mill price of their own, necessarily charge delivered prices meeting those calculated from existing bases. Such a mill may be regarded as the limiting case of a base mill with a base price so high, relative to those of surrounding bases, as to govern no destinations. If there are no nonbase mills, freight absorption or freight equalization may be practiced, without being classed as "basing-point pricing."

This group of practices covers a wide and perplexing complex of problems for the solution of which, as shown in the preceding chapter, traditional theory offers little help and some misleading preconceptions. Practices may be concerted or individual. Results range from competition so hard as to be destructive, to competition too soft to be effective, according as a firm may price regularly or irregularly, and may meet, "match," or beat (undercut) a competitor's price. Either one may expose a firm to criticism as harming competition, according to the circumstances which point to the intent and probable effect of the practice, including the size and market power or coverage of the firm, relative to its competitors. If it "systematically" meets and does not beat its rivals' prices, it may be criticized as eliminating price competition, while if a large firm undercuts its smaller competitors too deeply, too persistently (or perhaps merely too successfully), it may be charged with using its wider market extent or greater financial power to damage or eliminate competitors and thus lessen or impair competition or tend to create a monopoly.

The problem ramifies into the dilemma resulting from the fact that injury to a competitor may or may not be of a sort that injures competition, and any attempt to resolve this question is likely to hinge on a delicate balancing of incommensurables and uncertain probabilities. How tough or how soft should competition be? It is impossible to eliminate every unfair or undesirable element from competition, and a determined attempt to do so would injure it by making it too soft for its basic purpose, under which it is axiomatic that the less successful competitors get hurt.

This is an area of problems in which business would like a list of practices it may safely follow, and is not likely to get its wish fully. The law of the subject is case law, subject to very general "standards," and cases are decided in the light of particular situations, involving various combinations of specific practices, most of which are normal and legitimate if standing alone, assuming that the firms avoid agreement on what prices they will charge, or other practices of monopolistic character in themselves. What is held legal or illegal is commonly the whole complex, in terms of its setting, intent, and effect. Case law also has a tendency to extend settled principles to apply to new cases that may or may not be fully identical, thus calling for judgment whether they are equivalent in the relevant essentials.

The application of the antitrust laws to the trade practices of spatial competition has involved such extensions. It has followed the general method of the legal framework of individualism—telling people what they must not do and leaving them to devise a workable course of conduct from among the things not forbidden. But as this method has been extended into detailed trade practices, the original broad scope of permitted practice has been encroached on, until a business man may sincerely feel hard put to it to find a set of permitted practices with which it would be possible for him to carry on his business. If he wants to meet or "beat" competition, he must trust to finding ways of doing it that would escape condemnation, while the courts, and the Federal Trade Commission in its quasi-judicial capacity, are not in a position to furnish in advance precise specifications on where the boundaries of legality will be drawn in future cases.

There is a real dilemma here. Rigid rules, fixed in advance, are dangerous; and in this complicated field they are well-nigh certain to have unintended consequences, likely to be undesired and undesirable. An example would be any but the most carefully guarded statutory provisions dealing with the treatment of freight absorption, whether intended to broaden or to restrict its scope, to outlaw it or assure it unqualified legality. Yet there are unfortunate features resulting from the fact that orders in this field are regularly negative—to cease and desist from doing something that appears harmful. In the early stage of dealing with a problem, it is probably well not to form too definite a picture of the positive result desired, because at that stage such pictures are likely to be too doctrinaire and stereotyped for useful application. Later, increasing experience may lead to more pragmatic and flexible positive thinking about desirable forms of competition, adapted to the unavoidable conditions of modern industry. Such positive thinking is much needed and might help clarify the criteria applied in the case-by-case process. Needless to say, the independent student has a special place in this task of positive analysis, and it is this kind of contribution at which the present study aims, recognizing that success can at best be limited.

3. Key Stages in the Development of the Problem

A full historical account of the development of this problem is out of the question in the scope of the present study.[2] But it may be useful to trace a few of the main stages in the public recognition of the problem—which naturally lags behind the development of the problem itself—and to identify each stage with a particular phase of the problem that will be distinguished in the analysis which follows. The reader is trusted to recognize that this involves oversimplification and to make his own allowances.

This synopsis may start with the methods of localized "predatory" competition employed by the original Standard Oil Company to build a monopoly position by eliminating smaller local competitors: methods that figured as crucial evidence in the Standard Oil case of 1911. Here a firm with a nationwide market was able to quote, in the competitor's limited market, prices lower than the competitor was able to meet. Standard was able to price below its own average costs by virtue of its profits in its wider market, with the result that efficiency on the competitor's part would not protect it. In the 1911 case, the damage to

[2] For a fuller account, the reader is referred to Corwin D. Edwards, *The Price Discrimination Law* (1959), Chaps. 11-13.

competition had already been done, and the available remedy consisted of splitting the resulting consolidated firm into fractions that might compete with one another. These corporate entities have exhibited more genuine independence than pessimists at the time dared to expect. The Clayton and Federal Trade Commission Acts of 1914 and the Robinson-Patman Act of 1936 aimed at dealing with such tactics currently, before they could lead to monopolistic results.

Another aspect of the same principle was embodied in the amended long-and-short-haul clause of the railway act of 1910, which included a provision that if a railroad reduced its rates locally to meet water competition, the rates should not subsequently be raised except on a finding by the Interstate Commerce Commission that the increase rested on changed conditions other than the elimination of the water competition. This was obviously aimed at that feature of the practice that deprived the customer of the benefits of the reduction by recouping losses at his expense after the competition had been driven out. The provision was deterrent in character; if the competition was localized in space, it could not be also localized in time.

The 1911 Standard Oil decision appears to have effectively discouraged attempts to build monopoly by the method in question. But in the last decade localized competition by larger firms against smaller ones, though without prospect or intent of establishing monopoly, has been attacked as a form of discrimination injuring competition, because the larger firm's price cuts can be, in effect, subsidized by the profits from less actively competitive areas.[3] On this lesser degree of localized competition, economic judgment is less clear, since effective competition may require some freedom, not only to "meet competition where one finds it" but to take some aggressive initiative in doing so, instead of being limited to meeting a competitor's "equally low price," as suggested in the unfortunately precise wording of the Robinson-Patman Act. This wording was inserted with a view to ensuring that, under freedom to "meet competition" (the Clayton Act phrasing) predatory undercutting should not be unintentionally sanctioned. But the limitation points toward confining locally differentiated competition to the meeting or "matching" of prices, which is held to impair competition in a different and contrary way. The balancing of these opposite considerations is at present an unresolved dilemma, leaving legality dependent on an exercise of judgment that is difficult and necessarily unprecise.

[3] *Ibid.*, especially p. 452.

4. Single Basing Points and Discrimination Between Customers

This brings us to the next major stage of the problem, in which differentiated area pricing structures were used in an opposite way, not to destroy competitors but to cushion competition so that it would not go to destructive lengths. (Opponents of these practices charged that they eliminated price competition.) The methods used include basing-point pricing and kindred practices. Interwoven with the economics of these cases is the legal-factual problem whether concerted action has been used in connection with the pricing structure, in one of two main ways. If prices are fixed directly, by agreement or concerted price leadership, it is the price agreement that is illegal, not the spatial pricing structure; but the pricing structure may serve as a facilitating instrument whereby many prices may be controlled by one or a few acts of agreement, or price leadership may be conveyed in codified form.

Concerted action may be used in implementing or policing the relative price structure without fixing the prices that are to be charged under it, so that it promotes more precise meeting of prices than would happen naturally, after which the structure may operate to lessen or injure competition, affecting prices in ways not wholly predictable, but not fixing them. These two relations of the pricing structure to the amounts charged are distinct, though often confused; and emphasis has shifted from the first to the second during the development of this group of practices.

The economic effects include injury to competition among customers through charging them discriminating prices, and lessening of competition among sellers through the systematic meeting or "matching" of the delivered prices made by base mills, which thus have automatic price leadership in the areas in which their base prices plus freight are lower than the corresponding combination figured from any other base.[4] The first issue may be called the discrimination issue and is

[4] If the base includes a group of mills, the leadership of no one is automatic. And there have been pricing structures, notably under N.R.A. codes, in which nonbase mills were equally free with base mills to initiate prices based on the

naturally most prominent in the case of nonbase mills under single-base structures. The second may be called the price-meeting issue and would remain if every producing point were a base. The first issue was featured in the "Pittsburgh plus" case and later in the Corn Products and Staley cases, all involving single basing points and stressing "phantom freight" charged by nonbase mills to their nearby customers in meeting the delivered prices of base mills. The second issue—the first having been decided—dominated the Cement case, dealing with a multiple-base structure. Both issues were present in all these cases, but were not equally crucial. The present sketch aims to introduce these issues with emphasis on their legal setting, leaving fuller economic analysis to the chapter that follows.

By way of prelude to Pittsburgh plus, it may afford an enlightening comparison to recall an earlier period before the rise of Pittsburgh as a dominant center of iron and steel production, when iron was produced in relatively small, decentralized plants in eastern Pennsylvania, and Philadelphia was the dominant market. The product lacked the uniform quality of later times, and the pricing structure lacked the correspondingly precise regularity, but in a general way the value of iron at various points of production in the area tributary to Philadelphia was governed by the Philadelphia price minus cost of transportation from the point of production to Philadelphia. Later, when iron and steel production became concentrated, with Pittsburgh the dominant producing center, the pricing structure underwent a corresponding change, becoming oriented to a dominant center of production instead of to a dominant consuming market.

---

base in whose pricing territory they were located, thus breaking up the automatic price leadership of the base mill, if others cared to act on their own. The iron and steel code was of this sort; and the N.R.A. report on the basing-point system under this code noted a tendency to increase the number of basing points and decrease the average number of mills pricing on any one base, as reducing this kind of competitive force. It urged that if individual mill pricing became the rule, some limitation on freight absorption would become a necessity, to put a different kind of competitive pressure on individual mill prices. (See "Report of the N.R.A. on the Operation of the Basing-Point System in the Iron and Steel Industry," Nov. 30, 1934, pp. 85-90, mimeo.) This problem has been revived in a different form under the present shift to mill pricing. The limited local price leadership of single mills has been made more absolute by two governmental actions: the requirement of mill prices, and the "equally low price of a competitor" as defining the limit on freight absorption in a way that debars mills from the good-faith defense if they take price initiative in one another's territory. Thus one avenue of possible price competition is handicapped.

The system called "Pittsburgh plus"—it was never as simple as the name implies—was condemned in the decision of the Federal Trade Commission in 1924. This system, established by the U.S. Steel Corporation on its formation in 1901, was a sequel of a period of vigorous competition carried on by Andrew Carnegie, who succeeded in keeping his plants working actively by a policy of cutting prices wherever and to whatever extent necessary to secure orders. Near the turn of the century, a movement toward vertical integration had resulted in substantially increased capacity, confronting the rest of the industry with a situation in which the Carnegie type of competition offered a serious threat of driving prices in general below costs. In the formation of the U.S. Steel Corporation, Carnegie was eliminated by purchase (on terms so profitable as to make it difficult for him to realize his ambition to die a "poor man").[5] Then the "live-and-let-live" form of competition was substituted, with price leadership featured in the "Gary dinners" and formalized in the "Pittsburgh plus" pricing structure, under which producers at other locations accepted the price leadership of Pittsburgh by selling at the Pittsburgh price plus freight from Pittsburgh to destination, thus discriminating against their own nearby customers, charging them what came to be called "phantom freight."

This discrimination, which had some claim to be natural when Pittsburgh was the dominant producing center and exported its products to the other areas, in decisive excess of any reverse movement, became increasingly open to objection as the Chicago and Birmingham areas, and others, became increasingly strong and self-sufficient. The outcome of the Federal Trade Commission's decision against "Pittsburgh plus" was the setting up of bases in the Chicago, Birmingham, and other areas, with base prices at first higher than those at Pittsburgh, but the main ones later reduced until they were finally equalized with Pittsburgh. The question may fairly be raised whether this equalization, taken by itself, tended to increase or to lessen competition, as compared with greater independence in the setting of base prices at other points than Pittsburgh. This was as far as the company felt it feasible to go in partial compliance with an order that was much more far-reaching.[6]

[5] He is said to have remarked: "The confounded interest keeps eating up my expenses."

[6] See Edwards, op. cit., p. 353.

It is ironic that the effect of this case should have been limited to an incomplete rectification of the discrimination issue, because at this time the F.T.C. had more sweeping and doctrinaire aims than it had later. At that time it held that competition would bring about F.O.B. mill pricing.[7] It was under the ideological influence of F. A. Fetter, whose theory of competition for industries of this type (briefly referred to in the preceding chapter) hinged on uniform mill pricing, under which a producer's marketing area would depend on its mill price, relative to those of surrounding mills, and it could enlarge its area only by a relative reduction of its own mill price. When the area can be enlarged by freight absorption, reduction of the mill price is not essential for the purpose, though there are still some competitive incentives to reduce it, which will be examined later. Fetter's claim that genuine competition between spatially separated producers would lead them to refrain from freight absorption disregarded the incentive arising from *this kind* of competition.[8] Be that as it may, this doctrine is no longer controlling.

The issue of the nonbase mill was renewed in the Corn Products and Staley cases, decided by the Supreme Court in 1945. These cases were brought under the Robinson-Patman Act, on charges of discriminatory practices by individual firms, though a conspiracy case was in the background. The Staley decision held that the nonbase mill in question was, among other things, depriving its nearby customers of their "natural advantages of location." The decision called for the setting up of a mill price sufficiently below the existing nonbase delivered price at the plant's location to escape condemnation as mere evasion of the order by quoting a mill price so high as to have only nominal application. But this mill price was not required to be equal to the price at the previously controlling base, though this equality was implied in certain unguarded language used, especially in defining the point at which "phantom freight" ended and freight absorption began.

Facts that might distinguish this from subsequent cases were: (1) the distance between base and nonbase mills and resulting dis-

[7] *Ibid.*, p. 353.

[8] On this point see Saul Nelson, "Basing-Point Problems: Comment," *American Economic Review* (September 1943), pp. 620-22. Fetter based his argument on a "principle of indifference," deduced from the fact that different units of an identical product are alike to the seller, overriding differences in the mill net at which different increments could be marketed.

crimination against nearby customers of the nonbase mill were substantial; (2) it was stated that no evidence on costs had been offered to show that this nonbase mill needed the revenues it got from "phantom freight"; and (3) it had made no attempt to set up a base price and thus was on a different basis from a former base mill whose base price had become inoperative (as sometimes happened) through reductions in prices of surrounding base mills. Thus the decision did not necessarily create a rule abolishing all nonbase pricing, but it set up a precedent creating a strong presumption in that direction.[9] It expressly disclaimed a general prohibition of freight absorption as individually practiced by a mill that has its own mill price.

5. *Multiple Basing Points and Price-Meeting*

The next landmark concerns the multiple-base system, the crucial decision being that in the Cement case of 1948, written by Mr. Justice Black. The issue of the nonbase mill having been passed on, the additional findings in this case pertained to the use of freight absorption or other methods of meeting competitors' delivered prices, whereby a mill can enlarge its selling area without the necessity of reducing its own base price for the purpose. As to this issue, it is essential that unlike the discriminatory prices paid by different customers of a nonbase mill, the decision of a base mill whether or not to absorb freight or how much to absorb has no effect on the relative prices paid by different customers. The problem has shifted from the discrimination issue to the price-meeting issue. This is qualified, of course, by the fact that a decision not to absorb freight, in time of shortage, can cause customers in a short area to pay the full freight from distant sources, instead of being able to buy from these sources on a freight-absorbing basis. However, in the Cement case this was not an active issue—not until *after* the decision.

The case hinged mainly on a charge of unfair competition through combined action, not—in my view—to fix prices directly, but to imple-

---

[9] The present writer has dissented from the legalistic reasoning used in these cases, and in that part of the Cement decision which relies on them; see "Law and Economics of Basing Points," *American Economic Review* (March 1949), pp. 430-47.

ment the meeting of competitors' delivered prices more promptly and precisely than market forces would automatically bring about and to police the system against deviations. The implementing included freight rate books, embodying a uniform method of converting freight rates from the 100 pound units in which rail tariffs are quoted into the trade units ("barrels") in which cement prices are quoted and the equivalent in the bags in which deliveries are made. The answer could differ according to the number of decimal places to which the unit-conversion was carried, before being multiplied by the number of units. Implementing included also the use of rail freights for calculating delivered prices, though truck or water transport might actually be used; and the placing of restrictions on the use of trucks, including common-carrier trucks, unregulated private trucks, and the buyers' own trucks, all of which could—and did—introduce wide uncertainty about the cost of cement at destination, if the buyer was allowed to take delivery at the plant and arrange his own transportation. Incidentally, a railroad car, spotted on the producer's siding, could be loaded at his convenience, while trucks had a way of turning up at odd hours, demanding to be loaded at once, thus often imposing overtime costs on the supplier—an additional argument for preferential treatment of rail shipment.

The "policing" included methods of responding to irregular pricing, largely based on encountering a number of prices by a competitor in the field, figuring them back to the mill price they represented and, without waiting to verify all the competitor's delivered prices in the area in which the prices were found, meeting the calculated delivered prices resulting from this calculated mill price. If the competitor was shading prices locally, this response generalized the shading over the competitive area affected and was spoken of as reducing a competitor's base price or, if the competitor was a nonbase mill, "putting in a base on him." This was explained on the ground that if prices were being cut, a firm might lose too much business unless it acted promptly, without the delay required for accurate verification covering all localities. A reduced base price thus introduced need not apply to the competitor's entire market; there have been instances of mills with different base prices applying in different areas, according to the state of competition in each. At present, any claim of meeting a competitor's equally low price must be backed by verification of the particular prices met.

The Federal Trade Commission's order in the Cement case, which the Supreme Court upheld, was limited to basing-point practices pursued as part of a planned common course of action, aiming at the meeting or matching of prices, including methods of implementing and policing it. The Court's opinion on count two of the complaint, under the Robinson-Patman Act, created the appearance of going much further and outlawing individual freight absorption if more than intermittent or sporadic, or if engaged in by all the sellers in an area. The last point resembles the commission's doctrine of "conscious parallelism," involved in a case pending on appeal at the time.[10] The resulting prospect threatened the normal practice of meeting competition and made it appear that, while no course of action could be guaranteed legally safe, uniform F.O.B. mill pricing was the least hazardous course.[11] During the ensuing agitation for amending the law, "the majority of the Federal Trade Commission found it necessary to consider for the first time the possible meaning of concepts that had been employed in basing-point cases if they were to be applied generally to American industry."[12] This commentary is revealing.

In the outcome, it appears that there is room for individual freight absorption that is much more than intermittent or sporadic, but not as unrestricted as before the Cement decision. The extremely restrictive language of the opinion on count two appears to be clearly a dictum, the essential finding being that the good faith defense can be invoked for meeting a specific competitive situation but not for "adopting a system." This in turn appears to hinge on verifying the specific prices met, not inferring them from salesmen's reports of a limited sample, on blanket assumptions about the competitor's pricing structure. The result presumably sets substantial practical limits on the generality with which freight absorption can be practiced; but if the standards of verification are as reasonable as indicated in the Staley case (on which the Supreme Court's opinion on count two of the Cement case is based), a firm could meet them and still absorb freight much more continuously and widely than the Cement opinion indicates. Aside from this, there appears to be no binding quantitative limit on the amount of freight that can be absorbed or the number o

[10] Cf. Edwards, *op. cit.*, pp. 402-03.

[11] See Corwin D. Edwards, "The Effect of Recent Basing Point Decisions Upo Business Practices," *American Economic Review* (December 1948), pp. 828-4 especially p. 837.

[12] Edwards, *The Price Discrimination Law*, pp. 413-14.

cases. And the doctrine of "conscious parallelism," which might threaten simultaneous freight absorption by competitors, is not apparently being pushed.

Another consideration working in the same direction is that freight absorption does not alter the prices paid by different buyers, hence does not injure competition by discriminating between competitors; the injury that may be apprehended is the price-meeting type, and this does not occur unless freight absorption far exceeds the narrow limits of the dictum in the Cement decision which created so much apprehension. Count two of the complaint, which called forth this dictum, was brought under the Robinson-Patman Act, and it appears likely that this act will cease to be used against "systematic" freight absorption, though continuing to be used against irregularly localized pricing. Corwin D. Edwards has said that it was used in basing-point cases, not as a substitute for a charge based on concerted action, but as a supplement, to enable action to be taken against individual firms, especially if a pricing method, originally concerted, is continued after the concerted action has nominally ceased. This power has now been assured by the National Lead case, without need of Robinson-Patman findings for the purpose.[13]

Theoretically, individual freight absorption can be defended as meeting competition in good faith. But this defense is a strange example of a legal right so hedged about with obstacles that up to 1955 "not a single seller in a recorded case to date has succeeded in finally justifying a challenged discrimination by recourse to Section 2 (b)'s 'meeting competition' defense."[14] Where the discrimination is held not to

[13] The Price Discrimination Law, pp. 437-38, and 404 n. stating that members of the commission staff "undoubtedly hoped that if their view of the law was sustained, they would subsequently be able to attack industry-wide use of basing-point formulas without incurring the burden of proving that the use had been conspiratorial." The Staley case, on which the decision on count two of the Cement case relies, found discrimination between buyers who paid "phantom freight" and buyers paying freight-absorbing prices as a group, but an earnest search reveals not a word about discrimination among buyers who do not pay phantom freight: that is, the kind of discrimination which freight absorption in itself involves, in the absence of phantom freight. Count two of the Cement case raised a fresh issue, not decided in the Staley case.

[14] U.S. Attorney General's National Committee to Study the Antitrust Laws, Report (1955), p. 181. Since then the defense has been successfully made in the Standard of Indiana case, by a 5 to 4 decision, overruling the Federal Trade Commission. Cf. Edwards, The Price Discrimination Law, pp. 318-30. This is a kind of exception that hardly disturbs the rule.

injure competition, the defense is not needed; and where competition is held to be injured by the price-meeting route, the authorities appear extremely indisposed to admit the existence of good faith.

The commission is thus left with more legal weapons than it now proposes to use, while business firms, anxious to keep on the safe side of legality, have been influenced toward eliminating freight absorption or limiting it more narrowly than appears to be legally necessary under the commission's present ideas about injury to competition. In view of the drawbacks, discussed earlier, of mill pricing with unlimited freight absorption, such caution may be a lesser evil than incurring the risks of a statutory amendment. Industries are invited to experiment with freight absorption at their own legal peril, until they reach the (unpredictable) point at which the commission will hold that competition is injured. They are also invited to experiment with occasional undercutting of a competitor's delivered price, thus abandoning the protection (such as it is) of the "good-faith" defense of the Robinson-Patman Act, in the not-too-certain hope of meeting the commission's alternative test, of avoiding the impairment of competition that results from unduly perfect meeting or "matching" of competitors' delivered prices.

This last dilemma would be helped if the phrase "equally low price of a competitor" were construed with some latitude of approximation, as suggested by the Attorney General's National Committee to Study the Antitrust Laws.[15] But to make this authoritative would require a judicial test, in which some firm would assume the costs and risks of serving as a legal guinea pig, with the presumptions arising from a literal construction of the language of the statute all against it. Such a case might arise where a firm has been exploring the limits of the latitude indicated in Federal Trade Commission statements of policy, and has encountered commission action. Its defense might rest on evidence furnishing it with a basis for a reasonable belief that it was meeting an equally low price of a competitor, where precise equality is not ascertainable. If it were admittedly beating its competitor's price, relying on statements of the commission that occasional beating may improve rather than injure competition, it could hardly sustain this against the commission's judgment that in this case competition is injured—a matter on which judgments of the commission carry a presumption of finality, if within reason and supported by evidence. In such a situa-

[15] See *Report*, p. 183.

tion, there appears to be a strong probability that a firm would accept a consent decree, and the case would not reach final adjudication.

To sum up, it appears that the limits of permitted freight absorption are fairly wide, but not fully explored. It seems further that the basing-point cases, and the subsequent agitation for clarification of the law, have ushered in a new phase of the question in which the commission is paying more positive and balanced attention to the results of the general application of its doctrines. It seems to be adopting a wait-and-see attitude toward the consequences of the basing-point cases. This may mean allowing time to test the theory that without the implementing and policing activities that were banned in the Cement case, the meeting of prices could not be precise enough to bring about the harmful lessening of price competition at which that case was directed. Such a test is complicated by the uncertain possibility of the persistence of narrower limits on freight absorption, derived from Black's opinion on the Robinson-Patman count of the Cement case. Meanwhile the Federal Trade Commission is shifting active attention to enlargements of the older issue of too-tough localized competition of varied sorts, by larger against smaller firms.[16]

6. *Some Conceptual and Terminological Casualties*

This story illustrates in emphatic form the principle, earlier discussed, that in the kind of competition now under discussion, a horizontal individual demand function is not favorable to effective competition, but leads instead to the oligopoly stalemate. It goes further and presents in equally emphatic form the proposition that the perfectly informed market, in which only one price is possible, eliminates price competition instead of promoting it, because it leaves the buyer with no chance of finding a better bargain by canvassing the offers of competing sellers. If these conflicting ideas are to be reconciled, it must be done by recognizing both the tendency to iron out price differences and the importance of opportunity for differences to arise and to lead to new competitive price levels in the process of being ironed out. If a one-price market results from such a past process of adjustment, and is subject to change through a similar future process, it is not non-

[16] See Edwards, *The Price Discrimination Law*, Chap. 13.

competitive merely because at the moment there may be no differences of which an alert buyer can take advantage. It is striking that the regulatory authorities hold that basing-point systems make market information too precise, and their orders are aimed to promote less exact knowledge, with the burden on sellers to discover and verify rivals' price offers, instead of relying on systematic regularity. They aim to strengthen competition by making the market more imperfect. This exemplifies a problem that runs through this complex of problems: What is a desirable scope for price-differences, as against the tendency of competing sellers to charge the same price at any point of delivery?

Turning to phantom freight, it can mean two things, and the elimination of nonbase mills would eliminate one of them. True phantom freight occurs when a mill that quotes destination prices by adding freight to its own mill price, adds more freight than it has paid—for instance, charges rail freight when it used water. Fictitious or imputed phantom freight occurs when a mill that has no mill price of its own, quotes a delivered price equal to that charged by the base which rules the price at the destination in question, figured as *that mill's* base price plus the freight *that mill* charges, when this is more than the freight from the nonbase mill to destination. This is fictitious because it rests on the fiction that the nonbase mill has a base price equal to that of the ruling base mill, when it has no such base price, and if it establishes its own mill price, it is under no legal obligation to make it equal to the base price of the former ruling base.

By way of illustration, assume two mills distant freightwise $2.00 from one another, mill A quoting a mill price of $9.00 and mill B one of $10.00. Assuming—as one may for the present purpose—freight rates uniform with distance, their prices will meet at a point we may call C, distant 50 cents freightwise from B, and $1.50 from A. If B sells beyond this point—say halfway to A, it will be absorbing freight in the added area. Now let A reduce its mill price to $8.00, while B's remains at $10.00. This makes B a nonbase mill. Now, though it is charging less than before, it is charging phantom freight not only as far as C, but beyond, from C to the half-way point, an area in which it was formerly "absorbing freight." This is according to the dicta in the Staley case, and its arbitrariness appears self-evident. The example would work the other way around if mill B started as a nonbase mill and set up its mill price of $10.00 in compliance with the Staley case, A's mill price being $9.00.

Now consider point D, distant freightwise 50 cents from A and $1.50

from B, where A, with his mill price of $9.00, sells at $9.50. If B wants to sell there, he must accept a mill-net realization of $8.00, or $2.00 below his mill price. Has he absorbed $2.00 freight? The total freight he has paid is only $1.50, and it may seem illogical for him to be reckoned as absorbing more than 100 per cent of freight. Yet if that last 50 cents of concession is not freight absorption, what is it? It might not appear worthwhile to spend time on such verbal questions, but they would have become substantial legal issues if the O'Mahoney Bill had not been vetoed by President Truman in 1950. It legalized individual freight absorption in terms pointing to wider latitude than the Black limitations, but defined it so that it would not cover any greater concession than the amount of freight actually paid.

Thus if, in our example, B wanted to sell at D, where A's delivered price was $9.50, he must either reduce his own mill price to $9.50 or he would be operating in a legal no-man's land that the protection to freight absorption would not cover. He could operate in this no-man's land if he were willing to take the chance that his super freight absorption would not be held to injure competition. This was an unobtrusive and ingenious way of putting quantitative limits on what had been thought of as freight absorption, backed by noncompulsory pressure to stay within these limits and to quote mill prices equal to, or lower than, those of surrounding mills if one wanted to be able, without running too many legal risks, to penetrate those mills' home markets. This method should receive ample discussion—more than it received when the bill was before Congress—in terms of its probable economic effects. It has distinct advantages over, say, a flat dollar limit on freight absorption, as a way of limiting the competitive practice by which mills interpenetrate one another's market areas by accepting net realizations lower than their mill prices.

7. *Remaining Economic Problems*

The two main economic objectives of public policy in this field are: to minimize discrimination between customers and to promote a healthy degree of competitive pressure on the prices of different suppliers. Requiring nonbase mills to set up mill prices does something toward the first objective and injects into the discussion the idea of the customer's claim on the advantages of his location near his supplier, without defining the extent of this claim or formulating a theory of its basis, legal or economic. Its rationale should surely be explored. But mill prices for nonbase mills, by themselves, do nothing toward the second objective; indeed, as pointed out, they may in some cases impair it, where the result is to break up groups of spatially separated mills that price on a basis permitting each to initiate prices covering the market area of the whole group. The resulting competition would be in essentials like that between a group of producers at a single location and would be liable to the oligopoly stalemate unless the numbers and divergent perspectives in the group were sufficient to prevent. This would hardly be a feasible type of pricing behavior to require as a way of establishing competitive pressures between spatially separated producers. But if it exists voluntarily, it might be more competitive than mill pricing with unlimited freight absorption.

I had knowledge of a case of this sort in which domestic producers were few, but one was on the point of initiating a price reduction at the common base governing all the domestic producers, when an antitrust action was begun. The outcome was a consent decree requiring the setting-up of mill bases, after which this producer, being hundreds of miles distant from the others, was no longer in a position to initiate a price reduction that would govern their prices. Thus, in the interest of lower prices for a minority of customers relatively near the mills, one competitive factor, capable of affecting the whole industry, was rendered ineffective.

The key problem, bearing on effective competitive pressures, is posed if one assumes mill pricing with full freedom to absorb freight with the result that the area over which a mill can sell is not affected by whether its mill price is high or low. This does not mean that its total sales volume is unaffected by the level of its mill price, especially in the long run; and the most neglected question in this controversy-ridden field is: What competitive forces act on the level of a mill's mill price under such conditions, enabling it to sell more at a lower mill price than at a higher one? Since the nonbase mill is the limiting case of a base mill with a mill price so high that it governs no sales, the question might include the reasons why, for example in the cement industry, mills which started as nonbase mills showed a distinct tendency to become base mills as they got more firmly established. These forces did not operate strongly enough, and dependably enough in different cases, to warrant relying on them to bring about a satisfactory price structure, if one may accept the general judgment; and an analysis of their nature would probably bear out this judgment. But it would help toward understanding the competitive forces at work, much neglected by both sides in these controversies, for opposite reasons—one side does not want to admit that they exist, the other does not want to admit their shortcomings.

The attempt to make competitive forces stronger uses two main methods, which may take various forms and may be variously combined. One is to promote more irregular pricing, thus tending to weaken or break up the oligopoly stalemate, and to make collusion more difficult. The other is to reduce, limit, or eliminate freight absorption as a means of expanding a mill's selling area without reducing its mill price; the extreme and absolute form of this being the requirement of uniform F.O.B. mill pricing, so long and persistently advocated by F. A. Fetter. These two methods interact on one another, and this interaction needs to be taken acount of in judging their effects. For example, compulsory uniform mill pricing would leave little scope for irregular pricing as a means of increasing sales, by making it extremely difficult to conceal or disguise competitive chiseling, and this might be one of its most important effects. Again, if the buyer gets the option of taking delivery at point of origin and furnishing his own transportation, while freight absorption is permitted, the chief effect would not be the Fetter effect, but introducing irregularity and uncertainty with regard to the total delivered cost of the goods to the buyer.

In the other direction, a firm may want to compete for a larger share of its nearby business, on which its net yield is its full mill price, instead of accepting lower yields on freight-absorbing sales, while other mills are doing the same and taking some of its nearby customers. But it may find an open reduction of its mill price relatively ineffective (for reasons discussed in the following chapter) while irregular reductions might expose it to legal hazards. Under basing-point procedures, it might also be exposed to a reduction of its base price by a competitor located elsewhere, thus generalizing its local reductions which were not intended to be general. As the law now stands, the competitors would be required to verify the particular prices they were meeting, instead of generalizing them in the way indicated; and this may afford some protection to a mill that wants to use price-shading as a way of competing for more business in its home territory and reducing the wastes of cross-freighting. Its gains might not be so promptly and completely canceled. But the legal hazards would remain, since the mill is discriminating without the excuse of meeting a competitor's price.

It is not possible in a single analysis to cover all the possible gradations, varieties, and combinations of policies, and of the pertinent features of the businesses to which they may be applied. But we have at least made a sampling of the problems on which an analysis, if it is to be useful, needs to shed light.

CHAPTER 14

Industrial Competition Over Distance: Analysis

1. Introduction

In starting to analyze this problem in terms of economic theory, it may be well to remind the reader of the distinctive features of the group of cases involved, these being the ones in which transportation costs are a decisive factor. First, the products are primarily either homogeneous, or nearly enough so to make price differentials decisive; or, secondarily, habitual differentials may be strongly maintained, so that changes will be met. Second, production is localized, some points of production including several producers, others only one, in which case all of its competition necessarily comes from a distance. Third, costs of production contain substantial "constant" elements; when there is unused capacity, short-run marginal cost is enough less than average cost to leave room for differences in mill net realizations. Fourth, transportation costs are substantial, but not so high as to prevent mills from selling in one another's territories. Frequently cost of transport from one mill to the next is less than the spread between average cost and short-run marginal cost, permitting one mill to sell in another mill's dooryard while still covering marginal cost. These factors have their combined effect in the light of a fifth: namely, that expanding sales by a general price reduction, on the one hand, and by *sub rosa* price-shading or freight absorption, on the other hand, are governed by radically different criteria of profitability, especially as to the minimum yield which is necessary if the operation is to improve the seller's financial showing. In the latter case, the limiting minimum yield is short-run marginal cost, in the former it is much higher.

If one reduces the price applying to one's main market, one may gain added sales (especially if not all competitors meet the reduction); but against the revenue from these added sales, there must be offset the reduced revenue on all the previous volume of sales. In the terminology of economic theory, the marginal revenue is less than the price, and may easily be less than short-run marginal cost, so that the price reduction would not pay, even if the price were well above marginal cost. But where added sales are gained by freight absorption, the revenue from existing sales is not reduced, so that the mill-net realization on the added sales is a clear increase in sales revenue. In theoretical terminology, the marginal revenue equals the price (in the sense of mill net). Added sales are a gain at anything above marginal cost. Business men understand this distinction with the utmost clearness. They do not absorb freight out of perversity, but as the most feasible way of making some use of unused capacity.[1]

Of course, if for every sale secured in this way in a rival's territory, the rival were sure to respond promptly by making a sale of equal size in the first mill's territory, this kind of competition would reach a stalemate. But it does not appear to do so. A, who is taking sales in B's territory by absorbing freight, may expect B to absorb freight also, but not exclusively or primarily in A's market, and not necessarily because of A's freight absorption. A may expect that B will absorb freight whether A does or not and for the same reason A does, so that A would not escape B's freight-absorbing sales by refraining from his own.

Now let us pursue the analysis by imagining a model in which three such independent producers are arranged in a triangle, and ask the question what relative spatial pricing pattern is imposed on each of the three by the competition of the others. If freight absorption is permitted, the answer is that there is no determinable, natural, and inevitable pattern. The only certainty is that, in the absence of abnormal shortages, prices at different points cannot differ by more than the cost of transportation between them. If we add data about the capacities and

[1] One feature of the case was illustrated during the defense drive of 1941. Eastern steelmakers had been utilizing some of their unused capacity by selling some steel on the Pacific Coast, at a heavy absorption of freight. The defense drive brought demand that overtaxed capacity, including heavy shipments to the Pacific Coast, heavier than the producers would have undertaken for ordinary business reasons. Now, instead of yielding a little extra revenue, they were displacing more profitable orders; and the companies asked the privilege of filling the Pacific Coast orders on a non-freight-absorbing basis.

costs of the different mills and the distribution of demand in their tributary areas, we can create some approximate probabilities, but no inevitable certainties, as to which mill will price higher and which lower and how much, or whether one will act as a nonbase mill, and if so, which.

If we require uniform mill pricing and supply full data as suggested, it would be possible to deduce an approximate distribution of prices and sales, though not a precise and inevitable one; and we should be troubled with questions about long-run and short-run cross-elasticities of demand, and the time perspectives of the different producers in responding to them. There could be no nonbase mills, except for ones so small that a strictly local market would suffice for them; and if mills as small as this were viable, there would be more of them, and the triangular pattern would change. It assumes that the economies of large-scale production in the industry in question rule out production for purely local markets. Each must carve out a market for itself. If uniform mill pricing is not required, and if one mill chooses to act as a nonbase mill, it is likely to be a young mill, not well-established marketwise and with relatively high costs. But it may not be all or any of these things. In any case, it will be "discriminating" against its nearby customers, and this raises the question of their "advantages of location" and what claim they have on that account.

2. The Discrimination Problem and "Advantages of Location"

If the high delivered prices charged by the nonbase mill are necessitated by extra-high costs that are unavoidable, on economic grounds there is no vested claim on the part of the customer to prices lower than costs justify. This might happen, for example, if costs are dominated by essential heavy materials that have to move longer distances to reach the location of the nonbase mill. Let us suppose the costs of the nonbase mill are $1.20 above those of the base mill and the delivered price at the nonbase mill is $2.00 above the base price of the base mill, but as the nonbase mill sells at points farther removed from its own location, its net realization drops rapidly, and its average may well be less than $1.20 above that of the base mill, or not enough fully to offset its cost handicap. Such a mill may still perform a useful function in terms of service and prompt delivery to its local customers; and they might prefer its presence to its absence, though they pay the same price in either case. But if the nonbase mill lacks this kind of cost justification, the question of a claim to the advantages of location, or to some share of them, becomes a real issue.

In defining the "advantages of location" of a customer near a producer, one may first try to give precision to the actual ideas of those who use the phrase. As used, it seems to mean the difference between the transportation cost from the base mill that makes the price, and the cost from the nonbase mill, which is nearer the customer. If the nonbase mill has higher costs of production due to its location, this cost differential might be subtracted, but at first we may disregard this. If the nearby mill meets the delivered price from the ruling base (that is, acts as a nonbase mill) it absorbs all the "advantage." If it quotes a mill price equal to that of the ruling base, the customer absorbs all the "advantage." Or if one includes differences in production costs between the two mills, the customer absorbs the advantage if the mill prices reflect the difference in mill costs. If the nearby mill quotes a higher mill price than this, the advantage is shared, the nearby mill getting an amount equal to the difference in mill prices (or in their relation to mill costs) on those nearby sales on which it does not have to absorb freight, and its nearest customers get the remainder, if any. The alert reader may note that in defining the advantage in terms of cost, one adopts a criterion bearing on the question of equitable or economically useful sharing. The extent and character of its relevance will depend on the standards of equity or serviceability adopted.

Of these underlying standards, there seems to be no real discussion in the available literature. Negatively, the suggestion in the Staley case that cost data *might* have affected the decision if they had been offered, looks, as far as it goes, toward giving all the advantage to the customer unless the producer needs it all to cover his costs. But the decision, by refraining from requiring that the mill price which it called for should be equal to that of the governing base, left room for a sharing of the advantages—once more negatively. There seem to be two possible approaches to the search for a standard: one derived from the concept of the results of competition, the other based on the conception that the spatially separate mill has a limited natural monopoly of location—limited by the competition of more distant mills—and that this advantage is affected with a public interest, involving responsibilities appropriate to the features of this kind of case, including the situation of the mill and the exposures of the customer. It should be stressed that these are approaches, not final formulas, though they do lean toward different answers.

In the approach via the results competition might actually bring about, it is basic that competition should mean the kind of competition that exists or can exist in these situations: namely, competition between spatially separated producers. Appeal to any other kind of competition can be relevant, not under the competitive approach but under the limited-monopoly approach, under which a theory of public interest may be applied that gives the customers the benefit of a kind of competition that does not exist in these cases: namely, pure or at least effective competition at every point of production. The only statement of the competitive approach I have seen is that of Commissioner Mead of the Federal Trade Commission, replying to questions from a Senate committee, during the period after the Cement decision, when amendments to the law were being pushed, and the commission was attempting to allay apprehension by disavowing drastic intentions.

On this point Commissioner Mead, with the concurrence of three colleagues, wrote:

> The Commission does not consider that either buyers or sellers have a legal right to exclusive benefit from the advantages of location. Buyers and sellers alike have a right to seek to enjoy these advantages by competitive bargaining and to be protected from conspiracies, monopolies or unlawful discriminations that deprive them of the opportunity to benefit from such advantages.[2]

The phrase "competitive bargaining" appears to be here used as a formula whose sacrosanct standing might cover its lack of relevant meaning for the purpose of settling the division of the advantages in question between seller and buyer. If it is granted that competitive bargaining cannot determine this division, what remains is the intent of the commission to intervene in the buyer's behalf if the seller captures the advantages (by the unlawful discriminations involved in acting as a nonbase mill), and to ensure the buyer's getting some undetermined part of these advantages, but not necessarily the whole. This describes the effect of the Staley case.

[2] Cited by Corwin D. Edwards, *The Price Discrimination Law* (1959), p. 417.

Critical analysis of the role of competition in this adjustment hinges on the existence of two grades or levels of competition, which may be called direct and indirect or immediate and deferred, and they work differently. Direct competition is that between existing mills for the existing custom of present customers and is the kind that might be actuated by short-run perspectives. If direct competition is the governing criterion, a customer's "advantages of location" have nothing to do with his nearness to a single supplier, but with his nearness to an adequate number of competing suppliers to afford effective competitive alternatives. From the standpoint of the results direct competition would bring about, a location near an isolated supplier and far from competitors is a disadvantage, not an advantage.

Under competition, the seller is presumably free to exercise his judgment as between short-run maximizing of profits and more moderate and far-sighted perspectives. The nonbase mill is simply a mill that decides to exact from its nearby customers the maximum that direct competition—from the more distant base mill—permits. In the Staley case this was found to have injured competition among the customers, and the supplier was ordered to do better by his nearby customers than the minimum treatment which direct competition alone would compel him to give them. This result may be economically desirable in the light of its effects on competition among customers—indeed it almost certainly is if not made into too rigid a rule—but there is no evidence that "competitive bargaining" between supplier and customer would bring it about. Customers might ask for it, and their persuasion might have some effect, backed by a sense of inequity in the phantom freight that accompanies nonbase pricing. But this is hardly competitive bargaining in the usual sense. Direct competition gives no guide for the sharing of advantages of location, but suggests that the nearby supplier is free to absorb them.

Indirect competition—sometimes called "market competition"—has a more useful bearing and can exert a more positive force. It represents the longer-run dependence of a mill's volume of business on the prosperity and expansion of the customers naturally tributary to it, as conditioned by their success in their competition with their rivals. It embodies a recognition of interdependence between supplier and customer, such as might actuate firms with long-run perspectives. This interdependence can have competitive force to the extent that the customers can convince their suppliers of it and the suppliers have enough freedom from immediate pressures to be able to act on it. In its strongest form, it would conceive suppliers and customers as a team, competing with other supplier-customer teams in different locations: a team that is handicapped unless the customer gets terms that enable him to compete successfully, while the supplier is better off with flourishing customers nearby than if he is more dependent on more distant ones, for whose trade he must compete harder and often accept lower net realizations. In the Staley case, the nonbase mill had not acted to give effect to this interdependence and was ordered to do something substantial in this direction, in the absence of evidence that it could not afford it.

This appears to be the substance of the competitive approach to this problem. It discloses a real competitive force and one which is probably largely responsible for the tendency which nonbase mills have shown to convert to base-mill status as they became stronger and better established. But the existence of numerous nonbase mills showed that this force was not uniformly dependable in its operation. Now it has the force of a legal order behind it. Insofar as this order can be considered to rest on a competitive criterion, it decrees that the seller must act as if governed by indirect competition, rather than by direct only. That matter is not left to his free choice.

The limited-monopoly approach throws light from a different angle but fails to furnish a key to the proper level of a mill price that would embody a correct sharing of the advantages of location. The difficulty arises because in this theory it is only the supplier's differential advantage of location that is affected with a public interest, not his whole operation. On this basis, he would clearly be obligated to charge his nearby customers actual freight, not phantom freight, and this implies a mill price of some sort. But the effect could be nullified by an unduly high mill price; and if the mill price were regulated, that would apply a public-service obligation to the mill's entire operation, instead of merely to a freight differential which he enjoys with respect to a part of his customers. Surely it would be premature to treat as a public utility every industry in which competition is effectively conditioned by distance between competitors; the case of spatial competition does not appear that hopeless.

Reverting to our three-cornered model, we have still not found a determinate relative price structure dictated by the three-cornered competition. But if the sense of indirect competition is strong, with its long-run interdependence between supplier and nearby customers, it will tend to eliminate not only nonbase mills but extortionately high mill prices and large and arbitrary differences between them. This would not apply to group bases, in which the distances between mills in the group are not substantial, phantom freight is economically unimportant, and the nearby customers of the various mills are on a reasonably equal competitive basis so far as costs for transportation are concerned. In such cases, mill prices at each mill seem less serviceable toward effective competition than if every mill is equally eligible to quote a base price applying to the common trading area of all the mills in the group.

3. The Price-Meeting Problem and Freight Absorption

One key question in the price-meeting problem is: What competitive forces act on mill prices when freight absorption is unlimited?[3] We have just been examining forces of indirect or market competition, as they would act under these conditions, but the forces of direct competition were not exhaustively canvassed. The direct effect of a reduction of a mill price hinges on discouraging competitors' freight-absorbing sales. It has often been suggested that it would be rational for a mill to reduce its mill price enough to exclude all freight-absorbing sales, thus keeping for itself its "naturally" tributary territory, instead of reaching out into the territory of other mills. However, this is not economically feasible, under the conditions of marginal cost and marginal revenue, which have already been examined. This is especially inescapable if we follow the suggestion through and picture all the mills in the area as trying to do it.

For simplicity, let us ignore differences and assume that the average cost of each mill, under average operating conditions, is $9.00 and its short-run marginal cost $6.00 and that some of them, at least, are

---

[3] To avoid burdensome verbiage, this term will be used to cover the acceptance of mill-net realizations less than one's mill price, as a means of expanding one's sales area, without limiting it, as the O'Mahoney bill of 1950 did, to cases in which the delivered price is at least equal to the seller's mill price.

operating substantially below capacity. Assume that mill prices have been reduced to $9.00, as successive mills have successively reduced them in the attempt to shut out one another's freight-absorbing encroachments. There is still a margin of $3.00 within which a mill can gain by freight-absorbing sales, and this leaves room for plenty of freight absorption. Not until the mill-prices go to $6.00 will freight-absorption be positively excluded; and by that time all the mills will be in the red, and the industry will have ruined itself in the attempt to rationalize its pricing.

While a yield equal to short-run marginal cost is the limit beyond which freight absorption will not go, most freight absorption goes only a fraction of the way to this limit, especially in fairly active times when the pressure of unused capacity is not heavy. For one thing, the selling cost per dollar of gross sales added probably rises as a mill reaches deeper into the natural territory of surrounding mills, while the net return from a dollar of added gross sales shrinks, so that cost per dollar of mill-net yield rises doubly. This feature of selling cost was not taken account of in the oversimplified marginal cost figure of $6.00 with which our example started, and it could easily make the heavier ranges of freight absorption a losing venture, considerably before they approach the theoretical limit calculated on the basis of uniform marginal cost per physical unit sold. Figures for freight-absorbing sales in cement during 1929 and 1932 showed, as one would expect, that there were more freight-absorbing sales in the depression year, and average concessions in mill-net were greater. While the figures did not show marginal costs of particular mills, for comparison with mill nets, the minimum mill nets appeared to lie close to the general range of magnitude of marginal costs for the industry, but very few sales came at all close to this limit, and these few are the only ones that would be absolutely precluded by any moderate reduction of mill prices.

What could happen instead is that one mill, by reducing its mill price relative to those of surrounding mills, tends to make its area less profitable than theirs as a place in which to make freight-absorbing sales, thus tending to divert from its territory to others' the bulk of the sales on which only a small amount of freight is absorbed. Suppose that A and B have had equal mill prices and their delivered prices have met at the midpoint where each pays $1.00 freight. Now let A reduce his mill price, say from $9.00 to $8.80. The meeting point will be pushed 10 per cent freight-wise toward B, who now begins to need to absorb freight where his freight is 90 cents and A's is $1.10. B has to absorb 20 cents more than before, reducing his mill net on freight-absorbing sales by that much. A can sell past the midpoint with 20 cents less freight absorption than before, but his mill net on his freight-absorbing sales is unchanged. He may abandon his least profitable freight-absorbing sales, taking on instead the customers in his own area whom his freight-absorbing rivals have abandoned to him. On his former non-freight-absorbing sales he will get $8.80 instead of $9.00, and on his new non-freight-absorbing business he will get $8.80 in place of mill nets ranging from that figure down perhaps to $6.00, though the bulk of them would have lain in the mid-range. It would serve no useful purpose to draw up a more elaborate model in order to define with precision the conditions under which this kind of move would or would not be profitable for B. He faces a competitive incentive of a decidedly imperfect sort, which does not appear to be dependably positive and calculable in its action.

To turn the picture around, if A raises his mill price to a really high level, relying on the theory that this will not limit his selling area because he can always absorb freight, he will enable surrounding mills to sell in his natural territory without absorbing freight, and to sell over the whole of his territory with relatively small freight absorption, such as they might be willing to incur. As a result, his competitors may be expected to sell largely increased amounts in his natural territory, and he will not sell as much there as he would at a lower mill price. As a further result, in order to build up sales volume, he may be driven to reach out with more distant and less profitable freight absorption than he would feel the need for if his mill price were lower. Thus there is some direct competitive force, as well as indirect, which urges a far-sighted nonbase mill to set up a mill price, and to make it comparable with those of surrounding mills—or not too noncomparable. Basing-point structures in steel and cement have shown this tendency: also a tendency of a price reduction at one base to induce reductions (not necessarily equal) at surrounding bases.

Nevertheless, if a mill price is reduced for competitive reasons, this is on the whole more likely to have resulted from irregular price-shading of one sort or another and to represent an attempt to regularize a price reduction that has already taken place in an irregular fashion. While this form of competitive pressure acts somewhat intermittently, it is probably more powerful than those competitive forces just discussed, which act through direct inducements to reduce mill prices in the first instance. Therefore, in appraising the probable effects of measures designed to strengthen direct competitive pressures on mill prices, it is important to avoid unduly weakening the scope for irregular price reductions. For this latter kind of competitive pressure, an essential favorable condition appears to be substantial areas in which the sales of competing firms can overlap. And for this, considerable freedom to absorb freight is necessary. Within such an area, opportunity for irregular price-shading is increased by debarring the implementing mechanisms such as freight-rate books, used to promote precise knowledge of what regular delivered prices would be, and by requiring that firms that meet competitors' irregular prices should verify the prices they are meeting at each local destination.

Irregular price-shading is, of course, discrimination without the "good faith" defense of the Robinson-Patman Act; and if it is challenged in a given case, there seems to be no dependable rule by which to predict whether it would be held to have injured competition or promoted it. It may have both kinds of effect at once; and the outcome may depend on which appears more important to the Federal Trade Commission, whose judgment will carry great prima facie weight with the courts. The conclusion to which this analysis points is that some discrimination of this sort promotes competition and therefore does not need, in the logic of the law, to be defended as "in good faith meeting an equally low price of a competitor," in which case the defense would hold good, even if there were some incidental injury to competition. If this logic appears complicated, the author pleads that he is not responsible.

One effect of freedom to absorb freight arises in connection with the fact that demand in particular areas fluctuates differently from demand in the nation as a whole. If each area were required to furnish its own reserve of capacity to meet such fluctuations, the total of unused capacity would be greater than it is under a system that permits peak demands in one area to be met in part by imports from other areas. Supposing that there is such a peak, of a temporary sort, in one area, if mills in surrounding areas are to compete for the peak business, they must be able to meet one another's delivered prices, involving differentials in their mill nets. For the moment, this may be noted and fuller discussion postponed until the question of limitations on freight absorption is discussed.

A more enduring occasion for freight absorption arises where a producing area has capacity for more production than the immediate area will absorb, so that it needs to be a net exporting area, and producers located in it must ship a significant amount of their product past the locations of intervening producers in order to reach an adequate market. The delivered prices such a mill encounters are likely to be different in different directions, and the mill may need the benefit of a normal mill price for nearby business plus adaptable concessions for more distant sales, rather than being forced to an abnormally low price to its nearby customers, in order to quote a price enough lower than surrounding mills to enable it to sell past them without absorbing freight. The same principle is involved where different mills supply a concentrated market area of dominant importance to all of them, and they are located at different distances from it. Here the structure of tapering freight rates could produce absurd allocations of marketing areas unless there is enough latitude of freight absorption to permit reasonable flexibility. For this purpose alone, not much would be required. If no freight absorption were permitted, some of the burden of providing needed flexibility might be shifted to the structure of freight rates. This would not eliminate discrimination; it would merely call on a different party to do the discriminating.

The problem takes on a fresh aspect when a mill in an exporting area increases its capacity in the face of the need to absorb freight. Unless the new capacity is warranted as a modernization, the relevant cost is close to average cost, and price concessions based on short-run marginal cost are not warranted to dispose of the output of the excess capacity that has been deliberately created. Perhaps the best way of looking at this case is to assume that the new capacity is superior and will be operated full time, while the more obsolescent capacity may be worth operating if the marginal sales (which involve freight absorption) cover the short-run marginal cost of operating this older capacity. The factors that might bear on the judgment whether the new capacity might more economically be located nearer to markets and outside the exporting area are too manifold to be reasoned about a priori; but it seems that the judgment of firms in such a case is often swayed by noneconomic motivations, and that the preference for expanding in an existing location can lead to unnecessary amounts of freight absorption.

An obvious objection to freight absorption is the wasteful transportation from mutual interpenetration of market areas, often spoken of as the waste of cross-freighting. This term is misleading, however, since it conveys the image of identical products moving simultaneously in opposite directions over the same route of transport, and this is not the typical situation. In the case of unbalanced movements such as have been discussed, there is no way of simply canceling exports against imports and eliminating overlapping sales. In such cases, freight-absorbing sales include many shipments that are useful in bringing supply to demand and are not offset by equal movements in the other direction. A special case would be that of a chain of mills that selects the mill from which to fill a given order according to available unused capacity, and if a more distant mill is chosen on this account, charges the customer the same price as if the order had been filled from the nearest mill. Assuming all the mills quote mill prices, this is in effect the reverse of the situation condemned in the Corn Products case, in which a company owned two mills, one of which was a nonbase mill, so that when its nearby customers were served from the nearest source, they were charged the same price as if they had been served from the more distant one. Any excess freight resulting from this chain-mill policy is presumably more than made up for by the economy of better use of existing capacity. It registers as freight absorption, but does not mean that the chain mill organization is reaching into unnaturally distant areas for customers, nor does it affect the competitive situation one way or the other.

Chiefly for such reasons as these, the total amount of freight absorption, which the Federal Trade Commission has used as a rough and tentative indication of the amount of waste involved, is beyond reasonable doubt a substantial overestimate, but an accurate measure appears unattainable.[4] In any case, when freight absorption is unlimited, the resulting waste is large and is a heavy price to pay for whatever competitive services freight absorption renders. This, in addition to a desire to strengthen competitive forces, is back of moves to limit freight absorption, in one or another of various ways.

[4] For a review of evidence tending to this conclusion, see Carroll R. Daugherty, Melvin G. de Chazeau, and Samuel S. Stratton, *Economics of the Iron and Steel Industry* (1937), pp. 676-701. The most thorough conceivable examination of data as to shipments still falls short of answering all questions as to equivalence of products and alternative sources of supply, with allowance for presence or absence of unused capacity.

4. Ways of Limiting Freight Absorption

A number of different things may be done that have the effect of putting limits on freight absorption. The most drastic, of course, is outright prohibition, such as Professor Frank A. Fetter favored. In the early days after the Cement decision of 1948, steel and cement, as well as corn products, went over to uniform F.O.B. mill selling, as being in effect required by the decisions. It was clear, of course, that the decisions did not make this an absolute requirement, but it seemed highly probable that no other method of pricing was reasonably safe for a firm to use as its *general method,* and that while exceptions were allowed, it would be dangerous to let them appear to be becoming the rule. This change was made at a time of shortage, and it is highly probable that the industrialists realized that at such a time they would not lose sales by refusing to absorb freight; and that it was not necessary to meet the delivered prices of competitors when there was unfilled demand, and buyers would pay the extra freight to get the goods. As the shortage ended, freight absorption reappeared, but tentatively, and in cautiously limited amounts. As already noted, no outright quantitative limits have been imposed, but limiting conditions have been imposed that have had quantitative effects.

Limitations may take effect on the precision with which freight can be absorbed, on the number of cases of freight absorption, on the continuousness with which it is practiced, in a particular area or in the market in general, or on the amount of freight that may be absorbed in any given case. The precision with which general freight absorption can be carried on is reduced by eliminating the information services that went with full-fledged basing-point systems. A producer cannot tell by consulting a book what a competitor's delivered price at a given destination will be. This combines naturally with the requirement that he verify particular prices that he proposes to meet, where this means accepting reduced mill-net realizations. The resulting quantitative limitation consists in the number of prices he can effectively verify, and this can be greatly affected by how exacting the standards of verification turn out to be, when this issue is thrashed out in the courts.

Rigorous requirements of proof could act as effective limits on the number of cases that could be successfully defended as meeting a competitor's equally low price. In that case, one is tempted to wonder whether one limiting factor might be the filing space necessary to record and store the requisite evidence.

Limitations on the continuousness with which freight absorption may be practiced, as well as on the number of cases, are indicated in stringent terms in Mr. Justice Black's dictum on count two of the Cement case decision. As already pointed out, it appears highly doubtful that these extreme limitations will take effect as law. But in the meantime, freight absorption has been sharply reduced, with the result that the area in which a majority of a mill's sales are continuously and generally made is limited by its mill price, relative to those of surrounding mills.

Limitations on the amount of freight that may be absorbed in any given case are more difficult to define and enforce. The definition of freight absorption, coupled with the (limited) legal protection afforded it in the O'Mahoney bill, already discussed, might exert considerable pressure on mills to quote mill prices equal to those of surrounding mills, because this would at one stroke open up to them the entire area beyond these surrounding mills, while still acting within the legal definition of freight absorption; and this area might be larger and more important economically than the area which freight-absorbing sales could cover if the mill's home price were higher than those of the surrounding mills. On account of the tapering of freight rates with distance, it might be possible for a mill to quote a slightly higher mill price than those of surrounding mills and still reach this wider market without exceeding the limits of "freight absorption" as defined. And a mill was not, in this bill, forbidden to go beyond this limit. It was merely deprived of a somewhat indefinite legal protection if it did so.

The economic effect of a limitation of this general sort would seem to depend on a delicate balance in the degree of pressure exerted; it needs to be strong enough to have substantial effect, but not so rigorous and precise that any mill reducing its mill price will be sure that all the surrounding mills will follow suit, since then the incentive to reduce the price is stalemated. In the O'Mahoney bill, the force of the incentive toward (approximate) equality of mill prices satisfied one of these requirements: it was unpredictable.

There has been little discussion of the policy of allowing continuous and regular freight absorption but setting direct limits on it in dollars and cents per unit of product. That is, a producer could not sell to destinations at which the mill-net realization would fall short of his mill price by more than this limiting amount. This would leave zones in which producers' selling areas would overlap, to an extent determined by the amount of freight absorption permitted. It would enable a mill to enlarge its selling area by reducing its mill price, at the same time shutting out or limiting competitors' freight-absorbing sales in its own territory more effectively than it can do if freight absorption is unlimited, but not so rigorously as under strictly uniform mill pricing. This, and other ways of limiting freight absorption, were discussed in the N.R.A. report on the basing-point system in the iron and steel industry, in the context of a code incorporating a basing-point system with numerous nonbase mills, all filing prices on the base governing their locations and eligible to initiate changes at that base.[5]

This is a kind of limitation that might be considered for voluntary adoption by an industry already working under a code organization that could be adapted to carry it out. Otherwise, we should properly shrink from the amount of regimentation involved. The N.R.A. report called for more study before espousing a plan, but suggested a limit of $5.00 per ton as a basis for discussion, and urged that some limit would be necessary to create competitive pressure on mill prices, if all mills should set them up; otherwise they would have the position of local monopolies. The actual course, needless to say, has followed a different route.

This leaves for discussion the criterion of uniform mill pricing, which has not been unqualifiedly espoused by any responsible regulatory agency since the early years when the Federal Trade Commission regarded it as an essential requirement of a competitive price structure. As already noted, leading industries went over temporarily to this kind of pricing after the Cement decision, and at a time of shortage, when this did not cause them to lose sales, but enabled them to collect higher delivered prices than if they had continued to absorb freight. The effect would have been different if the elimination of freight absorption had been a binding rule, continuing into a subsequent period when unused capacity was prevalent.

The effect under such conditions can only be conjectural, but one

[5] "Report of the N.R.A. on the Operation of the Basing-Point System in the Iron and Steel Industry," Nov. 30, 1934, pp. 85-90, 127-33, 144 (mimeo.).

thing that would necessarily happen would be some readjustment of marketing areas and relative volumes of sales between producers. Producers who had been depending heavily on freight absorption would find their relative sales volume declining and would be under pressure to reduce their mill prices to restore their volume. This could be a hardship on producers in an area that produces more than it consumes and where the producers must sell past the locations of surrounding mills in order to reach markets that will enable them to dispose of their output. As already mentioned in connection with reasons for freight absorption, a rigid uniform mill-price rule might, in connection with freight rates that taper with distance, cause absurd allocations of market territory, especially where mills are located at different distances from some dominant market that all of them must reach. And if manufacturers were prohibited from discriminating, pressure for discrimination would to some extent be shifted to the railroads, chiefly pressure for more blanket rates that would enable manufacturers' selling areas to overlap. But such freight adjustments could not fill all the needs that would be felt.

Reverting to the situation of producers who are under pressure to reduce their mill prices in order to restore their sales volume, such reductions would, under the uniform price rule, expel surrounding producers from the outer fringes of their market territory unless they met the reductions, providing a well-nigh compelling incentive to do so, much stronger than if freight absorption were permitted. The result might be to touch off a price war, which could not go on forever, but must necessarily end in some kind of equilibrium of prices and selling areas. If the price war had been disastrous, firms might fear to disturb this equilibrium, once reached, and it might be stubbornly resistant to change, especially if the relative demand in different areas were stable. If it were variable, shifts might exert pressure for revising of price structure, unless room were left for enough sporadic freight absorption to take care of such fluctuations as might occur in the relative demand in different areas, without requiring a producer to reduce his mill price in order to secure business in an area he does not ordinarily serve, but in which demand is temporarily enlarged.

If the area distribution of demand were stable, the ultimate equilibrium might become so fixed that any reduction of the mill price of a major producer would be sure to be met by those surrounding, and this prospect would deter the making of any reductions. Irregular price-shading would afford no escape, because it would take visible shape in shipments to destinations outside the area the producer could reach with his regular price; hence it would be detected. The trail might be covered by manipulations connected with the use of buyers' trucks; and this might yield a crop of abuses. If area distribution of demand varied, as is the case with major construction materials, and if pricing rules were rigid, producers might be under pressure to try to circumvent the rules in other ways, for example by price reductions kept in force just long enough to negotiate a large order in the area where demand is temporarily high, the reduction being technically open to all, but not made the basis of active solicitation. If this were done crudely, it would presumably be forbidden as an evasion of the one-price rule.

If such devices did not work, mills outside the high-demand area might simply wait for the high demand to turn into a scarcity that would make the customers in the area willing to pay a premium for delivery, enabling the outside mills to sell there without cutting their mill prices. It is extremely unlikely that situations would arise in which mills outside this area would find it to their interest to reduce the mill price applying to their entire output, in order to compete for a temporary localized increase in business. To sum up the various possibilities, uniform mill pricing does not appear likely to bring active competitive pressure to bear on mill prices, in the long run. More flexible limits on freight absorption appear more promising.

5. Conclusion

In conclusion, it appears that industrial competition over distance, especially where transportation costs are a decisive factor, is one of those problems of which it has been said that they are not solved, they evolve. The principal reason is that it is not one problem, but a complex of interrelated problems, and what is done about one causes another to take on a new form, and can create fresh difficulties for it. This is especially true about things done in relation to the three main ends which policy seeks to serve: avoidance of discriminations injurious to competition between customers, bringing about competitive pressures on sellers which are effective without being destructive or demoralizing, and reduction of wastes of "cross-freighting." Since the problem, despite major common elements, takes different forms in different industries and areas, and especially since the rules of the game have been drastically changed in the past fifteen years, a fourth end may be added: namely, freedom of experimental adaptation to these changed rules, without attempting to embody the conditions of effective competition in a formula that is expected to fit all cases.

As to discrimination between customers, the kind involved in non-base pricing is condemned, where the discrimination is substantial; but the same general condemnation has not been extended to the kind of discrimination involved in irregular price-shading, because this is one way in which a price-meeting stalemate can be loosened up or broken up, and competitive pressures activated. The objective here is activation of competitive pressures among the sellers without carrying them to destructive lengths and demoralizing the market, and so far as possible, without enabling favored customers to gain advantages which injure competition among customers. Between these two ends there is some conflict. The decision against nonbase pricing, virtually requiring every mill that is not a member of a local group to set up its own mill price, changes the form of competitive pressure on the sellers. This pressure cannot hinge on the number of sellers who quote in the same "market" and may regularly meet or beat one another's prices, since this number is now reduced to one, or at most to a limited number constituting a local group. Accepting this change, competitive pressure between sellers comes to hinge on scope for irregular pricing, and on some of the various kinds of limitation on freight absorption—which incidentally reduce the wastes of cross-freighting.

Scope for irregular pricing is increased by eliminating the joint circulation of precise market information, so that the tendency of a competitive market to eliminate price differentials depends, as it does in theory, on the individual buyer's preference for the lowest price available, and on the seller's alertness to discover if any lower prices than his own are being offered. Scope for irregular price-shading appears also to be dependent on the existence of substantial zones within which the selling areas of spatially separated producers overlap, and this in turn requires some freedom for freight absorption. The requirement that a freight-absorbing seller verify the prices he is meeting not only restricts the scope for freight absorption in an elastic way rather than by a rigid quantitative formula, but also restricts the retaliatory tactics which freight-absorbing mills have used against irregular price-shading by base mills within their own home territory. There should be no need to point out that these conditions are matters of degree and of balance between opposing considerations. It is also obvious that the conditions not only diverge from the requirements of "perfect competition" and a "perfect market," but that these "imperfections" are essential for effective competition in this kind of industry.

The alternative that concerns us here is not that between competition and no competition; where that is the alternative, it raises no question of principle—the judgment is clear. The problems that concern us involve comparisons of different kinds and degrees of competition, and should be faced in the light of the possibility that competition may be unduly strong, in a given industry, as well as unduly weak or unequal in its incidence. There may be little or no room for an idea of unduly strong competition in the antitrust laws, but government officials in other roles have recognized it with respect to agriculture, bituminous coal, and crude oil. And industrialists operating under basing-point systems undoubtedly thought that without such systems competition in their industries would be unduly severe as well as chaotic, and that with such systems it operated with a healthy degree of effectiveness.

However that may be, the analysis of the present chapter has indicated, with respect to mill pricing with unlimited freight absorption, that although it enables a mill to extend its selling area without reducing its mill price, its volume of sales is still affected by the level of its mill price, relative to those of surrounding mills. As a result, there are competitive pressures at work on these prices, from both short-term direct competition and longer-term indirect competition; and these pressures can be fairly strong, and tend to keep mill prices from getting too far out of line with one another, though they are not dependably guaranteed to bring about a desirable level of competitive prices. And we have seen that these competitive forces can be strengthened, though care is needed that in strengthening one force, we do not undo the good effects by weakening others.

The desiderata of policy include balance between different ends, and moderation and flexibility in restraints imposed on genuinely individual business policies and trade practices. Following the recent far-reaching changes in the rules of the game, it is probably desirable to have a period of adaptation and shaking-down, in which industry may digest the result of these changes in the rules, while the regulatory authorities may watch these adaptations from their own standpoint, and may appraise their effect on competition with the deliberation appropriate to such far-reaching change. If, during such a breathing-spell, the objectives back of the recent major decisions appear in danger of being nullified, or if fresh injurious effects appear, it seems that the law of unfair competition gives the Federal Trade Commission ample authority for intervention.

CHAPTER 15

"Full-Cost Pricing" and Target Returns

1. Disagreement Over Full-Cost Pricing

More than twenty years ago, Hall and Hitch, at Oxford, inaugurated the method of studying business pricing by asking a sample of business firms how they do it, and analyzing the answers against the background of accepted theory—this at a time when the Chamberlin-Robinson type of analysis was in the full tide of its early dominance.[1] What emerged as the most typical pricing pattern in the busi-

---

[1] R. L. Hall and C. J. Hitch, "Price Theory and Business Behavior" Oxford Economic Papers No. 2 (May 1939). The authors use a "kinked" individual-demand curve (p. 23) with the caution that it is "more precise than the circumstances it purports to explain." The form used has some slope in each arm, implying differentiated products. Roy F. Harrod credits the authors with originating this curve (*Economic Essays*, 1952, p. 163). The writer recalls an earlier conference of the National Bureau of Economic Research at which Willard Thorp suggested that the situation under discussion was as if a firm faced a kinked individual-demand curve.

Among other writings on the subject, the following deserve mention. Harrod, *Economic Essays*, Pt. II, traces the development of Harrod's thinking on competition from 1930. Pp. 84-85 contain the pioneer use of the marginal revenue curve (though Joan Robinson gave it the name) and of its intersection with the marginal-cost curve; but in Essay 8 he treats the tangency theorem as only one possibility, and accepts full-cost pricing as representing long-run maximum profit if entry is free. C. Clive Saxton, *The Economics of Price Determination* (1942), and P. W. S. Andrews, *Manufacturing Business* (1949), develop and extend the investigation. Oswald W. Knauth, *Business Practices, Trade Position and Competition* (1956), is relevant though not a systematically quantitative study.

Most recent is A. D. H. Kaplan, Joel B. Dirlam, and Robert F. Lanzillotti, *Pricing in Big Business* (1958). (Cited as the Brookings study.) Lanzillotti has presented his own interpretation of the results of this study, in "Pricing Objectives in Large Companies," *American Economic Review* (December 1958), pp. 921-40. Cf. critical discussion of same by M. A. Adelman and by A. E. Kahn, and reply by Lanzillotti, *American Economic Review* (September 1959), pp. 669-87. Cf. also Maybelle Kohl, "The Role of Accounting in Pricing," a doctoral dissertation in the

ness firms' answers was the method that has been designated by the (oversimplified) term, "full-cost pricing." This method of inquiry surely deserves to be pursued, carefully and critically. It raises many questions, as to the characteristics of the firms responding, the extent to which their pricing agrees with their conscious policies, and the modifications and exceptions to which any such policy is necessarily subject in practice. The first thing the present writer notes, as Harrod points out in his Essay 8, is that the indicated finding agrees in general with the traditional view of the long-run results of competition, even as analyzed by Chamberlin, if the results of free entry are included, especially if the firms in question are approximately "representative" in the Marshallian sense. In view of this approximate agreement, it is a trifle ironic that these findings should have been treated as a theoretical heresy, and should have precipitated something like a war of theorists. In view of this attitude, a plea for a fair hearing for the "full-cost" ideas appears to be in order.

As usually presented, the full-cost price is one that will cover costs under normal conditions of operation, disregarding minor fluctuations. This means that it does not espouse the anomaly of raising the price if a downward fluctuation of demand reduces the operating rate and raises unit cost by spreading the overhead over a smaller number of units.[2] This anomaly is avoided if standard costs rather than current costs are used; and "full-cost" may accordingly be construed as covering standard accounting costs, plus some conception of a normal return on investment. On the other hand, if the normal rate of operation seems to have undergone an *enduring* reduction, it might appear consistent with the full-cost principle to raise the full-cost price to cover the resulting increase in unit cost—provided competition would permit. This proviso explicitly underlies "full-cost" pricing; and back of this is the more basic implied condition: if demand permits. (The

---

Columbia Graduate School of Business, 1954. Joe S. Bain, *Barriers to New Competition* (1956), finds correlations between these barriers and differences in rates of earnings. Relevant also is the growing array of intensive studies of single industries.

[2] The question of raising prices when demand declines is discussed by John M. Blair, "Administered Prices: a Phenomenon in Search of a Theory," *American Economic Review*, Supplement (May 1959), pp. 431-50. Blair includes cases in which dealers are allowed larger margins as incentives to push lagging sales and cases in which a premium is charged for keeping products in stock after sales become inactive.

idea that full-cost pricing disregards demand is completely unwarranted. It is more nearly true to say that it presupposes adequate demand to support a substantial volume of sales at a full-cost price, and is conditioned on the existence of such a demand.) As to changes in the prices paid for the factors of production, especially of course wages, it seems safe to say that a firm pricing on this basis would not follow every minor fluctuation in these prices, but would be expected to follow substantial and continued movements, especially if they are general to the industry.

As to the firms responding to the Hall and Hitch inquiry, out of a total of thirty-eight, three were classed as monopolistic, three as oligopolistic, and the rest as instances of product differentiation, classified by Chamberlin as "monopolistic competition." This means that they all had some latitude for price policy; but this says little about whether the latitude included policies of aggressive leadership, or policies of followership with limited room for divergence in one direction or the other from prices initiated by the leader. Later studies have examined larger numbers of firms, some including small firms, and the results have elicited a wider assortment of competitive situations and of pricing policies corresponding to them.

Reverting to the warfare between theorists and exponents of "full-cost pricing," one of the notable points is that one of the grounds of controversy is the very lack of any essential disagreement. The disagreement is over the rationale of the process by which the result is reached. Theorists conceive a firm as "maximizing its profits," within the limiting conditions symbolized by the curves of marginal revenue and marginal cost and their intersection. This mechanism, qua mechanism, leaves room for some variety of outcome, according as the firm may or may not have a degree of monopoly power, according as entry may or may not be free, unobstructed, and effective, and according as the firm's policy is or is not farsighted enough to anticipate new entries and thus to be governed by potential competition. If it is farsighted to this extent, and if entry is free and effective, the firm will in effect be following some variety of "full-cost" pricing policy. We have seen that this degree of foresight is not to be taken for granted. In fact, Chamberlin's "tangency theorem," discussed above, was seen to hinge on a more shortsighted policy.[3] And I have argued that a curve of demand

[3] See above, Chap. 3, Sec. 10. Cf. Chap. 10, Sec. 5.

as a function of price alone has a short-run relevance, since in the long run other things than the price of the product will change, while elasticities, however defined, change their character. I have also contended that the U-shaped cost curve employed in these theoretical models behaves as only short-run cost curves behave and yields different results from those that long-run cost curves would yield.[4]

For a firm to claim that it prices to cover full cost may mean one of two things. If the firm has a degree of real monopoly power, including some shelter from the potential competition of new entries, then it is saying in effect that it does not maximize its profit. Granted the existence of firms of this sort, they would be highly likely to refrain from maximizing their profits; but whether they would be likely to limit themselves to the precise extent indicated by the term "full-cost," some skepticism is warranted. On the other hand, if the firm is exposed to competition, of the sort that leaves it some latitude of policy, then it may be assuming that these competitive forces would in the long run limit it to a normal competitive rate of return, and it may be deliberately accepting this limit from the start. It might or might not consciously equate this with pricing to maximize profit in a long-run perspective. Or it may be pursuing a goal in which literal maximizing of profit is supplemented and modified by other objectives, such as maintaining or increasing its market share, or aiming at satisfaction derived from a sense of the sound reasonableness of its policy.[5]

In either case, ground for disagreement concerns not so much the result as the method the firm uses to arrive at it. Suppose we assume a firm pursuing a goal in which long-run maximum profit, as limited by competitive forces, plays at least a major part. Should such a firm be conceived as following the calculus of marginal revenue and marginal cost and their intersection, or is it legitimate to conceive the firm's reckonings as by-passing this analytical mechanism and directly adopting some conception of a long-run normal cost-price relationship?

[4] For costs, see above, Chap. 6, Secs. 5 and 7; for demand schedules, see Chap. 7, Sec. 5. It may be argued that such matters of slope and curvature merely exaggerate the results for legitimate purposes of exposition, without changing their character. As against this, the present writer would contend strongly that there is a real difference in kind in long-run cost functions between a theoretical curve with a precise optimum and substantial diseconomies for smaller and larger outputs, and a statistical function with no precise optimum, most of the output being produced by firms showing no decisive differences in cost due to scale alone.

[5] Cf. Brookings study, pp. 129-30.

Prima facie, the latter seems the more likely answer, subject to modifications by the more immediate pressures of short-run situations, in which short-run forces of demand and marginal cost must be reckoned with. Here it is fair to assume that successful framers of business policy understand the logic that the theorist expresses in his curves of marginal revenue and cost, but that they are unlikely to conceive it in these terms. The general character of the long-run normal cost-price relationship is simpler, more germane to their ways of thinking, and its data more available to them, than the theorist's curves. If the business manager does seek aid from this apparatus he will, as contended above, find curves that are pertinent to short-run adjustments, but are misleading for the purpose of the long-run projections that are here in question. For purposes of long-run general policy, some variant of "full-cost" pricing brings out an operational meaning that may be latent in the abstract formula of "profit-maximization," but is not manifest.

As to costs, "prime costs" of direct labor and materials are estimated and used by business and vary approximately with output, but the marginal element in indirect costs and capital outlays is considered indirectly and indefinitely, if at all. And the allocation of costs between different products is often highly arbitrary, so that competing multiproduct firms may attribute quite different costs to the same product, with the result that its price may be governed by that one among the relatively large firms that makes the smallest assignment of overhead to this particular product. Some firms allocate overhead quite systematically; but the bases used cannot be perfectly relevant to every different pricing problem; and these firms must compete with others whose methods are different. As to individual-demand schedules, firms depend mainly on judgment, only a few backing this with experiments in price differentiation, and such experiments as are tried are necessarily short-run affairs.[6]

Saxton reports that one firm found that a price 10 per cent above those of close competitors would bring a decline in sales of 20 per cent, but estimated that if this price differential persisted "for a considerable time," sales might decrease 30 per cent. Another estimated that a 10 per cent price reduction would need to increase sales volume 30 per cent to increase profits, and judged that it would not increase

[6] For the discussion that follows, see Saxton, *op. cit.*, pp. 45-49.

volume that much. It is of interest that the 20 per cent reduction in physical volume would show a net gain if marginal cost were more than 60 per cent of the competitor's price, which may be taken to represent the market, while the 30 per cent reduction would not show a net gain unless marginal cost were over 76 per cent of the competitor's price. If these figures are correct, it would be seldom that a 10 per cent price differential in either direction would increase net earnings. This also suggests that the latitude for price differentials in this differentiated-product industry is quite narrow, and that if a firm of substantial size were to establish an aggressive price differential of as much as 10 per cent below its competitors, it would capture enough business to impel them to follow suit or to make some other countermove; though Saxton reports that the effect on sales volume of a 5 per cent price change was commonly considered negligible. This would indicate that price reductions of this size might very likely not be met and would therefore be within the zone of discretionary maneuver.

The Brookings study reports a different kind of case, in which General Electric was introducing a novel product—a portable dishwasher—and experimented in three different markets with three prices and correspondingly different methods of distribution, the highest price being accompanied by home demonstration.[7] The company believed that in the introductory stage, when potential customers were not fully persuaded of the service value of the innovation, a price of $200 would sell no more than 5 per cent more washers than a price of $250, and economy models had little sales appeal. Later, with the hurdle of initial acceptance surmounted, and substantial numbers of machines in use, demand became more sensitive to price. This suggests an initial policy of wide margins and high promotional costs, followed by more modest margins as the product is established. Of course, the prospective elasticity of an individual-demand schedule depends on whether the firm making the move expects it to be met, either promptly or after it gives evidence of continuing; and this likelihood varies directly with the size of the initiating firm relative to the size and number of competitors, the size of the price-change and its apparent enduring character (an enduring price differential will have progressively increasing effect). This combination of factors leaves enough uncertainty to make the individual-demand function thoroughly conjectural.

[7] See Brookings study, pp. 59-60.

To sum up, a firm having some special reason for seeking a price that will maximize profits in the short run can base its pricing on a fair though incomplete knowledge of marginal cost, and on shrewd guesswork on elasticities of individual-demand schedules, but it can be given to few firms to know their profit-maximizing price with any real approach to accuracy. Many firms, however, can have quite well-founded ideas about a long-run normal, and the likelihood that it represents the highest rate of return they will be able to make in the long run. For a firm with some latitude of policy, a normal course would be to give itself the benefit of the doubt by pricing a little above the estimated norm, on the chance of being able to make this much, but with the prospect of making concessions where and when they might be necessary and hoping to wind up with a fair average return.

2. Does "Full-Cost" Include Excess Profits?

This may serve to introduce another source of objection to the full-cost idea: namely, skepticism whether it is really limited to a long-run competitive normal. The allowance for net return, which is necessarily included in full-cost, is open to the suspicion of being, in actual use, arbitrary and more generous than a typical theorist's conception of the minimum necessary supply price of investment and enterprise, which is included in his idea of normal cost. This objection has sub-stance and is not easy to appraise, chiefly because a competitive net return is not so simple as theoretical models make it appear and in practice includes various elements which such models are likely to omit.

In the first place, firms reporting in these surveys are to a prevailing extent large and successful ones, whose market position enables them to earn more than the strictly minimum return necessary to enable a firm to operate continuously. Weaker firms earn less; a minority are generally losing money at any one time. The reporting firms regularly describe their full-cost standard as one they aim to equal where com-petition permits, but competition may force them to accept less, either on particular products or on their total output over the run of favorable and unfavorable market conditions. This implies three levels of return: levels enforced by immediate competitive pressures where they are extra strong, leading to returns presumably below the firm's idea of full cost; the average level the firm hopes to make after accepting some subnormal returns; and the higher return which it must aim at, and must make wherever competition permits, in order to bring the average up to its idea of a normal return. This last return may be called the nominal full-cost goal; it is impliedly supernormal, but only by enough to bring the average up to normal or to the return necessary to attract adequate capital and enterprise. This hoped-for average may be called the real, as distinct from the nominal, full-cost goal.

In a dynamic economy, this normal return itself includes some elements not found in models of static equilibrium. A succession of new products and new processes means functional obsolescence in excess of physical wear, and research and promotional outlays which may need to be recouped in a limited "payoff period." Physical replacement at increased prices is also an element of cost not included in orthodox accounting, while the ideas held among such firms include provision out of earnings for growth, and some shifting of the business income tax. These enlargements of the full-cost concept will be discussed later.

If a firm does price with a view to some selected return, large or small, thought to be consistent with conditions in the industry, its prices would be expected to change in response to changes in costs affecting the industry generally—as oligopoly prices are said to do. The timing of such changes includes, among others, the practice of dealers who, after a rise in price, dispose of their existing inventory at their customary markup on its actual cost before raising their prices on the new inventory. After a price reduction, they may be forced to act sooner, if competitors begin pricing on the new basis. Manufacturers may or may not reckon their costs on a "last-in, first-out" basis, while changes in their prices, even if based on changes in their costs, may not be simultaneous with cost changes.

The sharpest clash between full-cost pricing and theoretically orthodox pricing occurs in the case of a monopoly, chiefly because a monopoly price is not supposed, even in the long run, to tend toward a cost standard, but toward a standard of maximum profit which is supposed (with insufficient reason) to be always above the level of a normal competitive price. Most monopolies are inventions or innovations, and only a minority are successful: the majority never reach the point of earning as much as a normal competitive return. The monopoly as conceived in the conventional theories is an enterprise that has passed this first test and is assumed to have the added power of excluding competition, the combination assuring the firm the economic ability to make more than a competitive return.

But in general industry, subject to the antitrust laws, single-firm monopolies are exceptional and practices aiming to exclude competition are limited in effectiveness and exposed to the charge of unfair competition. The firm is subject to some degree of potential competition and the need for good public relations and is probably somewhat affected by a sense that organized labor and the tax gatherers between them will absorb the lion's share of any really conspicuous profit. All this is not the setting for the profit-maximizing policy to act in the way represented by the conventional diagrammatic models. What it points to as a natural outcome is the selection of a rate of return, higher than a competitive rate by an amount that represents chiefly the difficulties faced by new entries, and the quoting of prices calculated to approximate that rate of return, generally in a setting of an expected succession of innovations, each presenting a fresh problem of the dynamic sort already suggested.

As to demand functions, for the short run a monopoly or near monopoly may be guided by its estimate of the industry demand function, which can be approximated with fewer uncertainties than an individual-demand function in an imperfectly competitive industry. And business men appear typically to think that they face an industry-wide demand that has an elasticity considerably less than one. If they are right in this estimate, this in itself means that they are pricing below the maximum-profit level. They could increase profits by raising prices until the price elasticity of demand increases to considerably more than unity. This might happen when the increased price comes within the range at which some substitute becomes an effective alternative, or merely by reaching the point at which the customer's willingness to buy falls off sharply enough to reduce net profits. The reader will remember that maximum profit is reached when margin elasticity, not price elasticity, reaches unity. If at this point the margin above relevant marginal cost were one third of the price, this would call for a price elasticity at this point of three, or much higher than the typical business man's estimate of the industry-wide elasticity of demand which he faces.

So far as this rough reckoning goes, it points to the conclusion that monopolists or near monopolists set lower prices than would be indicated by the profit-maximizing calculus, at least in the relatively short run to which estimates of the price-elasticity of demand are ordinarily relevant. It is consistent with the view that such pricing is governed by longer-run considerations, including a desire to forestall potential competition, or by motivations other than the strict maximization of profits. To this extent it is consistent with the view that such prices are set to cover cost, including what the firm conceives as a sound or fair net return. What has been said of monopolies or near monopolies is true in higher degree of firms exposed to effective competition of differentiated products. The allowance for net return included in their conception of full cost would be bound to be smaller in proportion to the strength of the competition they face.

3. Varieties of Situation Affecting Pricing Policy

Firms capable of practicing full-cost pricing or something like it must in the nature of the case be firms whose situation permits a margin of discretionary policy. They may be monopolistic or close to it, or firms large and strong enough to be capable of at least attempted price leadership, or merely firms producing differentiated products that stand well in the market. Producers of products with inferior market appeal might have some room for policy, but it would be defensive and unlikely to include the power to cover full cost on such products.

The original Hall and Hitch study was dominated by firms classed as engaged in "monopolistic competition"—signifying product differentiation. Later studies have undertaken to examine larger numbers of firms, some including small firms, and the results have elicited a wider assortment of competitive situations and of pricing policies corresponding to them. One may omit the permanently secure monopoly as an unreal limiting case and, on the other side, the firm engaged in active competition with numerous close and fairly equal rivals and the firm which, for the time at least, has to accept the status of market weakness or high cost, or the product which, at least pending improvements, is competitively inferior and on the defensive, and firms which for these or other reasons are forced to act as price followers.

All these add up to a majority of the firms in a typical market, which are not in a position to follow an independently conceived full-cost pricing policy, though some of them may, by the competitive tactics which their position forces on them, prevent stronger firms or stronger products from being free to follow their own conception of full cost. The remainder, who are in a position to follow such a policy if they choose, have different degrees of latitude for discretionary policy, and different expectations, time perspectives, and other features of motivation affecting the way in which they use this latitude. The same is true in much greater measure of particular products as handled by multiproduct firms, especially new and differentiated products, with the qualification that a firm's latitude may be limited by a competing product to which the competing producer allocates smaller amounts of overhead costs, or which the competitor chooses to use as a "leader," perhaps even a loss leader.

Turning to firms that are in a position to follow a full-cost pricing policy, either for their output in general or for particular products, we may start with a firm that has a large enough patent advantage to give it a monopolistic position for its product as a whole. This protection is temporary, unless it can be renewed by maintaining a continuing lead of a similarly decisive character, and this is unlikely, since subsequent patents are likely to be of a secondary character, as compared to the basic patents on which the original monopolistic position rested, while competitors are likely to acquire substitute patents, unless the antitrust laws have failed to prevent these from being consolidated in the hands of the original monopoly in such a way as to keep them out of competitive use. In the absence of successful and massive preclusive methods, substitute patents and imitations short of infringement are likely to encroach on the economic power of the patent monopoly before the basic patents expire. Thus, to an extent varying markedly from case to case, the patent monopoly tends to be subject to limitation and erosion, and its full measure of economic power is likely to be temporary, aside from the expiration of patents.

Hence the prudent patent monopolist who expects to continue in operation indefinitely is well advised to employ his period of full power with a view to building volume demand and a strong market position, rather than increasing his exposures by exacting short-run maximum profits. However, within such a volume-building policy, there is considerable latitude for taking profits while feasible and expecting to become competitive in proportion as the appearance of effective competition makes this necessary. Thus such a firm might price on what could be liberally construed as a full-cost basis, or might seek a return higher than this, but lower than short-run profit-maximization. As to different degrees of exposure to probable future competition, it appears impossible to say a priori whether greater insecurity tends to a high-price or a low-price policy.

Next we might consider the firm with a highly distinctive product-variant for which strong and apparently dependable customer preference has been established. Or in place of a single product-variant, a large firm is likely to put out a "line," with basic and recognizable common features but vertically differentiated over some part of the range from luxury to economy models. Such lines are, on the average, subject to closer rivalry, from competing lines located in the same general sector of the price-quality range, than are monopolies producing patented products. Those with superior market attractiveness hold this superiority subject to the efforts of rivals who are free to put out duplicate or equivalent attractions if they can. Nevertheless, Bain rates the difficulty of imitating a successful product variant as on the whole a more substantial obstacle to new entry than economies of scale or heavy capital requirements.[8] This may be subject to discount because throughout most of his study "entry" does not include an existing firm taking on a new product or line. Such a firm might find it easier than a wholly new firm to overcome the obstacles, not only of size and requirements of capital and technique, but also those of the established preferential position of existing brands. These latter might still, on a comparative basis, be the most substantial obstacles.

To sum up, for this type of firm or product, pricing is likely to be below the theoretical profit-maximizing level, with its comparatively short-run relevance, but there is latitude for pricing above a theoretical competitive level while the market advantage lasts. One rational policy might be of a full-cost character, including a liberal allowance for accelerated obsolescence of capital outlays, including research and introductory sales promotion, identifiable with the particular product or product line. For such outlays, the method of a "payoff period" is

[8] Bain, op. cit., pp. 114-43, 204, 215-17.

likely to be used. Firms producing a line of differentiated products, but lacking any clear competitive advantage, might still have latitude enough to follow a more conservative full-cost pricing policy, subject to more frequent exceptions arising from the necessity of meeting strong competition on particular products or in particular markets.

Low-cost firms in general have the kind of latitude in price policy that permits them to price on a full-cost basis and enables them to meet competition while doing so. If their cost advantage is moderate and competition strong, the rate of return embedded in their concept of full cost will be correspondingly close to the minimum competitive rate of return. This is true of the Marshallian "representative firm." At the other extreme is a low-cost firm in an industry that is so highly concentrated that effective competitors are few, and the low-cost firm must permit them to survive or face the odium of monopoly and the antitrust action that is likely to follow. Its advantages may include not only low production costs but advantages of size in distribution outlets. If these advantages are large, the firm may find itself under virtual compulsion to hold an umbrella quite high over its competitors. This would probably be the most secure setting for an umbrella policy, exempt from the kind of instability envisioned by Dean A. Worcester, Jr.[9] Needless to say, an industry is in a healthier condition if the minor producers offer stiffer opposition—the recent success of American Motors is an important service to the automobile industry as a whole.

Another type, already considered, is a firm sheltered by distance, to a limited degree, from direct competitors, but impelled to charge its nearby customers less than the maximum which direct competition would permit in the short run, because it has an interest in the growth and prosperity of those nearby customers who will, other things equal, prefer the nearby supplier. This indirect form of competitive pressure does not always work, as the Staley case attests.[10] Where it does work, its pressure is likely, though not certain, to be moderate enough to permit full-cost pricing on the part of the supplier.

[9] See above, Chap. 7, Sec. 2. Cf. Brookings study, p. 132 and footnote on umbrella pricing by General Motors in the low-price field.
[10] See above, Chap. 14, Sec. 2.

4. The Full-Cost Principle Working Backward

There is a considerable group of cases in which full-cost calculation works backward from the expected selling price of the product to the costs the producer will incur, either by way of prices paid for key materials or for labor, or in the form of quality features built into the product. The commonest case of adjusting the product itself to the price is that of "price-lined" goods, as exemplified in the women's garment trades; though here competition is so close that producers have little power to protect a chosen rate of return. Industrial firms, without formal price-lining, may decide on a price the market will support, for a contemplated product, and work out the design of the product to be attractive at that price and at a cost which the price would warrant. Or the adjustment between price and product may be simultaneous and mutual.[11]

If the cost turns out higher than the intended price will justify, the product may be redesigned and some costly elements of quality eliminated, if its appeal still seems likely to warrant the intended price, or added quality features may be sought that would warrant a higher price. If neither adjustment appears promising, the projected product may be abandoned.[12] Or a firm may find an unoccupied "niche" in the price-quality scale among existing products, and may design a product variant to fit it.[13] If a product is developed to sell at an "optimum consumer-indicated price," and costs are subsequently reduced, the benefit may be put into adding features to the product, rather than reducing the price.[14] This, be it noted, borders on the problems of "product inflation," discussed in connection with the automobile industry.

Where the price of a key material is at stake, the price of the product may be a highly sticky oligopolistic one, as in the case of cigarettes, or it may be the price structure necessary to clear the market, as in

[11] Cf. Brookings study, pp. 58-59, 67-68 (General Electric); pp. 70, 254 (farm machinery); pp. 131-32 (General Motors).

[12] *Ibid.*, p. 75 (International Harvester).

[13] Cf. Lawrence Abbott, *Quality and Competition* (1955), Chap. 11, especially p. 147.

[14] Brookings study, p. 262.

the meat-packing industry, where the amount of livestock placed on the markets determines the amount of packing-house products that will have to be disposed of, and these determine the prices that can be charged for dressed meat and the multitude of minor products. Then estimates of these virtually dictated product prices, minus costs of processing, determine the price a meat packer can pay for livestock and cover his full costs. If more livestock comes to market, the prospective scale of selling prices is reduced, and Swift, for instance, tries to protect its return in the light of this prospect, via the prices at which it feels it can afford to buy its requirements.[15] If competition narrows the margin, the initial and less determinate element on which it acts consists of the buying prices, which are subject to upward pressure from the attempts of different firms to maintain or increase their share of the market, with regard to their qualitative as well as their quantitative requirements. The market situation faced by the meat packer subjects him to more likelihood of miscalculation than the cigarette manufacturer.

It is safe to assume that Swift wants to cover full cost and can do so only by arriving at correct buying prices, which dominate its total costs; but is handicapped with respect to accurate fulfillment by the fact that packers are committed to a scale of production substantially in advance of marketing, and then market their output at prices determined by what the balance of supply and demand turns out to be. This, one recalls, is one of the reasons agricultural competition commonly yields returns to the grower that are, by industrial standards, below full cost. And it appears that this feature is to a less extent shared by meat packing, and is responsible for the fact that among the twenty-two big firms for which returns on investment are tabulated in the Brookings study for the years 1947-1955, inclusive, Swift shows one of the two lowest average percentage returns on investment, after taxes.[16]

[15] *Ibid.*, pp. 184-88.
[16] Data given in *ibid.*, Appendix IV, pp. 313-17.

5. Further Modifying Factors

The question whether an industry is rapidly growing, slowly growing, stationary, or declining has, of course, a great influence, not only on the ability of firms in the industry to earn a liberal return, but also on the rate of return that firms feel is needed to meet their requirements, so that they tend to embody it in their conception of full cost. Even more important at times is the past and prospective course of prices, which determines whether an established firm has the benefit of relatively low-cost structures and equipment, compared to the prices new competitors must pay for their facilities, and whether, when structures and equipment have to be replaced, it will take more money to replace them than the equivalent of orthodox depreciation accounts would amount to, so that surplus must be accumulated for the purpose if the firm does not want to raise fresh capital for the physical replacement of existing facilities.

The growing firm wants more than physical replacement, but often fears the loss of control if large amounts of securities are floated in the markets. If this is the only way to provide for the desired rate of growth, such a firm might reluctantly choose to grow more slowly. It is in such a situation that the firm feels that its own net earnings must provide the major part of its growth, in addition to dividends sufficient to satisfy its existing stockholders, when sweetened by the prospect of long-run growth in the value and earnings of the equity securities, this being often regarded as a hedge against inflation. Then funds for growth may come to be thought of as part of "full-cost," which firms aim to recover if they can.[17] If this is offset by a low rate of cash dividend, it may be merely a matter of the form in which returns are taken. But if powerful firms add it to a liberal rate of cash dividend on investment, it may represent a target return raised by monopoloidal power.

Heavy taxation of corporate net income introduces a further factor and a controversial one. The logic of orthodox marginal analysis argues that such a tax cannot be shifted, because the conditions de-

[17] Cf. *ibid.*, p. 204, citing leaders in aluminum, steel, and oil.

termining the most profitable price—marginal revenue and marginal cost—are not affected by it, so that the most profitable price is the same, with or without the net income tax. But numerous industrialists are convinced that they have, in fact, shifted this tax, and the logic of full-cost pricing makes this entirely plausible, even if full-cost pricing is not a wholly arbitrary policy, but is merely maximum-profit pricing as governed by long-run rather than short-run expectations. In the latter case, the long-run minimum return is the rate necessary to induce the investment of capital and the incurring of the risks of enterprise; and there is at least an arguable case that these depend on the reward that is left after taxes, at least more than on the net income before taxes. The rates of return reported by large and strong companies, capable of full-cost pricing, are liberal enough to suggest strongly that the corporate income tax has, in effect, been treated as a cost and included in the price charged the customer.[18]

One thing that stands out in this sketchy account is that there is so much diversity between different situations, and within any one situation so much gradation in the amount of discretionary latitude it allows as to a liberal or a narrowly restricted rate of return, that one would expect a great deal of variety in the outcome. The idea of "full-cost," including some conception of a minimum return to capital and enterprise, as the maximum that could be earned in the long run, might be expected to have some standardizing effect, but not enough to outweigh the differences between industries and firms in all the factors that make for diversity in attainable long-run rates of return, in plausibly tenable concepts of full cost, and in cost-price relationships for particular products. This diversity is perhaps the outstanding feature of the Brookings study, already referred to.

6. The Brookings Study: "Target Returns" and Other Objectives

This is a study of pricing aims and methods as reported mainly by twenty giant companies, selected partly on the basis of their importance and partly on the basis of their willingness to furnish full

[18] *Ibid.*, pp. 313-17, for rates of return on investment before and after taxes.

cooperation. Other companies supplied information on particular matters. The company-wide policies of different companies, as reflected in the returns, were combinations or resultants of diverse elements; and within single companies there was clearly much decentralization and diversity of decision on particular products. Different companies might be price-leaders or price-followers or meeters of competition, or leaders who meet competition where necessary, or leaders on new products and meeters of competition on mature ones.

In place of "full-cost" pricing, this study employs the concept of pricing for a "target return" on investment, finding this to be the most prevalent single type of general company policy. Four others were distinguished: stabilization of price and margin, pricing to maintain or improve market position, pricing to meet or follow competition, and pricing subordinated to product differentiation. Then each of the twenty firms on which the study concentrated was identified with one or another of the five policy objectives as the one that on the whole mainly characterized that firm. This was done with full realization of the oversimplification involved, and of the existence of reasonable ground for different classifications. The accompanying discussion contains material that might afford some basis for classifying different parts of a single firm's business under different headings or under a combination: for example, following the market on mature products, while policy for new products combines a dynamic form of target return with orientation to product differentiation. With these reservations in mind, we may review the classification presented in Chapter 2 of the Brookings study.

Under target return, one finds General Motors, International Harvester, Alcoa, du Pont, Standard of New Jersey, Johns-Manville, and Union Carbide. One notes that a majority of these firms are among the most profitable of the twenty.[19] The targets of this majority, so far

[19] For data, see table, Brookings study, pp. 313-17, giving returns on investment, after taxes, of twenty-two companies, for 1947-55 inclusive. Returns ranged from approximately 6.45 per cent for Swift to approximately 18 per cent for du Pont and approximately 24 per cent for General Motors. The over-all nine-year average for the twenty-two companies was 11.65 per cent. Averaging (unweighted) between years is by the present writer. The twenty-two firms included sixteen of the twenty analyzed in Chapter 2. For these twenty, Lanzillotti, one of the co-authors of the Brookings study, has presented somewhat different figures in his own summary interpretation of the study: see "Pricing Objectives in Large Companies," *American Economic Review* (December 1958), pp. 921-40; cf. discussion, *American Economic Review* (September 1959), pp. 669-87.

as indicated in figures, and their attained returns, are too liberal to be easily classed under "full-cost." International Harvester is an exception, with a modest 10 per cent target return and a more modest actual return.[20] It has a tradition of leadership in the field of farm machinery, but its formerly dominant market share has diminished, though its absolute volume has multiplied. It now meets close competition and faces a market of limited buying power, with buyers forced to figure closely on a basis of economically serviceable performance.

Alcoa is also in a special position, having operated under a court order of 1946, aiming to protect the opportunity of efficient nonintegrated fabricators to compete with the integrated Alcoa. It must not charge more than a "fair price" for ingot if that results in squeezing the nonintegrated fabricator, and as fabricator it must charge a margin sufficient to cover the costs of an efficient nonintegrated competitor.[21] The situation includes an integrated firm supplying materials to fabricator customers on terms that enable them to compete with an integrated rival. The felt need for a quasi-umbrella requirement may have diminished with reduction of Alcoa's commanding position, while aluminum ingot moves nearer to the status of a low-margin mature product.

Under stabilization of price and margin, the study classifies United States Steel and Kennecott Copper, apparently for two almost opposite reasons. U.S. Steel may fairly be rated as a successful follower of a policy of stabilization, while Kennecott is preoccupied with this problem precisely because it faces a fluctuating world market which makes instability a stubborn and troublesome problem, and its efforts at stabilization appear to have achieved only very limited results.

Under pricing to maintain or improve market position, the study lists A. & P., Swift, Sears-Roebuck, and Standard of Indiana. A. & P. has subordinated any target return to attainment of a desired market share. It has been enjoined against loss-leader tactics, but short of that it apparently follows a policy of using leaders for customer appeal. Sears-Roebuck relies on pricing below the general retail scale, accepting a modest rate of return. The particular position of Swift has been discussed in an earlier section. Standard of Indiana has followed a policy of meeting competition, in the face of reductions in its market share, which forced its policy to concentrate on the defense of its

[20] Brookings study, pp. 69-73.
[21] Ibid., pp. 31-36, 143-44, 267.

share against encroachments. Thus this group shades into the next: those who meet or follow competition. Firms in either group are hardly in a position to price for a particular target return. A further question is whether a policy directed to maintaining a market share sometimes includes setting a maximum limit on the share aimed at. This will be discussed later.

In the category of pricing policy subordinated to product differentiation, the study names American Can, General Electric, and General Foods. The foregoing discussion has indicated that the ability to maintain a target return is itself related to successful product differentiation, as with du Pont, Johns-Manville, and Union Carbide, if not others; the classification depending on whether a general target-return policy appears strongly amid the diversities imposed by product differentiation. In this connection it appears worth noting that the business executives whose reports figure in this study appear to minimize the distinction between rivalry of substitutes, such as a patented product faces, and competition of unpatented variants of the "same" product.

American Can, in addition to adapting its product to customers' requirements, rendered technical service on the can-closing machinery which it leased, and stressed readiness to meet uncertain seasonal demands. They held that if their customers, the canners, received equal treatment, they were not keenly sensitive to the amount of the price charged. Since the antitrust order of 1950, contracts have been limited to one season, can-closing machinery has been made available for sale, and "open-order buying has increased."[22] In the outcome, American Can has been moving in the direction of the meeting-competition type of policy. With regard to General Electric, we have already noted cases of interaction between the design of the product and the price that the market will support. General Foods has laid stress on specialties, and the price premiums they permit; but apparently these market advantages are dwindling, and with them the scope of pricing discretion exercised by General Foods.

If one may dare attempt to generalize on the basis of this study, one conclusion would be that very strong firms can aim at a liberal return and can roughly approximate it; while in other cases the range of pricing discretion that goes with product differentiation appears to be encroached on by competition, and firms are prudent if they aim at

---

[22] *Ibid.*, p. 210.

maintaining their market share, rather than attempting to "maximize profits" in the limited time perspective which this concept seems to imply in application. And firms that can make only a modest return appear to be preoccupied with meeting competition or maintaining their market share and, with some exceptions, seem not to have the kind of range of discretionary policy which "full-cost pricing" appears to imply. The picture includes more variety than was indicated by the original Hall and Hitch inquiry.

7. Further Comment

Maintaining a firm's market share raises the question whether there are upper limits to the share a firm aims at, either in its industry as a whole or in major segments of it. Various indications of this possibility are scattered through the Brookings study. Wherever an umbrella policy appears, it might be construed as implying such a limitation. However, when this implication was pressed on President Curtice, relative to General Motors' position in the low-price field, he refused to be drawn into admitting any maximum limit on the market share he would welcome.[23] It is common opinion that U.S. Steel has as large a market share as is consistent with its own interests; and the company itself indicates a willingness to accept reductions of its share in sectors where the share has been dominant, if accompanied by offsetting increases in other sectors where its share is low, with the implication that its total market share would be maintained.[24] Johns-Manville indicated a similarly selective preference for expansion of its market share in the field of new products, while in established products "they were even prepared to say that 20 per cent of a market was as large a share as they strongly desired."[25] International Harvester prefers not to have a market share so large as to confer monopoly power over price.[26] Actual or potential antitrust action has its impact in reducing desire for a dominant market share.

[23] *Ibid.*, pp. 132-33.
[24] *Ibid.*, p. 174.
[25] *Ibid.*, pp. 160-61.
[26] *Ibid.*, p. 136.

But this in turn raises problems of internal morale. These companies appear typically to want goals that will keep the members of the organization on their toes—"management is afraid of becoming lethargic."[27] To that extent they appear to shun the "quiet life" which has, rightly or wrongly, been spoken of as one of the aims of some heads of English businesses. Yet if such a firm accepts a limited objective as to the market share it aims at, it might seem to be softening by that much its scheme of incentives, and moving closer to the goals of the "quiet life." There seems to be a real ambivalence in that the firm wants its sales force to be working energetically and effectively to expand its sales volume, but does not want it to be too successful; since part of its picture of a healthy state of the organization is that the majority of the market should be held by competitors strong enough so that the sales staff will have its work cut out for it to maintain or increase its market share. If this condition is self-maintaining, well and good; but if one firm has superior efficiency, the balance may not be self-maintaining. Then the firm may want to set a limited goal, without causing the selling organization to relax its efforts if the goal is approached. One General Electric official is quoted as saying: "The Company would rather be pushing to expand a 25 per cent share than defending a 50 per cent share."[28] One escape from this dilemma is afforded by diversification, moving into fields in which there is room for vigorous expansion without approaching undue dominance.[29]

The objection to a conspicuously large market share, however, does not apply to new products in which the firm has initially a position of innovational monopoly or something approaching it. Market power does not interfere with the incentives to increased efficiency in productive processes—or it has two-sided effects, as was earlier indicated. And growth resulting solely from such efficiency is unlikely—with possible exceptions—to lead to such a decisive advantage over competitors as to weaken competition substantially, or to create the condition that has been spoken of as compulsory umbrella holding. Growth brought about by mergers, by preclusive massing of patents or by other methods preclusive of competition is, naturally, a different matter.

A broader question may be raised, whether the desire to minimize

[27] *Ibid.*, p. 265.
[28] Lanzillotti, *op. cit.*, p. 933.
[29] Brookings study, p. 265.

legal vulnerability is one form of the search for a "quiet life," and whether it tends toward soft rather than vigorous competition, and a wish to avoid doing too much harm to one's rivals. Insofar as the antitrust laws may have this effect, is it compatible with their main purpose? To answer this question would call for a monumental study in itself. It appears clear that there are elements working in both directions, and that any attempt to strike a balance involves a weighing of multitudes of disparate impacts, on which judgment is often a matter of degree and contains unavoidable subjective elements. I stand with those who hold that the toughest competition is not necessarily the best or the most effective in its long-run effects, but that under present conditions shelters against the rigors of tough competition are on the whole more likely to be carried too far rather than not far enough. Like most economists, I am opposed to competitive advantages of size of a bargaining sort that are not bound up with technical progress and serviceability to customers. I would even be willing to see some slowing of technical progress if it were the necessary price of greater decentralization and competitive equality, except for the judgment that in view of the current world struggle leading western nations cannot afford to pay this price. By and large, my judgment would be that the effect of antitrust policies is more favorable than unfavorable to a salutary kind of balance between tough and soft competition.

Selling below cost with intent and effect of eliminating competition is an offense, though it would not be desirable, if it were feasible, to forbid all selling below cost. As to the treatment of margins that affect the terms of competition between integrated and nonintegrated producers, the law induces a circumspect regard for fairness without incurring the burdens and responsibilities of general and continuing regulation of such margins. One real dilemma of antitrust policy concerns price discrimination. This may result in bargaining advantages for large and powerful customers, thus impairing the quality of competition at the customers' level, while it may serve to avoid the drying up of active competition among the sellers.

Cost-plus pricing, or stabilization policies, being practiced more by large and strong sellers than by their smaller competitors, tends to leave aggressive price discrimination to the smaller firms. The larger firms may respond defensively, if discriminatory encroachments become substantial, but in the interest of price stability they may not meet the lowest prices set by any of their rivals. Moderate product differentiation helps to make this degree of elasticity of policy feasible. Such a policy does not court antitrust difficulties, since defensive discrimination is unlikely to be held to lessen or injure competition, though the line between aggressive and defensive discrimination may become uncertain in practice. Insofar as the presence of the antitrust laws may tend to moderate the aggressiveness of competition by large and strong firms, the softening effect is probably outweighed by freeing competitors from "unfair" handicaps and making umbrella-like policies less secure than they would otherwise be.

CHAPTER 16

Some Remaining Problems and Practices

1. Competition of Business Firms as Buyers

Since buying and selling are equal and opposite, it may seem anomalous that in this volume sellers' competition should occupy an array of chapters, while buyers' competition is compressed into a fraction of one. However, something of the sort is a rational middle way between twin errors: one of assuming that the study of sellers' competition contributed nothing to that of buyers' competition, so that the whole analysis needed to be done *de novo*, and the opposite error of dismissing buyers' competition by assuming—as is sometimes done—that it is adequately covered by simply reversing what is said about sellers' competition. The simplest form of this latter thesis would assume that, while sellers' competition drives prices down toward costs, buyers' competition on the part of business units drives costs (in the sense of prices paid for productive factors) up toward selling prices, resulting in an equilibrium in which excess profits are squeezed out and the benefits of increased efficiency diffused both to consumers and to suppliers of materials, labor, and other productive factors.[1] There is of course a measure of truth in this, and it may be useful as a starting point for inquiry; but it is oversimplified, begs too many questions, and ignores too many differences which are operationally important.

On the other hand, the whole analysis does not need to be done over, because what has already been said about sellers' competition covers many of the facts and forces involved in buyers' competition, including markets of the supply-and-demand type and those in which prices are the active factors, bargaining and negotiation, and the character and competence of business firms and consumers as buyers. But

[1] Cf. discussion of diffusion, above, Chap. 4, Sec. 6.

in buyers' competition these elements are differently combined and take variant forms. Business does not demand goods for their own sakes, as consumers do, but as means to the ends of profitable selling of its products. This means, among other things, that the amounts business firms want to buy are gauged by the amounts they expect to be able to sell. In contrast to consumers, much of what they buy consists of materials that have been reduced either to effective homogeneity or to differentials the value of which the business buyer can ,quantify dollar-wise. This is reinforced by the fact that business buyers are better informed and more calculating than consumers.

This is true of the manufacturer buying productive equipment, as against the housewife buying household equipment. The dealer buying consumer goods for resale may know their performance capabilities better than the average consumer, but his problem is whether they will sell; and the dealer may in some cases be taking the greater risk, in that goods that perform moderately well may still become comparatively unmarketable in the dealer's hands. Business buying involves larger transactions on the average (though not invariably) than business selling, since the latter includes sales to individual consumers. Though the business buyer may be either smaller or larger than his supplier, business includes fewer monopolistic buyers than monopolistic sellers. This is because a firm may have a monopoloidal position in the sale of its product, but generally uses materials that are also used by numerous other industries, so that as a buyer of means of production it is in a competitive position. Monopoloidal fabricators of specialized metal products may compete for the steel they use with makers of totally different products.

Examples of the contrary sort, in which concentration in buying parallels concentration in selling, would include the buying of leaf tobacco and the sale of its products, buying of livestock and sale of dressed meat, and to a slightly less extent, buying of wheat and sale of flour; the test being that the use of a single basic material is virtually confined to a single industry, so that in that industry a monopoly seller would also be a monopoly buyer, and a competitive buyer would be a competitive seller. As to the monopoloidal buyer who is a competitive seller, perhaps the chief example would be an employer dominating a limited local labor market, but selling his product in competition with producers located elsewhere. But such semi-isolated local labor markets appear to be a diminishing feature of the economic landscape.

The usual treatment of the curves representing the behavior of business costs with varying output is consistent with the assumption that business firms are competitive as buyers of the factors of production, whether they are competitive or monopolistic as sellers of their products. This is in harmony with the fact, mentioned earlier, that these curves are intended to reflect changes in the amounts of productive factors used, at given prices, but not to reflect changes in the prices of the factors occasioned by variations in the amounts used. Hence they correspond to the situation of a producer who faces a horizontal supply schedule, as an individual competitive purchaser would.[2] However, buyers' competition, while favorable to this result, is not necessary to it. If the supply of the factor of production in question can be materially increased without increasing its cost of production, an increase in the amount demanded by one large user, or by all the users, might not raise the price, except perhaps temporarily.

Actually, an extra-large user might be able to use his larger volume of purchases as a leverage in bargaining for a price concession, if the total demand were not large enough to create a general shortage. If demand were to decrease, the suppliers' costs might be less flexible, if they had fixed investments. Thus a firm with a buyer's monopoly might be in a position to squeeze down the prices of its major supplies if it were actually willing to bring about an absolute reduction in its physical volume of output—something that happens far oftener in theoretical models than in reality. Where the factor in question is labor, it does not appear to be characteristic monopoly policy on the employer's part to squeeze down wages below the going rates; rather the opposite, for reasons that are hardly mysterious. It is in such industries that unions are strong enough to make the employer ready to share his gains with them. More likely to be exploited are workers in poorly organized, locally fragmented markets, whose employers are small and subject to extra-severe competition.[3] In such cases, the employer's competition as seller is not balanced by equally effective competition as buyer of the services of labor, and the supplier—the worker—suffers.

A local union may decide to accept a wage reduction where that is necessary to enable a hard-pressed employer to stay in business and

[2] Cf. P. W. S. Andrews, *Manufacturing Business* (1949), p. 84.
[3] The prevalence of this kind of wage differential is shown in Chap. 18, Table 2, below.

continue the jobs of the union members. Whether this will be done, and whether it is economically sound, appears to be a matter on which judgments might vary from case to case. The opposite method is for the union to maintain its standard rates and let particular employers go under if they cannot pay them. This is generally rationalized by the idea that all or most of the displaced workers will be reabsorbed as the trade of the defunct employers is taken over by more efficient ones who can pay standard rates. In the garment trades, unions have assisted hard-pressed employers to raise their level of efficiency. The United Hatters, Cap and Millinery Workers' International Union has twice given economic help to employers in difficulties; in a recent case taking a controlling interest in the Merrimac Hat Corporation of Amesbury, Mass., to save the jobs of the workers.[4] These represent a variety of different ways in which unions may protect the workers' interests when employers' competition as sellers threatens their capacity as buyers of the services of labor.

Probably the chief example of competition unbalanced in the opposite direction is the use by a strong union of the technique of striking against one selected employer, leaving his competitors free to take his business away from him. When he has been forced by this pressure to grant a wage increase, this may become an industry pattern, and can occasion an increase in prices. This method of playing competition of buyers (employers) against unified action by sellers of labor is currently impelling employers to make common cause in one way or another—including airlines reimbursing a struck competitor for the business transferred to them as a result of the strike. In the steel wage negotiations of 1959, the union proposed to apply this squeeze play if industry-wide negotiation should fail to yield them gains they were willing to accept. The industry responded by contemplating a possible mutual reimbursement arrangement; and the union countered with a suggestion of invoking antitrust action against such an arrangement by the industry. These tactics were not carried out: the fact that they were proposed appears to come close to a *reductio ad absurdum* of the present state of collective bargaining between a union exempt from the antitrust laws and a group of employers to whom these laws are applicable, when a stubborn dispute uncovers the ultimate power-leverages available to both sides. If a business firm were to pursue tactics parallel to the union squeeze play, it would clearly be guilty of

[4] *New York Times,* Jan. 18, 1959, pp. 1, 42.

discrimination injurious to competition and tending to raise prices by coercive power.

It appears that a monopolistic seller may or may not be in a position to compound the profits he gets from raising selling prices with profits gained in his capacity as buyer by limiting his demand for factors of production and reducing the prices he pays for them. If he is to compound his profits in this way, his factors of production must have supply schedules that slope upward, so that increased amounts cost more, and vice versa for decreased amounts, thus reversing the behavior of sloping demand schedules. It appears that the supply schedule seldom behaves like a demand schedule in reverse, that while a monopolistic seller may also be a monopolistic buyer of the factors of production, he is more often not; and that if he is, various forces may prevent him from using this position to squeeze down the prices of the factors of production, especially labor. This squeezing down can happen, but various other outcomes seem more likely.

A simple reversal of the quoted-price method of selling would imply that the buyer quoted a buying price and the sellers could take it or leave it. There are cases in which the buyer takes initiative, such as leaf tobacco and the purchase of livestock in central markets. These appear to have a hybrid character, sharing features of the supply-and-demand type of market and of buyers' quoted prices. Differences in the qualities of different lots offered cause the buyer to make individual offers, and the auction method is used for tobacco. Cases in which the buyer takes the initiative in quoting a price might seem most likely to occur where the buyer is large and the supplier relatively small; but even here it would seem that a genuine buyer's quoted price is not a frequent phenomenon. In construction work, the large buyer may call for bids, placing the price initiative with the seller; and there may be two-sided negotiation.

Another kind of initiative that may come from the large buyer is an offer to the supplier of a volume of business that is large or steady or both, in return for a price concession. If there were active competition between buyers in the making of such offers, the price concession that can be gained in this way by the big buyer would in theory be limited to the economic value to the supplier of the large, steady volume of orders. However, measurement of this advantage appears difficult or impossible. If the big buyers are very few, it may be questioned whether competitive checks on such concessions are effective, and a problem might arise of the sort that occasioned the provision in the Robinson-Patman Act that the quantities for which discounts were given might be limited in case so few could qualify for them that they would tend to promote monopoly.[5] A similar principle for a long time caused quantity discounts in rail freight rates to be limited to carload lots. A more natural limit is likely to be set by the reluctance of some big buyers to incur the quasi-public-service responsibilities that would go with taking so much of a single supplier's output that the supplier does not have adequate alternative market connections, and becomes dependent on the big buyer.[6]

Some particular forms of pricing where buyers are large and few will be mentioned in the sections that follow. In general, this situation tends to cause sellers' competition to be the more immediately active force, but the buyers' competition in the ultimate sale of their products will, if effective, impel them to maintain their volume of demand for the means of production they need if they are to hold their market position.

In a market of the supply-and-demand type, a single big firm's volume of purchases will affect the price, since his demand is an appreciable fraction of the whole; but this effect may be confined to the short-run, and the long-run effect will normally depend on the elasticity of the supply in response to the total demand at the current or expected future price. In a market in which suppliers sell at quoted prices, the relation between immediate and long-run effect may be reversed; an increase in buyers' orders, even those of a big buyer, need not have any immediate effect on price, if there is enough unused capacity to fill the increased total of orders. But the price may rise (1) if there had been more than normal unused capacity, which had driven price below normal "full cost," and the pressure is now relieved, especially, (2) if unused capacity is reduced so far below normal as to bring early expansion of capacity, and accompanying long-run marginal cost, into contemplation.[7]

If there is not enough unused capacity to fill the increased total of orders, delays in delivery, followed if persistent by premiums for

[5] See U. S. Attorney General's National Committee to Study the Antitrust Laws, *Report* (1955), pp. 176-77. The majority of the committee opposed the provision, but some members favored it.

[6] Cf. above, Chap. 5, p. 91.

[7] This factor has been discussed above, Chap. 7, Sec. 8.

prompt delivery, are a natural result. In such a market, if the firm that increased its orders gets its increased deliveries, it will encroach on the requirements of its competitors, causing them to respond with defensive price increases. If these succeed, the first firm's attempted expansion will be limited or defeated. This could lead to a contest in outbidding, until the resulting increase in costs, from higher prices of means of production, discourages enough of the planned expansion of production to bring total demand for means of production down to the supplier's capacity, meanwhile stimulating the suppliers (unless there is definite reason for thinking the expansion temporary) to install increased capacity.

One special class of transactions of growing importance is the sale of durables with a turn-in of a used unit, automobiles being the largest instance.[8] Here purchase and sale are tied together in one transaction, and competition in setting the buying price for the used unit is subsidiary to the sale of the new item and is connected, with some leeway, with the ultimate resale (or scrapping) of the used item, with or without reconditioning before resale. This last price is a hybrid, which may in form be a seller's quoted price on a differentiated commodity, but in which the controlling factors are supply and demand, and supply equals the turn-ins on replacement sales of new units, minus scrappings of used units. The leeway between the turn-in allowance and the ultimate resale price of the used unit is a way of shading the seller's quoted price of the new unit, rather than an independent instance of buyers' competition. Naturally, such shading is greatest in a buyers' market, in which the dealer may expect to take a loss on the turn-in, which acts as a deduction from his nominal markup.

It may begin to appear why competition of business units as buyers offers a smaller field of investigation than competition of sellers, once the latter has been examined—chiefly because the former is subsidiary to the latter—but still presents problems that cannot be disposed of by simply reversing the models of sellers' competition. From the standpoint of this inquiry, the distinction between a buyers' and a sellers' market acquires added pertinence, despite the imprecise character of the terms; because it brings out the different grades of activity or urgency of sellers' and buyers' competition, sellers' competition being most active in a buyers' market and vice versa.

[8] Cf. above, Chap. 7, Sec. 8.

In markets of the supply-and-demand type, the two states of the market might be distinguished according as supply is greater or less than demand at current prices—this of course decides the direction in which prices will move in the short-run. A more important criterion would be whether supply is greater or less than demand at prices that cover a representative producer's average costs, determining the direction of longer-run movements. In markets of the sellers' quoted-price type, literal supply is less important than productive capacity. It is not easy to find a descriptive term for the grade of competition represented by buyers in a buyers' market or sellers in a sellers' market. "Passive" or "quiescent" suggests too complete a cessation; "competitive bargain-hunting" as distinct from "competitive offering of bargains to stimulate the movement of goods" conveys more of the nature of the difference.

The point is that competition is a two-sided activity, and it is only one side that becomes quiescent in a favorable market. It still presupposes that a firm tries to get as good a bargain as the market affords and at least as good a bargain as its competitors get. This kind of competition continues in a favorable market; but it is always subject to the condition that the goods must move—the firm must obtain the supplies necessary to meet its orders, or must sell enough to be economically sound, and for this purpose it must ordinarily sell at least as cheap or buy at least as dear as its competitors do. If this is not sufficient, it must sell cheaper or buy dearer. This is the kind of competition that becomes active, or even urgent, in an unfavorable market, and it is this that causes the market price to change. This does not necessarily mean that the tactical initiative, for example in a sellers' market, rests with the buyers. It may, but a seller may instead lead prices upward, recognizing that demand is so strong that such a lead will probably be followed, and without waiting for actual shortages to cause buyers to take the initiative by offering premiums for early delivery.

Some would say that in a sellers' market, for example, sellers' competition ceases; but this does less than justice to the competitive element in the "bargain-hunting" stage, or the dependence of a price leader on being followed by his competitors; also the extent to which large and strong firms may deliberately restrain swings in prices, believing that more nearly stable prices are more healthy for business, and therefore exerting their market power to keep prices in a temporarily unbalanced market from getting too far out of touch with longer-run average or normal levels. This involves restraining increases as well as decreases, and in an extreme sellers' market it may call for rationing shortages. In the absence of such restraints on price fluctuations, a strong buyers' market, under pressure of large amounts of unused capacity, would tend to drive prices below average costs, with short-run marginal cost as the only minimum limit. On the other side, it is possible for the competition of buyers who have orders to fill, in a sellers' market, to drive their buying prices up to the point at which their prospective profits are turned into losses.[9] This has been observed as one of the factors playing a part in the downturn of a cyclical expansion.[10] Chamberlin notes an equivalent phenomenon when firms pack added value into a product until cost exceeds return.[11] Intermediate between strong buyers' and sellers' markets, one might identify a balanced market as one in which the amount of unused capacity is small enough so that the long-run cost of expansion will have to be considered if output increases further.[12]

From the standpoint of desirable conditions, this analysis emphasizes the need for two-sidedness in competition over the long pull that includes buyers' and sellers' markets, plus the desirability of moderation, so far as possible, in the degree of fluctuations. Yet shifts of this sort in the balance of supply and demand, in moderation, can play a useful part in breaking up one-sided conditions of bargaining power and bringing about a fresh start in the working-out of bargaining relations, which might otherwise harden to the disadvantage of one side or the other. Great disparities of size can generate dependence for the smaller firm, yet dealings between large and small firms also have their very useful place in the economy. We have already noted the problems created by vertical relations, including agency and integration, in altering the buyer-seller relation in the direction of a captive or dependent status for either supplier or customer. The most conspicuous current instance of this group of problems is the one created by du Pont's ownership of 23 per cent of the stock of General Motors. Perhaps the most general requirement that can be set up is that both

[9] Cf. G. E. Putnam, "Unit Costs as a Guiding Factor in Buying Operations," *Journal of Political Economy* (1921), pp. 663-75.

[10] See W. C. Mitchell, *Business Cycles* (1913), pp. 475-83, 494-98.

[11] See "The Product as an Economic Variable," *Quarterly Journal of Economics* (February 1953), pp. 4-5.

[12] Cf. above, Chap. 7, Sec. 8.

buyer and seller should have the benefit of genuinely independent competitive alternatives and should use them to protect their interests in their dealings with one another.

2. Auctions

A brief comment may be in order on auctions, since they are an obvious form of buyers' competition, though their significance for the present study is confined to the part played by buyers who are dealers or industrial firms purchasing means of production. This method is characteristically used for commodities that are differentiated, not only between brands but between single units, in ways that do not lend themselves readily to identification by market grades, and the supply of which is irregular or occasional—generally a sale of used durables. Household goods and antiques furnish most of the examples. A sale may be of one owner's goods, conducted on the premises, or conducted at an auction dealer's regular place of business, combining lots from various sellers. Sale to the highest bidder may or may not be limited by sellers' reservation prices.

Tobacco auctions, already mentioned, are exceptional, the buyers being manufacturers; and the concentration among them introduces some of the features of sellers' quoted prices. It is not clear that effective grading is not feasible, though it faces obvious difficulties; and it might afford some protection against inequities to particular sellers, such as may result from the vagaries of unsystematic bidding. Demand is reflected back from consumer demand at sticky prices, and supply is the more active variable and is affected by the features common to agricultural products.[13] The buyers have the advantage over the sellers in market information; and the balance of supply and demand presumably favors them more often than the sellers, though the average prospect, taking one season with another, may find some reflection in the quoted prices for the finished products.

In the more usual types of auctions, the more significant prices for our purposes are those offered by dealers, as representing the expenses on which they must seek to secure a return, and limited by some kind

---

[13] Cf. above, Chap. 12, Sec. 3.

of estimate of the prospects of resale, these estimates being made by buyers whose basis of market information, though imperfect, is at least better than that of the general run of consumers attending the sales. In the case of household goods, the unskilled consumer may recognize an offering specially suited to his needs, and may rationally outbid a dealer in such a case, while in antiques and objects of art the occasional connoisseur may exceed the average dealer's knowledge. The prices offered by dealers represent amounts on which, in the dealer's best judgment, a sufficient margin may be earned by a resale price—necessarily conjectural—with allowance for the uncertainty of the resale price, which will probably be of the negotiated type, and for the uncertain time elapsing before resale. Competitive forces are presumably at work, but they clearly operate with wide margins of indeterminateness.

3. *Purchasing on Sealed Bids*

Purchasing on the basis of sealed bids is a method of reaching an agreement for purchase, the essential feature of which is that a large buyer tries to secure a favorable price—meaning one below the openly quoted price if the product has one—by requiring suppliers to bid individually on a single transaction, instead of adhering to their regularly quoted scale of prices that are open to all buyers. Thus the buyer puts the suppliers in competition with one another's *unknown* offers instead of with offers made either openly or under market conditions that permit them to be discovered and met. Under sealed bids, negotiation of agreements is either excluded or employed in a limited and subsidiary capacity. Insofar as it is employed, it alters the character of the method of pricing. This method is used both by large private firms and by government, but is more characteristic of government, both because of its huge total of purchasing operations and because of its preference for minimizing the scope of discretionary negotiation by its purchasing agents, coupled with the publicity of government prices, which restricts the effectiveness of negotiations.[14] It is only natural

[14] For an enlightening account of these procedures and the accompanying problems, see Dickson Reck, *Government Purchasing and Competition* (1954). Negotia-

that as used by government this method takes a more rigid and rule-bound form than in the hands of private firms, which employ it with more latitude for flexible policy, and with certain accompanying differences in the procedures followed.

The essentials of the procedure include the invitation to bid; the definition of the product, including checks on quality delivered; the kind of award made and the criteria governing it; and the alternatives available if bids are unsatisfactory. The differences between governmental and private procedure stem largely from the arm's-length character of legislative checks on integrity and efficiency in executive agencies. This leads government to combat favoritism and corruption by formally prescribed procedures, in contrast to the more direct and personal disciplines and incentives available to a private firm.[15] The differences begin with the fact that governmental agencies are legally required to use sealed bidding regularly in major classes of cases, while it is optional with private firms. Private buyers may use it occasionally, to feel out the market for procurement of a novel product, or intermittently when competition seems to need activating, and then go back to negotiation when bidding has served its temporary purpose. Government bidding is intended to be open to all qualified suppliers, including any who are sufficiently interested to ask to be put on the list, and to bid occasionally thereafter.[16] Private firms typically prefer to restrict invitations to six or eight suppliers well known to them.

Government bidding must be based on specifications wherever feasible, the general rule being that the lowest bidder who meets the specifications receives the entire contract, while private firms make freer use of lists of acceptable products, and are not restricted to the bid that is lowest in money terms, but may give heavy weight to differences in quality in selecting the most advantageous bids, and they typically divide awards among favorable bidders with a view to protecting continuity of supply. Government bids are opened publicly, while private firms prevailingly keep them confidential, thinking that

tion is widely used for specialized military items or items in critical supply. For government's civilian purchasing, the sealed-bid procedure is the general rule, subject to numerous exceptions; notably perhaps small items and cases of identical bids, all unsatisfactory. See *ibid.*, pp. 30, 84.

[15] See summary of these differences, *ibid.*, pp. 26-33, 88-89.

[16] A firm can be removed from the list if it does not bid on three successive invitations, *ibid.*, p. 80.

this makes bidders more likely to quote their lowest price.[17] Government bears a burden of showing cause in rejecting a bid on the ground that the bidder is not responsible, while private firms are under no such restriction.[18] If bids are tied, the award may go to a firm offering advantages above minimum specifications, or to a small firm in preference to a large one, or may be made by lot. If all bids are unsatisfactory—meaning worse than might be gotten by other methods—government may reject them and readvertise or authorize agencies to purchase locally. Bids that are identical and unsatisfactory may be met by rejection and resort to negotiation, on the ground that the bidding has failed to elicit competition.[19] Awards may be distributed where the amount is so large as to require it, or where bidders limit the amount they offer to supply to less than the total that is to be purchased.[20] Private buying is naturally free from the restrictive rules that condition the government's freedom of action in these and other circumstances.

Among the reasons for expecting bids to be below the general market are low costs resulting from the large volumes involved in a single order, which may mean large product runs (though not always). Or the bidder may limit the amount he undertakes to supply to what he needs to fill up his expected unused capacity. Or the procedure of bidding may be less expensive for the supplier than the usual private methods of sales promotion. This does not apply where contracts for indefinite amounts are distributed among suppliers who must compete for subsequent orders from different purchasing agencies.[21] And costs may be increased if the government specifications call for a product that differs from that regularly produced. However, in the case of venetian blinds—typically an assembled product—it was possible to specify a product different from that made by any firm, using parts that were standard and obtainable but of high quality, with the result that established producers could assemble it economically and were willing to bid on it, while the government got improved performance for its money.[22] Where a government specification is thus an improvement on prevalent market practice, it may be adopted by knowledge-

[17] Ibid., p. 88.
[18] Ibid., pp. 81-82.
[19] Ibid., pp. 82, 154, 160-61.
[20] Ibid., pp. 147, 157-58.
[21] Ibid., pp. 158-59.
[22] Ibid., pp. 153-54.

able private buyers.[23] On the other hand, government specifications may have gotten out of date and may conflict with current practice without corresponding benefit.

Where products are differentiated, government may treat all that meet specification requirements as equivalent, disregarding minor quality factors in excess of requirements. Or it may attempt to quantify the service value of such differences, so that it may rate the lowest bid as the lowest per unit of service value, which might not be the lowest per unit of physical product.[24] Such quantification is an outgrowth of the need to conform to the requirement of awarding the contract to the lowest bidder. Private buyers are naturally freer to use their judgment as to which bid is more advantageous in terms of service value. Even government makes some concessions, such as getting the kind of office machines the staff in question knows how to use, or prefers, or the brands of drugs the doctors in question consider best.[25]

It is only in the case of government purchasing that the results of the sealed-bid method are matters of public record and are thus fully available for economic analysis. These results depend in a peculiar way on the key feature of the special type of competition involved: namely, the unknown character of rival offers. In the case of government buying, the bidder knows the past bids, and can draw inferences from these as to the lowest bid he is likely to have to meet. Results also vary with the nature of the product—homogeneous or differentiated slightly or strongly, quantifiably or nonquantifiably—and with the concentrated or nonconcentrated structure of the industry, prevailing methods of pricing in the regular market, and, last but not least, the state of the market.

The bids express a wide variety of attitudes on the part of the bidders. A general call for bids may smoke out the supplier who is ready to make the largest concession, doing it more simply and cheaply than it could be done by negotiation. However, since this supplier does not know just how low he will have to bid to win the award, and does know that if he always bids his ultimate minimum, he will lose money on this class of business as a whole, he and others like him may mostly not bid their lowest prices, but rather a kind of price that might bring an award once in awhile, without cutting so drasti-

[23] *Ibid.*, p. 145.
[24] *Ibid.*, pp. 141-44.
[25] *Ibid.*, pp. 170-71, 173.

cally that a single award is barely worth taking on a stop-gap basis, and a series of them would add up to a class of business not worth taking.

In addition, then, to the bidder who is making a serious or eager effort to secure this contract in the face of strong expected competition, there are gradations of less eager bidders, who are willing to take a contract, but only if it comes to them on terms that satisfy them, generally well above short-run marginal cost and sometimes above the prevailing market price. There may at times be a suspicion that some of these higher bids are submitted with an idea that they will furnish a standard of comparison, relative to which the bargain character of the lowest bids may be appraised. The highest bids may come (one infers) from bidders who have no desire or expectation of securing a contract, but who bid for the sake of keeping their names on the invited list, in case they should want to try for future awards. Some bid so high as to appear anxious to make sure they will not secure the particular contract on which they are bidding.

In some kinds of cases, the bidding has simply reflected an unwillingness to make any concessions from the going prices already quoted to private purchasers, the unwillingness being fortified by the apprehension that strong private buyers would demand similar concessions and that they would spread. This adherence to quoted prices has occurred both in the case of highly differentiated products and of homogeneous ones. In such cases it may be said that the sealed-bid method has failed to elicit competition—meaning competition beyond whatever level of competitive forces may be active in the general market. The implication that the general market is monopolistic may or may not be warranted; and the level of competitive pressure aimed at by the sealed-bid purchaser may be one that would be ruinous if applied to all the sales of an industry. It may be that in the open market, unpublicized price-shading has brought the prevailing *de facto* price scale below the openly quoted scale of list prices; but sellers may not be willing to make their shaded prices a matter of public record as a government bid would do. This may cause bids to government to be higher than the *de facto* market, for a reason that would not apply to private buyers who keep bids confidential. In such cases, bids might be identical without direct collusion in the making of the bids; bidders might merely be adhering to the going list price or price structure.

The trade may or may not regard a specially low price quoted to government as something apart from the general market and not necessarily indicating the *de facto* market level, or likely to spread to the general market. Only where this separateness is accepted can purchasing by sealed bids achieve its characteristic purpose of securing prices below the general market. In the case of electric lamps, the producers had a regularly quoted scale of different prices to purchasers for use and for resale. They charged higher prices to purchasers for use, presumably so as not to undercut their dealers. Contract purchasers for use received discounts according to quantity purchased. By consolidating its purchasing, the government was able to secure the maximum discount openly quoted to contract purchasers for use; but it was not able through sealed bids to elicit departures from these regular discounts.[26] In other cases it has secured prices similar to those charged to dealers.

In the case of tires, market practice includes extra large discounts on original-equipment tires as compared to those sold through dealers for replacement. Sears Roebuck has secured terms enabling them to underprice the replacement dealers with tires lacking the big makers' brands. Here government encountered identical bids of a sort which appeared exposed to antitrust action. It circumvented them first by negotiating with Sears Roebuck and later, after bids were no longer identical, employed an irregular procedure involving negotiation after receiving price proposals. "Target prices" were named, based on the lower proposals, and suppliers whose offers were higher were given a chance to meet the "target prices." Prices were secured "the same as those paid by all but the largest original-equipment manufacturers."[27] Government had used a special method to deal with a special situation: a method probably best described as quasi-negotiation adapted to dealing with large numbers of suppliers. It departed from the basic principle of sealed-bid purchasing, since the incentive to submit a low bid is undermined if higher bidders are allowed to revise their bids downward and share the business.

The most conspicuous instances of identical bids have occurred where a basing-point pricing structure existed, the delivered price to any destination being the lowest combination of base price plus freight to that destination, and mills at all locations other than the

[26] *Ibid.*, pp. 155-58.
[27] *Ibid.*, pp. 160-62.

ruling base met this delivered price. In the case of cement, for in-stance, if all producers used the same freight-rate book and if in con-verting from the hundred-pound units in which freight rates were quoted to the theoretical "barrels" in terms of which prices were quoted, they all carried the unit conversion to the same number of decimal places before multiplying by the number of "barrels," the bids would be identical to the last decimal place to which the con-version was carried. In some areas, when land-grant freight rates were still in force on government shipments, these complicated the reckon-ing, often being different for different sections of a rail route that had been pieced together out of parts of different original rail properties. Competent traffic men might figure rates differently unless they used a common rate-book and common conversion methods. The cement producers, having much unused capacity and heavy constant costs, in a cycle-sensitive industry, were genuinely apprehensive that any com-plete breaking away from this price-meeting method would lead to cutthroat pricing. Localized price-shading was frequent, and was a fre-quent prelude to open price reductions, but it played a negligible part in bids on government contracts.

Under Interior Secretary Ickes, pressure was put on the companies to bid on an F.O.B. mill basis.[28] This would have meant that, to any one destination, delivered costs from different origins would no longer be identical, and from any given origin, delivered costs to some des-tinations would be above, and to others below, the prices from other points of origin. If a base mill, bidding on this basis, wished to win a contract in the territory where the price was governed from some other base, it would have to quote an F.O.B. mill price below its own base price, so that the buyer would benefit by reductions to some other destinations besides the one the reduction was aimed to reach. Some bids on this basis were elicited, but the practice did not become general at this time. After the Cement decision of 1948, it would ap-pear that the former method of calculating bids would be forbidden, being clearly a case of calculation by formula and not of freight ab-sorption to meet the individually verified prices actually charged by competitors. Thus the practice of bidding on an F.O.B. mill basis (as well as on a delivered basis) has greatly increased, though freight absorption is not explicitly forbidden.

[28] Ibid., p. 165.

Homogeneous products, produced by numerous competing firms, show interesting patterns under sealed-bid purchasing.[29] The spread between low and high bids is commonly wide, the high bid ranging from 27 per cent to 122 per cent above the low bid in certain examples, with an extreme instance of 200 per cent. If one ignores scattering extremely high bids as being submitted with no intent to secure the award, the spread is less, but still substantial, say roughly from 17 per cent to 28 per cent above the low bid in the same examples. On the average, low bids are below the price charged to private buyers, but in a strong sellers' market they may rise above this level. This appears to indicate that the suppliers, when their capacity is fully occupied, give preference to the regular customers who will presumably continue to buy from them when demand is less strong, as against taking a government contract that has no implication at all in regard to future orders.

A shift to a buyers' market brings in more bidders and causes the range of bids to move downward by moderate steps, as a bidder who wants to be low tends to bid a little under the previous low bid, which affords his standard of comparison. This goes on until the low bids reach something like a floor, affording the minimum margin above short-run marginal cost that is necessary to make the most eager seller consider the contract worth taking. In some exceptional cases a seller may be willing to bid below short-run marginal cost, if he is ready to incur a temporary out-of-pocket loss for the sake of keeping his basic working force together. In such a market, some of the bids that are higher than the previous low may rest on the rather unlikely chance that the former low bidders may be tired of working on such subnormal terms; and that a bid that covers a more generous allowance for overhead may have some chance of securing an order. Such a bidder would presumably not be sad if his bid did not turn out to be low, being willing to take a contract, but only if it yields more than the previous low bids.

In such a market, the lowest bids characteristically come from among the smaller firms. Where the bids are close to short-run marginal cost, one may conjecture that they come from firms that have enough existing business to finance all or most of those overhead costs

[29] *Ibid.*, Chap. 6, especially pp. 99, 106. In the cases, fully tabulated, of toilet tissue and white enamel paint, the former showed a stronger tendency for the serious bids to cluster near the bottom of the range.

that call for actual monetary outlays, and enough unused capacity to need more business badly, while they are small enough so that the increment of business involved in the contract in question is important to them. To very large firms, the amount of business involved, for example, in miscellaneous office supplies, may not appear important enough to make the necessary close shaving of margins worth while. When the buyer is successful, he gets the benefit of a discriminatory price concession; and this often appears to be his main objective.

Quite different is the use of competitive bidding to explore the supplier market for a new and distinctive product. As an example, the Brookings study mentions a "canned pump motor," designed to operate submerged, for pumping radioactive materials from nuclear reactors.[30] Specifications were precise, and not comparable to ordinary commercial motors. In such a case, bidders are likely to be few, and it is likely to be the big supplier who has the resources of engineering and operations research that are needed for estimating and encountering the contingencies of such an unaccustomed job. The policy of the motor department of General Electric toward this type of case, as described to the Brookings investigators, was to estimate the value of the product to the customer, so far as possible, and then "determine whether it can be produced at an economical cost that will allow a fair return on the necessary investment."

This statement of procedure indicates a kind of target-return pricing working backward, but it is bafflingly incomplete, and one wonders whether it fits the case of the "canned pump motor," the value of which to the government must have been highly elastic, to say the least. One wonders also what would happen next if the calculation indicated either that the item could not be profitably made at the initially estimated price, or that it would be so highly profitable that vigorous bidding from rival suppliers could be expected. In any case, suppliers' estimated costs include overhead special to this job; and there would be little pressure to squeeze bids down to utilize existing capacity, although the opportunity cost of diverting resources to this job would be affected by whether the pressure of other orders was strong or slack. The initial result could hardly be more than a first approximation on both sides, with closer competitive adjustments remaining to be made if the item later becomes more nearly standard.

[30] A. D. H. Kaplan, Joel B. Dirlam, and Robert F. Lanzillotti, *Pricing in Big Business* (1958), p. 68.

To sum up, sealed-bid purchasing is a method suited to a large buyer, and brings its most characteristic results when dealing with numerous sellers, though large suppliers may respond better in the introduction of new products on the buyer's initiative. The method has various uses, not all available in all situations. It requires a definition of the product, to assure adequate and sufficiently uniform quality; and this function can become creative in specifying a more serviceable product than the market affords, smaller buyers not being in a position to exert such quality control. As to price, the most characteristic function of this pricing method is to give the buyer the fullest benefit of any substantial unused capacity that may exist, especially in a buyers' market, including discriminatory concessions if the market is one in which they can be granted without spreading and leading to general cutthroat competition. The feeling-out of a tentative competitive suppliers' market for a new product is also an important function.

The method may be useless for animating extra powerful competition in a strong sellers' market, or one marked by price leadership or a firmly established price-meeting structure. It may be worse than useless where suppliers are afraid to grant publicly the concessions they give confidentially to private buyers. In such cases, the government may be forced to fall back on negotiation—the method preferred by large private buyers, who use sealed bids intermittently, and more flexibly than government. The rules controlling government buying, which require sealed bids if feasible, reflect efforts to combat apathy, favoritism, and corruption in government purchasing agencies. It would appear fortunate that these rules have not too narrowly restricted the initiative of the purchasing agencies.

4. Forward Contracts

This subject will here be narrowly construed, since otherwise volumes might be written about it. We are interested, of course, in practices that make a difference such as a fairly general theory of competition needs to recognize. The extension of credit to purchasers is part of the terms that affect the attractiveness of an offer of sale, and if competitors' offers are strictly equalized, this may involve equality in credit terms as well as prices. It has been noted above that a backlog of forward orders is normal in many industries, and that variations in its amount, plus promptness or delay in deliveries, constitute adjusting factors in the balancing of fluctuations in supply and demand. What will be considered here are contracts for forward delivery running for a substantial period, during which conditions in the spot market are likely to change; and attention will be focused on the effect of forward contracts on competition in the light of such liability to market changes.

The mutual usefulness of such contracts to buyer and seller is clear: the advantage of continuing relations is fortified by a definite obligation. To an extent varying with the terms and the conditions affecting fulfillment, the seller is afforded assurance of ability to dispose of at least part of his product, and the buyer is afforded assurance of supplies which may be tailored to fit his needs, and timed to suit his requirements. No less obvious than the mutual benefit is the fact that it is paid for by undertaking obligations on both sides which may involve some risks. The buyer may find that he does not want, or cannot profitably use, as much as he has undertaken to purchase (if the contract is for a definite amount, and especially if it calls for a definite price). With the same proviso, the supplier may encounter difficulties in making deliveries, and may incur losses in meeting his obligations to deliver. Either one may, through a standing agreement, lose the benefit of subsequent market changes in his favor, or suffer additional damage from changes of the opposite sort.

The stipulations of such a contract include the product, the duration of the contract, the amount contracted for, which may be fixed or adjustable, including "requirements contracts," the times of delivery (likely to be adjustable), and the price (also fixed or adjustable). The extent to which terms are likely to be fixed is limited by the mutual interests of the parties in the light of the extent of the changes they are likely to encounter, and modified by their relative bargaining strength. It is not to the interest of either party to bind himself to terms that might prove ruinous. And since forward contracts normally are based on the desirability of continuing relations, and these are likely to extend beyond the duration of a single contract, it is not in the interest of either party to exact terms that might prove really harmful to the other, because then the damaged party will not wish to renew.

The need for adjustability varies with the extent of disturbances likely to be encountered: in proportion as these are violent and un-predictable, rigid terms are unsafe. Competition of sellers has often led them to allow buyers to cancel contracts in a heavily depressed market. Furthermore, the existence of forward contracts and the proportion of total transactions to which they apply has an effect on the stability of the market, increasing stability in that portion covered by such contracts, with the possibility of concentrating fluctuations on the remainder and increasing the violence of price changes resulting from a given change in the balance of demand and supply, or demand and productive capacity.[31]

In connection with this, the existence of forward contracts at fixed prices creates ambiguity in the meaning of price indexes, since the current market price may differ from the price at which many deliveries are being made. The importance of this obviously varies with the proportion between forward and spot transactions, and its operation varies according as the forward contracts in an industry are mostly made at one time, or at staggered or irregular intervals. I examined the pricing structure of the potash industry at a time when there were three domestic producers, with whom the buyers—producers of fertilizer—contracted for the bulk of the output on a seasonal basis, most contracts being made at one time of the year. The result was that the market prices current at other times of the year applied to an extremely small fraction of total deliveries.

As to the relation of forward contracts to competition, where competition for customers exists, the securing of a customer on the basis of a forward contract is clearly a competitive act. The seller has to meet the attractions of rival offers, and is bidding also against the buyer's option to remain uncommitted. He must offer the buyer an inducement to alter his uncommitted status. From such alteration, the seller gains a larger volume of business than would ordinarily be involved in a single sale for current delivery. If a seller has been deterred from atempting to gain business by an aggressive price reduction because it would be promptly met, the use of forward contracts may enable him: (1) to gain enough business, projected into the future, to make the reduction worth his while, and (2) to hold the business he has gained,

---

[31] This is spoken of as a "thin market." The theory of this effect includes the fact that the holder of a contract may, in time of scarcity, be in a position to use the scarce product more liberally than he would if he had to procure it in the open market at increased prices, thus increasing the scarcity in the open market.

even if his initial reduction is met. He may hold it even if competitors undercut his original reduced price, though in this case he may be under pressure to meet their reduction.

As to the buyer, once he accepts a forward contract, the competitive leverage available to him is converted from an option to retain his uncommitted status to an option to resume it at the end of the contract, or by cancellation if the seller permits. If this option is to be actively effective to the full extent, the buyer must maintain multiple market contacts. The same holds true even more forcibly for the supplier: if he is to get the active benefit of competitive alternatives, he must maintain contacts with alternative purchasers. Otherwise, his competitive safeguard is of the potential sort, and to make it active he must switch from a customer with whose requirements he is familiar, and must recreate with a new customer the intangible assets that constitute trade contacts. He might do this if he became sufficiently dissatisfied with his existing relations, or saw sufficient chance for improvement, but there is some resistance to be overcome.

On the other hand, if the supplier has become dependent on a single big customer and has let his alternative market contacts lapse, he may have acquired a noncompetitive kind of protection, as the dominant customer may feel a responsibility for the dependent supplier's essential needs for business. The big customer would naturally retain discretion in safeguarding a particular supplier when others might be more economical or more desirable to deal with. With this in view, it is the part of caution for the large customer, if he is sensitive to such responsibilities, not to allow a firm supplier-customer relation involving virtual dependence to become established. Some large buyers make it a general policy to avoid taking more than a part of any supplier's output. In such a matter the competitive interests of the large customer leave him much latitude of policy, while the general interest in a competitive economy leans toward limiting the extent and duration of such forward commitments.

The basic reason is that every forward contract is, to the extent of the business it covers and the extent and duration of its terms, a restriction on competition: it takes that particular item of business out of the competitive market, to the extent that its terms are binding. The competitive force that persists stems from the need to keep the opposite party satisfied with the arrangement, and willing to renew it on expiration, in the face of the competitive alternatives that are open to him. Accordingly, while most such contracts do not go to lengths that would be regarded, in a reasonable view, as "restraints of trade" and contrary to public policy, they leave room for the question whether the restriction, in a particular case, is so general as to outweigh the advantages gained by the participants in the transaction in question. This factor has been recognized in some antitrust orders which have included, among other stipulations, a limitation on the duration of such contracts, for example, to one year.

5. Forward Contracts with Adjustable Prices

If the product is one dealt in on a market in which the current price is determined by the balance of demand and supply or demand and productive capacity, forward contracts may call for payment at the market. It does not appear clear that such a provision, in such a market, has any identifiable effect on the price that would prevail with quantity buying but without forward contracts of a formal sort. A theorist might reason that the market price will be set by the residue of uncommitted transactions, and that the requirements of the marginal buyers and sellers are presumably unaffected by the fact that a given amount of demand and an equal amount of supply move under price-adjustable contracts. In that setting, the thinness of the open market might have little effect.

If prices are "administered" or oligopolistic, there is more ground for expecting forward contracts to have an effect on the movement of prices. They might increase the likelihood that a price increase by an important producer would be followed, thus making the increase more likely to occur. Or if the contract takes the form of an escalator to compensate for increased costs, there is an inherent possibility of reducing the bargaining resistance to cost increases, because of the automatic provision for passing the increase on to the purchaser. This appears to be a possibility rather than a certainty; it depends on the existence of a zone of indeterminateness in which bargaining factors might determine the outcome.

Operating in the opposite direction is the practice of guarantee against price decline: a practice that has been much neglected in economic analysis. It bears on the central problem of competition—the incentive to reduce prices; but it appears capable of operating so differently in different variant forms and circumstances that it is extremely difficult to do more than identify different effects which appear possible, and the circumstances that are conducive to them, all in highly tentative terms. Thus one might take a few uncertain steps beyond the agnosticism that leaves each case to be determined on its own state of facts. In 1920, the Federal Trade Commission had received enough complaints about the practice to cause them to invite expressions of opinion from some 2,000 firms, the published result being a 68-page digest of replies. A majority of these were favorable and a large minority unfavorable, but the digests were too brief to convey adequately the differences of reasoning and circumstances responsible for the differing views. It appeared that the effects, and indeed the nature of the issues raised, might vary widely from situation to situation. The practice has been briefly mentioned in a few other studies.[32]

The occasion for the practice is the fact that a purchaser on a forward contract calling for a fixed price, or one who has accepted delivery in advance of his needs, accumulating enlarged inventory, may find himself at a disadvantage after a decline in price, in competition with rivals who bought after the decline. If the seller himself has lowered his price, and is selling at different prices to earlier and later purchasers, the ground for complaint of discrimination is obvious; but the purchaser may suffer just as much if the lower price is made by other suppliers, or results from a general buyers' market. The insertion of a provision giving him the benefit of any subsequent decline makes a forward contract safer and more attractive for the buyer, while adding a contingent liability for the seller. Or it makes it safer for the buyer to accept deliveries in advance of need, at the convenience of the supplier and in accord with the requirements of stability and economy in the supplier's production schedule. In order to meet that situation, the privilege of the reduced price would apply to inventories remaining unused or unsold after the price went down, and the precise terms

[32] See Federal Trade Commission, *Digest of Replies in Response to Inquiry Relative to Practice of Giving Guarantee Against Price Decline* (May 27, 1920). See also E. A. Lincoln, *Applied Business Finance* (1929), pp. 642-44; Leverett S. Lyon, *Economics of Free Deals* (1933), pp. 111, 127, 133; E. R. A. Seligman and Robert A. Love, *Price Cutting and Price Maintenance* (1932), p. 75; N.R.A., Division of Review, "Trade Practice Provisions in the Codes," pp. 50-51; H. A. Toulmin, Jr., *Trade Agreements and the Anti-Trust Laws* (1937), pp. 75, 167.

obviously need careful specification. The buyer, getting the benefit of a fixed price if the market rises, and a reduced price if it falls, is in a favorable position for contracting ahead—some have thought too favorable, as inducing undue accumulation of inventories, and enabling strong suppliers, who can afford the risks of forward contracts with guarantees against price decline, to sell so much of the market so far ahead as to limit unduly the free market available for others.

For the market in general, the practice spreads the incidence of price reductions: something which competition is supposed to do and which forward contracting would not do without this adjustment. It does not, of course, have this spreading effect on increases in prices, leaving in force the terms of previous forward contracts. And the spreading of price reductions takes place in a fashion different from that brought about by competition in the absence of the contractual guarantee, factors of timing and expectations being different and possibly tending to different results, in ways that call for further examination.

Factors that may influence the results include the terms of the guarantee, the proportion of the industry's total business to which it applies, the question whether the forward contracts that include the guarantee are made at about the same time and for the same term or at different times and for different periods, and especially the question whether the market is one in which the firm in question has a margin of discretion regarding its individual price on current transactions, or whether this is determined by market forces beyond its individual control. This in turn is related to the degree of differentiation of the product and the degree of concentration in the industry. Does it approach the oligopoly model or are sellers numerous? As to terms, the chief difference is between a guarantee covering only the producer's own reductions in price, and one that extends the benefit to reductions made by others. The former, limited type would be distinctive to about the extent that the producer's product is unique or sufficiently differentiated to afford its producer substantial independence of price policy. Otherwise, he might be virtually forced to follow reductions made by his major competitors, disregarding perhaps a fringe of minor firms over whom the major ones could afford to follow an "umbrella" type of policy.

The extreme opposite to this limited guarantee would be one guaranteeing the lowest price prevailing in the market. It may be noted that such a guarantee would be dangerous unless it were given by producers generally; otherwise a single firm with large outstanding forward contracts not bound by the guarantee could inflict losses on its rivals who were so bound, at small cost to itself. This might be one reason for the use of pressure to make the guarantee general in the trade or industry. Such pressure has been held to be unfair competition; also pressure by a wholesale grocers' association to make a supplying manufacturer grant such a guarantee or, failing that and after a price decline had occurred, to exact a rebate on stock left in the dealers' hands.[33] In the Federal Trade Commission's digest of replies, mention is made of unfairness to suppliers who cannot afford the guarantee, especially if they may find the whole market pre-empted by forward contracts, fortified by the guarantee.[34] If the unpre-empted fraction of demand is quite small, and if the guarantee undertaken by the major sellers does not apply to price reductions made by the remaining fringe of sellers who have not made forward contracts, the major sellers can afford to disregard price reductions made by sellers in this fringe. In such a case the thin current market may fluctuate considerably without affecting the prices at which the bulk of deliveries are made. This would apply where the bulk of the forward contracts are made at one time, in which case competitive forces bearing on the bulk of the business would operate at the time the forward contracts are being made. If the forward contracts are made at staggered times, competitive forces might act on them more continuously.

From the standpoint of competitive theory, the main effect of a price-decline guarantee on subsequent competitive forces may be summed up as a reduction of the elasticity of the individual-demand functions of firms that have given the guarantee. This tends to reduce the incentive to subsequent price reductions in two ways: one reducing the ratio of net gain from added business secured by such subsequent reductions, the other narrowing the scope of added business that can be thus secured. As to the first, the guarantee increases the expense of a price reduction aimed to secure added business by extending it to business already held under contract, thus increasing the ratio of reduced average unit revenue to increased physical vol-

[33] Toulmin, *op. cit.*, p. 75, cites anti-hog cholera serum code; also p. 167, cites *F.T.C.* v. *St. Louis Wholesale Grocers' Association et al.*, 7 F.T.C.D. 1; and *F.T.C.* v. *Wisconsin Wholesale Grocers' Association et al.*, 7 F.T.C.D. 489.

[34] Lyon, *op. cit.*, p. 133.

ume. The extension is not necessarily wholly unproductive in volume of business, since it may enable the firm's existing customers to do more business in competition with their rivals: thus the competition involved is of the indirect sort discussed above in Chapter 14 in connection with nonbase mills. It might not be an effective incentive to initiate a price reduction, though in defensive terms a firm would wish to prevent its existing customers from losing business to rivals who are being supplied at reduced prices.

Secondly, the firm's opportunity to gain new customers by a price reduction is limited to uncommitted purchasers: as to those who already hold similar contracts with its competitors, it is assured in advance that its price reduction will be automatically met by their present suppliers, so that they will have no incentive to change their allegiance. It would seem to follow that the competitive incentive to reduce prices hinges on the existence of a large volume of uncommitted business, either most of the time, or at a time that is decisive for the setting of the prices at which the bulk of the business is done. If the uncommitted volume is of major amount, the forward contracts may not substantially diminish the competitive pressures, especially if the sellers who count in the market are numerous. In the opposite case, something like the oligopoly stalemate may come about.

The practice in question appears clearly to have a stabilizing effect on prices, qualified by fluctuations in the current open market. This stabilization is undoubtedly welcome to industry and trade in general and carries mutual advantages in trading which even economists may recognize, within limits. The stability becomes self-defeating if it turns into the kind of rigidity that can set up a dike against market pressures until they become so strong that the dike breaks and the resulting change is more severe than it need have been. Overstocking induced by the guarantee is presumably contributory to this danger. A degree of shelter from the incidence of short-term fluctuations is not undesirable, if it does not block the essential longer-run adjustments between costs and prices. It appears important that these adjustments should be responsive, in volume of commitments and in prices, to the indications of economic conditions afforded by the movements of the current market or of uncommitted transactions, even if they do not follow its short-term fluctuations.

In conclusion, it appears likely that the effect of the price-decline guarantee may vary widely according to the structure of the industry, its marketing practices, and the prevalence of the guarantee in the industry. It appears to be, not so much a primary factor of independent importance as a collateral factor, consistent with competition if other conditions in the industry are favorable to effective competition, or capable of strengthening oligopolistic tendencies if they exist. Overly simple judgments on the effect of the practice per se appear risky. The examination given in this chapter, of this and other practices, may serve not so much to point to definite conclusions, as to call attention to a neglected group of problems and to indicate some of the conditions bearing on their effects on competition. The effects of these practices may vary according to the underlying conditions or accompanying practices that influence the incentives to aggressive or defensive competitive action.

CHAPTER 17

Some General Aspects of a Differentiated Economy

1. Dilemmas of Diversity

It has become a familiar idea that we live in a "mixed economy"—better described perhaps as a differentiated one, or a balanced one if this is understood to refer to an uneasy and imperfect balance between the forces of private and of community interest. The conception is commonly taken to mean a mixture of three main elements: private enterprise, subject to laws aiming to maintain competition, public service industries, and public economic activities which may render services free or for a charge which is generally intended to cover costs. In the private sphere, while we depend heavily on competition, what we aim to preserve is not competition of any and all sorts, but competition that makes for serviceability, since we recognize that there is no magic by which success in uninhibited competition necessarily goes to those whose qualifications and practices are serviceable to their customers, their workers, or the economy as a whole. Therefore controls in these interests are an inherent part of an enlightened and constructive competitive system, as indicated at many points in the present study. Such controls limit the consumer's "sovereignty" while aiming to improve its essential exercise and to mitigate the inadequacies of the mixed structure of guidance by which it is implemented.

The whole economic structure is subject to pervasive regulation in the interest of health, safety, limited hours of work, and minimum wages and assurance of minimum income in unemployment, old age, and other disabilities, lumped under the headings of "social security," the "social minimum," or the "welfare state." To this has been added support for distressed industries, positive promotion of labor organization under exemption from the antitrust laws, and the attempt to combine the promotion of high and reasonably stable employment with avoidance of substantial peacetime price inflation. The reader does not need to be reminded that methods of promoting high and stable employment are still in an exploratory stage, despite important advances. Features of their Keynesian basis have gained increasing acceptance, even, to an extent, among supposedly non-Keynesian business men; while confidence in our ability to apply these methods is increasing. But the accompanying form of the problem of inflation remains a realm of uncertainty.

In the present study, we have been examining further differentiation within the area of private industry, finding multiplying differences between different industries and within single industries: differences in the kinds and degrees of competitive situations and the corresponding competitive activities and pressures. These ramify into differences in flexibility of output and price in response to change in the balance of demand and supply, and changes in costs. The question of degrees of competitive pressure may be taken up first. Here the range runs from monopoly limited by substitution, through various degrees of oligopoly and competition of differentiated products, down to substantially pure (but imperfect) competition, which is frequently judged unduly or destructively severe, not only by those engaged in it, but by public officials or legislators. The pattern shows not only variety but instability: we observe competitive industries acquiring monopolistic characteristics, and "natural monopolies" either displaced by substitute services or suffering severely from their competition. Single products and whole industries are born, mature, and die; and accompanying changes in industrial structure suggest the more disturbing question whether the competitive system itself may be a temporary phase of economic evolution, and may be in process of losing that dominant character which gives the distinctive tone to an historical period. It is well to be aware of this question, while avoiding answers which are unduly sweeping—and necessarily unproved.

We have been emphasizing this diversity, envisaging many more differences or grades of difference than are included in the generally accepted theories of "pure" competition, oligopoly, and competition between differentiated products, viewed as analytical models. And while we have stopped considerably short of the variety of cases distinguished by leading inductive students, we have come uncomfortably close to the kind of multiplicity that baffles generalization or reduces it to the conclusion that each case must be settled on its own merits. As a means of escaping this conclusion we have been examining, not single cases, but classes of cases, the classification being based on important conditioning factors, such as supply-and-demand versus quoted-price marketing, homogeneous versus differentiated products, consumers versus firms as customers, differences in industry structure and in relevant time-perspectives, new versus mature industries and products, competition over distance, etc. And we have considered effects on products as well as on cost-price relationships. To some extent we have been looking at these differentiating features separately, but we have not been able to isolate their effects, since their full import appears only as they work in combination.

Behind all these diversities, many wise students have long thought that competition is marked by common features and is a pervasive and unifying force. They also thought that it works toward something called equilibrium, combining somehow with the forces of disturbance and disequilibrium (which are not only inseparable from progress but are one side of the routine equilibrating process of competitive give and take). If W. C. Mitchell failed to find evidence of the existence of this tendency to equilibrium in a dynamic economy, finding instead tendencies to self-reinforcing movement, overreaching itself and leading to reversals, this is rather evidence that theorists had not succeeded in defining the reality underlying the equilibrium concept as an operating process in combination with forces of disturbance. This is a challenge to reformulation.

Thus, before closing this survey, it appears incumbent on us to take an over-all view of the organic whole of which these diversities and disequilibria are parts. We should look first at the diversities, seeking some understanding of their extent, of the ways in which they fit together if they do fit together or, where they do not, the seriousness of the resulting misfits. We should be alive to both harmful and serviceable features. Finally, we should look for features common to the diverse forms and degrees of competitive forces, in terms of which the essential requirements of effective competition may be described, and the diverse forms brought together in a common framework.

This twofold task will be attempted in the concluding chapters. Such an attempted conspectus implies normative criteria: general ones such as those discussed in Chapter 4 above, and more specific ones suggested by particular problems. These criteria include desirability from a variety of standpoints, some of which may be in conflict with others, indicating the necessity of compromise. One decisive criterion is the feasibility of remedies, in the light of a variety of conditioning factors, difficulties, and obstacles. A study as general as the present one cannot dispose of all questions of feasibility, but it needs to take account of them—so far as feasible.

2. Generalized Indicia: Structure, Behavior, Performance

Available tests of "effective competition" have often been classified into "structure" and "performance"; and such a classification is a useful beginning, of the sort that serves its purpose by revealing that it is an oversimplification, and by pointing the way toward more discriminating analysis. This service has been effectively performed by E. S. Mason in two extremely useful articles.[1] These reveal possible conflicts between these standards and the insufficiency of either by itself. An obvious conflict occurs where optimum size of firm may be too large to permit the numbers that are optimum from the standpoint of competitive incentives and pressures; but this in turn is an oversimplification, since optimum size is different for different functions, not all of which need to be combined under one management.

The giant firm's department of research and development may need to be combined with marketing by the firm of the results of its innovations, to enable du Pont, for example, to recover the millions it has spent, over decades, in developing plastics; and Alcoa's integration into the field of fabrication was a means of speeding the growth of demand for aluminum. On the other hand, pioneering in the field of

[1] See "Price and Production Policies of Large-Scale Enterprise," *American Economic Review,* Supplement (1939); and "The Current State of the Monopoly Problem in the United States," *Harvard Law Review* (1949). References herein are to these articles as reprinted in American Economic Association, *Readings in Industrial Organization and Public Policy* (1958), pp. 190-204 and 376-92, especially pp. 198-202 and 377-81. Cited hereafter as American Economic Association, *Readings.* More recently, Joe S. Bain's *Industrial Organization* (1959), gives a rounded and penetrating analysis.

electronics, distinct from large-scale exploitation, appears to be successfully done by very small and personalized units; and a similar firm making fine pistols has recently scored advances over the leaders in that field, causing the leaders to make improvements.[2] No sweeping statement can define the boundaries of efficient small-scale specialization; the safest statement being that all opportunities for such specialization should be kept open.

The outstanding performance tests deal with reduced costs, improved products, avoidance of excessive unused capacity or insufficient reserve capacity, avoidance of selling costs that encroach on product improvement and price reduction. Every one of these either presents a problem rather than an answer, or cannot be dependably applied without due allowance (and what is "due"?) for the different factors that condition these features of performance in different industries.[3] Opportunity for progressive economies differs in different branches of production. And this, as we shall see, imposes really serious difficulties on our present type of economy in maintaining a non-inflationary price-level, this being one of the most important desiderata for the economy as a whole.

The writings on this subject already referred to reveal the need of an intermediate category between structure and performance, which might be called "behavior."[4] For example, Mason classed collusion versus noncollusion under structure, where it could logically be placed on the ground that the number of firms has no competitive meaning except as the firms act independently. But it seems more appropriately classed as behavior, along with attempts by such firms to increase or defend their shares of the market. This is not performance, in the sense of increased efficiency, reduced prices, and expanding volume of sales, but it leads to it.

The importance of behavior is well illustrated in the National Lead Case.[5] Here industry structure included four firms, two of which did 90 per cent of the business, while there were indications that the share of the smaller firms was tending to increase rather than diminish. The

[2] Described in Westport, Conn., *Town Crier*, Feb. 1, 1959.
[3] Cf. American Economic Association, *Readings*, pp. 203-04, 389-90.
[4] Since reaching this conclusion, I find Joe S. Bain expressing it explicitly. *Op. cit.*, Chap. 8. Bain uses the phrase "market conduct," treating it as a link between structure and performance which may work in both directions. I have allowed my own discussion to remain as originally written.
[5] American Economic Association, *Readings*, p. 385.

homogeneous character of the product should presumably also be classed as structure. Behavior included efforts of firms to increase their market shares, while performance included repeated reductions of prices of titanium pigments and great increase in total volume of sales. This was in the setting of a "vigorous, comparatively young, but comparatively large, worldwide industry." It clearly does not follow that in another industry, especially a more mature one or one not affected by a worldwide market, such a highly concentrated structure would tend naturally to produce the observed vigor of competitive behavior and performance. It is not true, as contended by some lawyers engaged in antitrust practice, that structure is irrelevant and behavior is the only thing that counts—specifically, that two firms are sufficient if they behave competitively. If they do (in terms of price), it is because they choose, not because their economic situation impels them. On the other hand, thirty firms in an industry are not enough to ensure competition, if they elect to behave noncompetitively, though even in that case thirty are better than three, on the score that collusion among thirty is more unstable.

As to collusion if it merely means concerted action for an agreed end, such action may be needed to set up the conditions and practices of an effectively competitive market, or to bring about noncompetitive behavior, in price or any of the other dimensions of competition; and its character depends on which kind of purpose it is used for.[6] No difficulty need be created by the concerted action that is involved in setting up an organized exchange, despite the fact that its facilities may be used, among others, by traders trying to corner the market. The purpose and effect of other uniform trading practices may be more ambiguous, raising questions whether their intent and effect is to make the market more effective by making it more orderly and informed, or to reduce unduly the effectiveness of competition—for example, by facilitating the neutralizing of rivals' moves. We have seen that discrimination is one of these ambivalent practices.

To sum up, "structure" represents a group of conditioning factors, and "performance" suggests results, impliedly judged by normative standards. But conditions are broader than structure, and results include more than is generally suggested by "performance." And there are mutual interactions: conditioning factors are results of prior actions

---

[6] As used, "collusion" is like "conspiracy" in being a double-barreled word, indicating both concerted action and an illegitimate purpose.

and include anticipated results of contemplated actions. Business behavior—the intermediate term here proposed—is both result and cause; and insofar as it is not precisely determined, it has room to act as an independent causal factor.

We are forced to examine the complex of conditioning factors precisely because we are determined to minimize direct control of market performance in general industry and trade, except in war or comparable emergency, and therefore we must try to influence the results indirectly, via the character and force of competitive pressures, which we attempt to influence through the conditioning factors. Even under direct controls of performance, conditioning factors need to be taken into account in devising means of enforcement and introducing degrees of latitude into regulations, under which allowance may be made for special and local conditions. A fortiori, in indirect controls, the conditioning factors are the heart of the matter. But in attempting to understand their action, we face a baffling difficulty because these factors act in combination, and a single one may act differently according to a considerable assortment of others in connection with which it operates. If an observer wants to "predict" the natural tendencies of one conditioning factor, he needs all the understanding he can get of the way in which its operation can be altered by the presence or absence of other factors. The effect often turns out to have some unexpected features, making it unsafe to rely implicitly on deductive analysis. One needs the light shed by numerous particular cases. Yet, as shown in Chapter 3, the number of significant combinations is too great for exhaustive inductive analysis; and a progressive growth in understanding calls for an endless interplay between the two kinds of approach.

The problem of analysis starts at some existing point in our endless economic evolution, and is precipitated by some change from previously existing conditions. The change may become evident in existing performance, such as behavior of prices which appears undesirable; or in existing conditioning factors, such as increased concentration, leading to an inherent probability of monopoloidal behavior; or the change may occur in our analytical thinking, such as imperfect-competition theory, making suspect some condition that had previously been accepted, such as increasing concentration, and creating dissatisfaction with earlier crude attempts to answer the question what percentage of control by a single firm is monopolistic. If the process starts with some problem of unsatisfactory performance, it goes on to a search for causes in terms of the inherent tendencies of the conditioning factors. Or if it starts with the conditioning factors, it goes on to a search for the seriousness of the actual or inherently probable results in terms of performance. Results alone are not decisive in a given case, for reasons already indicated, but especially because we want not only satisfactory performance, but an assurance that such performance is imposed by the conditioning factors. We are not satisfied if the results are good merely because the holder of insufficiently limited power chooses to use the power beneficially, when he might choose to use it otherwise. But this attitude has to make terms somehow with the necessary existence of some degrees of discretion in the use of market power, and to balance this against the degrees of effectiveness of the limitations within which such discretion is exercised.

Thus the analysis of conditioning factors remains more basic than the scrutiny of results. One conditioning factor we are sure we do not want is unchecked private monopoly power; and we are bound to search for feasible means to prevent it or to break it up where it exists, within the limits of means we are willing to use. To this the outstanding exception to date is the degree of monopolistic power that organized labor has come to possess and exercise within the past quarter century. This is partly because of legal exemptions and the structure of legally permitted practices that have multiplied on the basis of these exemptions, and partly because prevailing criteria for the use of such power (which in turn influence judicial decisions) have not developed limitations commensurate with the degree which the power has now attained.[7]

Public opinion is just beginning to realize that the kind of power possessed by the teamsters and various other unions has no place in the economy of a "free and democratic" society, aside from the cynically unmoral use made of this kind of power by some unions and the internal abuses that have accompanied it. This question of power is unfinished business, and not to be disposed of, either by accepting union power as it is, or by transplanting into the labor field the particular answers that are applied to business firms. Here is a wide di-

---

[7] Cf. C. O. Gregory, *Labor and the Law* (1946), especially Chaps. 7-10. Cf. Philip Taft, *Economics and Problems of Labor* (1942), Chaps. 19 and 20. More recently, this legally sanctioned power structure has been forcefully analyzed by Roscoe Pound; see *Legal Immunities of Labor Unions* (1957).

versity of standard which needs to be reduced but appears both impossible and undesirable to eliminate. It affects, be it noted, the largest single "component part of price," composing roughly two thirds of "value added" in industry and trade.

Reverting to differences in the business field, we have noted that the Chamberlinian system, with its emphasis on pure or perfect competition, oligopoly, and "monopolistic competition," lumps the conditioning factors into fewer categories than need to be taken account of, and suggests sharper differences between the cases than appear to prevail in practice. Another attitude is that of Stigler, who falls back on the older categories of "monopoly" and "competition" and appraises industries according as they are prevailingly one or the other, necessarily on the basis of inductive examination that falls far short of being exhaustive. A third attitude is that of R. B. Heflebower, who recognizes a wide variety of conditioning factors, giving attention to their effects in the combinations in which they characteristically operate, and concluding that the results are not as widely different as the diversity of conditioning factors suggests.[8] My own attitude is, in general, most like that of Heflebower, though I would add that this view of the results is true because the situations with respect to incentives resulting from the conditioning factors are not as different as they appear in the more sharply delimited models.

This conclusion may be consoling to persons disturbed by ideas about the omnipresence of important degrees of monopoly, but it is not the end of inquiry. In Chapter 7, above, we identified the most pervasive common feature of the various types of competition as a demand function for the product of a single firm, enough more elastic than that applying to the whole industry or other relevant group, to afford incentive to competitive actions, initiatory or defensive, aiming to improve the firm's bargaining offers relative to those of its rivals. Or, more simply, it centers in the possibility of a firm's securing an increase or avoiding a decrease in its volume of business, relative to that of the group, sufficient to cause competitive tactics to offer a prospect of improving its financial prospects. But this unified statement covers a multitude of differences, bearing on whether in a given case or kind of situation the "cross-elasticities," and the corresponding

[8] See R. B. Heflebower, "Toward a Theory of Industrial Markets and Prices," *American Economic Review*, Proceedings (1954), pp. 121-39; reprinted in American Economic Association, *Readings*, pp. 297-315.

incentives to competitive action, are strong enough to be effective. These differences need far more investigation than can be given them in what remains of the present study.

3. Sources of Different Performance

The scope of the problem is indicated by an attempt to list the conditioning factors, classifiable under "structure," which lead to different results in different industries and trades. First comes the structure of the market, primarily the supply-and-demand market versus that of quoted prices. Allied to this, and even more important for the inequalities that result, is the distinction between self-employed or family units, whose costs consist mainly of their personal efforts, and firms whose dominant costs are the prices paid for the factors of production, and are dependent on all the forces that govern the behavior of these prices, which are also the incomes of those who furnish the factors of production. Some of the greatest inequalities occur between these two groups.

The lowest incomes occur in areas of really unmitigated competition or insufficiently equipped self-sufficiency in which an inferior living is gained by those who are excluded from, or have not found their way into, the areas of more mitigated competition. But an inferior living is better than none; and so long as sheltered areas exist, escape-hatches may be necessary, even if they afford "substandard" incomes. Attempts to improve the inferior livings have this problem to reckon with. This lends force to the demand for stronger competition in the sheltered areas and increased freedom of access to them. As things are, we appear to have two unassimilated economies, and the less-favored one affords a necessary, though unsatisfactory, outlet for those not assimilated into the other, but who still need some source of livelihood.

Next come differences in the character of the product—homogeneous or differentiated—and in the character of the customer—business firm or ultimate consumer. Then comes the size and concentration of sellers and buyers—the most emphasized feature of "structure." The latter accounts for price differentiations some of which are surprising in amount, automobile tires being an outstanding example. From our present over-all standpoint, the seriousness of this depends on whether the benefit of these special prices is transmitted to consumers; and this depends on the competitive pressures that affect the recipients of these favored terms.

Next come different forms of combination: horizontal, vertical, and diversifying. These are all departures from the single firm specializing in one product, one stage of production, or one restricted productive function; and they present problems on the relations of the specialized firms with the combined ones. Diversification enables a successful firm to grow, and perhaps to make larger use of its managerial and technical resources, without acquiring monopolistic dominance over any one product. Hence this kind of growth is likely to be preferred under the antitrust laws. This is one way of avoiding the dilemma of competition mentioned in Chapter 15, Section 7, above. It makes possible a competitive structure without intensifying the competition into a battle of giants, in which a substantial gain in market share by one is a threatening degree of encroachment on the others and provokes reactions accordingly—or leads to a truce of giants in which room for growth may be limited. The firm also reduces its total risks by combining those of diverse products. A special kind of hedging occurs when it combines two substitutes, one of which might displace the other, wholly or partially. If monopoly is involved, then obviously a monopoly of two substitutes has more power than a monopoly of one; but if no monopoly is involved, the advantage gained by diversification does not appear inherently objectionable.

Vertical integration raises more obvious problems of competition with one's own customers or suppliers. The opposite of integration—specialization—affords the small firm a chance to attain viable economies in a limited field. Whether the specialization sacrifices some of the economies of vertical integration depends on whether the specialized firm's contractual relations afford coordination with the requirements of its suppliers and customers that does not suffer too much by comparison with the supposedly superior coordination possible within the structure of the integrated firm. The coordination may naturally suffer somewhat if the specialized firm is a supplier meeting the requirements of numerous customers because it is unwilling to become dependent on a single customer, or because the customer is unwilling to assume the paternal obligations involved in such dependence. It is obvious that such relationships involve problems of fair and equal treatment by integrated firms. This, however, is also true of the relations between a big firm and its distributors, whether or not it is integrated.

Another conditioning factor is the age of the industry, in which four periods may be distinguished. First is the introductory period, dominated by its problem of establishing the viability of a new product against existing products. Second is the period of youthful growth, when viability is established and demand for the new product is expanding—possibly at the expense of older products. Third comes maturity, when major displacements of alternative products have gone about as far as they will, and expansion proceeds more nearly apace with that of the economy in general. Fourth comes old age or decline, when a firm's situation is dominated by the need of defense against the encroachments of newer alternatives, or finding some more viable alternative of its own. These stages affect the problem of numbers adequate to effective competition. The first stage may present no problem. In the second, the problem may arise of converting an original innovational monopoly into a competitive industry. Ample room for growth may afford competitive incentives, even if firms are few; while larger numbers may enter, some of which will be weeded out. A conspicuous example was the automobile industry in its first two decades. In the mature stage, fewness of firms may interfere seriously with well-rounded competitive incentives. In the final stage, reduced numbers are natural, but not necessarily desirable from the standpoint of trying out a variety of adaptations, some of which may make survival possible.

As we have seen, the same problem occurs in the life-history of a single product in the product-mix of a diversified producer, with two important exceptions. One is that the firm's existence does not depend on the survival of a particular product, and a switch to a viable product may be feasible. The other is that the diversified firm may sustain an obsolescent product, or ease its exit, out of its other profits. Thus diversification may work in opposite directions. It may delay abandonment of nonviable products, but is unlikely to do so permanently. The firm wants products with a future.

Finally, one may conclude that the effect of the conditioning factors is likely to be different for different forms of competitive activity. One might, tentatively and for illustrative purposes, hazard the conjecture that in a given industry two or three firms of not-too-unequal strength would be enough to afford plenty of competitive incentive to improvements in the efficiency of productive processes. A few more might suffice to afford incentive for competitive product-differentiation but, as indicated above, in Chapter 10, Section 3, larger numbers and vigorous competitors of smaller size relative to the total industry, might be needed in order to afford incentives to a well-balanced assortment of offerings which would do justice to the desire for economy models. This was discussed with reference to the state of the automobile industry during the fifties, when it had passed through the stage of the Model T Ford and into the stage of mature demand, dominated by replacements and annual models; in which stage the demand for economy models was ignored by the big three until its importance had been demonstrated by the small foreign cars and by the "compact" models pioneered by one of the smaller and struggling domestic competitors.

It is pertinent also that the example is drawn from the realm of durables, mainly sold to consumers and having outstanding prestige value, affording room for styling appeal, once the more basic mechanical dependability had been achieved. And it has been earlier noted that the method of distribution by exclusive agents affords marketing advantages to size beyond the scale dictated by the requirements of productive efficiency. The resultant is an industry in which great advances have been made, some of which may in the present stage appear misdirected, the reason for misdirection being that the number of firms is small enough to distort competitive incentives from the standpoint of well-balanced differentiation in quality with due regard to the reflection of the costs of "quality" in price. And the differences between firms in competitive strength and profitability appear greater than desirable, from the standpoint of assured survival of healthy competition.

If, in differentiated products, well-balanced competition on the price-quality scale calls for moderate but substantial numbers, price competition in homogeneous or near homogeneous products appears to call for still larger numbers in a given market area. Where numbers are small, an imperfect alternative may be furnished by some forms of discrimination in price, which rates as a market imperfection from the standpoint of prevailing economic theory. The resulting difficulties of diagnosis and policy are treated in the recent volume by

Corwin D. Edwards.[9] The above unduly brief treatment may serve to illustrate the ways in which different conditioning factors combine to affect the resulting performance, the seriousness of some of the resulting differences between industries and firms, and the tentative character which must attach to attempts at appraisal on a priori grounds alone, even where such attempts take fairly large numbers of conditioning factors into account.

4. Conditions Affecting Usefulness of Defensive Competition

The basic relation between initiatory and defensive competition can be briefly stated: without initiatory moves, competition does not begin, without defensive responses it does not spread. This relationship takes different forms in agriculture, where the active variable is supply, from those which it takes in industry and trade where the active variable may be price, product, or selling effort. It has been indicated that a firm, the structural situation of which does not give it enough incentive to initiate a competitive move, will take defensive action to meet another firm's move, always provided that move is shown to be effective. The point has been made that the prospect of a defensive response can impair the incentive to initiate such a move, but that it does not always do so.

In fact, the extreme case of this deterrent effect—the familiar oligopoly stalemate—is rather rare, applying to openly quoted prices of homogeneous products produced by small numbers of firms, in markets where the bulk of customers are free to change suppliers and are not committed by standing contracts that would constitute obstacles to such free transfer of their trade. (The binding force of such contracts on the customer is highly elastic and variable with business conditions, and literal enforcement is seldom resorted to.) In such a case, the effectiveness of the competitive move is beyond question, and the response can be instant and precise. But change the single condition

[9] Corwin D. Edwards, *The Price Discrimination Law* (1959).

of an openly quoted price: let it be understood in the trade that actual transactions depart from the openly quoted prices—as they commonly do—and the stalemate is no longer automatic or absolute. The deterrent effect of a prospective defensive response may still exist, but becomes weaker and more uncertain and is less likely to prevent price-shading than to set limits on it, keeping it for considerable periods within the limits that competitors will meet by similar shading, and avoiding such extreme demoralization of the price structure as would lead some strong firm to slash the openly quoted scale of prices.

Where products are differentiated, the effects of changes in price are much slower and more unpredictable, except (as already indicated) where the products have remained essentially unchanged long enough for the market to establish a price equivalence between them, so that a price change by one is fairly sure to be met. Otherwise, the stalemate effect is unlikely. Still more unlikely is it in the case of a change in the product, in the selling appeal or in both together. The new product variant may or may not catch on, and this it will take time to reveal, and further time to mobilize the defensive response, giving the initiator an interval in which to capitalize on his success— if he does succeed—and a possibility of more enduring gains. We have spoken of "defensive preparedness" as being desirable for a firm that does not want to be too slow in its responses; and have suggested that the research and planning department which furnishes this preparedness is likely to come up with things that are too good to keep in cold storage and will be installed as innovations. In such a case, defensive competition (in which every firm must engage) turns into the aggressive variety, and this possibility increases the likelihood that aggressive competition will occur, and that any stalemate of mutually defensive attitudes will be upset. Thus the existence of defensive preparedness is a form of potential competition that may turn active; and thus the likelihood of the initiation of active competition is increased.

So far, it has been assumed that defensive responses are attempts to protect a firm's sales volume or share of the market in the face of other firms' initiatory moves, the latter being taken for granted. Then any effect which the prospect of defensive responses may have in deterring initiatory moves is a by-product. There remains the class of cases in which the deterring of active competition is the main purpose of the response. In strongly marked instances the responding firm may be directly concerned to ensure that its rival loses by its initiatory move, and to this end it may be willing to incur, temporarily, reductions of income greater than would be necessary if it were concerned only with defending its own net earnings. This is the kind of response to which it is appropriate to apply the terms "retaliation," or "disciplinary" or "punitive" measures. The distinction between this and normal defense is clear in terms of principle or purpose, but may be hard to identify in practice, especially where normal defense includes irregular pricing that meets competition where it finds it. Short of extinguishing the competitor, the practitioner of trade discipline may be protecting standards of price or price policy. He may be protecting fat profits in a sellers' market or substandard earnings in a buyers' market: neither suffices to identify the disciplinary policy. As an antitrust problem, it may need to be interpreted in connection with other features of particular cases.

To sum up, defensive competition performs the essential service of ensuring that competition becomes general, even though only a relatively small contingent in an industry has incentive enough to take an aggressive initiative. The prospect of defensive responses may exert no deterrent effect on initiatory competitive moves, or may exert varying degrees of deterrent effect in proportion to its promptness and precision in neutralizing initiatory moves; but the extreme case of the oligopoly stalemate requires quite special conditions and is therefore not common. This, and the disciplinary type of response, constitute special problems.

5. Changes in the Role of Patents

A patent system is a characteristic feature of a mixed economy, but is necessarily a somewhat undiscriminating instrument: its general rules cannot afford just the kind and degree of protection that is optimal for the conditions of each case. It means one thing to a small inventor, another thing to a huge firm, able to hold competitive patents out of use, and still another thing to a diversified giant firm whose massed patents reach into a variety of industries and which may join with other giants in a patent pool covering the essential techniques of these industries. The terms of such interchanges are affected with a public interest, and the uses of patent rights have figured in orders issued in antitrust cases in which misuse of patents had played a part in building monopolistic power beyond the intent of the patent system.

Where compulsory licensing has been employed in the attempt to establish wider competition, the problem has arisen of requiring the sharing of "know-how" that goes beyond the technical disclosures required by the patent itself. Some giant firms are becoming wary about acquiring overly numerous patents, even where they may be better situated to exploit them than the existing holders. In various ways the simple temporary legal monopoly is becoming complicated and the exclusiveness of its monopoly rights is being eroded piecemeal. But no wholesale substitute has been found for the principle of the temporary monopoly, as a selecting test of the value of innovations and a protection to the first developer.

6. Flexible and Sticky Prices

How important and how serious are the problems affecting the over-all action of our economy which arise from the coexistence of flexible and sticky prices? For this purpose, "prices" include price components, especially wage costs. Among the effects that have been attributed to these diversities in price behavior are effects on stability of production and employment, inequalities between different groups of producers in their ability to cover costs, including normal returns, and a tendency to a creeping inflationary bias in the economy as a whole. As to the first, the economy is divided into groups that respond differently to discrepancies between supply and demand. If demand is insufficient, one group is pictured as maintaining production and cutting prices to whatever extent necessary to move the output, the other as restricting production to whatever extent necessary to maintain prices. The inference may be drawn that the latter course makes for instability of production and employment. The connection of this with unequal ability to protect costs and normal returns is self-evident. The connection with a possible inflationary bias will be taken up in the chapter that follows.

Discussion of this subject begins properly with the work of Gardiner C. Means.[10] He examined the frequency and amplitude of price changes, finding that as to frequency of change, prices fell into two sharply separated groups, concentrating at or near the opposite ends of the scale he was using. Amplitude was positively correlated with frequency, though it appears that on a scale of amplitude of changes, prices are dispersed less discontinuously.[11] It is obvious that products dealt in on organized markets of the various supply-and-demand types are bound to change with maximum frequency, and it is scarcely less probable that their changes would show more than average amplitude. Remembering that they include many agricultural products, with one-family farms playing a large part in their production, they have the further characteristic that their costs are largely the personal efforts of the producers and their families, for which no fixed contractual remuneration is stipulated, and this, as we have seen, greatly increases the feasible amplitude of price flexibility.

Among products sold at quoted or negotiated prices, it is inevitable that prices would not change nearly as frequently as those of products sold on supply-and-demand markets, but the statistics presumably fail to do justice to the amount of irregular price-shading, and therefore understate the flexibility of these prices. In general, their flexibility appears to depend more on the nature of the product than on numbers of sellers, though with homogeneous products, oligopoly makes for low flexibility. Strong product differentiation also makes for low flexibility, while less pronounced product differentiation, especially if also less stable, may actually be favorable to price flexibility, as compared to oligopolistic selling of homogeneous products.

Quoted prices do not follow closely the minor fluctuations of demand, and they may be insensitive to fairly large fluctuations. Price reductions are likely to take place via irregular price-shading when demand is weak; and when it is strong the trade is likely to be willing

[10] The basic reference is his study: *The Structure of the American Economy* (1939). For frequency of changes, cf. U. S. Joint Economic Committee, *Frequency of Change in Wholesale Prices* (1959). Critical comments include E. S. Mason's writings, referred to above; and especially A. C. Neal, *Industrial Concentration and Price Flexibility* (1942); also his "Pricing Aspects of Business Cycle History," *Economic Institute on Pricing Problems and the Stabilization of Prosperity*, Chamber of Commerce of the United States (1947), pp. 32-39. Cf. F. C. Mills, *Price-Quantity Interactions in Business Cycles* (1946).

[11] This correlation of Means' has not been discredited, though critics have discounted its significance.

to follow an upward lead, and such a lead is likely to come from some strong firm. The trade is also likely to follow a lead that conforms to recent changes in costs. On this score one would expect relatively high price flexibility in the prices of processed foodstuffs, reflecting the flexibility in the prices of their basic materials. But the prices of the products will not change with anything like the frequency of the prices of the materials; they will follow only substantial changes. As seen in the case of meat packers, the packer gauges the price he can afford to pay for live animals with reference to his estimate of the price at which the demand will take the product in the volume at which the animals are being offered. He acts in the light of his need to maintain or increase his share of total sales, at margins that will cover his full costs, if possible. He commits himself to a scale of output in advance of marketing, and thus literal supply and demand affect his selling price to an extent not found in the case of inanimate materials, making for greater flexibility and reduced accuracy in the attempt to cover "target returns."

One of the chief differences between prices directly governed by supply and demand and prices that warrant the term "administered" is that the former are flexible both upward and downward, while the latter, though slower to respond in either direction, are genuinely resistant to downward pressures, but merely sluggish in responding to upward pressures. As a result, their response to a fluctuating series of upward and downward pressures exhibits a "rachet action" with a net upward resultant. In this connection, it appears that the price most rigidly resistant to downward pressures is the rate of wages paid to organized labor. This introduces a "rachet action" into the behavior of costs, and therefore into the behavior of those prices that are responsive to changes in costs. The net outcome for a given product seems to depend on whether elements of cost that have two-way flexibility account for a larger fraction of costs than those prices of materials or factors of production that are mainly flexible upward. This points toward varying degrees of upward bias in quoted prices as a resultant of their responses to upward and downward movements of demand and cost.[12]

This affects the behavior of the indexes in which flexible prices and others are combined, in ways that appear during the period from

[12] Cf. Gardner Ackley, "Administered Prices Reconsidered," *American Economic Review* (May 1959), pp. 419-30, especially p. 425.

1952 to 1958-59. The consumer price index was stable from 1952 to 1956, mainly because the heavily weighted food prices were declining, while the less flexible prices were rising. In 1956-57 both kinds of prices rose, and in the recession of 1957-58 the index kept on rising. Thus there may appear to be two kinds of periods: one in which the price index is stable because the flexible prices are falling while the others are rising, and another in which the flexible prices—chiefly influenced by agriculture—are rising and leading the index upward. This may misleadingly tend toward attributing the rise to the flexible prices, disguising the fact that the reason the price index winds up higher is the rachet action or the persistent upward drift of the less flexible prices.

As to the effect of these discrepancies on stability of production and employment, there is a little evidence that moderate price flexibility in particular industries may somewhat mitigate fluctuations of production; but no ground for thinking that full stability of production and employment could be brought about by the kind of prices that move as much as may be needed to "clear the market."[13] ("Clearing the market" is a misleading phrase, lacking definite meaning, as applied to industry and trade.) The balance of economic judgment would surely class this unlimited kind of flexibility, in response to cyclical fluctuations of demand, as unstabilizing.[14] If one makes the violent assumption that business payments for interest, rents, and wages share in this flexibility, the income-generating aspect of prices would shrink along with the demand-limiting aspect; and the net balance would probably act to deepen depression through uncertainties and inequalities of timing and incidence and a decisive discouragement of business outlays.

A more realistic assumption would be that prices entering into costs are either rigid or subject to only limited decline, including wages and the prices of industrially processed materials. Then the price reductions that sellers could make in the attempt to revive demand would be limited to their profit margins. A moderate reduction of prices, absorbed out of profits, might have a slight net tendency to increase consumer expenditures. Except as to current items like

[13] E. M. Doblin, "Some Aspects of Price Flexibility," *Review of Economic Statistics* (November 1940), pp. 183-89, especially p. 188.

[14] It is noteworthy that Edwin G. Nourse, the outstanding advocate of a low-price policy as a way of diffusing the gains of increased productivity, rejects the idea of slashing prices as a remedy for recession: see his *Price Making in a Democracy* (1944), Chap. X.

food, the net effect would depend largely on whether buyers expected prices soon to rise again, in which case the present would be a good time to buy; or whether they construed the reduction as a forerunner of further reductions, in which case a shrewd buyer would wait; or whether their buying was not affected by expectations, one way or the other. If the price reduction were an expression of the "clear-the-market" kind of pricing, and if in most industries the market was not "cleared" (as it would not be), increased buying might wait until some kind of bottom had been reached. "Clearing the market" in this context must mean not only disposing of excess inventories, but putting idle facilities to work, up to some rate of operation that could be called normal.

The question now shifts to heavy and sustained price reductions, approaching the limits of what can be absorbed out of profits, and their efficacy to revive demand. Here the decisive factor would appear to be the drastic impact on profits, while bankruptcies of weak firms would increase out of proportion to the over-all shrinkage of profits, causing some immediate unemployment and a reduction of capital outlays. In a longer perspective, this process of "going through the wringer" might clear the ground of some weak firms and prepare the way for a stronger industry structure when revival should come, but at the expense of letting the recession run its course, rather than acting as an effective stabilizer.

If the stimulation of investment is a decisive factor, it might seem that it is more important that the prices of capital goods should be reduced than the prices of consumer goods. One difficulty here is that these prices are especially inflexible downward; another is that after a recession has become clearly evident, demand for capital goods is likely to show extra low price elasticity. If price reductions are to be effective as a means to revival, the indicated conclusion is that they need to be used, not as stimuli by themselves, but as reinforcing factors in connection with other measures for stimulating demand. If slack-time work were planned to the point of being ready to be triggered if its cost were reduced, this might make it worth while for the capital goods industries to cooperate by offering such reductions, in a setting affording them some assurance of a response in revived demand, which they would not otherwise have. Thus limited price flexibility might play a useful role as part of a stabilization program, but it appears misleading to expect unlimited price flexibility to bear the whole brunt of stabilizing production and employment.

The second effect of the coexistence of flexible and sticky prices is inequality in the ability of producers to cover costs, in the different types of production. This is a serious defect in our economy, but we have seen that it is due, not to the behavior of prices alone, but to a combination of this with other factors, including large numbers of competitors and advance commitment to production which must later be disposed of on a market of the supply-and-demand type. In the leading case of agriculture, a more fundamental source of difficulty has been greatly increased productivity in face of an inelastic demand, calling for displacements of producers at a greater rate than is easily feasible on social and economic grounds. The part which price flexibility plays in this complex has, of course, been greatly restricted by price supports. The accompanying restrictions of acreage appear to have stimulated competition in increasing yields per acre and per worker, and to have been largely frustrated by the enormous increase in these yields. This was accomplished by means of achievements in plant biology which developed ultra-productive strains, by mechanization, and by lavish use of increasingly efficient fertilizers. The economic impact of all this represents a serious, and so far unsolved, problem of disparity in the ability of major sectors of the economy to sustain themselves in reasonable prosperity unaided. Antitrust action in industry and trade attacks the disparity from the other end, and might set limits on it; but it would be unrealistic to expect competitive pressures in industry and trade to become as severe as those natural to agriculture.

This discussion has one further corollary. Prices move in response to changes in the balance of demand and supply, or to changes in cost. The ultra-flexible prices show their high flexibility in their responses to demand and supply, while in respect to the relation of prices to cost, their adjustments are not flexible but sluggish, inaccurate, and inadequate. For industry and trade, selling on quoted prices, the ultra-frequent changes that occur on organized exchanges would perform no particular function. Quoted prices are relatively deliberate in rising in response to increased demand, and this deliberateness has its good points. The trouble comes, as has been shown, from their being less flexible downward than upward. And in response to changes in costs and in margins of net earnings, these prices are definitely more flexible than farm prices, supposedly the extreme type of flexibility. Clearly, "flexibility" by itself is an oversimplification.

Clearly also, the combination of ultra-flexible prices with sluggish adaptation on the side of costs and earnings places the producers at a disadvantage in protecting normal net returns. This effect would appear to extend in lesser degree to the more highly flexible prices of the quoted price type. It is compounded with the effects of large numbers and small size. Where firms are large, as in meat-packing, the handicap of having to do with flexible prices, though felt, is less serious.

CHAPTER 18

Inflationary Impact of Unequal Increases in Productivity

1. Methods of Diffusing the Gains of Progress

During the period 1952-59, the continuance of inflationary trends, in the absence of war spending or equivalent sources of excess demand, has raised the question whether we are facing a "new" inflation, "pushed up" from the side of costs and prices rather than "pulled up" from the side of demand and built into the nature of our mixed economy. This problem is receiving so much and such competent discussion that it requires some hardihood for a fresh writer to add his bit.[1] However, it might be more conspicuous to omit the subject; and something might be contributed by treating it primarily as a problem of assimilating different rates of increase in productivity in different parts of our mixed economy, possessing different degrees of market power; also by trying to define the requirements of a noninflationary model for assimilating these differences, the model being defined with the latitude that is necessary for active adjustments in an imperfect market.

---

[1] Among pertinent references are the following: *Challenge Magazine* (December 1957); John T. Dunlop, *The Theory of Wage Determination* (1957); Harold G. Moulton, *Can Inflation be Controlled?* (1958); G. L. Bach, *Inflation* (1958); Committee for Economic Development, *Defense Against Inflation* (1958); W. L. Thorp and R. E. Quandt, *The New Inflation* (1959); The American Assembly, *Wages, Prices, Profits and Productivity* (1959).

The two last-named studies came to my attention after the present chapter was substantially written, and between them they cover much of its content; the study by Thorp and Quandt expressing conclusions especially similar to those of the present chapter. I have embodied the substance of this chapter, amplifying some points, in *The Wage-Price Problem* (1960).

The basic facts may start with the long-run annual increase in real income or real net product per worker. Studies going back seventy years and more indicate an upward trend of about 1.7 per cent per year, with evidence pointing to speeding-up in the latter part of the period. Signs of slowing down have appeared in 1954-58, but this period is too short for confident diagnosis. Output per worker has been increasing considerably less than 2 per cent per year; but the National Bureau of Economic Research finds that output per weighted man-hour increased 2.3 per cent per year during 1919-57, while for 1889-1953 the rate was 2 per cent.[2] The weighting of man-hours takes account of the increase in the proportion of the more highly paid types of workers, which would increase average earnings if wage rates were unchanged. Real earnings per man-hour follow the course of output per man-hour very closely, indicating approximate long-run stability in the division of real product between wages and other shares. The present study may at times use 2 per cent as an illustrative round figure to symbolize the order of magnitude of the limit set by productivity on the over-all annual trend of increase in real earnings.

The increase in productivity is an average of different rates in different industries. The differences are no accurate gauge of the merit of the performance in the different industries and processes, but are more basically the result of the fact that the economies of mass production and applied science are more available in some kinds of production than in others—more available in assembly-line industries, steel making, and plastics than in general repair work, school teaching, and barber shops. The more rapidly advancing group—we will call it "leading"—includes agriculture, but its main character is set by

[2] For these figures see especially Solomon Fabricant, *Basic Facts on Productivity Change*, National Bureau of Economic Research, Occasional Paper 63 (1959), especially pp. 5, 11, 19, 29. This study shows, among other things, a more rapid increase for 1919-57 than for 1889-1919. The notable study by the Twentieth Century Fund, *America's Needs and Resources* (1955), indicates a long-term increase in real income (or real net product) per capita of the population of a trifle under 2 per cent per year. The rate per worker is lower because an increasing percentage of the population is gainfully employed. The rate per man-hour is greater, since man-hours per worker have decreased greatly. The most adequate figures are available for manufacturing, in which productivity has increased faster than the average for the economy. In manufacturing, output per production worker has increased faster than output per head of the total working force, because nonproduction workers have increased relative to production workers (and this has aided the increase in output per production worker).

large-scale industries, marked by high concentration and relatively sticky prices, and by the presence of powerful labor unions.

The simplest method of sharing the gains of such differentiated progress would be in the form of price reductions where increased productivity has reduced the costs of representative firms. The outstanding advocate of more prevalent use of this method has been E. G. Nourse, following a lead given by H. G. Moulton.[3] If this were the sole or dominant method of diffusing the gains of progress, it would mean a declining price level, which would share the gains among all members of the economy in proportion to their purchases. Pensioners and other recipients of fixed dollar incomes would share the gains along with those actively engaged in current production. If this were the exclusive method, it would mean that basic money wages would not increase with increasing productivity, thus depriving labor unions of their most tangible function and the one that appeals most strongly to their membership.

The present analysis supports the view that the current effect of unions in raising real wages, as distinct from money wages, is greatly exaggerated in the prevalent ideology of collective bargaining. This strongly suggests that their more important function, which is genuinely essential, lies in the realm of protecting human rights on the job. It is even arguable that this latter function is so important as to justify the existence of strong unions in spite of, and not because of, the complications resulting from their power to raise money wages

[3] See Harold G. Moulton, *Income and Economic Progress* (1935), especially pp. 161-62; and Edwin G. Nourse, *Price Making in a Democracy* (1944); cf. Edwin G. Nourse and Horace B. Drury, *Industrial Price Policies and Economic Progress* (1938). These are all Brookings Institution studies. They deal with an economy of imperfect competition in which there is a considerable range of discretionary price policy, and policies of price stabilization interfere with competitive reduction of prices. The 1938 volume presents examples of economically successful policies of price reduction by strong firms: successful apparently because they increased the firm's proportionate share of industry sales—that is, on a competitive basis. Naturally, an entire industry could not gain at the same rate, though the other members might be forced to follow suit defensively. To generalize this as Nourse proposed, it appears necessary to look beyond the industry-wide impact to the economy-wide effect of increased real incomes resulting from a reduced price level. Nourse dealt with internal corporate incentives, stressing professionalized management and a shift of emphasis from the current preoccupation with dividends toward increased stress on incentive payments to key workers, not confined to top executives. Interesting in this connection is a current revolt by a shareholders' organization against the size of incentive payments to top management.

beyond the limits imposed on real wages by increased productivity. This does not mean that this kind of power over money wages on the part of unions must be accepted as untouchable; but it is firmly entrenched, and stands as an effective obstacle to handing all the gains of progress to customers via price reductions that would reduce the general price level. Nourse himself, in a discussion in 1957, limits himself to the prevention of price inflation.[4]

As already suggested, a procedure more in accord with prevailing mores is for the gains made in leading industries to be wholly or largely shared between wages and profits in these industries. If these same industries hold on to their position of leadership, this would build up for them the status of a favored group. The workers in this group would get their share in the shape of wages higher than those of workers of equal grade and quality in relatively lagging industries. Property income would get its share in terms of a larger aggregate return on the larger investment per worker which has been necessary to the increased productivity, without (in most cases) any notable increase or decrease in the percentage rate of return. The improvements take effect in finding ways in which increased capital per worker can be used without the drastic and precipitous decline in its "marginal productivity" which would result from such massive increases in capital per worker in the absence of such improvements. This is the chief enduring form in which "capital" gets its share and does not ordinarily require an increase in its fraction of the product. "Enterprise," as distinct from capital, may get an increased profit, which competition (where it is effective) tends to limit to the period before the improved processes become standard practice, available to the "representative firms" whose costs determine prices.

This favored status of enterprise and capital in "leading" industries may be ironed out by competition, but the favored status of labor in these industries tends to be, not ironed out, but partially and laggingly offset in a different way: by increases in the wages demanded and secured by unions in the lagging industries; in other words, wage increases in excess of increases of productivity in these latter industries. Such wage increases raise wage costs of production, and, since the presumption is that profits in these industries would not have much capacity to absorb increased wage costs, this means that their prices

[4] See his "Prices and Policy-Makers," *Challenge Magazine* (December 1957), pp. 39-44.

will rise. Some of this increase may flow back in the shape of increased money costs on purchases made by the leading industries; but its chief impact is in increased cost of living, for which workers throughout the economy will seek offsetting wage increases so far as their bargaining strength permits. As a result, the cumulative effects include price increases in the original leading industries, which we assumed did not initially raise their prices.

Of course, if the unions in these leading industries are able to exact wage increases in excess of their above-average increases in productivity, thus raising *their* wage costs of production, the rise in prices follows a fortiori: these industries are virtually sure to raise prices to offset their increased costs and restore their former profit margins if possible. There will be controversy whether the price increases were needed, or whether the wage increases could and should have been absorbed; but this is not likely to deter the employers if market conditions are such as to make the restoration of profits feasible. The cumulative effect is further increased if the leading industries anticipate the flow back and raise prices further to offset some part of it in advance—as U. S. Steel has apparently sometimes done, in a policy that has exposed it to widespread criticism.[5]

Characteristic behavior in twelve industries or industrial groups is exhibited very revealingly in the following table, in which the twelve groups are arranged in the order of their rates of increase in productivity (measured in terms of total employees), and this is correlated with changes in wages and in prices. Even if one has reservations about the precise accuracy of the figures, certain relationships stand out with surprising clearness. Changes in productivity differ widely; changes in wages differ by only a fraction as much, though higher wages accompany higher increases in productivity with remarkable, if rough, consistency. Iron and steel is the outstanding departure from type, being seventh in increased productivity and first in increased wages. In every industry but one, wages increased faster than productivity, indicating an increase in wage costs per unit; and these discrepancies were naturally greatest where the increase in productivity was least. With some exceptions, the six industries showing greatest

[5] See Gardiner C. Means, *Administrative Inflation and Public Policy* (1959), pp. 26-31, referring to U. S. Steel's price increase of July 1957 and citing Roger Blough's testimony, in *Administered Prices*, Hearings before the Senate Committee on the Judiciary, 85 Cong. 1 sess. (1957), Pt. 2, pp. 211, 244.

Table 1[a]

Percentage Changes in Productivity, Output, Wages, and Prices for Twelve Manufacturing Industries, First Quarter 1955 to First Quarter 1959

Industry	Productivity	Output	Wages	Prices
Tobacco......................	30.2	18.1	23.0	8.7
Nonferrous metals..............	22.9	0.6	26.4	1.9
Chemicals.....................	20.0	24.8	22.2	2.7
Petroleum and products.........	17.8	9.8	24.8	6.7
Paper and allied products.......	14.7	17.7	21.2	13.0
Food and kindred products......	14.0	10.2	20.8	4.8
Iron and steel.................	11.3	11.6	34.8	26.5
Rubber.......................	9.7	7.6	20.0	5.6
All manufacturing..............	9.3	12.0	20.2	10.6
Nonelectrical machinery.........	8.9	9.6	20.6	23.2
Fabricated metal products.......	8.2	17.7	19.5	13.8
Electrical machinery............	0.0	5.4	19.5	20.7
Motor vehicles.................	−1.7	−25.1	17.7	17.7

[a] From exhibits of T. A. Anderson, in *Employment, Growth, and Price Levels*, Hearings before the Joint Economic Committee, 86 Cong. 1 sess. (1959), Pt. 7, p. 2156. The data are identical with those of Mr. Anderson's Table I, merely rearranged in the order indicated, the better to bring out the relationships that hinge on differences in the rate of increase in productivity. Anderson's table also shows changes in profits: all downward (presumably cyclically) except for tobacco, food, etc., and the iron and steel group, these three all being among the upper seven in terms of increase in productivity.

increase in productivity (and in wages), showed the least increase in prices, and the converse was true with a single exception for the six industries showing the least increase in productivity (and in wages). The excess of increased wages over increased productivity—signifying increased wage cost per unit—was least where both increased productivity and increased wages were greatest, and vice versa.

Naturally, this comparison does not cover all the important variables. The industries included are all marked by relatively high concentration, strong unions, and high wages; and in another comparison of seven such industry groups with seven groups marked by low concentration and low wages, Martin Segal finds that wages in the latter group are in a lower range than all the wages in the former group, and are rising more slowly, so that their disadvantage is widening.[6] One notes also that wage differences within this latter group are greater than within the former group, but that their rate of increase (for the period covered) is fairly uniform, and while less than that of the for-

[6] See *Employment, Growth, and Price Levels,* Hearings before the Joint Economic Committee, 86 Cong. 1 sess. (1959), Pt. 8, pp. 2635-40.

Table 2[a]

Percentage Increases in Average Hourly Earnings, 1953-58

	Average Hourly Earnings, 1953	Percentage Increase, 1953–58
Low-Wage and Low-Concentration Industries		
Lumber..............................	1.62	17
Furniture............................	1.54	16
Apparel.............................	1.33	13
Leather.............................	1.37	15
Cleaning plants.......................	1.14	16
Laundries...........................	0.98	15
Retail stores.........................	1.40	21
High-Wage and High-Concentration Industries		
Petroleum...........................	2.21	24
Rubber.............................	1.93	22
Chemicals...........................	1.83	26
Primary metal........................	2.06	29
Machinery...........................	1.96	21
Transport equipment..................	2.07	21
Electrical machinery..................	1.76	22

[a] Exhibits of Martin Segal, in *Employment, Growth, and Price Levels*, Hearings before the Joint Economic Committee, 86 Cong. 1 sess. (1959), Pt. 8, p. 2639. An even more impressive showing of wage gains in strongly unionized sectors of the economy in excess of those in weakly organized sectors, at selected dates from 1929 to 1958, is presented by E. C. Budd, *ibid.*, pp. 2522–27. During this period, the advantage of the strongly organized sectors is shown as having grown from 9 per cent to nearly 41 per cent. If the limit on increase of total real wages is 2 per cent per year, these figures suggest a gain in the strong sectors of 2½ per cent, against 1½ per cent in the weak sectors, these percentages being merely indicative of ranges of magnitude. Compared to these differentials among workers, gains at the expense of the employer's relative share become insignificant

mer group, it is greater than the economy-wide average increase in productivity and is therefore high enough to be inflationary, even though lagging and moving defensively. See Table 2.

2. Requirements of a Noninflationary Model

If the method of adjustment we have been examining is inflationary, what method would be consistent with general stability of the price-level? The basic condition is that the sum of realized claims to income should increase at the same rate at which real product increases; and that the more rapid increase of productivity in the "leading" industries should not accrue to either wages or profits in these industries as differential, favored-group incomes, to such an extent that other groups would be bound to take action in an attempt to catch up. As we have seen, even if they do not succeed in catching up, the pursuit raises unit costs. The conditioning factor here is that differences in rates of increase in productivity, and of immediate bargaining power, are much greater than differences of income in which the market will acquiesce without moving to reduce them.

A noninflationary adjustment requires, then, that income in the leading industries shall absorb only a fraction of their increased productivity: in fact, assuming that they will be able to secure gains exceeding the economy-wide average, their differential, compared to others which are below the average, must be not only limited to a size that will be tenable market-wise but one that will not lead to countervailing movements. A 41 per cent differential in favor of strong industries may be tenable, but only in the sense of ability to keep that far ahead in an inflationary pursuit race. A noninflationary differential must not start a pursuit race. How big a differential is noninflationary? Available evidence cannot answer, but it seems amply certain that it is much smaller than the differentials that actually exist.

The simplest model, which can be taken as nothing more than a point of departure, would be one in which wages rise at the rate at which product per worker or per man-hour increases in the economy as a whole, while the over-all proportion going to profits does not increase. In some respects this model is not too unrealistic. It seems fairly probable that wages and profits in the lagging industries as a group will not fall much further behind those of the leading industries than they have already fallen; though there will, of course, be departures from any norm in particular instances. These departures may furnish useful incentives to mobility or to acceptance of improvements, or may remedy particular inequities—or may create fresh inequities. The bulk of such departures from norm are bound to be upward. As to the relative division between wages and profits, it may shift in particular industries, one reason being unequal changes in the amount of capital per worker.

In manufacturing as a whole, the relative division has shifted in favor of labor in recent years. This may have been facilitated in part by the fact that real product has increased faster than real investment. (This has not been true in all periods.) This could mean that if capital received its former share of product, the percentage return on investment could rise; or the former percentage return could be maintained with a slightly smaller share of value added.[7] This may not apply to other sectors of the economy than manufacturing; and it is not safe to count on it as an important continuing feature of our system. As far as it goes, it affords a margin out of which special departures from the over-all wage formula could be met without raising prices. But it appears virtually certain that this margin would not suffice to finance any major part of the special departures that would be successfully bargained for.

The basic rate of increase, which we are estimating as less than 2 per cent per year per worker, or 2.3 per cent per weighted man-hour, may seem skimpy to workers who have been making nominal gains, in money terms, at something like twice that rate, and then have felt they had a grievance because inflation robbed them of the excess—as it was bound to do. For the increase in real product sets the limit on the economically possible increase of real wages (except for such small and nonprogressive gains as may be made at the expense of the proportion going to profits). That is approximately what labor as a whole had been getting as a long-run trend.[8] The reason was that, with the minor qualifications just mentioned, this was all there was available in the economy which labor could get. Moreover 2 per cent per year, if sustained, is far from a skimpy rate of increase. It doubles the original amount in thirty-five years, just as inflation at 2 per cent per year halves the real value of fixed money incomes in thirty-five years. The one is a notable gain, the other a formidable loss.

If money wages rise at something like the economy-wide rate of

[7] Cf. Albert Rees, "Patterns of Wages, Prices, and Productivity," The American Assembly, *op. cit.*, p. 24.

[8] Cf. Fabricant, *op. cit.*, especially p. 29. Of the units Fabricant uses, the relevant ones for this purpose are wages and product per man-hour, weighted or unweighted according as one is concerned with wage rates or man-hour earnings. Fabricant also employs a compound unit of labor and capital input. Since capital increases faster than labor, and often faster than product, productivity in terms of this compound unit increases more slowly than product per man-hour. Accordingly, Fabricant finds that real wages have increased faster than productivity *in terms of this compound unit of input.* This is logical, and indeed necessary: if it were not so, labor's proportion of total product would have been steadily shrinking, with serious results for the economy. But the finding that is significant for our purposes is that real wages follow closely the course of productivity per man-hour. The form in which capital and enterprise get their share of increased productivity has been discussed above.

increase in productivity, this reduces wage costs per unit of product in what we are calling the leading industries, and increases them in the lagging ones. Prices must rise in the lagging industries, and if the price-level is to remain stable, prices must fall in the leading industries, which must pass their reduced wage costs on to their customers. These conditions of price-level stability appear, to say the least, highly unlikely to come to pass. The industries in question include too many with restricted downward price flexibility, facing competitive forces that act too sluggishly to compel the prompt reductions of prices which, at this strategic point in the economy, are demonstrably necessary to a stabilized price level by the inescapable logic of arithmetic.

As for unions, there are some competitive forces tending to set limits on the wages they can obtain; but where unions are strong, their most powerful competitive forces tend to raise wages: namely, the competition of leaders with potential rivals, or of unions with rival unions, in offering gains to their members. This is competition in making the most of monopolistic bargaining power. In the light of this power, which is at its strongest in leading or highly concentrated industries, and in the light of the pressures exerted on union leaders by their strategic situation, it seems well-nigh inevitable that wage adjustments should be based on the ability of these leading industries to page wage increases above the average. This would mean that the employers' wage costs might not be reduced, so that there might not appear to be any occasion for them to reduce their prices. Then the noninflationary model would have failed to be realized; and the most that could be hoped for would be that the progress of education in the economics of this brand of inflation would result in some kind of compromise, which would stop short of the full inflationary effect that results when the various participants in the leading industries succeed in absorbing as their own property or perquisite the above-average gains that accrue in these industries.

The relation between wages and the introduction of improvements which increase man-hour productivity is a two-way one. Where wages rise enough to raise wage costs of production, they afford the employer an incentive to adopt more labor-saving equipment, in order to economize the expensive labor and raise its productivity. Or he may develop improvements in order to be able to increase productivity enough to pay the wage increases which experience tells him are coming. And if he installs an improvement, its success may hinge on having the willing acceptance and cooperation of the workers affected, and this may be promoted by a wage increase that shares some part of the gains with these workers. This is clearly a rational basis for departing from the strict average-productivity standard, but appears capable of being harmonized with it if the incentive premium is moderate enough to be acquiesced in without starting an inflationary pursuit race, or is allowed to remain unchanged long enough for others to catch up by the normal, gradual increase of productivity. This calls for restraint on the part of the recipients of the premium, whose natural tendency would be to regard it as establishing a higher relative place in the country's scale of differential wages, to be made permanent if possible, by keeping that far ahead of others who might be trying to catch up.

In competitive industry, it is sound economics that improvements are a source of special differential gains only until they have become standard practice, available to those "representative firms" whose costs set prices in the industry; after which the improvement is in the public domain and not a source of differential gain to the user. What is here suggested is that the same principle is equally sound with respect to any differential gain that may accrue to workers from incentive payments made in connection with any particular innovation; but with whatever differences are called for by the acceptance of the principle that the labor of a human being should not be subject to the same competitive forces that apply to commodities. In that light it is suggested that in general such innovational premiums should be retained, but their differential character ironed out gradually by the rise in the general level of wages.

Another important inequality in our economy concerns agriculture, and has led to policies of support, aiming to lessen its disadvantages relative to industry and trade in general and focusing on the concept of parity as a past historical relation between prices paid and received by farmers. Its effect must be interpreted in the light of agriculture's extra-high increase in productivity, along with the unrestricted price flexibility that is natural to it. These make it only natural that the ambition to maintain agricultural prices at parity has proved unattainable, and that the warehouses have been clogged with unsalable products, even at prices substantially below parity. The supporting of agricultural prices at levels that rise when other prices rise contributes its bit to the cumulative process. It takes effect on food prices, which are an important element in the consumer price index, even though the price received by the grower is only a minor fraction of the final cost of food to the consumer. One of the major difficulties here arises from the differences in cost of production between large corporate farms, family farms that are amply equipped and efficiently managed, and smaller, less efficient family farms, ranging down to submarginal units which, because they produce little in the way of a "cash crop," get correspondingly little benefit from price supports. Here the greatest agricultural poverty is found.

To revert to the more general picture, the conclusion to which it points is that, existing economic forces being what they are, some inflationary trend is well-nigh inevitable in the course of the adjustments to different rates of increase in productivity. One can understand the position of S. H. Slichter and others, that the best we can hope to do is to hold the trend down to a creep—say, less than 2 per cent per year. Incidentally, a 2 per cent annual inflation, superimposed on a 2 per cent annual increase in real income per worker, would mean that money incomes are increasing twice as fast as real incomes do or can increase; also that anyone whose money income is not increasing at that rate is falling behind the procession in relative terms. In the above discussion, the tendencies leading to this kind of result have been analyzed in a way that attempts to show the parts played by the behavior of "administered prices" and by the bargaining power of strongly organized labor, both of which are involved, and both share in causal responsibility, but in different ways.

3. The Tough Problem of Causal Responsibility

Thus the noninflationary model makes a contribution to the identifying of causal relations: in a direct sense any behavior that departs from the requirements of the model is a proximate cause of inflation. But for the student the question does not end there; it moves on to the underlying causes of the proximate behavior and, with remedies in mind, inquires how far they are modifiable. Meanwhile parties at interest dispute over whose behavior is to blame. Here a key question is whether certain inflationary behavior was voluntarily initiated or was a response to the behavior of others; and in the latter case, whether the response was necessary. And since there are discretionary margins of policy in these cases, the question of the necessity of a particular response is endlessly arguable. When the issue is thus joined, the reasons for failure to agree are not mysterious.

Spokesmen for business naturally identify increased wage costs as the main causal factor and affirm that offsetting increases of prices are an unavoidable necessity, commonly including the controversial item of capital expansion out of plowed-back earnings. In this connection they sometimes add that the necessity of raising prices to cover increased costs holds for the weaker firms in an industry, if not for the strongest ones; and that if the strongest firms reduced their profit margins to absorb increased costs, too many weaker firms would be extinguished, and the resulting increased concentration would invite antitrust action.

This argument raises a problem of economic differentiation, for the investigation of which the necessary data are not available in the general statistics of industries. Insofar as this argument is valid, it points toward the probable existence of undesirably large differences of economic strength among firms in concentrated industries. It appears inescapable that a progressive increase in wage costs, at the rates we have been recently experiencing, if absorbed out of profit margins— already a minority share—would in less than a decade reduce these margins below the minimum necessary to the function they perform in our kind of economy, whatever allowances may be made for the imprecise character of that minimum. The greater size of the wage share ensures this result.

On the other side, spokesmen for organized labor, including its able staff economists, and other economists whose sympathies lie with that side, go far toward placing the entire causal responsibility on "administered" prices, citing detailed statistical analyses in support of this position. A few theoretical economists, whose predilections favor neither side as such, but are strongly on the side of a competitively ruled economy, have decided that the most strongly intrenched monopoly power in the country is that of labor unions, and are ranking this, along with anticompetitive business conditions and practices, as twin problems to be at least mitigated if we hope to avoid the replacement of private bar-

452   COMPETITION AS A DYNAMIC PROCESS

gaining by direct public controls.[9] Specific remedies generally remain insufficiently defined. It is earnestly to be hoped that the issues involved can somehow be dealt with on the basis of the requirements of a properly operating economy, rather than on the basis of the relative political power of organized pressure groups, or the issue-obscuring epithets and generalities that prevail in too much public discussion.

As indicated, the question of causal responsibility is often entangled with the normative question of the reasonableness of the share which each side is trying to protect or to increase, or whether a given wage increase warrants a proportionate price increase or only one that is equal in dollar terms. In the case of the steel price increase of July 1957, following a wage increase in 1956, Gardiner C. Means argued that the price increase greatly exceeded any increase in wage cost of production traceable to the wage contract, and was therefore an independent inflationary move in an industry of a "bellwether" character.[10] The argument includes some telling points of statistical interpretation. But after an able and at least partially successful attempt to deflate the company's figures on increased wage cost of production, Means is left with a finding that the contract did increase wage costs somewhat. And if the preceding analysis is correct, any increase in wage costs in an industry with a more-than-average rate of increase in productivity is inconsistent with the requirements of a noninflationary adjustment. It is inflationary, though the price increase that followed it may have been inflationary also, beyond what the wage increase necessitated.

The attempt may be made to assign causal responsibility to one share or the other according to which increased first, or which increased the most, in each case from some selected starting point. There is even some reason in assigning greater causal importance to the larger share, merely because it is larger. The argument from priority of movement is the basis of a disclaimer of causal responsibility by one group on the ground that they are merely catching up with an initial disequilibrating movement originating elsewhere. Here the nature of

[9] Cf. E. H. Chamberlin, *The Economic Analysis of Labor Union Power* (January 1958); also "Can Union Power Be Curbed?" *Atlantic Monthly* (June 1959), pp. 46-50; also Fritz Machlup, *Monopolistic Wage Determination as a Part of the General Problem of Monopoly* (1947); also papers by various writers in *The Impact of the Union*, D. McCord Wright, Ed. (1951); and *The Public Stake in Union Power*, Philip D. Bradley, Ed. (1958).

[10] *Op. cit.*, pp. 28-29.

the starting point is crucial, and it is too temptingly easy to select a starting point which contains some initial inflationary disequilibrium, favorable to one group. Then the first move after this starting-point is likely to be one that reduces this disequilibrium: that is, one that impairs this group's former favorable position. Then this group will try to catch up with its former position, quite sincerely unconscious that this means restoring an inflationary imbalance.

The same thing is true, whether it is a case of a business corporation raising its prices to restore its former profit margin and catch up with the effect of a wage increase, or whether it is a case of a union whose 4 per cent annual wage increase has been cut in two by a 2 per cent annual rise in the cost of living, and which demands further wage increases, to catch up with the rise in the cost of living and restore the (inflationary) 4 per cent increase, figured in dollars of stable buying power. The fact that one party is catching up is meaningless until the observer not only knows what this party is catching up with, but knows enough about it to be in a position to judge whether the catching up is in the interest of balance or the opposite. Attributing causal responsibility on the basis of priority of movement has much in common with the problem of priority between the chicken and the egg. As qualifying this negative view, there appears to be some truth in the "bellwether" theory of the strategic importance of particular industries, notably steel.

One major example of the inflationary point of departure, or standard of comparison, is the level of what passed statistically for "real incomes" during the war, which was cut loose from its normal dependence on volume of consumer goods produced. Statistically, of course, "real income" is not volume of goods received, but money income, deflated by a price index. During the war, money incomes vastly exceeded goods available at existing prices, which were controlled and prevented from rising as they would otherwise have done. The result was an enormous volume of involuntary saving, which became a wholly abnormal part of current "real income," destined to be realized later, after inflation had dissipated much of its real value. But as of the year in which it was received, it counted as "real income" at the level of prices then prevailing. Thus "real incomes" rose while productivity did not. Then followed an interval without price controls and before productivity caught up with the unreal "real incomes" of the war period. This interval was marked not only by more dollars seeking goods than goods seeking dollars, but by the psychological aftermath of a period in which it had been possible to increase "real income" by raising money incomes beyond the limits normally set by productivity. This was presumably not a primary force, but such as it was, it reinforced the pressures toward inflationary wage demands to which strong union organization is naturally subject.

If priority of movement is an uncertain guide to causal importance, relative extent of movement might furnish more meaningful evidence, if either share had increased notably at the other's expense; but neither has, to a convincing extent. If anything, wages have gained on profits in recent years, but, as already noted, the increase of product per unit of capital has made room for a small shift of this sort. In itself, it does not prove that either share is responsible for inflation. The over-all picture is at least consistent with the analysis given above, which assigned some causal responsibility to each share.

4. Normative Criteria

The prevalent normative criteria in terms of which these movements are appraised include, as indicated in Chapter 4 above, something of the nature of a double standard with respect to the shares of wages and profits. Increased wages are regarded as desirable as ends in themselves; hence the approved standard is the maximum wage consistent with the necessary rewards to capital and enterprise. The latter share is regarded as a means to an end; hence the approved standard here is, the minimum reward necessary to stimulate and to enable capital and enterprise to perform their essential productive functions, of furnishing improved processes and products. If these two standards are both construed realistically, it is not clear that there is any necessary conflict between them in application, though it is clear that they give increased wages the benefit of whatever doubt there may be. Back of these standards relating to the rewards of the actively productive factors, lies a more general standard which approves of incomes for all, irrespective of their current contributions to production, sufficient to meet their essential needs. By this standard, the most seriously insufficient incomes are mostly not found in the ranks of organized labor; but they do include incomes that suffer from price inflation, regardless of its source.

There may have been a tendency to accept the argument that particular wage increases won by strong unions, which raise their wages above the general level, are a benefit to the rest of labor because they tend to spread, raising the general level of wages. It is probable that money wages in lagging industries are higher than they would be if wages in leading industries had not risen faster, but are real wages higher? Remembering that real wages depend on real productivity, remembering also the large and growing differentials between these two wage groups, exhibited in Table 2 above, the process looks uncomfortably like a struggle for shares of a limited total, in which the group with less market power gets the smaller share. Our analysis of the inflationary pursuit race casts heavy doubt on the idea that those who are outstripped in the race owe a debt of gratitude to those who have outstripped them. If this argument has validity, it must be because increased wage costs are a stimulus to increased productivity. This is possible; but it is hardly credible that such a stimulative effect could outweigh wage differentials of the size and increasing character that have been observed. This argument is a form of the "trickle-down" theory, relying for its acceptance on the powerful feeling of the solidarity of labor.

Another normative criterion is, of course, growth in total productivity accompanied by a high level of employment. It is on this ground that some observers justify a mild degree of inflation as affording a stimulus to growth. It is argued by some that such growth makes it possible to compensate many or most of those who suffer from inflation, through social security and in other ways, and to increase their compensation enough to leave them better off than they would be in a less rapidly growing economy.[11] This argument is necessarily conjectural. The stimulative effect of mild inflation, as compared to a stable price level, is hardly subject to proof. Equally conjectural is the extent to which the increased compensation is a result of changing social attitudes and

[11] One limited and tentative expression of this view was given by Robert Eisner, in *Employment, Growth, and Price Levels*, Hearings before the Joint Economic Committee, 86 Cong. 1 sess. (1959), Pt. 4, p. 789: ". . . I might raise the question as to what these pensions might likely be or have been if over the past 25 years the Government had not followed an expansionary policy. . . . The price increases have not prevented probably 95 per cent of us from being much better off than . . . the people who were comparable to us in the social scale were 25 years ago." The conjectural 5 per cent of the population remains a problem.

would have taken place equally (in real terms) under a stable price level, which would avoid an initial shrinkage of the real value of these compensations and a delayed offset via an increase in their money value. Social security has become more adequate, and the increasing productiveness of our economy has helped to make it able to afford increasingly adequate social security while still permitting other incomes to increase in real terms. This increasing productiveness may have been promoted by a policy that refrains from interfering with private bargaining arrangements, which afford scope and incentives for progress, and incidentally tend to bring about creeping inflation. But this is open to the inference that abstention from direct controls of wages and prices makes for increased productivity, in spite of and not because of the creeping inflation that may result under existing conditions.

Another view is that creeping inflation of the sort we have been analyzing cannot be counted on to remain creeping, but has an inherent tendency to speed up, as people come to expect it and take measures to hedge against it in their investments and purchases. Such an intensifying effect is a feature of the boom phase of business cycles and of the more violent wartime type of inflation, both of which are expected to be temporary. What we are dealing with at present is an expectation of a trend that is milder but more enduring, and that seems to have created apprehensions which, because of this expected continuance, are out of proportion to the modest effects so far visible. One apprehended effect is the bidding up of the prices of assets which would be expected to rise in value with future inflation, thus adding to a "pushed-up" inflation something that Winfield Riefler calls a superstructure of demand-induced inflation, against which the classical weapons of credit restriction remain pertinent, "in principle," with due regard to the difficulty of distinguishing the two kinds of inflationary forces in any given case.

The outstanding instance of this at present is the rise in the prices of equity securities until their current yields on these prices are less than those of good bonds. The buyer is paying for current yields plus expected appreciation. One fear is that this must end in a revulsion. If the expected appreciation shrinks, this might squeeze that part of the current price that is based on it, causing prices to fall. However, if the basis in physical growth persists, and especially if some inflationary trend in prices of products is expected to continue, any such revulsion might be moderate rather than disastrous.[12] As to effects on business investment, a high-priced stock market favors the raising of capital by issuance of equity securities, which is in itself desirable. A shift to speculative purchases at the expense of productive investment has been mentioned by R. J. Saulnier as a danger.[13] It could have inflationary consequences, largely dependent on the ways in which the sellers of such assets spend the proceeds of the sales. In general, however, the effects so far considered appear unlikely to intensify substantially a trend toward rising prices of commodities that enter directly or indirectly into the cost of living.

The kind of reaction that would have such an effect is a flight from cash to commodities, such as occurs in the more violent forms of inflation. On balance, a creeping inflation does not appear likely to precipitate such a flight. To bring about this result, the risk of loss from holding cash would need to outweigh manifold uncertainties about the prices of particular commodities that might be chosen as a hedge, plus costs of storage and any risk of deterioration to which some of them might be subject. A milder form of the same effect might consist in an abnormal accumulation of business inventories; but the resulting increase in demand would naturally be a single-shot affair, reaching its natural limits fairly soon, after which it would subside to the replacements needed to maintain the inventories at their enlarged amounts, such replacements being no greater than if the inventories were smaller. Up to the autumn of 1960, there has appeared to be no sign of pathologically large accumulations of inventories, such as would be symptoms of a tendency toward a real flight from cash. On the whole, unless the loss of confidence in the dollar leads to something like panicky conditions, it appears unlikely that creeping inflation, of the sort involved in our methods of assimilating unequal rates of increased productivity, would automatically and without other aggravating causes turn into the more menacing rapid variety.

[12] Since the above was written, the market witnessed a prolonged decline during 1960, involving a mild business recession, followed by a regaining of a majority of the lost ground. The original problem appears to remain.

[13] See his speech to American Bar Association, Corporation, Banking and Business Law Section, August 25, 1959. The address was reported in the *New York Times* of August 26. Mr. Saulnier's address also sets forth the rationale whereby a necessary condition of a stable general price level is price reductions in industries in which productivity increases faster than the economy-wide average.

5. Fiscal and Monetary Conditioning Factors

So far, nothing has been said about the part played by fiscal and monetary conditions and policies in the kind of inflation we are considering. Some, notably the "Chicago group," tend to hold that these constitute the whole story: that the adjustments of administered prices and negotiated wages could not bring about an inflationary price movement unless the fiscal and monetary conditions of inflation were present, and if these conditions were present, inflation would come in any case. The extreme form of this view focuses its analysis on the quantity theory of money.[14] As to this, the importance of the volume of means of payment is undeniable. Nevertheless, the truth seems to be that the volume of credit has considerable capacity to respond to the requirements of trade: in fact, that it is the normal thing for it to accommodate itself to the increased requirements generated by an increase in prices of the sort we have been envisaging. And if the volume of means of monetary payment lags in this accommodation, it is normal that the lag should be made up for by an increase in the velocity of circulation. The figures and charts presented in the hearings just referred to show peaks and troughs of money stock lagging behind those of business volume, and income velocity taking up the slack.[15] Thus they appear consistent with the hypothesis of changes in monetary volume and its velocity of circulation induced by changes in monetary volume of business, the latter being capable of including as independent causes the kind of price adjustments we have been analyzing.

[14] See testimony of Milton Friedman and R. T. Selden, *Employment, Growth, and Price Levels*, Hearings, Pt. 4, pp. 605-719, especially pp. 649-68, 688-719.

[15] Cf. Thorp and Quandt, *op. cit.*, p. 29; and Lloyd G. Reynolds, "Wage Behavior and Inflation: An International View," in The American Assembly, *op. cit.*, pp. 116-17. Selden, in *Employment, Growth, and Price Levels*, Hearings, Pt. 4, pp. 706-18, attempts to dispose of this adaptive behavior (which his own figures indicate) by failing to find causes for it *of the sort his theory recognizes*—these being long-run causes rooted in the desire for money balances, such as might lead to a long-run change in the equilibrium-velocity of circulation. This appears to rule out the question here at issue: namely, whether there are causes other than his theory envisages.

6. Appraisal of the Problem

If one discounts the danger that creeping inflation may speed up, should one be disturbed about it? There appear to be two reasons for such concern. One is the fact that it affords a continuing prospect for our normal peacetime economy, as distinct from self-limiting cyclical movements or temporary national emergencies. This would involve continuing maladjustments to the disadvantage of fixed money incomes, which are undesirable even at a slow rate of inflation, if continued, and would become serious unless the rate were kept substantially below, let us say, 2 per cent per year.[16] The other reason is that the remedies we know how to apply do not appear adequate or appropriate to this kind of problem.

Direct controls of wages and prices can be used with considerable effect in national emergencies, mainly because they are expected to be temporary, and also because unusual cooperation can be secured at such times. But to employ them permanently would involve a change in the character of our system which we are not willing to contemplate. And if we are tempted to employ them because other remedies have failed to eliminate slow creeping inflation, it is well to remember that the wartime experience affords no basis for thinking that they are capable of doing this. During the war, they demonstrated the capacity, under wartime conditions, to slow down what would otherwise have been a runaway inflation, to something best described as an accelerated creep. They showed no ability to eliminate this creep, despite a general freeze order and a subsequent "hold-the-line" order. There is no reason for expecting more of them in peacetime.

Another set of remedies consists of restrictive fiscal and credit policies. Such policies would be unqualifiedly appropriate if inflation did not occur except when the economy had passed the point of full employment. Unfortunately, the kind of inflationary pressure we are con-

[16] It may be significant that the experts have been predicting an increase of 1¼ per cent. This is on the margin of the rate which is clearly serious in itself, but is sufficient, if continued, to create the kind of expectations that could add the superstructure of demand-induced inflation mentioned by Riefler, resulting from hedging purchases by buyers.

sidering occurs well short of that point, and has proved—in 1957-58— that it can persist in the face of a moderate, but definite, recession. In such a case, the desire to check inflation by these methods comes into conflict with the desire to stimulate production and employment. If the alternative were clear and unambiguous, it would take the shape of balancing higher or lower employment against more or less inflation. If it were accurately predictable, we should be deciding what percentage of unemployment we would tolerate as an alternative to what percentage of annual increase in the price level.

Unfortunately, the alternatives are far from clear or accurately predictable. The line between a policy that adds to inflation and one that subtracts from otherwise-attainable production and employment is not surveyed and staked out. Restrictive policies, if strongly applied, can restrain the monetary volume of business, but there is no guarantee that this will take its main effect on the price dimension of the monetary volume. They are not certain to restrict supply and demand equally. But chiefly, if wage costs and business' target returns have as much force behind them as seems likely under present conditions, and are as resistant to reductions, there is a disquieting likelihood that the main effect will be to restrict physical production and employment, and not prices. Any policies that demonstrably have this effect are unlikely to be tolerated. Therefore, against an inflation in which excess demand is not the moving cause, it is doubtful how much can be usefully attempted in the way of control by restrictive fiscal and credit policies, though restriction of excess demand will always remain an essential safeguard.

If wages, by rising faster than productivity, force up wage costs of production, can the discrepancy be remedied by a more rapid increase in productivity? This is to be distinguished from an increase in output matched by increased employment; which is much to be desired for its own sake but is not a remedy for the kind of inflationary problem we are considering. It is a more rapid increase in productivity which would make it possible to raise wages without increasing wage costs of production and hence without creating pressure to raise prices in the particular industry affected. But if this industry is already one in which productivity is rising faster than the average, the result would naturally be to accentuate the inequalities between industries: inequalities out of which this particular problem arises. From this standpoint, the most useful place for increases in productivity would be in the lagging industries, reducing their relative disadvantage. But the same characteristics responsible for their lagging character would presumably stand as obstacles to their achievement of better-than-average increases in productivity and thus reducing the relative disadvantage which is the source of the difficulty.

If a determined drive in this direction were made and were successful, there would be a danger that the overemphasis on quantity output in the lagging industries might result in sacrificing important elements of quality. A further possibility is that there is a limit—presumably elastic but real—on the rate at which the market can absorb an increasing volume of products. One vital conditioning factor is the rate at which new products can be devised and brought into market acceptance—products in which a progressive increase in output can be successfully embodied. The remedy via increased productivity may raise as many problems as it solves. Perhaps the least questionable approach to this objective would be through improving the existing means for making scientific and technical knowledge available to small firms which do not command the resources necessary for a division of research and planning comparable to those of giant firms. The furtherance of even this clearly commendable goal might get into controversial territory if it should appear that one of the necessary ways to promote it involved really basic alterations of the patent system. However that may be, any way of facilitating improved productivity in the lagging industries would have peculiar advantages from our present standpoint. It would reduce an especially troublesome kind of inequality.

Another logical direction in which to seek remedies is that of doing things to business firms and unions which, without controlling prices and wages, would aim to alter their behavior in a less inflationary direction. As to business firms, more vigorous antitrust policy is an obvious suggestion; but it is hard to identify specific actions which promise to deal effectively with the inherent difficulties which have been already indicated, especially the nonflexible character of full-cost or target-return pricing. Even fairly drastic dissolutions do not appear likely to go far enough to transform sticky-price industries into the flexible-price type. Stiffer wage bargaining by employers has been suggested; but without considerable modification of pricing policies, it does not seem likely to get far in moderating either wage or price trends. In the steel strike of 1959—the culmination of a postwar series of strikes—the companies appear to have attempted a more drastic resistance than is feasible in terms of present attitudes, including proposals on working rules and conditions which gave the union the feeling that its legitimate and hard-won powers in this field were being attacked. And the companies defended a target return that included capital expansion out of earnings.

As to unions, some of their coercive powers and methods may be limited, but suggestions that have been made for weakening them structurally would rouse such fierce opposition as to lead to more intransigeant attitudes, probably reversing a hopeful if gradual and spotty trend toward more maturely accommodating attitudes.[17] This would surely be true of proposals to break unions up into units coextensive with the employing firm as a competing unit, thus transmitting to labor bargaining the competitive forces to which the firm is subject. Actually, such forces do have some effect where regional competition plays a part, but the trend in "bellwether" bargains is in the opposite direction. The proposed change would be promptly identified as a form of "company union" and rejected accordingly. Proposals for greater internal democracy in unions would probably aggravate the problem in hand, since the rank-and-file are likely to take less broad-gauged and far-sighted views than their leaders, and the latter would be under increased pressure to compete by promising greater gains.[18] This question of bargaining policy is distinct from the need for protection of individual members against arbitrary action by union authority.

Finally, there is the attempt to induce bargaining parties to adopt more responsible attitudes in the use of their market power, refraining from using it to push prices and wages up to inflationary levels. Urgings in this direction by neutral parties, including public figures, have been characterized by Ben W. Lewis as "economics by admonition,"

---

[17] Cf. R. A. Lester, *As Unions Mature* (1958).

[18] The General Electric strike of October 1960, may appear superficially an exception, in that the largest local refused to support a strike called by the national union. At issue here was apparently the company's bargaining method of making a thoroughly good offer, and refusing to do more than minor higgling on it. This method requires a strong basis in employee relations to gain acceptance, because it minimizes the union leader's opportunity to claim credit for gains made. It would appear that this practice was the real *casus belli* in the strike in question. It is widely regarded by unions as an "unfair" practice and resisted—usually with success.

and dismissed as futile.[19] Actually, in President Eisenhower's appeals in connection with the steel strike of 1959, the element of economics appears to have been limited to the need of reaching some compromise settlement that would start the industry working again. As to the efficacy of mere admonition, skepticism is warranted, but this need not carry utter defeatism about the prospects for increased responsibility. Some progress has been made, though such ideas and their purport infiltrate slowly. But admonition or entreaty, while it may be all that is feasible once an emergency arrives, is going at the matter from the least promising end.

What is needed is to build the necessary basis for responsible action in the shape of an understanding by the principal parties of the economics of the problem, humanized but not emasculated by mutual understanding of one another's feelings of right and necessity. This needs to be implemented by setting up conferring bodies. A wide variety of such proposals have been made, several of which appear likely to be acted on.[20] Among the questions involved are: whether the bodies should be official or unofficial, or both, how closely their deliberations should be focused on the problem of inflation; how best to correlate material from the fields of fiscal and monetary matters, price-making and wage-bargaining; and if nongovernmental representatives of public and consumer interests are included, what two-way connecting links might be set up between them and the broad and amorphous interests they would represent; also whether the conferring body should have continuing existence and its own staff to pursue lines of investigation that might not be covered by the existing staff materials to which it would have access, or to recombine, digest, and interpret material from the standpoint of its particular interest. The basic necessity is, probably by a combination of methods, to promote understanding of the requirements of a noninflationary adjustment—understanding of the kind that combines recognition of com-

[19] See Ben W. Lewis, "Economics by Admonition," *American Economic Review* (May 1959), pp. 384-98. Professor Lewis pictures the admonition as calling for the substitution of altruism for self-interest, and for correct solving of many-faceted social problems. This appears to the present writer a straw man. Wise self-interest *is* responsible; and it seems possible, not to guarantee perfect solutions, but to identify sticking points and the directions in which they need to come unstuck.

[20] See John T. Dunlop, "Policy Problems," in The American Assembly, *op. cit.*, pp. 137, 148-49, 160.

plexities with a firm grip on the essentially simple fundamentals—and to bring this understanding to bear both on public opinion and on the bargaining and price-making processes themselves. This will not be quick or easy.

The saving grace is that quick solutions are not a matter of desperate urgency. It will not bring calamitous harm on the country if the problem is not solved in three years, or five. We can afford to work with a variety of possible remedies that take time and no one of which offers a complete solution; and to avoid committing ourselves to those more drastic and untried remedies which might backfire. We need to be working actively on the problem, but we can afford to be, within reason, cautious and patient.

CHAPTER 19

Common Requirements of
Healthy Competition

1. Is There Unity in This Variety?

It is time now, in closing this study, to seek an answer to the question that has underlain it and has become evident repeatedly throughout its course: Has the study succeeded in the difficult task it set for itself, of producing a framework for the study of competition which might assist toward more effective treatment of those factors of dynamic process that present such difficulties to theoretical analysis? Such a framework would stand somewhere between the models of theoretically precise equilibrium prevailing in the Chamberlin-Robinson period and the current inductive examination of diverse cases, each in terms of its individual facts, and might, if successful, afford a useful bridge between these two approaches. Having noted that observed results appear to diverge less than the prevailing diverse theoretical models would lead one to expect, can we identify common features underlying the divergences that help explain their relatively limited extent, and afford a better approach to the understanding of the observed behavior than the existing equilibrium models do?

Have we developed hypotheses which, without furnishing a basis for precise prediction, lend themselves to prediction of a tentative and approximate sort, or failing that, at least afford guides to what to look for and what general kinds of results to expect under various conditions? Underlying all the rest, have we developed conceptual tools of analysis that may lend increased order and system to the study of particular cases? Can they also aid the normative task of defining the requirements of competition that may be both feasible (and therefore imperfect) and reasonably and usefully effective? These are searching questions, and the tests they impose are not easy to meet.

2. Prerequisite: Customer Competence, Implemented

Customer competence is generally either taken for granted or dismissed as outside the sphere of economic analysis. But we have seen that it is a prerequisite to healthy competition and does not take care of itself in an age of new products and applied science, but affords many problems of policy and implementation. The recognition of these problems and of the inevitable differences in success in different parts of the economic field form part of the assumptions necessary to realistic thinking about competition. We have seen that the purchaser's competence varies with his status and character—big firm, small business man, consumer—and is different for matters of price and quality. The latter may be visible or invisible, disclosed by dependable information or not so disclosed, concerned with desires that are properly treated as matters of "taste" or matters of safety and health, in which risks are objectively determinable and are subject to a valid social judgment that the customer must be protected against products that could be dangerous or fatal. This last can be taken as a kind of social minimum principle of general application, akin to other minima that competition is not allowed to contravene.

In the area above this minimum, the unifying principle would seem to be that information and guidance, furnished on a nonmarket basis, should supplement deficiencies in the guidance otherwise available or in the customer's ability either to furnish it for himself or to get the benefit of a set of market offerings that are safe to accept by virtue of the canvassing done by a quota of competent buyers sufficient to discipline the sellers and eliminate most of the offerings that are substandard in an important degree. Obviously, minimum standards of truth in advertising are part of such a standard for implementing customer competence. Obviously also, such protections can only minimize or mitigate, and not eliminate, the exploitation of buyers whose negligence and incompetence invite exploitation and who, according to P. T. Barnum, have a birthrate of one per minute.

It depends on customer competence whether competition improves quality or debases it, debasement being none too precisely distinguished from useful economizing of high-quality materials that are expensive and limited in supply. Equally indefinite is the line between luxury products for customers who prefer them, and what we have called "product inflation," in which the alternative of economy products is not offered, or not on an equally favorable basis, for the customer to make his choice. As we have seen, this may occur when "competition of the few" reduces the effective cross-elasticity of demand until it is too low to afford an effective competitive incentive to produce economy products.

The goal of implemented customer competence might be defined as including a set of market conditions in which customers of normal judgment are afforded the necessary means of looking after their interests effectively enough to avoid gross and demonstrable errors. Competition is healthy in proportion to the quality of customers' judgment, combined with the adequacy of these environmental conditions of customers' choice; the combination causing the responses of demand to producers' various offerings to reflect adequately the relative values of these offerings in terms of existing standards. These standards are a mixture of objectively determinable criteria of performance, including effects on safety and health, socially generated standards of value, individual vagaries of preference and desire for experiment with novelties (preferably without undue risk), and accidents of exposure to momentary and fortuitous stimuli or interested appeals. The whole complex varies from day to day and evolves through an individual's life. All of this is subsumed by formal theory under the impliedly inscrutable caption of "tastes" and is swept under the rug by the assumption that customers' choices are final data that economists can only accept and must not scrutinize. By implication this inscrutability covers the widely differing external conditions and pressures under which choices are made, including the things business does to facilitate or to stultify them.

3. Tools of Economic Analysis

The study of competition starts with a paradox in which a group of producers, each trying to maximize his profits, end by minimizing them. The first task of such a study is to explain the existence of this paradox. The tools of analysis used need to furnish this elementary explanation before going on to refinements in defining the indicated result. In the case of agriculture, the paradox is easily explained by the simplified model, which in this case approximates the essential facts well enough to explain them. In this model the individual farmer has no control over price, only of his individual supply. After he has selected his most profitable product or combination of products, he gains more by raising more, down to the point at which he covers only his individual marginal cost. Similar action by other farmers adds up to enough to raise the aggregate output and bring down the price, until each producer reaches his limit.

But in the conditions characteristic of industry and trade, the paradox presents more of a problem, partly because the individual seller selects his price as well as other features of his offering, and sells in a market in which price is the active variable, rather than "supply" in the literal sense, and partly because he nearly always faces a demand function in which there is some room for setting a lower price and selling more, or setting a higher price and selling less—this instead of being unable to make any sales at a price ever so slightly above the ruling market level. The seller can even influence his individual demand function by differentiating his product or his selling appeal. The discussion that follows will have to do with these more complex conditions characteristic of industry and trade. Producers' range of policy will mostly be spoken of in terms general enough to cover variations of price, product, or selling effort, though price alone may sometimes be mentioned for simplicity. Our first approximation will run in imprecise terms appropriate to the business man's view of his situation.

Basically, a producer facing effective competition cannot increase his profits by raising his price without improving the attractiveness of his product enough to hold his customers. Nor can he do it by skimping in his product in ways that reduce the attractiveness of his offering below those of competing producers. If he acquiesces in their outbidding him, they will take business away from him; and even if the process is not rapid, if it continues, it will reach a point at which they are taking more business from him than he can afford to lose. So he will try to meet the appeal of their offerings, even if he might make more money, say, over the next two or three months, by not reducing his price or improving his product, and accepting a somewhat smaller sales volume. This describes the kind of perspective that accounts for the compelling force of defensive competition, even where the firm's individual demand function has the sloping character that theory associates with an "element of monopoly." A real monopolist is not subject to this compelling kind of pressure. The pressure is the greater because a firm's short-run marginal cost is generally below its average unit cost; so that if its volume shrinks, its costs will not shrink proportionately; and vice versa if its volume expands, at least within the limits of existing capacity, its average unit cost will be reduced.

If the firm outbids its rivals, it is normally reducing its profit margin per unit of sales and hopes to increase its sales volume by a larger fractional amount ("margin elasticity" greater than unity) and thus increase its total profit (or reduce its total loss or forestall a reduction of profit). In practice the competitor may think more in terms of maintaining or increasing his market share than in terms of a close calculus of profits. For the latter purpose, theoretical analysis introduces its apparatus of demand functions and cost functions, giving the profit calculus greater formal precision than it possesses in practice. In the resulting models, the profit maximizing point is uniquely determined by the single-firm demand curve and the corresponding curve of costs at different rates of output.

In these simplified analyses, the essential feature of a competitive situation is a single-firm demand function which, whether flat or sloping, is more elastic than the demand schedule for a group or industry including the firm's close competitors. This implies cross-elasticity of demand. This common feature underlies the diverse forms and degrees in which competition is found, ranging from unduly severe to unduly weak and sluggish, as judged chiefly by whether it leads to general losses or permits unnecessarily large profits. If a firm whose profits are already moderate is to increase them by reducing its prices, this implies a highly elastic single-firm demand schedule—how elastic depends on whether the marginal cost that is relevant to the particular situation is below the firm's average cost, equal to it, or above it.

The ideal of the most simplified abstract models, in which the firm's most profitable price equals its own cost at its optimum scale of production, where its marginal and average costs are equal, requires a single-firm demand curve that is strictly horizontal *at that level*, implying a homogeneous product, identical costs for all competitors, and absence of fluctuations. Departures from these conditions are of the essence of situations in industry and trade. Where costs differ between firms, not every firm can just cover its own costs. Where rates of operation vary, with marginal cost below average cost a considerable part of the time, a horizontal demand function is not necessary to prices that, on the average of fluctuations, approximate no more than normal returns to "representative firms."

For this purpose the long-run forces are more important, and they differ less than short-run. Long-run cost functions are flatter than short-run, and we have seen that they may be relevant in a growing industry, even when output is not strictly equal to capacity. And we have seen that the defensive competitive demand function is, in effect, flatter than short-run functions, because the firm may lose business progressively over time. But if it gains an aggressive advantage, it cannot count on this to endure in the face of the efforts the others are sure to make to offset it. What remains in the long run from any such single advantage will be an uncertain residuum, which may be substantial or negligible unless renewed. Thus there is an asymmetry between aggressive and defensive incentives, making it inherently probable that the forces back of defensive responses are more general and more compelling than the incentives to aggressive moves—admitting that aggression and defense interpenetrate. It is not necessary that all firms should have the perspectives and market situations that lead them to initiate aggressive action. If a minority of reasonably strong firms do, they will set the pace the others will perforce follow. All of this carries us a certain distance toward explaining why observed diversities of competitive behavior are not as large as theoretical models suggest.

However, the short-run responses remain, with all their diversity. If they are to be integrated with long-run adjustments, it seems necessary to take account of how changes take place in time: rates of change, changes that are shortly damped down or continue progressively, actions and responses that may be prompt or delayed and may range from inadequate defenses to more than adequate counteroffensives. These, plus demand functions in which character of product and selling effort are active variables, introduce inescapable uncertainties, and render theoretically precise "profit maximization" unattainable. To make up for this, uncertainties act, as we have seen, along with delayed competitive reactions, to make competition of limited numbers possible without ending in the oligopoly stalemate, while sloping single-firm demand schedules may mitigate tendencies to drive prices below cost, without always eliminating such tendencies, and without necessarily protecting excessive profits, for firms of average efficiency. These, all of which are "imperfections" in the realm of precision models, become useful or even necessary in the realm of actual competition, in which adaptation to change is ever present and "perfect" equilibrium is seldom if ever reached.

4. Competition as a Sequence of Moves and Responses

We have seen that in the field of industry and trade, competition as an activity (as distinct from a state of hypothetical equilibrium) may be viewed as a series of initiatory moves and defensive responses; and much of the explanation of the basic competitive paradox in this field resides in this sequence, and is to be explained in terms of the character of the moves, the character and timing of the responses, and the uncertainties of their timing and their efficacy. Defensive responses hardly need explaining; but it is not self-evident why firms should initiate actions of sorts calculated to elicit responses that would leave the industry as a whole less profitable than before. The initiating firm presumably hoped to improve its relative standing, but in this it may or may not have succeeded. To say that it expected to encounter a highly elastic single-firm demand function, at least in the short-run, is presumably true but does not explain the factors responsible, or the behavior of the function over time. The rivals' expected responses are the chief factor determining the character of the function.

In the prevailing theory, this crucial matter of the rivals' responses is regularly simplified into two extreme cases, the firm acting either as if other firms would not respond, or as if they would respond so promptly and precisely as to neutralize any gain the initiating firm might expect to make (as with an open reduction in the price of a homogeneous product in a market with unused capacity). This simplification misses the really characteristic cases, which lie between the extremes and need more to explain them than can be represented in a curve on a diagram. A more generalized summary may be worth attempting.

A successful move, if there were no response, would bring the initiator (or initiators) progressive gains, largely at the expense of the shares of rivals in the market or submarket in question. The speed of the encroachments varies with the homogeneous or differentiated character of the product, the nature of the move, and the state of the initiator's capacity and his ability and readiness to expand it while maintaining his competitively advantageous offerings. The extent of threatened encroachments depends on the initiator's unused capacity in the short run and in the longer run on his potential expansion; and for differentiated products it may be subject to uncertain limits on the extent to which buyers' preferences can be shifted. The pressure on competitors to respond varies with all these factors, from a move by a negligible hanger-on, which may be ignored, to a formidable threat that must be met if competitors are to retain a place in this market. If the threat depends on pricing that will not cover full costs of expansion, competitors may judge that it cannot endure, but may still reckon that they would lose less by meeting it, hoping that it will be temporary. If the responses neutralize the initiator's gains, but he remains competitively minded, this in turn is a challenge to him to devise a type of competitive move that will not be exposed to such neutralization. All of this leaves room for considerable variety in the tactics selected. The outcome to which it points is neither a perfect equilibrium nor an oligopolistic stalemate, but a continuing give-and-take of moves and responses.

The initiator naturally has the best chance if his product is differentiated. Then when he brings out a new offering or merely reduces his price, it takes time for the customers to respond, more time for competitors to appraise the customers' response and decide whether it needs to be met, and still more time to decide on the most promising competing response, after which the effectiveness of this response remains to be determined. Thus the initiator has a good chance for a gain before the response materializes, and a fair chance for a continuing gain after it does materialize if his new appeal was really effective. In such an industry, the most successful offerings will yield profits and the least successful will incur losses. For one of the latter group, the nature of his demand, with its delayed reactions, may give him time to devise something that will improve his showing. If he does not succeed, in the long run he is, as we have seen, about as badly off as if he were facing a flat demand curve and could not meet his competitors' prices. Thus the position of the differentiated product is not as strongly sheltered from competition as sometimes represented. Even the shelter from potential competition afforded by the difficulty of new entries, emphasized by Bain, appears to be mitigated by the growth of large diversified firms with versatile resources that reduce the cost of starting a new product line, and that are on the lookout for fresh openings.

It may be that only a few firms will initiate fresh moves, and they may not do it often, but to the extent that they are pace setters for the others, the effect spreads and continues. In the annual model situation, this pace-setting effect would apply chiefly to substantial and successful departures. As we have seen, when competition of the few is in its early stages, and firms are unaccustomed to its pressures, it is likely to have a destructively severe character within limits set by short-run marginal cost; and because a relative gain in volume by one large firm means a substantial encroachment on the business of particular competitors, defensive response is virtually mandatory, even if full costs are not being covered. An initiatory move may come from a firm with unused capacity and with short-run marginal costs well below its average costs, hard pressed financially for lack of sufficient volume of business and under pressure to gain some added volume—perhaps only temporarily—at prices above its short-run marginal cost but below its average cost, and possibly below the average costs of even quite strong competitors. This pressure is naturally intensified if there is much excess capacity; and in the depression of the thirties, it was more than the "sentiment against spoiling the market" could cope with. Reduced severity of business fluctuations has moderated the strength of these competitive pressures.

Under these more moderate conditions, with average cost playing a larger part in the reckonings of competitors, an extra-strong firm has opportunities to gain business at prices that afford it a normal return, but that are below the average costs of its weaker competitors. Some of the latter may be driven out. This is a normal competitive process. But if it goes too far, because differences in competitive strength are unduly great, and leads to a high degree of concentration, the strong firm may be deterred from seeking further relative gains by the fear that elimination of too many weaker competitors, and acquisition of too large a percentage of the industry's business, may invite unwelcome attention from antitrust authorities. Or a representative firm may see an opportunity to secure some particular item or category of added business, contingent on making a price concession or offering some particular attraction. Such opportunities may also be taken advantage of by firms so unimportant that their out-of-line tactics will be tolerated without response by the leaders, who will hold an umbrella over them, so long as they do not threaten to step out of their class.

More generally, initiatory moves may be made by firms that see opportunities for a particular gain, are aware that they are starting a game of moves and responses, if it has not been started already by others, and who have enough self-confidence to expect to be able to keep ahead in the game, or at least to be better off than if they neglect the game and thus let others get ahead of them in it. In another widespread pattern, moves may be started by sales organizations under pressure from top management to increase their market share, the management in turn believing that an organization that stands still is not in a healthy state. This may happen without close profit-maximizing calculation. Thus initiatory moves may come from a variety of sources and from variants on the common motivation of hope for increased profit. It is not necessary that all firms, or most, should take competitive action of an initiatory sort; nor is it necessary that fresh action of this sort should be going on continually.

If a substantially successful move has been made by an important competitor, attempts at some sort of response on the part of the others must be the rule, with few exceptions; even though in most cases the response is not so compulsory as the meeting of a competitor's price for a homogeneous product in a market containing unused capacity. We have seen the various kinds of time lags and uncertainties that may affect the defensive responses. Their character will naturally be responsive to the nature of the initial move. They will be different according as it consisted of landing a single big contract, or bringing out a new model or a new selling campaign or a general campaign of undercover price shading. The resulting level of competitive offerings is likely to have some persistence between renewals of initiatory action.

Such intervals of stabilized offerings do not mean that competition has lapsed; but it is probably healthier if there is some minor feeling-out of the market going on most of the time. In the case of special flare-ups of price warfare, of which the occasional price wars of gasoline dealers are the most conspicuous examples, the subcost competition ordinarily ends with a return to a more stable market condition in which some price differentiation is acquiesced in between brands of gasoline and types of dealers and exerts some check on the higher-margin brands and dealers. In more moderate cases, the level of offerings the members of an industry or trade are forced to meet in self-defense may be one the bulk of them are able to maintain, and in that case something like it is likely to persist. The more aggressively competitive firms impose their competitive pace on the others, by reducing prices or failing to follow increases; but except for temporary price wars or exceptional conditions of chronic subcost competition, the pace is pushed only as fast as the bulk of the trade can follow. If strong demand has left a fair amount of slack in profit margins, it may not all be ironed out at once. First moves may be small, and when they are met, other small moves may follow, stiffening the competitive pace by degrees. The useful service of the more aggressive initiators is to set a competitive level that puts pressure on the bulk of the industry, but that all but an inefficient few of them can manage to meet.

How do these ideas about prevailing competitive levels of offerings compare with Marshallian long-run normals? An adequate answer would reflect many changes of conditions since Marshall's *Principles* took definite shape, or in less degree since his *Industry and Trade*. But the preceding "descriptive analysis"—to use W. C. Mitchell's term—has more in common with Marshall's treatment than with the more recent emphasis on rigorous equilibrium models. Common features include active recognition of differences between firms in the same industry, tendencies to concentration and to unduly severe competition, somewhat restrained by what Marshall called a "sentiment against spoiling the market," and lack of reliance on a strictly horizontal single-firm demand function. Differences, while important, are largely matters of degree or emphasis, appearing in the descriptive picture of conditions to which his more general formulations apply and which gives them their real content. Present conditions include greater concentration and more massive use of applied science in guiding production and in innovation in processes and products. The advantage of very big firms as against merely big firms seems today to call for more attention than Marshall gave it. Similarly, Marshall's "representative firm" may have been conceived as more representative of a sizable group, closer to top efficiency, than are the "bulk" firms whose defensive competition is stressed in the present analysis.

One pregnant change, contributory to this result, is the increased dominance of corporate business, plus the achievement of the potentialities of indefinitely continuing growth that are inherent in its approach to perpetual life. An outstanding feature of Marshall's treatment is his picture of the typical life history of growing and declining vigor in the "private" type of firm, which did much to prevent firms of this class from growing to entrenched dominance. He recognized that the "public" joint-stock company had more capacity for growth, but dismissed this with no appraisal of its importance; and the general tone of his comparison of the two forms of enterprise is one of evenly balanced weighing of advantages and disadvantages on both sides.[1] In this country the antitrust laws, plus the shift of giant firms to diversification, appear to have partially taken the place of the Marshallian limit on concentrated growth, but only partially. Entry is presumably more difficult today than under the conditions Marshall contemplated, especially in technical forms of industry, with the diversified giant firm having an advantage, and the new firm likely to find its niche as supplier of a specialty product to the larger firm, which is representative of the industry in the full range of its products. Successful giants get higher rates of return than the bulk of firms. The averages for industries or industry groups, as reported, are mostly not as far out of line with Marshallian standards as one might expect from the altered conditions since his time. But the diversities grow in importance as one examines them.

[1] See Alfred Marshall, *Principles of Economics*, 5th Ed. (1907), Book IV, Chap. 11, Sec. 5; Chap. 12, Sec. 5; Chap. 13, Sec. 2.

5. Dynamic vs. Relatively Stable Industries and Trades

The dynamic industries and trades are those in which techniques and products are changing rapidly, also those in which youthful expansion is going on, the two conditions being likely to occur together. Here it is natural that there should be marked differences between firms, advantages being gained by those most successful in taking the lead, and the responses of the others are not likely to be fully successful in equalizing their market position. This is, of course, all the more true if the leaders' position is heavily fortified with patents. Here one would not expect a competitive equilibrium to be closely approximated. If innovation is more widely distributed in an industry, it may serve a further purpose of keeping technical and commercial practices stirred up and preventing them from settling into a rut in which every firm would know about what to expect of its competitors, and competition, being mutually defensive with nothing fresh to be defensive against, would lose its important dynamic character.

On the whole, it appears that American industrial management resists these stagnating tendencies quite effectually, under the widespread conception of top management that an organization, to be healthy, must be kept on its toes, under pressure to meet goals that are always ahead of its performance. Where management does not resist stagnating tendencies, it is jolted out of them by the impact of fresh techniques and fresh competition in products or in prices. It is conceivable that competition in this country might run down. Then the quiet life may become the prevalent goal, but the prospect does not appear imminent.

House construction and retailing had fallen into ruts, for reasons too familiar to need elaborating; but both have recently been jolted by new techniques, with some effect. Being "in a rut" is here intended to designate, not a complete oligopolistic stalemate, but a condition in which initiatory competitive moves that disturb or at least stir up the prevailing level of mutually defensive offerings, are of a minor character and make no radical departures from familiar and customary appeals. Curiously enough, it appears to be this sort of competition of minor moves and responses within conventional channels that can most closely approximate the model of normal competitive equilibrium, neither too strong nor too weak; always provided it does not become too static and subside into a real stalemate. Most people would prefer more progress at the expense of wider departures from models of theoretical equilibrium, especially if they can have reasonable confidence that differential advantages from innovation will be limited to their proper temporary character.

On that condition, dynamic departures from "pure and perfect" competition are welcome. The gains will pass into the public domain and will be diffused. It appears that "perfect competition" is a special case of the paradox of "rational" economic behavior in general. It is supposed to result from a perfectly informed appraisal of each situation the individual or the firm confronts. But such appraisal can be approximated only to the extent that the situations become routinized; in which case the individual's response also becomes routine, and routine reactions take the place of the exacting and unwelcome labor involved in "rational choice." Accordingly, the latter faculty lapses. So with "profit maximization"; under dynamic conditions it is highly uncertain and imperfect; under thoroughly routinized conditions it lapses and tends to be replaced by routine responses. The uncertain and imperfect behavior appears clearly preferable, so long as it represents a shifting balance between effectively opposing forces of change and adaptation: of disturbance and (uncompleted) equilibration.

6. Requirements of Effective Competition: Imponderables

The requirements of effective competition hardly need summarizing since we have been talking about them continuously. We started with customer competence, the promoting and implementing of which becomes a many-sided enterprise for many types of agencies, commercial, governmental, and professional. As to business attitudes, we started with the firm's desire to increase profits or to reduce losses, under the conditions imposed by rivals' offerings. Back of this lie the antitrust laws. If they are to be successful they need to be supported by a widespread acceptance of the general idea of competition as a way of business life, a willingness to compete and to accept the policing of violations and borderline cases, even though business men may disagree with the authorities about numerous particular practices. This is in addition to conformity with the basic morals of trade, including furnishing dependable information and guidance to customers, or at least not misleading them. Harder to define is the obligation not to compete in debasing standards of taste and morals, either in advertising or entertainment. Between them, these requirements define a large area of responsible conduct.

Further, the present analysis, especially of the relation between aggressive and defensive competition, points to the usefulness of diverse attitudes among business men. One puzzling phase of this is the relation between firms animated by a sense of responsibility to the trade as a whole or the economy as a whole, and firms characterized by a degree of competitive "cussedness," which may contribute nothing to the embryonic codes of responsibility that are so essential, but which may contribute to the element of competitive aggressiveness that is also indispensable if competition is not to run down and become ineffective. The attitude of responsibility may have a certain conjectural affinity for standards of "soft" competition, which the attitude of nonconformist "cussedness" may serve usefully to offset, provided it does not become dominant enough to displace the sense of responsibility—which is indispensable—and replace it with completely irresponsible attitudes. The relation between these two groups of attitudes and the feasible and serviceable degrees of each, constitute an important area of imponderables, study of which tends to fall between stools. One stool is the inductive reporting of observed behavior, without primary attention to shades of motivation. The other is the building of deductive models each of which will undoubtedly continue to be based on a single concept of motivation, because this makes a determinate result possible. As against this, an interpretation based on interplay of contrasting attitudes has only one advantage: it gives a truer picture of the essential facts.

7. More Formal Requirements

In formal terms the great common feature of competitive pressure can be defined as single-firm demand functions more elastic than those of groups or industries—that is, those that include the products of competitors. This does not tell how high elasticity needs to be in order to make competitive pressures adequately effective; and if measurement were possible, no single figure would be found to fit all cases. Examination of this problem calls into view many diversities: of size (affecting cross-elasticity), of time perspective, of aggressiveness or defensiveness, and of expectations of the results of a competitive move and of the responses to it. In these terms the requirement of effective competition is that some one of these variant opportunities for a profitable increase in a firm's market share, viewed in some one of these perspectives, should appear favorable enough to one or more firms to induce them to improve their offerings to their customers; that this should lead to defensive reactions by the industry or trade in general; and that this should go on until profits for the bulk of the firms—not including the very strongest or the weakest—approximate the minimum necessary supply price of capital and enterprise.

This implies giving the customers (or the workers) the benefit of gains in the level of technique available to this bulk group of firms. The effectiveness of the competition will depend on how far this level of technique lags behind the best that is achieved by the strongest firms; and whether the differential advantage of the strongest firms is an appropriate temporary reward for technical leadership, or whether it depends on other sources of power and is unduly wide and unduly enduring. In the latter case, the technical level of which the public gets the benefit is an unduly lagging one. But if the generally available state of the arts is able to follow the leaders reasonably closely, so that their differential returns depend on their keeping ahead in a moving procession, there need be no quarrel with substantial differential profits, as they are part of a mechanism that gives the public the benefit of a level of technique that is better than the leaders' was a few years ago.

In terms of structure, favorable conditions include a substantial number of firms small enough, relative to the whole market in which they compete, to have strong competitive incentives (though there is no need for atomistic smallness) and economically strong enough to make their competitive pressure count. They may make their distinctive contribution to variety and innovation, especially in products. Larger firms, necessarily fewer, can make a different kind of distinctive contribution. In fact, it appears that the service of competition in securing, for the ultimate benefit of the general public, the gains of advancing techniques, is substantially furthered by the presence of firms large enough to devote resources to research and planning in amounts hardly conceivable to the world of the nineteenth century; but it is not proved that giants of the present size are necessary for this purpose, and they appear to threaten a companion requirement: namely, the presence of competitors that are more numerous and necessarily smaller, but strong enough to be effective checks. Extreme concentration is consistent with strong competitive pressure for efficient production, but it is not favorable to the kinds of competition that make for rapid and adequate diffusion of the benefits.

The structural requirements toward which this discussion points are exacting. There can be no guarantee that they will come about naturally, or that antitrust laws will suffice to steer development to the indicated goal. They involve differential advantages, but imply also that these be not so great as to divide the firms in an industry into an aristocracy and a handicapped proletariat, with the aristocrats making high profits and the customers paying prices that are high because based on the proletariat's inferior level of efficiency, insufficiently mitigated by the low rates of return the proletariat makes. A further implication is that differential advantages should be fluid, not fortified against change. Leaders should need to go on displaying the qualities that brought them leadership if they are to hold their position without decline. And there is need that others should have a chance to improve their relative standing and corresponding incentives to try to do it.

8. Problems and Defects

The defects of the performance of a competitive system are implied in the exacting character of the requirements that have just been summarized, as it is a foregone conclusion that they will not all be satisfactorily met. In accord with the basic position of this book, we are concerned here, not with failures to attain an unreal "perfection," nor with those "imperfections" that actually serve a useful competitive purpose, but with real and serious defects of function. One may start with qualitative defects, affecting the quality of the product, via the quality of the mechanisms that implement the customer's selection; or affecting the quality of the wants that get supplied—or, to be more accurate, the consumer susceptibilities to which competing suppliers find it profitable to appeal. And as a check on tendencies of the student to apply his own personal standards of taste and morals, he should keep in mind that the crucial question is a comparison of available marketing structures and methods, including different ways of implementing competitive consumer choosing, or the substitution of some variety of controlled or publicly operated monopoly, with the defects to which its nature renders it liable.

One major source of the difficulty is the very success of the economy. Multitudes of new products and of unfamiliar materials for products of all sorts, produced by applied chemical science, outgrow the capacity of the consumer to judge quality, and exceed the current resources of public agencies for testing it, with the result that responsibility is perforce thrown back on the producer. New products bring new ways of life—conspicuously the automobile, movies, radio, and television—and this imposes on the individual the really formidable task of organizing this way of life which has been virtually forced on him. He does not always succeed. The ampler level of living includes vital gains in the conditions of physical health, plus a much more immature stage of attention to the conditions of mental health. The latter is marked by an excessive tendency to view human nature primarily in terms of pathological conditions, which in varying degrees are omnipresent, and insufficient emphasis on the conditions of a reasonably healthy balance, to which imperfect human nature can aspire.

But in general, as we become better off, we advance the frontier of want-gratification from things that have the dignity of necessities to things less and less essential—entertainment, amusement, and vanities. Growing leisure gives people in general a new resource, which can be splendidly used, or wasted, or can be a corrupting force. These gains offer us the opportunity to give life the dignity of a purpose beyond the level of physical necessities, but only if we have such a purpose or can develop one and organize our enlarged level of living around it. Otherwise, more and more of our consumption, and the activity that goes with it, tends to become a disorganized and meaningless succession of experiences or sensations, adding up to futility in place of the potentially enlarged dignity we might have had.

The relevant point for the present study is the part business competition plays in this task of organizing the enlargement of living that increased productivity makes available to us. What it does is to pull us in all directions at once, with a force gauged by the dollar value of a sale; pulling with equal force toward things that might mean high fulfilment, sterilizing futility, or degrading corruption. And there is ground for suspicion that in the present uprooted state of our mores, there is a form of Gresham's law at work, favoring the appeals that are futile or positively debasing. There are signs that this tendency needs more effective social counteraction than it is receiving at present. It is a phase of the inherent dilemma of freedom, which means freedom to choose from among disinterested and interested sources of guidance: a dilemma that can be mitigated, but from which the individual cannot be wholly insulated without danger of the decay of the critical faculties that are essential to a free society.

Among more tangible perversions of selling appeals in business, the bribery of purchasing agents has grown with the growth of the impersonal corporation. Here competitive pressures on the purchasing firm give it a powerful interest in combating this form of corruption, and its facilities for testing the performance of rival materials and equipment afford a means of exercising a check, tending to safeguard its efficiency from being seriously impaired by use of inferior means of production. In retailing, the firm itself, as distinct from its purchasing agents, may receive undercover inducements to push favored products for reasons other than their superiority. Here the competitive check depends on the competence of the consumer as a shopper and is less effective than the checks exercised by the industrial firm as a purchaser. For this evil, the removal of competitive checks is hardly the appropriate remedy: improved means of identifying quality are a more constructive method, though facing inherent difficulties.

A still more structural dilemma of competition is the dilemma between firms too numerous (and hence too small) for efficiency and firms too few for strong competitive incentives. This dilemma was reflected in the requirement of the preceding discussion, that there should be firms small relative to the industry market but strong enough to exert competitive pressure on larger firms. This requirement may or may not be fulfilled. If it is not, either efficiency or competitive pressure suffers. We have seen three related reasons for a slackening of the competitive impulse to increase a firm's market share when it becomes one of a few giants. One is the lack of room to expand sales volume enough to increase total profit by tactics that reduce unit margins. This is fortified by the effective resistance the giant rivals are certain to offer; and finally by reluctance to grow large enough to become a conspicuous mark for the antitrust lightning. As a result, though market shares are still subject to variation, they tend to reach an approximate sort of stability, which the firms tend to accept, and to refrain from efforts to disturb them drastically. This somewhat elastic condition is reflected, with a rigor seldom found in full force, in the theoretical model in which a firm is discouraged from making competitive moves by the confident expectation that any such move will be neutralized by its rivals' responses.

This qualified acceptance of stable market shares can be reflected in the ability to earn a target return substantially above the rate earned in industries that are more strongly competitive, especially if it is fortified by conditions that handicap new entries. It can be combined with what we have called "product inflation," in which competitive incentives are distorted because there is too little room for a competitive increase in one firm's share of the market.

In that connection, the interesting question arises what will happen in the automobile industry if, after the spectacular gains scored by American Motors in pioneering the introduction of a compact model, its relative volume becomes stabilized as one of a big four or big five that has become established in the compact field, while the field of larger cars remains a big three. Will the tendency to "product inflation" reappear in the compact field, for the same reason as before, or will the momentum of success with an economy model cause this type of offering to persist, backed by the strong personality of American Motors' President, George Romney? And if so, could it last as long as the reign of the Model T Ford? Would it have a better chance if Mr. Romney's suggestion were followed, and the giants, with their multiple models, were broken up into firms numerous enough to have stronger competitive incentives, though large enough for the fullest operating efficiency?

As already noted, competition of the few does not weaken the incentives to strive for efficient production; but if there is not reasonable equality of access to the means of efficiency, including techniques not too far behind the best, the public may not get a satisfactory share of the benefit of the advances in the techniques of production. This inequality is likely to be combined with handicaps to new entries, which tend to protect such above-normal returns as may result from the softening of competition among the few. The result takes the shape of substantial inequalities in the severity of competitive pressure in different branches of production, which amount to serious defects in the institution as it operates, regardless of arguable disagreements about what a sound and desirable degree of competitive pressure is. In the light of the evidence, it appears to lie somewhere between the existing extremes, at a level that would probably be regarded by business men in general as unduly severe. These inequalities breed inequalities in wages and play their part in the "built-in" tendencies to inflation, which have been discussed.

As to this last, it remains for the future to determine how serious a threat it is. But it appears highly probable that if we are led to abandon our reliance on the forces of the (partially) free market and of (imperfect) competition, it will be because we have become convinced that this system is incurably addicted to a higher rate of "built-in" inflation than we are willing to tolerate. If this happens, it will be due partly to inequalities in the rate of progress and remuneration in different sectors of the economy, and very likely in greater part to the growing downward inflexibility of prices, which brings about a "ratchet action" and prevents differences in the rate of increase in productivity from being adjusted in a way consistent with a stable average price level. Such stability requires increases in some prices, roughly offset by decreases in others. The restoration of two-way price flexibility in response to changes in costs, where it threatens to disappear, is perhaps the most crucially needed single improvement in our imperfect market system.

9. Concluding Appraisal

It seems evident that no simple and sweeping statement can sum up the status and performance of competition between business firms, in our present mixed economy. In the aggregate, it fills a large place and has an enormous effect. But we have seen that this effect is uneven enough to create serious problems of disparity, even though the disparities in the force of competition are not as great as the diverse theoretical models would lead one to expect. Competition tends to be overly strong in some sectors of the economy and insufficiently effective in others; and where it is effective, it is often effective to perverted ends. But it does perform the dynamic function of mobilizing resources and allocating them, as is essential in providing for new products and for expanded production of familiar ones.

Where it is strongest, it elicits risk capital at what is probably in the aggregate less than full cost. Where a branch of production has become stabilized, competition sets the limits on the rates of return and is responsible for whatever approximation to normality they achieve. Where it does not work satisfactorily, preference is regularly given to attempting to improve the conditions of its operation, as against abandoning it and resorting to direct controls. The areas in which free and competitive market adjustments have been displaced by direct controls of one sort or another do not offer such conspicuous examples of success as to make us eager to increase their number unnecessarily.

The ultimate question the student is bound to ask, but to which he cannot hope for a proven answer in specific terms, is the question of the prospects for the persistence of reasonably serviceable competition in those sectors of the economy in which we are trying to keep it in operation. This breaks down into the question of the direction or directions in which it is evolving, the dangers to its continuance and serviceability, and the forces that are available to oppose these dangers. As for dangers, we are moving in directions that present two large problem areas. One is, obviously, the growth of giant units, with many smaller units coming to hold a subordinate or subsidiary position as suppliers or distributors, while the giants command such large fractions of their industries that they lack the kind of room for expansion, and incentive for it, that are the logical motive to vigorously aggressive competitive tactics. The second is the disadvantageous position held in the economy by those industries and trades composed of numerous small units, faced with harmfully severe competition, or tending to take refuge from it in guild-like behavior, in which the accepted custom of the trade takes the place of actively competitive determination of the terms of their offerings. Such behavior is more tolerantly regarded in these cases than where it involves big industrial firms.

In both types of industry, there are tendencies for the desirable interaction of aggressive and defensive competition to be replaced by a condition of mutual defense, becoming unduly passive for lack of the spark of reasonably frequent initiatory action and the continuous anticipation of such action. The condition that results is, as already indicated, more subject to competitive pressures than the theoretical stalemate of pure oligopoly, but partakes in lesser degree of the same tendency of aggressive adjustment of the terms of competitive offerings to lapse into a passive state.

As to the forces tending to the maintenance of effective competition, the outstanding ones include, first, the freedom of any individual, by himself or by forming an organization, to engage in any trade or industry; second, access to the necessary means of production, including funds, material resources, and technical knowledge; and third, a climate in which participants in an industry can and do maintain independence of attitude and policy, and in which there are enough independent firms to afford opportunities of substantial increase in the market share of any who compete successfully, and enough to create an inherent probability that there will be some among them whose situation and temperament lead them to initiate competitive action, thus breaking up any tendency for the market to settle into a passive condition of mutual defensiveness. Naturally, the climate needs to be one in which such competitive initiative will not be suppressed by effective trade discipline; for that, one must look to the antitrust laws.

In the evolution that we must expect, different aspects of competition will probably develop in different ways. We may distinguish first the *conditions* of competition: largely the market, the mores, and the structure of the trade or industry. Next come competitive *activities*, the most strategic of which consist of changing the character and terms of the firm's offerings, as to product, selling activities, or price, the change being an initiatory move or a response, aggressive or de-fensive. Less spectacular is the day-to-day activity of operating the in-dustry or trade with an aim to making it as strong, competitively, as possible, and of seeking and soliciting sales on the terms already es-tablished. This last may be separated from the making of changes in the offerings, or may be combined with it, in varying degrees. Finally, we may speak of the competitive *pressures* which result from these conditions and activities and which impel a firm to further activities, including the pressures of potential competition as well as of active competition.

Structurally, the trend is toward greater absolute size; and while the statistical indexes of concentration in different industries do not dem-onstrate any clear increase, there is ground for the conclusion that this negative finding is misleading in one respect that can be impor-tant. The bare statistics of firms in an "industry" need to be interpreted in the light of the extent to which the smaller firms, instead of being reduced copies of the giants, have a narrower and more specialized coverage. Thus it might take a substantial number of small firms, added together, to give one of the giants a single competitor in each of its divisions or departments, with the result that the effective num-ber of competitors in any one of the various sectors of the "industry" is a good deal less than the bare numbers for the "industry" as a whole would suggest. In that sense I am persuaded that effective con-centration is increasing, despite negative showings in the statistical in-dexes.

This has its advantageous side, in that the small but specialized firm can often equal the efficiency of the giant, or better it, in its special-ized field. It seems further possible that the relatively small and spe-cialized firm which has, let us say, 25 per cent of the business in its particular field, has more competitive incentive than the giant that holds 25 per cent of the entire industry, in that if the giant grows be-yond 30 per cent or 35 per cent, it may invite antitrust scrutiny and possible action, while the smaller firm would be less likely to attract the same unfavorable notice if it grew to the same relative size in its limited field.

How shall one appraise the effect of approximately stabilized market shares in softening incentives to the aggressive kind of competitive action? This is a problem, the full import of which may take time to show itself, because the motivations left over from the period of competition for relative growth may persist for a considerable time. There remains, of course, the incentive to maintain the market share already gained, including expansion if the industry is growing, but this rates as defensive and may not make great demands on the strength the firm has already demonstrated. The resort to diversification affords fresh challenges to the dynamic capacity of a successful and creative management and an opportunity to grow without exceeding the desirable or expedient market share in any one line of operation, but may end by increasing the number of fields in which the dynamic management will approach the limit of desirable size of market share.

This raises the further question: Is this cycle of growth of market shares to a limiting percentage, followed by diversification, the present-day substitute for the Marshallian cycle of growth and decline in the life history of a successful "private" firm? If so, does it perform a corresponding function? The answer seems to be: it does in part, but not completely. It prevents one firm from reaching unrivaled dominance, but does not dispose of the weakening of incentives to competitive expansion. In contrast, it seems clear that Marshall conceived his natural limit on the firm's expansion as typically coming into play while the firm is still trying to expand, even though with reduced vigor, and before it has reached a market share with which it is satisfied or beyond which it does not wish to grow. This difference, however, lends itself to diverse interpretations. It may be testimony to the stronger competitive motivation of American entrepreneurs that they carry the firm's expansion so far, while the British entrepreneurs of Marshall's picture reached the limits of vigorous expansion sooner, even if not fully converted to the pursuit of the "quiet life." This is consistent with the judgments of various highly qualified observers on the comparative competitiveness of American and European industry.

Be that as it may, diversification is playing an important part, and its ultimate effects have probably not been fully revealed, as they bear on concentration and the persistence of competitive incentives. Interdepartmental competition within great firms is an important factor, as is the competition for promotion in the executive ranks. This includes competition in enlarging sales volume at the expense of the firm's rivals, as well as competition in terms of records of efficiency in production; but it is not self-evident how much intrafirm competition adds to the forces that work toward passing the gains of increased productivity on to the consuming public. It is too early to predict that competitive incentives will be perverted to monopoly gain or will subside into the striving for the "quiet life," but this is a possibility to be kept in mind by those who realize that change is the law of life in business organization as elsewhere. If this change materializes, it will mean a further diminution of the difference between an imperfectly competitive economy of large business organizations and one that is controlled or collectivized.

Meanwhile it remains true that the imperfectly competitive mixed economy we have is better than the impossible abstraction of "perfect competition," largely because of its dynamic quality; and because, while competitive *processes* change their forms, competitive *pressures* continue to be forceful, including what is probably an increasing role for various forms and degrees of potential competition. The forces making for diffusion of the gains from increased productiveness are changing their character, and those emphasized by classical theory may be playing a diminishing part, but forces remain that do accomplish diffusion that is widespread, if not ideally equitable. The system has serious shortcomings; but there is room to hope that our performance in these respects may be substantially improved, if all the groups concerned attack the problems with a realization of their importance and with the necessary understanding and good will.

INDEX

Index